JBL 135, no. 4 (2016): 665–683
doi: http://dx.doi.org/10.15699/jbl.1354.2016.3111

Expanding Ecological Hermeneutics: The Case for Ecolonialism

TINA DYKESTEEN NILSEN
tin-nils@online.no
VID Specialized University, Stavanger, Norway

ANNA REBECCA SOLEVÅG
Anna.Rebecca.Solevag@vid.no
VID Specialized University, Stavanger, Norway

This article reviews current trends in ecological biblical hermeneutics and argues for a more expansive approach. As an alternative to the Earth Bible Project's "ecojustice principles," the Earth Charter is a cross-disciplinary and interreligious ethical framework for ecological biblical interpretation. We contend that ecological biblical hermeneutics may benefit from incorporating interdisciplinary insights and engaging with a variety of approaches and methodologies. As an example, we argue for *ecolonialism*, that is, an ecological approach that incorporates insights from postcolonial biblical hermeneutics. An *ecolonial* lens is applied to the *The Kautokeino Rebellion* (2008), a Norwegian movie about a Sami uprising in northern Norway in the 1850s. We show how the film's use of the Bible and biblical quotations brings out not only the colonial implications of the Norwegian state church and its minister but also the devastating effects of Norwegian colonization of the Sami population on ecological issues.

Ecological hermeneutics has undergone an explosive growth during the last few decades,[1] developing with an evolutionary speed few species outdo. Yet a couple of its stages dominate. In this article, we give some suggestions for how

[1] For research history, see David G. Horrell, *The Bible and the Environment: Towards a Critical Ecological Biblical Theology*, Biblical Challenges in the Contemporary World (London: Equinox, 2010), 124–27; Hilary Marlow, *Biblical Prophets and Contemporary Environmental Ethics: Re-reading Amos, Hosea, and First Isaiah* (Oxford: Oxford University Press, 2009), 81–95, http://dx.doi.org/10.1093/acprof:oso/9780199569052.001.0001; Ernst M. Conradie, "Towards an Ecological Biblical Hermeneutics: A Review Essay on the Earth Bible Project," *Scr* 85 (2004): 124–27, http://dx.doi.org/10.7833/85-0-941; Norman C. Habel, "Introducing the Earth Bible," in *Readings from the Perspective of Earth*, ed. Norman C. Habel, Earth Bible 1 (Sheffield: Sheffield Academic; Cleveland, OH: Pilgrim, 2000), 25–37, esp. 27–33.

665

ecological hermeneutics may develop further, making it relevant by extending its genetic layout and by introducing it to more habitats. In other words, our call is for expansion. We propose that ecological biblical hermeneutics would benefit from a broad-based starting point such as the Earth Charter (see below), from interdisciplinary exchange, and from an inclusive approach to methodology. As an example of how this may be done, we discuss the colonial situation of the Sami indigenous population with reference to a Norwegian movie, *The Kautokeino Rebellion* (2008).[2] By combining ecological and postcolonial approaches in what we term an *ecolonial* perspective, we offer a fresh interpretation of the film's use of the Bible and biblical quotations.

Our engagement with this field grows out of our own context. Norway faces a number of ecological challenges, many of them connected to the petroleum industry. This black gold has made Norway one of the strongest economies in the world today. This development has resulted in Norwegians using more than our fair share of the world's resources. Yet public debate in Norway has only very recently and reluctantly started to deal with the ethical dilemma posed by the fact that our economy—our wealth—is based on an industry that pollutes the atmosphere and causes global warming.

I. Current Approaches to Ecological Hermeneutics

It has been argued that interpretations of biblical texts that legitimate human dominion over creation (e.g., Gen 1:26–28) also legitimate the human exploitation of natural resources behind our current ecological crisis.[3] Ecological hermeneutics grew out of an effort to counter and/or come to terms with such views.[4] Before discussing our own contribution, we will give a brief overview of current ecological biblical hermeneutics. For more than a decade, two larger projects, the Earth Bible Project and the Exeter Project, have dominated the field, though other projects, as well as individual scholars, also have made significant contributions.

---

[2] *Kautokeino-opprøret (The Kautokeino Rebellion)*, directed by Nils Gaup, Borealis Productions & Rubicon Film, Norway, 2008.

[3] See, e.g., Lynn White Jr.'s seminal article "The Historical Roots of Our Ecological Crisis," *Science* 155.3767 (10 March 1967): 1203–7, http://dx.doi.org/10.1126/science.155.3767.1203. A summary of criticism of this article by other scholars is found in Marlow, *Biblical Prophets*, 16–18.

[4] David G. Horrell, "Introduction," in *Ecological Hermeneutics: Biblical, Historical and Theological Perspectives*, ed. David G. Horrell et al. (London: T&T Clark, 2010), 1–12; Conradie, "Towards an Ecological Biblical Hermeneutics," 124–27.

The Earth Bible Project

The Earth Bible Project was born at the turn of the millennium.[5] On the initiative of Norman C. Habel, a group of biblical scholars and scientists developed a set of "ecojustice" principles, which has since been refined through a series of SBL consultations on ecological hermeneutics. These scholars acknowledge that as Western interpreters they have inherited anthropocentrism, patriarchalism, and androcentrism as interpretative biases and are to be counted among those who exploit the earth.[6] They also acknowledge the need to change allegiances and commit to a participation in "Earth community" and work for justice for Earth (i.e., the total ecosystem).[7] While the project does not lay claim to any orthodox ecological hermeneutical *method*, six principles and three steps underlie the approach.[8] The principles, which were developed first, may be summarized as follows:[9]

1. *Intrinsic worth* of the universe and its components
2. *Interconnectedness* (and interdependence) of all living beings
3. *Voice of the Earth* as a subject, rejoicing or speaking against injustice
4. *Purpose* of the universe and all its components in a dynamic cosmic design
5. *Mutual custodianship* acting as partners with Earth, rather than rulers
6. *Active resistance* of Earth and its components in the struggle for justice

The principles have met with both approval and criticism. While not resulting in an abandonment of the principles, the criticisms have led to the development of three steps in the hermeneutical process that have become closely linked to the principles: suspicion, identification, and retrieval.[10]

1. *Suspicion.* The texts or the interpretations of the texts are likely to be anthropocentric, viewing human beings as superior to nature, which is regarded as an object rather than as having intrinsic value.
2. *Identification.* The reader must, before reading, acknowledge his or her interconnectedness. When reading, she or he must identify with Earth in

---

[5] See, e.g., Norman C. Habel and Peter Trudinger, eds., *Exploring Ecological Hermeneutics*, SymS 46 (Atlanta: Society of Biblical Literature, 2008); Norman C. Habel and Vicky Balabanski, *The Earth Story in the New Testament*, Earth Bible 5 (London: Sheffield Academic, 2002); Habel, *Readings from the Perspective of Earth*; Norman C. Habel and Shirley Wurst, *The Earth Story in Genesis*, Earth Bible 2 (Sheffield: Sheffield Academic, 2000).

[6] Habel, "Introducing the Earth Bible," 36–37; Norman C. Habel, "Introducing Ecological Hermeneutics," in Habel and Trudinger, *Exploring Ecological Hermeneutics*, 1–8, esp. 1–3.

[7] Habel, "Introducing Ecological Hermeneutics," 3.

[8] Habel and Trudinger, *Exploring Ecological Hermeneutics*, vii.

[9] Habel, "Introducing the Earth Bible," 24; The Earth Bible Team, "Guiding Ecojustice Principles," in Habel, *Readings from the Perspective of Earth*, 38–53, here 42–53; Habel, "Introducing Ecological Hermeneutics," 2.

[10] Habel, "Introducing Ecological Hermeneutics." Two of the steps, however, are present already in Earth Bible Team, "Guiding Ecojustice Principles," 39–40.

the text (rather than automatically identifying with the human characters), seek how Earth has suffered, and discern how Earth has resisted wrongs.
3. *Retrieval.* The voice of Earth or of its members is explicitly or implicitly present in the text as the voice of a subject. This voice has been ignored or suppressed in Western scholarship, for example, by being interpreted as anthropomorphism. This voice must now be retrieved, for instance, by reconstructing the narrative so that Earth is the narrator and the interpreter.

The Exeter Project

While the Earth Bible Project is by far the most influential approach in ecological biblical hermeneutics today, the Exeter Project has also drawn considerable attention from scholars worldwide. The Exeter Project, consisting of a team of six scholars led by David G. Horrell, was a time-limited project from 2006 to 2009, with major publications in 2010 involving several additional scholars.[11] Part of the project's motivation was discontent with overly positive evaluations of the Bible's ecological stance (such as, e.g., *The Green Bible*)[12] and also with the Earth Bible Project's perceived lack of communication with theology as well as its tendency to replace the Bible's normative authority with the project's own ecojustice principles.[13] Horrell—acknowledging Ernst Conradie's influence on their project, and particularly his call for a doctrinal link—draws out the necessity for a tripartite hermeneutics meant to safeguard a nuanced approach:[14] first, a historical study and informed exegesis (i.e., the text in its ancient context); second, interpretation informed by theological tradition but also reshaping it; and, third, engagement with contemporary science, ethics, and other fields of knowledge to illuminate the ecological issues.[15] Horrell also calls for interpreting a wider range of biblical texts, in opposition to the tendency of other ecological approaches to focus on a few favorite ones.[16]

While the aim of the Exeter Project was to examine how interpretations regarded biblical texts both as legitimizing human exploitation of nature and as

---

[11] Significant publications from this project include Horrell, *Bible and the Environment*; Horrell et al., *Ecological Hermeneutics*.

[12] Michael G. Maudlin and Marlene Baer, eds., *NRSV: The Green Bible* (San Francisco: HarperOne, 1989).

[13] Horrell, "Introduction," 1–11.

[14] This is understood as an approach rather than a method. See Horrell et al., *Ecological Hermeneutics*, viii.

[15] Horrell, "Introduction," 10; Horrell, *Bible and the Environment*, 121–27. Cf. Ernst M. Conradie, "What on Earth Is an Ecological Hermeneutics? Some Broad Parameters," in Horell et al., *Ecological Hermeneutics*, 295–313; Conradie, "Towards an Ecological Biblical Hermeneutics," 133–34.

[16] Horrell, *Bible and the Environment*, 12. See also Conradie, "What on Earth Is an Ecological Hermeneutics?," 295; Conradie, "Towards an Ecological Biblical Hermeneutics," 126.

promoting responsible stewardship, the final task was "to consider what kind of contribution the Bible might make to contemporary theological ethics … and to consider what kind of hermeneutic is justifiable and appropriate to allow the biblical texts to function constructively in the formulation of an ecological theology."[17]

Other Contributions to Ecological Biblical Hermeneutics

Another example of cooperative ecological hermeneutics is the *Green Bible*.[18] The *Green Bible* is a version of the NRSV with green print for those passages the editors consider ecologically relevant. Another example is Noah J. Toly and Daniel I. Block's edited volume *Keeping God's Earth*, which facilitates a conversation between ecological scientists and biblical scholars on a number of ecological/environmental issues, such as water resources, cities, diversity of life, and climate change.[19]

Individual scholars also analyze biblical texts from an ecological perspective.[20] Hilary Marlow's monograph *Biblical Prophets and Contemporary Environmental Ethics* is noteworthy for its extensive hermeneutical reflection.[21] Marlow does not feel at home with the Earth Bible Project and critiques their method, their lack of clarity with regard to terminology, and the ecojustice principles.[22] Reminiscent of the Exeter Project, but without situating herself in relation to it, Marlow follows the tripartite outline of tradition, text, and ethical and theological consequences. She draws up an "ecological triangle" that schematizes relations between God, humanity, and nonhuman creation, letting questions pertaining to this triangle guide the

---

[17] University of Exeter, "Uses of the Bible in Environmental Ethics: Project Outline," http://tinyurl.com/jbl1354c.

[18] Maudlin and Baer, *NRSV: The Green Bible*.

[19] Noah J. Toly and Daniel I. Block, eds., *Keeping God's Earth: The Global Environment in Biblical Perspective* (Downers Grove, IL: InterVarsity Press, 2010).

[20] See, e.g., Richard Bauckham, *The Bible and Ecology: Rediscovering the Community of Creation*, Sarum Theological Lectures (Waco, TX: Baylor University Press, 2010); Bauckham, *Living with Other Creatures: Green Exegesis and Theology* (Waco, TX: Baylor University Press, 2011); Frederick J. Gaiser and Mark A. Throntveit, eds., *"And God Saw That It Was Good": Essays on Creation and God in Honor of Terence E. Fretheim*, WWSup 5 (Saint Paul, MN: Luther Seminary, 2006); Terence E. Fretheim, *God and World in the Old Testament: A Relational Theology of Creation* (Nashville: Abingdon, 2005); Fretheim, *Creation Untamed: The Bible, God, and Natural Disasters*, Theological Explorations for the Church Catholic (Grand Rapids: Baker Academic, 2010).

[21] Marlow, *Biblical Prophets*. See also Marlow, "'What Am I in a Boundless Creation?' An Ecological Reading of Sirach 16 and 17," *BibInt* 22 (2014): 34–50, http://dx.doi.org/10.1163/15685152-0221p0003.

[22] Marlow, *Biblical Prophets*, 86–95. Note, however, her almost contemporaneous article in which she follows the Earth Bible steps, "The Other Prophet! The Voice of Earth in the Book of Amos," in Habel and Trudinger, *Exploring Ecological Hermeneutics*, 75–84.

textual analyses.²³ In addition, Marlow discusses the relation between contemporary environmental ethics from a Christian theological perspective and the environmental ethics of the biblical texts as interpreted through her ecologically focused historical-critical exegesis.²⁴ She points to similarities in the concerns of both, claiming that the present environmental concerns "invite" a rereading of the biblical texts, while the biblical texts are a "source" of reflection on interactions between human beings, God, and creation.²⁵

Another biblical scholar who has contributed extensively to ecological hermeneutics is Elaine Wainwright. Wainwright was a member of the Earth Bible team and a contributor to several Earth Bible publications.²⁶ She has further fine-tuned her own ecological hermeneutics in publications not connected with the Earth Bible. In *Women Healing/Healing Women*, she argues for an "ecofeminist, postcolonial reading perspective."²⁷ In some respects, this approach comes close to our own suggestion for an *ecolonial* reading, which will be explicated below. In recent publications, Wainwright has introduced the term "read ecologically" or "ecological reading" to describe her approach.²⁸ Her proposed methodology for doing so is to use *habitat*²⁹ as a key analytical category that highlights the "ecological texture" of the biblical text: "This is the texture that contains traces of the social, cultural and material worlds of the author/s and readers at different points in the text's history as part of Earth's unfolding and expanding."³⁰

---

²³ Marlow, *Biblical Prophets*, 109–11.

²⁴ Ibid., 244–78.

²⁵ Ibid., 277–78; see also Marlow, "'What Am I in a Boundless Creation?,'" 38.

²⁶ See, e.g., Elaine Wainwright, "Healing Ointment/Healing Bodies: Gift and Identification in an Ecofeminist Reading of Mark 14:3–9," in Habel and Trudinger, *Exploring Ecological Hermeneutics*, 131–40; Wainwright, "A Tranformative Struggle towards the Divine Dream: An Ecofeminist Reading of Matthew 11," in Habel, *Readings from the Perspective of Earth*, 162–73; Wainwright, "Of Borders, Bread, Dogs and Demons: Reading Matthew 15.21–28 Ecologically," in *Where the Wild Ox Roams: Biblical Essays in Honour of Norman C. Habel*, ed. Alan H. Cadwallader and Peter Trudinger, HBM 59 (Sheffield: Sheffield Phoenix, 2013), 114–26.

²⁷ Elaine M. Wainwright, *Women Healing/Healing Women: The Genderization of Healing in Early Christianity*, BibleWorld (London: Equinox, 2006), 31.

²⁸ See, e.g., Elaine M. Wainwright, "Place, Power and Potentiality: Reading Matthew 2:1–12 Ecologically," *ExpTim* 121 (2010): 159–67, http://dx.doi.org/10.1177/0014524609354740; Wainwright, "Images, Words and Stories: Exploring Their Transformative Power in Reading Biblical Texts Ecologically," *BibInt* 20 (2012): 280–304; Wainwright, "In Memory of Her! Exploring the Political Powers of Readings—Feminist and Ecological," *Feminist Theology* 23 (2015): 205–20, http://dx.doi.org/10.1177/0966735014555640.

²⁹ Wainwright ("Place, Power and Potentiality," 160) draws on Lorraine Code's use of the term *habitat* as "a place to know" (*Ecological Thinking: The Politics of Epistemic Location* [New York: Oxford University Press, 2006], http://dx.doi.org/10.1093/0195159438.001.0001).

³⁰ Wainwright, "Place, Power and Potentiality," 160.

II. Expanding the Horizon of Ecological Hermeneutics

Scholars participating in endeavors such as the Earth Bible Project and the Exeter Project, as well as individual scholars like Marlow and Wainwright, have produced and continue to produce valuable insights. They have brought ecological matters to the forefront of biblical scholarship and have painstakingly started the process of developing ecological reading strategies. Yet there are also some challenges, in particular with the dominating Earth Bible and Exeter Projects. In several respects, which will be elaborated below, we find these approaches to be too narrow. Our current ecological crisis is a global challenge, and the scholarly discussion needs to be inclusive as well as multifaceted. Hence, we suggest a broad definition of ecological hermeneutics and a global, interreligious starting point for reflection—the Earth Charter—that could serve as an alternative to the Earth Bible's guiding principles. Further, we propose that ecological hermeneutics work from an interdisciplinary theoretical framework rather than a strictly theological one. Drawing on this interdisciplinary framework, we also suggest the use of a wider range of approaches.

Defining Ecological Hermeneutics

The Earth Bible Project has never claimed a monopoly for its principles and steps.[31] Nevertheless, there is a tendency within the field to locate the Earth Bible Project's approach at the center of ecological hermeneutics—perhaps a result of its intimate connection with the SBL section on ecological hermeneutics.[32] Like Marlow and Conradie, however, we raise questions regarding the Earth Bible's three steps and its underlying philosophy—ideology criticism.[33] Its basic direction of "reading against the grain," coupled with "suspicion" and "retrieval," is inspired by the feminist biblical hermeneutics developed by Elisabeth Schüssler Fiorenza, among others, in the 1980s.[34] Although this model has served as a useful first stage

---

[31] Habel and Trudinger, *Exploring Ecological Hermeneutics*, viii.

[32] This SBL section, led by Habel and Trudinger, was a direct continuation of the Earth Bible Project; see Habel and Trudinger, *Exploring Ecological Hermeneutics*, vii; Horrell, "Introduction," 7.

[33] See Conradie, "Towards an Ecological Biblical Hermeneutics," 37–38; Horrell, "Introduction"; Marlow, *Biblical Prophets*, 89–95; Marlow, "'What Am I in a Boundless Creation?,'" 35–39.

[34] Habel refers only to "several approaches of well-known feminist hermeneutics" ("Introducing Ecological Hermeneutics," 3). There seems to be a close resemblance, however, to the approach Schüssler Fiorenza develops in *In Memory of Her: A Feminist Theological Reconstruction of Christian Origins*, 2nd ed. (New York: Crossroad, 1994). Cf. Heather Eaton, "Ecofeminist Contributions to an Ecojustice Hermeneutics," in Habel, *Readings from the Perspective of Earth*, 54–71.

in the development of ecological hermeneutics, the Earth Bible Project has not revised its use of the approach in light of recent developments and critiques.[35] As a result, the three steps of suspicion, identification, and retrieval now seem restrictive, forcing a certain kind of ecological interpretation that is overly occupied with retrieving the "voice of Earth." In our opinion, there are also many other interpretive steps that could be taken in order to investigate the ecological aspects of the Bible—hence, these three steps should not be equated with "ecological hermeneutics" per se.

Despite the tendency just described, there is no consensus as to how to define "ecological hermeneutics." Nevertheless, the following may be a useful working definition:

> *Ecological hermeneutics is defined as interpretation of texts or study of the interpretation of texts that focuses on ecology, that is, on interrelationships among and between plants, animals, and human beings and/or between them and the places in which they live.*[36]

Our definition of "ecological hermeneutics" includes any method or approach of textual interpretation or the study thereof as long as ecological concerns are to the fore. The definition is thus narrow enough to give criteria that specify what ecological hermeneutics is, but at the same time it is broad enough to allow for a large diversity of methods and approaches. It is inclusive rather than exclusive. We like diversity in nature—and in academia.

Our definition neither presupposes nor excludes a link to Christian theology, opening up for diversity also in this respect. While we agree with the Exeter Project and Marlow that theology should be informed by ecological biblical interpretation, we do not want to restrict ecological biblical hermeneutics to serving a theological discipline. We are convinced that we need a wider scope if we want to have an impact beyond the discipline, in societies that may be post-Christian, multireligious, or otherwise. The Earth Charter, we suggest, is such a broad-based starting point.

---

[35] Cf. Marlow, *Biblical Prophets*, 85–86.

[36] This is our own formulation, but drawing on definitions of "ecology" in Michael Allaby, ed., *Oxford Dictionary of Ecology*, 4th ed. (Oxford: Oxford University Press, 2010); A. S. Hornby et al., eds., *Oxford Advanced Learner's Dictionary of Current English*, 5th ed. (Oxford: Oxford University Press, 1995). Ecological hermeneutics is thus a sub-branch of environmental hermeneutics, which is constituted by "the intersection between philosophical hermeneutics and environmental thought.… Environmental hermeneutics may address any number of a wide variety of topics involving natural entities and ecosystems; land- and seascapes; wild, rural, or urban environments; and indeed any other conceptions or meanings of 'environment' where interpretation is involved" (David Utsler et al., "Introduction: Environmental Hermeneutics," in *Interpreting Nature: The Emerging Field of Environmental Hermeneutics*, ed. Forrest Clingerman et al., Groundworks: Ecological Issues in Philosophy and Theology [New York: Fordham University Press, 2014]: 1–14, here 4–5).

Introducing the Earth Charter

The Earth Bible team does not deny that there are challenges attached to their six principles,[37] yet we are not convinced by their attempted solutions. For example, we find it problematic that Earth (and its components) is a subject with a voice,[38] which seems based on the Gaia proposition that the earth "is a living entity, biologically and spiritually."[39] Moreover, we wonder with what authority an exegete can speak on behalf of Earth. For example, in an effort to give voice to Earth in Gen 1:26–28, Habel makes several interpretive moves that seem problematic. In particular, he decides to make Earth female (defying the Earth Bible's commitment against androcentrism), and she "gives birth" in anthropomorphic fashion.[40] Another concern is that the principle of purpose refers to a "dynamic cosmic design," which gives purpose to all the elements of the universe. This seems to come close (in wording, if not in intended meaning) to the evangelical idea of "intelligent design"—an idea that (unsuccessfully) tries to combine a fundamentalist understanding of the Bible and Christian religion with physics and evolutionary biology.

We would suggest that the Earth Charter may serve as an alternative ethical framework for ecological biblical interpretation. Like the ecojustice principles, the Earth Charter is a set of values and principles developed to foster a sustainable future.[41] The charter is a product of a decade-long, worldwide, cross-cultural dialogue among experts such as scientists, international lawyers, and religious leaders. The project started as a United Nations initiative in the mid-1990s and was continued as a global civil society effort. The text of the charter was launched in 2000, and since then the Earth Charter Initiative has worked to disseminate the charter and seek endorsement by organizations and governments. Despite some critical voices,[42] several religious bodies have endorsed the charter, as have a vast number of universities, religious organizations, and NGOs, as well as UNESCO, government authorities, and private businesses. According to the Earth Charter website, it is

---

[37] Habel, "Introducing Ecological Hermeneutics."

[38] Marlow, too, has critical remarks on this; see *Biblical Prophets*, 92–93.

[39] Earth Bible Team, "Guiding Ecojustice Principles," 46. The authors claim that Earth can still be regarded as a subject even by those who do not agree that it is a living entity, but they do not explain how.

[40] Habel, "Introducing Ecological Hermeneutics," 8.

[41] All references to the Earth Charter are from the Earth Charter Initiative, "The Earth Charter Initiative," http://tinyurl.com/jbl1354dd.

[42] For example, indigenous peoples did not initially endorse the charter but formulated "The Indigenous Peoples Earth Charter" in 1992. See Dialogue between the Nations, "Indigenous Peoples Earth Charter," http://tinyurl.com/jbl1354f. Since then, the Earth Charter Initiative has organized talks with indigenous peoples and amended the charter to include their concerns. Several groups of indigenous peoples now participate actively in the Earth Charter's activities. See Beatriz Schulthess, "Participation of Indigenous Peoples in the Earth Charter Consultation Process," Earth Charter Initiative, http://tinyurl.com/jbl1354g.

acquiring the status of a soft law document, like the Declaration of Human Rights. The charter consists of a set of principles around four main pillars:

- Respect and care for the community of life
- Ecological integrity
- Social and economic justice
- Democracy, nonviolence, and peace

Although it may seem that only the first two of these categories pertain to ecology, the Earth Charter makes it clear that "the goals of ecological protection, the eradication of poverty, equitable economic development, respect for human rights, democracy, and peace are interdependent and indivisible."[43] This is in line with the growing realization on the part of ecological initiatives that matters pertaining to biodiversity, preservation of habitats, and so on, cannot be isolated from issues regarding local culture, political history, power dynamics, social justice, and economic factors—as well as the rights of indigenous peoples.[44]

This integrative approach is one of the reasons why we find the Earth Charter to be a good platform for our view of ecological hermeneutics. Further, the charter is developed to include religious as well as nonreligious approaches. The Earth Charter does not supply us with a certain methodology for ecological biblical interpretation. Rather, the framework of the Earth Charter may inspire a number of different methodological approaches. We understand the Earth Charter to be a verbalization of our context—this is the place from which we do our reading.[45]

Widening the Range of Approaches

As we see it, ecological hermeneutics, like feminist or postcolonial interpretation, for example, is a normative approach; we want our research to have an impact.[46]

---

[43] The Earth Charter Initiative, "What Is the Earth Charter?," http://tinyurl.com/jbl1354h2.

[44] See, e.g., Monique Borgerhoff Mulder and Peter Coppolillo, *Conservation: Linking Ecology, Economics, and Culture* (Princeton: Princeton University Press, 2005). For an example of a conservation organization using the integrated approach, see WWF (World Wide Fund for Nature), "WWF's Social Policies," http://tinyurl.com/jbl1354ii. The rights and viewpoints of Sami people in ecological issues are emphasized in documents such as Ole Henrik Magga et al., eds., *Reindeer Herding: Traditional Knowledge and Adaptation to Climate Change and Loss of Grazing Land; Report for the Arctic Council and the Association of World Reindeer Herders* (Kautokeino, Norway: International Centre for Reindeer Husbandry, 2011); Ingunn Ims Vistnes et al., *Reindeer Husbandry and Barents 2030: Impacts of Future Petroleum Developments on Reindeer Husbandry in the Barents Region*, A report commissioned by StatoilHydro from The International Centre of Reindeer Husbandry (Kautokeino, Norway: International Centre for Reindeer Husbandry, 2009).

[45] See Fernando F. Segovia and Mary Ann Tolbert, *Reading from This Place: Social Location and Biblical Interpretation in Global Perspective* (Minneapolis: Fortress, 1995).

[46] Like those, for example, of Fernando F. Segovia, "Introduction: 'And They Began to Speak in Other Tongues'; Competing Modes of Discourse in Comtemporary Biblical Criticism," in

As ecologically engaged biblical scholars, we strive toward making the world a better place for all living beings. In line with the Earth Charter, we propose that ecological hermeneutics should widen its horizon to look at the interconnections between exploitation of natural resources, poverty, imperialism/colonization, and gender inequality. One way of doing this is to work from an interdisciplinary perspective, drawing on insights from power-critical approaches (such as gender, sexuality, race, disability),[47] ecological sciences (climate, biology, conservation), social sciences, law, and so on. Similarly, the methodology of ecological readings could also benefit from diversification. Methods such as contextual, reader-oriented, and cultural all hold unexplored potential as resources for ecological hermeneutics.[48]

In biblical hermeneutics, postcolonial approaches have been important for demonstrating how colonization processes and resistance to them play a role both within the Bible itself and in its history of reception.[49] In the following, we combine postcolonial and ecological lenses in what we term an *ecolonial approach*.[50] We find this perspective an apt tool for our analysis of a movie set in a colonial space but focused on the intricate connections between land, animals, colonizer, the indigenous population, and the Bible. This is but one approach among many, however, that we envision as belonging to ecological biblical hermeneutics. In other words, we have chosen an interdisciplinary space—the intersection of popular culture and the Bible—and a broadened approach—the combination of ecological and postcolonial—to test the possibilities of an expanded ecological hermeneutics.

Segovia and Tolbert, *Reading from This Place*, 1:1–32; Elisabeth Schüssler Fiorenza, *Rhetoric and Ethic: The Politics of Biblical Studies* (Minneapolis: Fortress, 1999); Musa W. Dube, *Postcolonial Feminist Interpretation of the Bible* (St. Louis: Chalice, 2000); Musa W. Dube Shomanah and Gerald O. West, *The Bible in Africa: Transactions, Trajectories, and Trends* (Leiden: Brill, 2000). This is in line with Wainwright's view of ecological readings in "In Memory of Her!"

[47] Ecofeminism is one fruitful example. See, e.g., Wainwright's publications mentioned above (nn. 26–28) and Laurel Kearns and Catherine Keller, eds., *Ecospirit: Religions and Philosophies for the Earth*, Transdisciplinary Theological Colloquia (New York: Fordham University Press, 2007), http://dx.doi.org/10.5422/fso/9780823227457.001.0001.

[48] Wainwright notes the necessity of including new readers of the Bible, mentioning agriculturalist writers, poets, and others, all of whom are professional writers. See Wainwright, "Images, Words and Stories." Contextual approaches, however, may also hold great potential.

[49] See, e.g., Stephen D. Moore and Fernando F. Segovia, *Postcolonial Biblical Criticism: Interdisciplinary Intersections*, Bible and Postcolonialism (London: T&T Clark, 2005); R. S. Sugirtharajah, *Postcolonial Criticism and Biblical Interpretation* (Oxford: Oxford University Press, 2002); Segovia and Tolbert, *Reading from This Place*; Dube, *Postcolonial Feminist Interpretation of the Bible*.

[50] The term *ecolonial* thus parallels *ecofeminist*. As noted, Wainwright also combines ecological and postcolonial perspectives in *Women Healing/Healing Women*. For a theological approach integrating these two lenses, see Marion Grau, *Rethinking Mission in the Postcolony: Salvation, Society, and Subversion* (London: T&T Clark, 2011).

III. An Ecolonial Reading of *The Kautokeino Rebellion*

Sami people have lived in the northern part of Fennoscandia[51] for thousands of years.[52] Traditionally, the Sami were hunters and gatherers, with an animistic and polytheistic religion. About five hundred years ago, in the face of a changing economy in Europe, some Sami developed reindeer husbandry. The Sami in Norway traded with Norwegians for centuries, but during the nineteenth century Norwegian authorities gradually adopted an ever more colonial policy in the northern territories, which seriously affected the lifestyle of the region's Sami population.[53] National borders, being subject to centuries-long dispute, were more firmly drawn, restricting Sami nomadic movements.[54] During some periods, use of the Sami languages was forbidden in school and Sami parents were told to speak only Norwegian to their children.[55] The Sami were regarded as an inferior race in need of Norwegianization if they were to "develop."[56] The Lutheran state church served colonial ends, as it was intricately tied up with law enforcement, education, health, and even commerce. The local Lutheran minister was often the Norwegian state's only representative in small Sami communities.[57]

The Kautokeino Rebellion builds on the true story of a conflict between the

---

[51] Norway, Sweden, Finland, and northwestern Russia.

[52] The time of their habitation is impossible to date precisely. For a history of the Sami people, see Odd Mathis Hætta, *The Sami: An Arctic Indigenous People* (Karasjok: Davvi Girji, 2008); Lars Ivar Hansen and Bjørnar Olsen, *Samenes historie fram til 1750* (Oslo: Cappelen Akademisk, 2004); Noel D. Broadbent, *Lapps and Labyrinths: Saami Prehistory, Colonization and Cultural Resilience*, Contributions to Circumpolar Anthropology 8 (Washington, DC: Smithsonian Institution Scholarly Press, 2010).

[53] Colonization began already in the second half of the thirteenth century. See Hansen and Olsen, *Samenes historie*, 165–69.

[54] A law called "Lappekodicillen" ensured the continued right of the Sami to cross the borders, but despite its never being abrogated, the borders were closed in 1852. See Hansen and Olsen, *Samenes historie*, 169–75, 261–81, 460–68, 497–508; Steinar Pedersen, *Lappekodisillen i nord 1751-1859: Fra grenseavtale og sikring av samenes rettigheter til grensesperring og samisk ulykke*, Dieđut 3/2008 (Kautokeino, Norway: Sámi allaskuvla/Sámi University College, 2008); Nellejet Zorgdrager, *De rettferdiges strid Kautokeino 1852: Samisk motstand mot norsk kolonialisme*, trans. Trond Kirkeby-Garstad, Samiske samlinger 18 (Nesbru: Vett & Viten and Norsk Folkemuseum, 1997), 89–118.

[55] Per Oskar Kjølaas, *Bibelen på samisk: En bok om samisk bibeloversettelse*, 2nd ed. (Oslo: Det Norske Bibelselskap, 1996), 33–34.

[56] Ibid.

[57] For the role of the state church as a vehicle of colonization, see, e.g., Zorgdrager, *De rettferdiges strid*, 130–31; Hætta, *Sami*; Tore Johnsen and Line M. Skum, eds., *Erkjenne fortid— forme framtid: Innspill til kirkelig forsoningsarbeid i Sápmi* (Stamsund: Orkana, 2013); Hansen and Olsen, *Samenes historie*, 333–35; Svein Malmbekk et al., eds., *Et helligt land for Gud: Hålogaland bispedømme 200 år*, Ravntrykk 32 (Tromsø: Universitetet i Tromsø, 2004); Central Synod of the

Sami of Kautokeino in northern Norway and the Norwegian authorities in the years 1848–1852.⁵⁸ The Sami population in Kautokeino kept reindeer and were seminomadic with a summer residence on the coast and a winter residence on the moor. A religious awakening started by the Swedish minister Lars Levi Læstadius had touched many Sami communities. Although religious and civil authorities at the time described the awakening in terms of religious fanaticism and ecstatic excess, Læstadius appealed to many Sami because he critiqued the liquor trade and encouraged Sami followers to read and study the Bible independently of the local church and minister.

In Kautokeino, the conflict between the Lutheran minister—as a religious leader and as a state representative—and the local followers of Læstadius grew because of tensions concerning politics (including the liquor trade) and religion (including Bible interpretation). The Læstadians disturbed church services, calling for repentance and conversion. In February 1852, several men and women were convicted of mocking the state's official religion, for taunting and yelling at a state official (the minister), for threats of violence, and for general disturbance of public order. As the months passed, the conflict escalated, reaching a climax in November 1852, when several Sami men and women marched on Kautokeino and, in the ensuing fight, killed the sheriff and the local merchant.

This is the historic "Kautokeino rebellion," for which thirty-three men and women were convicted and received harsh prison sentences. The leaders, Aslak Hætta and Mons Somby, were executed by decapitation in Alta on 14 October 1854—their heads were sent to the University of Oslo for research on race. The incident also caused a harshening of assimilation policies in the decades that followed. The heads were not returned to their families until 1997, almost 150 years later. That same year the Lutheran state church, the Church of Norway, for the first time acknowledged the role they played in the assimilation and colonial politics, asking for reconciliation with the Sami.⁵⁹

Elen and Her Flock

The Kautokeino Rebellion was produced in 2008 by Sami film director Nils Gaup.⁶⁰ In the movie, we meet the young couple Elen and Mathis, who experience

---

Church of Norway, "Urfolk i den verdensvide kirke med utgangspunkt i samisk kirkeliv," item 13/97, http://tinyurl.com/jbl1354k.

⁵⁸ For reconstructions of the historical events, see Zorgdrager, *De rettferdiges strid*; Hætta, *Sami*, 24–25; and *Store Norske Leksikon*, "Kautokeino-opprøret," http://tinyurl.com/jbl1354l.

⁵⁹ Central Synod of the Church of Norway, "Urfolk i den verdensvide kirke med utgangspunkt i samisk kirkeliv."

⁶⁰ For an analysis of the film with a focus on how it constructs the role of religion in Sami identity formation, see Cato Christensen, "Religion som samisk identitetsmarkør: Fire studier av film" (PhD diss., University of Tromsø, 2013). Christensen shows how international discourses of

a religious conversion after a meeting with Læstadius. Mathis overcomes his alcohol abuse and Elen becomes the leading figure in the local Læstadian community in Kautokeino. Elen is the narrator and the main character. We follow her, as a desperate wife, trying to make ends meet despite her husband's drinking problem; as a brave religious leader, leading Bible studies and talking to the minister on the community's behalf; and as a heartbroken mother, having to leave her son behind as she goes to prison. The many camera shots of nature scenery capture the Sami connection to the land: the vast sky, the ocean and the moors, and reindeer, birds, and wolves. In contrast, we mostly meet the Norwegian characters indoors—in the church, in the tavern, in jail, inside homes—but often with hints at the pristine life of the outside through windows or through the sound of the wind.

Biblical quotations and discussions about the Bible abound in this movie.[61] In one such scene, Elen argues with the minister, Stockfleth. Elen's husband and several other men in the family have abruptly been sent to prison (although not convicted yet) at a time of year when their help is crucial in order to get the flock of reindeer up on the moor before winter. In the Sami language of the region, Elen asks Stockfleth to have the men released so they can gather the reindeer and bring them to the moor before they fall prey to wolves. Stockfleth, answering in Sami, at first seems to listen attentively. Suddenly, however, he changes into Norwegian— the language of the colonizers—and, mimicking Elen's desperate plea for help, asks her, "Will you help me tend my flock?" Completely oblivious to her situation, he allegorizes her concern for her reindeer flock and makes the discussion revolve around his concern for what is, in his eyes, a wayward church congregation of "lost sheep" vulnerable to "wolves" (presumably the Læstadian preachers). Deeply shaken, Elen leaves Stockfleth, and, in the next scene, her reindeer break loose and are shortly afterwards attacked by wolves.

In his metaphorical reuse of shepherd and flock, Stockfleth draws on New Testament imagery of the good shepherd (John 10:11–16) and the parable of the lost sheep (Luke 15:1–7).[62] Although Stockfleth is intimately familiar with this

---

nature-based indigenous spirituality are linked to Norwegian postcolonial concerns in the film. His dissertation is based on four articles, one of which is Christensen, "Reclaiming the Past: On the History-Making Significance of the Sámi Film *The Kautokeino Rebellion*," *Acta Borelia* 29 (2012): 56–76, http://dx.doi.org/10.1080/08003831.2012.678720.

[61] For discussions about the Bible and film, see, e.g., Philip Culbertson and Elaine M. Wainwright, *The Bible in/and Popular Culture: A Creative Encounter*, SemeiaSt 65 (Atlanta: Society of Biblical Literature, 2010); Adele Reinhartz, *Bible and Cinema: An Introduction* (New York: Routledge, 2013); Erin Runions, *How Hysterical: Identification and Resistance in the Bible and Film*, Religion/Culture/Critique (New York: Palgrave Macmillan, 2003), http://dx.doi.org/10.1057/9781403973566; Richard Walsh and George Aichele, *Screening Scripture: Intertextual Connections between Scripture and Film* (Harrisburg, PA: Trinity Press International, 2002).

[62] The image of the shepherd served as a divine and royal metaphor in ancient Near Eastern writings, including the Hebrew Bible. See, e.g., Ps 23. There is not space to trace the background of the metaphor here.

biblical imagery of the good shepherd and clearly identifies as a shepherd, a *pastor*, he disregards the material level of the image. Is he blind to Elen's actual flock of reindeer and her utter despair at losing them to the wolves? Does he not grasp, or does he choose to ignore, his parishioners' connection to the land and to their animals? He seems completely consumed in a spiritual, allegorizing world, unaware of the ecological and colonial consequences of his stance. Yet he has strong ties to the merchant who benefits economically from exploiting the Sami and to the government's colonial assimilation politics and territorial encroachment.

In the film, Elen, too, is a metaphorical pastor. She uses the Bible to "talk back" when she opposes the liquor trade as well as in direct confrontations with Stockfleth. But Stockfleth does not see her as a pastor, only as a potential "helper" in his own endeavor. In conceiving of himself as a shepherd, Stockfleth identifies with the messianic, Christlike figure—the authority figure. In typical pastoral fashion, he calls Elen a child and refers to her as part of his flock. Through this imagery he conceptualizes her as an infant and an animal, a notion that reflects then current ideas about the Sami population as less developed racially and thus in need of guidance and integration into Norwegian systems of school, law, and church. This scene, then, through its biblical references, draws the connection between ecological and postcolonial perspectives. There is, of course, nothing unusual in Stockfleth's interpretive move. On the contrary, the allegorical interpretation he propounds is inherent in the biblical texts. By making the literal level so explicit in the following scenes, however, the movie draws out the devastating consequences of Stochfleth's interpretation. To us it is a reminder to move beyond such metaphorical and allegorical constructions and look at the material level, asking questions about who gains and who loses when imagery becomes an intellectualized game. Such a perspective resonates with the Earth Charter's statement about social and economic justice. The means to secure a sustainable livelihood is intricately connected to principles of nondiscrimination and the right of all living beings to be treated with respect.[63]

Slaughtered Reindeer

An earlier part of the film shows Elen's first meeting with Læstadius, the Swedish pastor behind the revival. In a sermon in church, Læstadius quotes two sentences from Deut 28, weaving together verses 42 and 31: "Aliens residing among you shall ascend above you higher and higher, while you shall descend lower and lower. Your ox shall be butchered before your eyes, but you shall not eat of it." The interpretation of the text in a Sami context is never explicated verbally in the film; rather, it is shown in the subsequent unfolding of the events. It becomes clear that the aliens referred to in Deut 28 are the Norwegians who colonize the area and its

---

[63] http://tinyurl.com/jbl1354m.

resources, as well as the lives and culture of the Sami, while the Sami themselves experience a loss of autonomy and resources. The slaughtering of the ox in front of their eyes, which they themselves will not eat, comes to fulfillment several times when the reindeer of the Sami are forcefully butchered by the Norwegians to pay for unjust debts and trial expenses.[64] The forced butchering destroys the economic foundation of the Sami, which is disastrous for their culture and way of life. The rise of the alien and the butchering of the ox are linked in the same textual unit in Deut 28. The film's use of the text makes an intrinsic connection between colonial practices and their effect on ecology. The film's subtle critique of this connection comes close to what we term *ecolonialism* and fits well with the Earth Charter's concern for ecological integrity. The charter encourages the adoption of "patterns of production, consumption, and reproduction that safeguard Earth's regenerative capacities, human rights, and community well-being."[65]

Reverberating Ecolonial Concerns

This connection between ecology, colonial politics, and the Bible is also relevant for Sami issues today. We mention one—potential oil extraction in the Barents region.[66] The Norwegian government is exploring the possibility of oil production in the Barents Sea. This is a politically contested issue, and opinion is also split within the Sami community. A number of Sami community leaders and religious bodies are among the most vocal protesters, together with environmental groups. The situation may be compared to the heated controversy around the construction of the Alta Dam in the late 1970s.[67] In spite of vigorous protests from the Sami population and environmental groups, Norwegian authorities built the dam, which was a very serious encroachment on Sami territory, causing loss of important grazing areas and reduced access to other natural resources, which the Norwegian state now wanted to exploit. If oil is extracted in the north in the future, accidents would be catastrophic for the entire Arctic region, as the ecosystem in such extreme climates is highly vulnerable.[68] Moreover, the day-to-day business of oil production in the Barents Sea will have consequences for nature and environment in northern

---

[64] The Sami relied on a barter rather than monetary economic system, so payment was made in reindeer.

[65] http://tinyurl.com/jbl1354mm.

[66] Other issues concern conflicts over predation, loss of grazing areas, and reindeer dying en masse from starvation. These issues involve a complex combination of factors that reindeer owners and the state regard differently. Moreover, climate change results in winters with ice-covered ground, which makes it difficult for reindeer to identify and penetrate to vegetation.

[67] For a brief overview, see Hætta, *Sami*, 70–71.

[68] A similar situation is facing the indigenous peoples of Alaska. For a discussion of their situation, see Marion Grau, "Caribou and Carbon Colonialism: Toward a Theology of Arctic Place," in Kearns and Keller, *Ecospirit*, 433–53, http://dx.doi.org/10.5422/fso/9780823227457.003.0022.

Norway and will therefore affect Sami reindeer husbandry and culture. A report commissioned by the Norwegian petroleum company StatoilHydro, and authored primarily by researchers from the International Centre for Reindeer Husbandry, concludes that extensive petroleum activity and piecemeal development in the Barents region will lead to a reduction of grazing areas, reduced herd production, increase of internal conflicts, and reduced quality of life for the indigenous populations. At the same time, the report sees the possibility of more sustainable outcomes than these if herders, their communities, and indigenous scientists become seriously involved in the process.[69]

The discussion about oil extraction has also reached the churches in Norway. In 2007, major and minor Christian denominations launched an ecumenical "decade for the environment," calling not only for a "green church" but also for a "green society." The churches base their commitment on what they consider a biblical view of "responsible stewardship of creation."[70] In line with this, the majority church in Norway, the Church of Norway, has repeatedly called for CO_2 reductions and innovation within energy production.[71] Its bishops have, on several occasions after 2007, argued in the media for decreased oil production and a prohibition against further oil drilling, as has the Sami Church Council, actively referring to the Bible for arguments.[72] At the time of this writing, the most recent example of this engagement is an op-ed in the national newspaper *Aftenposten* (9 February 2015), in which the two bishops who govern dioceses in northern Norway joined the leaders of an environmental group and a workers' association in warning against oil drilling in the north.[73] The op-ed caused political outrage; Tina Bru, a member of the Norwegian Parliament who is on the committee for energy and the environment, renounced her Church of Norway membership in protest against the

---

[69] Vistnes et al., *Reindeer Husbandry and Barents 2030*.

[70] Christian Network for Environment and Justice, "Grønn Kirke," http://tinyurl.com/jbl1354n.

[71] Church of Norway, "Klima og miljø," http://tinyurl.com/jbl1354o1 and http://tinyurl.com/jbl1354o2. At the time of writing, the most recent official statement is the Church of Norway Council on Ecumenical and International Relations, "Må styrke Norges klimainnsats," released 27 November 2014, http://tinyurl.com/jbl1354p. This statement complements an earlier one from 22 September 2014, in which leaders from eleven different religions in Norway called for a reduction in Norway's emissions; see Council for Religious and Life Stance Communities, "Sammen må vi ta klimautfordringene på alvor! En appell fra tros- og livssynsledere i Norge," statement released 22 September 2014, http://tinyurl.com/jbl1354q. For a critical evaluation of ecological statements from the Norwegian church from 1969 to 2007, see Tom Sverre Tomren, "Miljøetikk og økoteologi I [sic] Den norske kyrkja: Ein analyse av miljøfråsegnene til Den norske kyrkja i perioden 1969–2007" (PhD diss., MHS School of Mission and Theology, 2014).

[72] NRK, "—Ikke nok å bare be til gud [sic]," interview with Anne Dalheim, leader of the Sami Church Council, and Sami politician Ole Henrik Magga, 8 August 2013, http://tinyurl.com/jbl1354rr.

[73] John Leirvaag et al., "Erna, Tine, Tord og Siv smelter iskanten," *Aftenposten*, 9 February 2015, http://tinyurl.com/jbl1354ss.

bishops' clear political stance.[74] In the debate on petroleum extraction in the Barents region, biblical interpretation has become a burning issue at the intersection of ecological concerns, the rights of indigenous peoples, and the state's financial profit.

IV. Conclusion

In this article, we have presented some suggestions for a broader ecological hermeneutical approach to the Bible. Starting with a broad definition of ecological hermeneutics, we have suggested that the Earth Charter may serve as a framework for such ecological readings. As a global, interdisciplinary, and interreligious call to action, it integrates ecology with concerns for democracy, peace, and equal distribution of resources. In line with this, we have also proposed a diversification in methodological approaches, integrating ecological hermeneutics with other approaches to the Bible. As an example of one approach, we have argued the case for *ecolonialism*, an ecological approach informed by postcolonial insights. Looking at some uses of the Bible in *The Kautokeino Rebellion*, our *ecolonial* reading revealed how exploitation of land and natural resources cannot be understood without the context of Norwegian colonizing efforts toward the Sami population of northern Norway. The film shows how the Bible was used both as a tool to colonize and exploit *and* as a tool to talk back and fight the oppression. We end by quoting the lyrics of the movie's theme song, "Elle." To our minds this is an apt expression of an *ecolonial* stance, weaving together the forces of nature and the force of people who can no longer stay silent.

> Elle
>
> At last the spring river opened up again,
> At last we let ourselves drift with the flow.
> Finally the night of ice had to give in,
> my dearest son of the wind.
>
> For sure I flew with the bluethroat.
> For sure I danced with the northern light.
> In a powerful breath we exhaled as one,
> my dearest son of the wind.
>
> And so, the lips of the silenced people bursted out in speech.
> And so, the flood of words once again started moving
> overflowing the frozen riverbanks,
> as we finally came together,
> my dearest son of the wind.

---

[74] NRK, "Melder seg ut av kirken etter olje-kronikk," interview with Tina Bru February 11, 2015, http://tinyurl.com/jbl1354tt.

When you're walking alongside the reindeer-herd,
when you herd the beautiful bulls with the great antlers,
then all of the horizon comes alive and starts to sway,
my dearest son of the wind.[75]

[75] Original Sami lyrics by Rawdna Carita Eira, melody by Mari Boine. English translation by Rawdna Carita Eira. Reprinted here with the kind permission of Rawdna Carita Eira

New from
BAKER ACADEMIC

Paul the Ancient Letter Writer
An Introduction to Epistolary Analysis
Jeffrey A. D. Weima
978-0-8010-9751-5 • 288 pp. • $24.99p

"An outstanding book from a seasoned and much-respected scholar."

—**Paul Foster**, University of Edinburgh

Paul and Gender
Reclaiming the Apostle's Vision for Men and Women in Christ
Cynthia Long Westfall
978-0-8010-9794-2 • 368 pp. • $32.99p

"Guaranteed to inform and challenge readers to think of gender and sexuality in light of a genuinely biblical worldview."

—**Michael F. Bird**, Ridley College

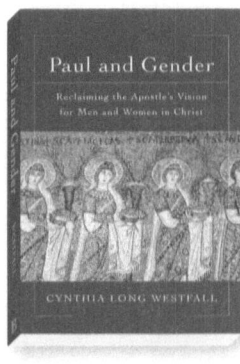

Hermeneutics as Apprenticeship
How the Bible Shapes Our Interpretive Habits and Practices
David I. Starling
978-0-8010-4939-2 • 256 pp. • $24.99p

"This is a book not to be missed by those who are charged with discerning God's word for the Christian people."

—**Stanley Hauerwas**, Duke Divinity School

Ⓑ Baker Academic

bakeracademic.com
Available in bookstores or by calling 800.877.2665

JBL 135, no. 4 (2016): 685–704
doi: http://dx.doi.org/10.15699/jbl.1354.2016.3091

A Study in Scarlet:
The Physiology and Treatment of Blood, Breath, and Fish in Ancient Israel

RICHARD WHITEKETTLE
rwhiteke@calvin.edu
Calvin College, Grand Rapids, MI 49546

Leviticus 7:26 and 17:10–14 state that the blood of land animals and aerial animals must not be consumed. These verses say nothing, however, about the blood of fish, implying that the consumption of fish blood is permitted. This difference in the treatment of land/aerial animal blood and fish blood is based on a belief that the blood of land/aerial animals is a breath/blood amalgam, while the blood of fish is simply blood. Thus, what Lev 7:26 and 17:10–14 prohibited was the consumption of a land/aerial animal's breath/blood amalgam. And, since it was breath that set this amalgam apart from the blood of a fish, it was really the consumption of a land/aerial animal's breath that was being prohibited. It was believed that the breath of a land/aerial animal was the essence of its life and that God had complete sovereignty over a land/aerial animal's breath. Consequently, by prohibiting its consumption, the Levitical/Priestly tradents hallowed the breath of a land/aerial animal and acknowledged that sovereignty over it belonged exclusively to God.

The consumption of animal blood is prohibited in Gen 9:4; Lev 3:17; 7:26; 17:10–14; 19:26; Deut 12:16, 23–25; and 15:23. The reason given for this prohibition is that an animal's blood is associated with its נפש (Gen 9:4; Lev 17:11, 14; Deut 12:23), which is usually understood as being its "life." As to why this meant that the blood was not to be consumed, scholars have generally argued that, because blood was equated with life, it was thought to belong exclusively to God, who is the creator of life.[1]

---

[1] Jacob Milgrom, *Leviticus: A Book of Ritual and Ethics*, CC (Minneapolis: Fortress, 2004), 105, 189; Roy Gane, *Cult and Character: Purification Offerings, Day of Atonement, and Theodicy* (Winona Lake, IN: Eisenbrauns, 2005), 63–64; Rolf P. Knierim, *Text and Concept in Leviticus 1:1–9: A Case in Exegetical Method*, FAT 2 (Tübingen: Mohr Siebeck, 1992), 56–57, 66. The meaning of נפש in Gen 9:4; Lev 17:11, 14; and Deut 12:23 will be discussed later.

685

Leviticus 7:26 and 17:10–14 state that the animals whose blood must not be consumed are land and aerial animals. In addition, Lev 17:13 states that it is edible wild land and aerial animals whose blood must not be consumed. If one assumes that the dietary regulations of Lev 11:2–23 are part of the thought world behind Lev 7:26 and 17:10–14 (reasonable assumptions given the Levitical/Priestly nature of all three texts), then Lev 7:26 and 17:10–14 prohibit consuming the blood of the land and aerial animals that are edible according to Lev 11:2–23. Curiously though, while Lev 7:26 and 17:10–14 prohibit consuming the blood of edible land and aerial animals, they do not mention the blood of edible aquatic animals, which, according to Lev 11:9–12, are fish.[2]

This article will explain why there was a prohibition against consuming the blood of land/aerial animals and why there was no prohibition against consuming the blood of fish. To do this, I will show the following. The absence of fish from Lev 7:26 and 17:10–14 was intentional and not accidental (section I). The Levitical/Priestly legists behind these texts believed that land/aerial animals breathed air but fish did not (sections II–IV) and that breath formed an amalgam with a land/aerial animal's blood. This belief is what lay behind (a) the prohibition against consuming a land/aerial animal's blood (which was a breath/blood amalgam) and (b) the permission to consume a fish's blood (which was only blood and not a breath/blood amalgam) (sections V–VI). I will then conclude with several observations about Israelite thought regarding blood, breath, and fish (section VII).

I. An Intentional Absence

There are two ways to account for the absence of fish from Lev 7:26 and 17:10–14. First, if the prohibition against consuming an animal's blood applied to fish, as the Qumran community believed, it would have to be argued that fish were ignored or overlooked in Lev 7:26 and 17:10–14.[3] Second, if the prohibition did not apply to fish, as the rabbinic community believed, it would have to be argued that fish were not mentioned in Lev 7:26 and 17:10–14 because the red fluid in their bodies (hereafter simply blood) did not qualify as blood, which must not be consumed.[4]

---

[2] As for the other blood prohibition texts, Lev 19:26 gives no indication of the animals at issue. Leviticus 3:17, Deut 12:16, 12:23–25, and 15:23 focus on land animals. Genesis 9:4 prohibits consuming flesh (בשר) with blood. The word בשר is used throughout the flood story, before and after Gen 9:4, to refer specifically to land and aerial animals (Gen 6:17, 19; 7:15, 16, 21; 8:17; 9:11, 15, 16, 17 [all of which, along with Gen 9:4, are often ascribed to a Priestly source]). It is likely, then, that Gen 9:4 prohibits the consumption of the blood of land and aerial animals, and not of the land, aerial, and aquatic animals of Gen 9:2–3.

[3] See Jodi Magness, *Stone and Dung, Oil and Spit: Jewish Daily Life in the Time of Jesus* (Grand Rapids: Eerdmans, 2011), 37–41.

[4] See Jacob Neusner, *A History of the Mishnaic Law of Holy Things*, 6 vols., SJLA 30 (Leiden:

Several things suggest that fish were not ignored or overlooked in Lev 7:26 and 17:10–14. First, the laws of Lev 11:2–23 regulate the consumption of land animals (vv. 2–8), aquatic animals (vv. 9–12), two-legged aerial animals (vv. 13–19), and four-legged aerial animals (vv. 20–23). Thus, Levitical/Priestly thinkers were well aware of the need to regulate the consumption of aquatic animals along with other animals. Second, the fact that aquatic animals occupy the second of four positions in the sequence shows that they were an integral part of Levitical/Priestly thinking about consumption. Third, as seen in the following chart, the laws of Lev 11:9–12 classify aquatic animals through three levels of taxonomic differentiation (levels 2, 3, and 4):

1.	aquatic animals		כל אשר במים
	2a.	with fins/scales (i.e., fish)	כל אשר־לו סנפיר וקשקשת
		3a. living in seas/lakes	בימים
		3b. living in streams	בנחלים
	2b.	without fins/scales (i.e., nonfish)	כל אשר אין־לו סנפיר וקשקשת
		3a. living in seas/lakes	בימים
		4a. שרץ activity	כל שרץ המים
		4b. non-שרץ activity	כל נפש החיה אשר במים
		3b. living in streams	בנחלים
		4a. שרץ activity	כל שרץ המים
		4b. non-שרץ activity	כל נפש החיה אשר במים

Thus, aquatic animals elicited careful and thorough scrutiny from Levitical/Priestly thinkers. Fourth, the laws of Lev 11:2–23 were revised and supplemented over time, indicating an interest among Levitical/Priestly thinkers in creating and enhancing clarity and precision in their dietary (and carcass) prescriptions.[5] Thus, if the prohibition against consuming blood applied to fish, it is likely that this would have been inserted into Lev 7:26 and 17:10–14 at some time or mentioned in some other text.

Brill, 1978–1980), 5:49–51 §5.1; Neusner, *Sifra: An Analytical Translation*, 3 vols., BJS 138–140 (Atlanta: Scholars Press, 1988), 2:90–91 §XCIII.IV; Magness, *Stone and Dung*, 37–41.

[5] Richard Whitekettle, "The Raven as Kind and Kinds of Ravens: A Study in the Zoological Nomenclature of Leviticus 11,2–23," *ZAW* 117 (2005): 509–28; Whitekettle, "One If by And: Conjunctions, Taxonomic Development, and the Animals of Leviticus 11,26," *ZAW* 121 (2009): 481–97, http://dx.doi.org/10.1515/zaw.2009.032; David P. Wright, "The Spectrum of Priestly Impurity," in *Priesthood and Cult in Ancient Israel*, ed. Gary A. Anderson and Saul M. Olyan, JSOTSup 125 (Sheffield: JSOT Press, 1991), 150–81, here 167–69; Jacob Milgrom, *Leviticus 1–16: A New Translation with Introduction and Commentary*, AB 3 (New York: Doubleday, 1991), 691–98, esp. 693–95 regarding 11:39–40 and 46–47. Milgrom observes that שקץ and טמא are used differently in 11:43–45 than elsewhere in Lev 11 (695), which suggests that, as a supplement, 11:43–45 may not have enhanced clarity (at least not to a modern reader).

In sum, Levitical/Priestly thought regarding consumption had a robust interest in aquatic animals and in clarity and precision. Fish would not, therefore, have been ignored or overlooked in the consumption laws of Lev 7:26 and 17:10–14.

It follows, then, that fish were not mentioned in Lev 7:26 and 17:10–14 because the blood consumption prohibition did not apply to them and that this was because their blood did not qualify as blood, which must not be consumed. But why would that be? If a fish is caught and injured so that it begins to lose blood, and the fish is returned to the water where it has everything necessary for a happy fish life, it will die, showing that its blood is just as integral to its life as the blood of a gazelle or a dove is to theirs. Since this is a readily observable phenomenon, and since Levitical/Priestly thinkers had a robust interest in aquatic animals, it seems reasonable to assume that they knew this.[6] What difference, then, did they see between fish and land/aerial animals such that they permitted the consumption of fish blood but prohibited the consumption of land/aerial animal blood?[7]

II. Animal Attributes

There are two ways to identify differences between fish and land/aerial animals in the Israelite textual record. One way is to see what characteristics are associated with land/aerial animals but never with fish or with fish but never with land/aerial animals. The problem with such an approach, however, is that there is no way to tell whether an attribute was not associated with certain animals because it was

---

[6] While it is reasonable to assume that the Israelites, through empirical observation, believed that fish had blood that was integral to their existence, the textual record is silent on this. As to the reason for this silence, in 112 of the 137 instances where animal blood is mentioned, the blood is that of the sacrificial animals used in the Israelite cult, a set of animals that does not include fish. In twenty instances, the discussion revolves around the consumption of land or land/aerial animal blood, with those particular animals mentioned (Lev 7:26, 27; 17:13, 14 [3x]; Deut 12:16, 23; 15:23; 1 Sam 14:32, 33, 34), understood from context (Gen 9:4 [see n. 2]; Lev 3:17; 17:10 [2x]; Deut 12:23), or understood from the Levitical/Priestly character of the text (Lev 19:26, Ezek 33:25, Zech 9:7) (since there is no evidence to indicate or suggest the contrary, it is assumed here that Levitical/Priestly thought was consistent regarding the types of animals whose blood was not to be consumed). In five instances, the blood belongs to specific land/aerial animals or land/aerial prey animals (Gen 37:31, Num 23:24, Job 39:27–30, Isa 66:3, Ezek 14:19). In sum, there was little interest in animal blood beyond that of sacrificial animals and edible land/aerial animals. What little interest there was involved the blood of specific land/aerial animals. Thus, the textual record is silent regarding fish blood because it was not relevant to the interests of the authors to whose thinking we have access.

[7] The aspects of blood on which this article focuses are the understanding of its physiology and the regulation of its consumption. The relationship between these matters and other matters involving blood (e.g., cultic and social matters [e.g., Lev 4:1–5:13, Deut 21:1–9]), will not be taken up here. For recent treatments of some of these other matters, see Yitzhaq Feder, *Blood Expiation in Hittite and Biblical Ritual: Origins, Context, and Meaning*, WAWSup 2 (Atlanta: Society of Biblical Literature, 2011); William K. Gilders, *Blood Ritual in the Hebrew Bible: Meaning and Power* (Baltimore: Johns Hopkins University Press, 2004).

not characteristic of them or simply because it was never mentioned. For example, the homes and sounds of land and aerial animals are mentioned in the textual record, but those of fish are not.[8] This could be because the Israelites believed that fish had no homes and made no sound or because there was never a need or occasion to mention these things.

The other way to identify differences between fish and land/aerial animals is to look at texts containing primary-level taxonomic schemas. More specifically, the other way is to look at texts containing *truncated-form*, primary-level taxonomic schemas.

A primary-level taxonomic schema encompasses a segment of a zoological classification system. In such a system, a society divides its entire animal inventory into several primary-level taxa (e.g., animals → land/aquatic/flying). These primary-level taxa are subdivided into several, more exclusive secondary-level taxa (e.g., flying animals → insects/birds), some or all of which are subdivided into several, more exclusive tertiary-level taxa (e.g., birds → sparrows/crows/warblers), and so forth. The process of subdivision ends in a terminal level of specificity beyond which categoric distinctions are no longer made (e.g., warblers → Blackburnian warbler/Worm-eating warbler).[9] Thus, a primary-level taxonomic schema consists of the taxa at the broadest level of differentiation in a classification system.

There are several primary-level taxonomic schemas found in the Israelite textual record:[10]

Schema I	Schema II	Schema III	Schema IV	Schema V
land	h-c land	domesticated land	domesticated land	land
	l-c land	wild land	h-c wild land	
			l-c wild land	
aerial	aerial	aerial	aerial	2-legged aerial
				4-legged aerial
aquatic	aquatic	aquatic	aquatic	aquatic

[8] Richard Whitekettle, "Of Mice and Wren: Terminal Level Taxa in Israelite Zoological Thought," SJOT 17 (2003): 163–82, http://dx.doi.org/10.1080/09018320410001001.

[9] Brent Berlin, *Ethnobiological Classification: Principles of Categorization of Plants and Animals in Traditional Societies* (Princeton: Princeton University Press, 1992), 16, http://dx.doi.org/10.1515/9781400862597; Ralph Bulmer, "Which Came First, the Chicken or the Egg-Head?," in *Échanges et communications: Mélanges offerts à Claude Lévi-Strauss à l'occasion de son 60ème anniversaire*, ed. Jean Pouillon and Pierre Maranda, Studies in General Anthropology 5 (The Hague: Mouton, 1970), 1069–91, here 1073–74. An example of such a classification structure in Israelite zoological thought can be seen in the chart in section I, which schematizes the classification of aquatic animals (a primary-level taxon) found in Lev 11:9–12.

[10] Richard Whitekettle, "Where the Wild Things Are: Primary Level Taxa in Israelite Zoological Thought," JSOT 93 (2001): 17–37, http://dx.doi.org/10.1177/030908920102509303. High carriage (h-c) land animals move over the ground (e.g., hares, goats); low carriage (l-c) land animals move along the ground (e.g., rats, snakes). See Richard Whitekettle, "Rats Are Like Snakes, and Hares Are Like Goats: A Study in Israelite Land Animal Taxonomy," Bib 82 (2001): 345–62.

As can be seen in the following chart, in some of the texts that contain a primary-level schema, all of the animal taxa that constitute the schema are mentioned (referred to as full-form below); in other texts, however, all of the animal taxa that constitute a schema are mentioned except aquatic animals (referred to as truncated-form below):

	Full-Form	Truncated-Form (i.e., without aquatic animals)
Schema I	Gen 1:20–25, 28; Job 12:7–8; Hos 4:3; Zeph 1:3	Gen 2:19; 7:2–3; 8:20; Lev 7:26; 17:13; 20:25a; Job 35:11; Jer 9:9 (Eng. 10); 12:4; Ezek 31:6, 13; Dan 2:38; 4:9, 11, 18 (Eng. 12, 14, 21)
Schema II	Gen 1:26 (MT), 9:2, Lev 11:46, Deut 4:17–18, 1 Kgs 5:13 (Eng. 4:33), Ezek 38:20	Gen 1:30; 6:7, 20; 7:8–9, 23; 8:17, 19; Lev 20:25b; Hos 2:20 (Eng. 18)
Schema III	Pss 8:8–9 (Eng. 7–8), 104:10–26	Gen 2:20, 9:10
Schema IV	Gen 1:26 (*BHS*), Ps 148:7–10	Gen 7:14, 21; Ps 50:10–11
Schema V	Lev 11:2–23, Deut 14:3–20	none

Since a text that uses a truncated-form schema situates land and aerial animals, but not aquatic animals, in a particular context, it is possible that some attribute shared by land and aerial animals, but not by aquatic animals, is the reason for the absence of aquatic animals.

The chart on the following page lists the texts containing truncated-form primary-level schemas (taken from the chart above), identifies the attributes of the land/aerial animals mentioned in each of these texts and groups texts involving similar characteristics together.

The only texts that mention a physical characteristic of land/aerial animals are those in group J. The characteristic in Gen 1:30 is נפש חיה. The phrase נפש חיה is used twelve other times in the textual record (Gen 1:20, 21, 24; 2:7, 19; 9:10, 12, 15, 16; Lev 11:10, 46; Ezek 47:9). In each of these instances, it is used as a label—living creature(s)—for the animals or human being mentioned in the text. In Gen 1:30, however, נפש חיה is not a label for animals but rather a label for something in animals (אשר־בו נפש חיה).

As to what this thing is, נפש can refer to desire, soul, or throat. It is unlikely, though, that any of these meanings is intended in Gen 1:30, since it is unlikely that such things would have been (1) associated in Gen 1 with animals and not also humans (e.g., soul of life/living soul), (2) associated with animals (e.g., desire of life/living desire), or (3) thought of at all (e.g., throat of life/living throat).

Group	Text	Attributes of Land/Aerial Animals
A	Lev 7:26	land/aerial blood must not be consumed
	Lev 17:13	land/aerial blood must not be consumed
B	Gen 2:19	land/aerial formed from ground and brought to the אדם for naming
	Gen 2:20	land/aerial named by the אדם
C	Gen 8:20	land/aerial that are clean are sacrificed to God
	Lev 20:25a	land/aerial are divisible into clean and unclean types
	Lev 20:25b	land/aerial that are unclean should be avoided
D	Job 35:11	land/aerial are wise but less so than human beings
E	Jer 9:9 (Eng. 10)	land/aerial are absent from a desolate land
	Jer 12:4	land/aerial are absent from a desolate land
F	Ezek 31:6	land/aerial live under/on tree
	Ezek 31:13	land/aerial live around/on fallen tree
	Dan 4:9 (Eng. 12)	land/aerial live under/on tree
	Dan 4:11 (Eng. 14)	land/aerial depart from under/on tree
	Dan 4:18 (Eng. 21)	land/aerial live under/on tree
G	Ps 50:10–11	land/aerial belong to God
	Dan 2:38	land/aerial under authority of king (Nebuchadnezzar)
H	Gen 9:10	land/aerial are parties in covenant with God
	Hos 2:20 (Eng. 18)	land/aerial are parties in covenant between them and humans
I	Gen 6:7	land/aerial will be wiped from earth by flood
	Gen 6:20	land/aerial will board ark to survive flood
	Gen 7:2–3	land/aerial will board ark to survive flood
	Gen 7:8–9	land/aerial board ark to survive flood
	Gen 8:17	land/aerial will exit ark after flood so they can multiply/fill the land
	Gen 8:19	land/aerial exit the ark after flood
J	Gen 1:30	land/aerial have נפש חיה in them
	Gen 7:14 (+ 15)	land/aerial have רוח חיים in them
	Gen 7:21 (+ 22)	land/aerial have נשמת־רוח היים in them
	Gen 7:23 (+ 22)	land/aerial have נשמת־רוח היים in them

The word נפש can also refer to breath. Breath would have been a recognized characteristic of land/aerial animals, as well as something that was thought of as being in them. Furthermore, there is a simple reason why this aspect of creaturely existence was associated with animals but not with human beings in Gen 1 (discussed in the first paragraph of section III). In sum, it is reasonable to assume that נפש חיה means "breath of life/living breath" in Gen 1:30.[11]

The characteristic in Gen 7:14–15 is רוח חיים. The expression רוח חיים is mentioned in association with animals also in Gen 6:17, though no particular types of animals are mentioned there. Whether one connects 6:17 with 7:14–15 through a common (Priestly) literary tradition or with 7:14–15 (and 6:7) by reading Gen 6–9 as a whole, it can be assumed that 6:17, like 7:14–15, associates רוח חיים with land/aerial animals.

Regarding the meaning of the phrase רוח חיים, רוח can refer to wind, breath, and spirit. Wind can be ruled out because רוח חיים is said to be in animals in 6:17 and 7:14–15 (אשר־בו רוח חיים). As for breath and spirit, 6:17 says that water will kill animals, while 7:14–15 understands that the animals on a boat will not be killed by water. Both of these texts, therefore, reflect a concern with drowning. Further, in each text, the animals that will or will not die by drowning are described as having רוח חיים in them. Thus, 6:17 and 7:14–15 create a direct connection between drowning and the רוח חיים in a land/aerial animal. It is reasonable to assume, then, that רוח חיים in Gen 6:17 and 7:14–15 is an animal's breath of life, the thing that would be viscerally affected by drowning.[12] This conclusion is strengthened by the fact that the verb used to describe the death of animals in 6:17 is גוע, a verb associated with the loss of breath (e.g., Job 34:14–15, Ps 104:29) and with a person's last action before death (i.e., taking a last breath) (e.g., Gen 25:8, 17; 35:29; 49:33).

The characteristic in Gen 7:21–23 is נשמת־רוח חיים. The most basic meaning of נשמה is breath. This is confirmed as its meaning in 7:21–23 by its presence in the nose of land/aerial animals in 7:22 (באפו), and the use of the verb גוע (see preceding paragraph) in 7:21 to describe the death of the animals that have נשמת־רוח חיים in their nose. Thus, נשמת־רוח חיים refers to the "breath of life" in Gen 7:21–23.[13]

In sum, Gen 1:30, 6:17, 7:14–15, and 7:21–23 reflect a belief that land and aerial animals breathe air. Does the absence of fish from these texts, however, reflect a belief that fish do not breathe air?

---

[11] See Claus Westermann, *Genesis 1–11: A Commentary*, trans. John J. Scullion (Minneapolis: Augsburg, 1984), 77; Gordon J. Wenham, *Genesis 1–15*, WBC 1 (Waco, TX: Word, 1987), 3; Josef Scharbert, *Genesis 1–11*, EchtB (Würzburg: Echter, 1983), 46; *DCH* 5:728, s.v. נֶפֶשׁ; Horst Seebass, "נֶפֶשׁ *nepeš*," *TDOT* 9:497–519, here 504–5. Note that in Gen 2:7 an object becomes a נפש חיה/living creature when it is given breath.

[12] See Theodore Hiebert, "Air, the First Sacred Thing: The Conception of רוח in the Hebrew Scriptures," in *Exploring Ecological Hermeneutics*, ed. Norman C. Habel and Peter Trudinger, SymS 46 (Atlanta: Society of Biblical Literature, 2008), 9–19, here 11–13; Sven Tengström, "רוּחַ *rûaḥ*," *TDOT* 13:365–96, here 375, 387; Horst Seebass, *Genesis I: Urgeschichte (1,1–11,26)* (Neukirchen-Vluyn: Neukirchener Verlag, 1996), 201–2, 215.

[13] See *DCH* 5:779; *HALOT*, s.v. נשמה; Hedwig Lamberty-Zielinski, "נְשָׁמָה *nešāmâ*," *TDOT* 10:65–70, here 66–68; Tengström, *TDOT* 13:375–79.

III. Fish and Air in the Israelite Textual Record

After land, aerial, and aquatic animals are created in Gen 1:20–25, they are merged into broader groupings, first in 1:26–28, where God places all three types of animals under human authority, and then in 1:30, where God gives two types of animals—land and aerial—plants for food. Given the movement from the entire animal inventory in 1:20–28 to just two-thirds of it in 1:30, the mention of breath in 1:30 serves (1) as a characteristic shared by land and aerial animals that explains why they can be treated together in the matter of plants as food (breathing air places them in the terrestrial world, which is where plants also live [Gen 1:11–12]), and (2) as a characteristic that distinguishes the animals that are mentioned (land and aerial) from those that are not (aquatic).

According to Gen 6:17, the flood will destroy the following:

כל־בשר אשר־בו רוח חיים	all flesh in which there is breath
מתחת השמים	from under the heavens,
כל אשר־בארץ	everything that is on the land

The phrase "all flesh in which there is breath" indicates that the flood will destroy all breathing animals (except those on the ark). The phrase "under the heavens" indicates that the destruction will envelop the whole of the habitable world. The appositional phrase "everything that is on the land" indicates that the creatures in the habitable world under the heavens that breathe are those that live on the land, identified elsewhere in the flood story as land/aerial animals.

Genesis 7:14 mentions the land and aerial animals that come on board the ark. Genesis 7:15 describes them as coming "from among all flesh in which there is breath" (מכל־בשר אשר־בו רוח חיים). As an echo of Gen 6:17, Gen 7:15 reflects the belief found in 6:17 that the creatures in the habitable world under the heavens that breathe are those that live on the land, identified elsewhere in the flood story as land/aerial animals.

Genesis 7:21–22 describes in the following way the animals that will die because of the flood (the content of verse 23 parallels the content of the a/b lines):

כל־בשר הרמש על־הארץ	a	all flesh that move on the earth
בעוף ובבהמה ובחיה	b	aerial, domesticated land, h-c land,
ובכל־השרץ השרץ על־הארץ		and all l-c land,
כל אשר נשמת־רוח חיים באפיו	c	everything in which there is breath
מכל אשר בחרבה	d	that is, everything on the dry ground

The a/b-lines define the animals killed by the flood, with the a-line giving the whole complement and the b-line listing the constitutive parts of the whole. The use of the word "everything" in the c-line indicates that death will encompass all breathing animals. Since the c-line is in apposition to the a/b-lines, and explicated in the d-line, the complement of "everything in which there is breath" equals the land and aerial animals of the a/b-lines and the dry ground inhabitants of the d-line.[14]

In sum, Gen 1:30, 6:17, 7:14–15, and 7:21–23 all reflect a belief that land and aerial animals breathe air but that aquatic animals, and therefore fish, do not.

Psalm 104, however, might be thought to reflect a different belief. The psalm mentions land (vv. 11, 14, 18, 20–21), aerial (vv. 12, 17), and aquatic animals (vv. 25–26). Verse 29 describes how, if God takes away "their" breath (רוח), "they" will expire (גוע). Since this follows the earlier mention of land, aerial, and aquatic animals, it might be inferred that the "they" includes all of those animals and, thus, that aquatic animals breathe air. In verse 29, however, when "they" die, they return to their dust (עפרם), a substance associated with the ground and dirt. This comports well with the bodily fate of dead land/aerial animals but not with that of dead aquatic animals.[15] In addition, in Ps 104:30, when God sends out his breath, "they" are created, which renews (with living creatures) the surface of the ground (פני אדמה), a location strongly associated with human beings and land/aerial animals (Gen 4:14; 6:1, 7; 7:4, 23; 8:8, 13; Exod 32:12; 33:16; Num 12:3; Deut 7:6; 14:2; 2 Sam 14:7; 1 Kgs 8:40; 9:7; 17:14; 18:1; 2 Chr 6:31; Isa 23:17; Jer 8:2; 16:4; 25:26, 33; 35:7; Ezek 38:20; Zeph 1:2–3) but not with aquatic animals (only Zeph 1:2–3). Thus, it is very likely that aquatic animals are not being referred to in Ps 104:29–30.

It might be argued, though, that the exclusion of aquatic animals from Ps 104:29–30 is unlikely, given the interest in the entire animal inventory earlier in the psalm. The treatment of aquatic animals in verses 25–26, however, is separated from the treatment of land/aerial animals in verses 10–23 by an expression of wonder in verse 24. In addition, the treatment of land/aerial animals in verses 10–23 is arranged chiastically (wild land – aerial – domesticated land – aerial – wild land), indicating that land/aerial animals constitute an independent section of the animal inventory from which aquatic animals stand apart.[16] Thus, the exclusion of aquatic animals from Ps 104:29–30 would be in accord with the handling of aquatic animals elsewhere in the psalm.

In sum, it is reasonable to assume that Ps 104, like Gen 1:30, 6:17, 7:14–15, and 7:21–23, reflects a belief that fish do not breathe air. Thus, the textual record is consistent on this matter. But who among the ancient Israelites would have held this belief?

---

[14] On the preposition מן in the d-line as explicative, see Ronald J. Williams, *Williams' Hebrew Syntax*, 3rd ed., rev. and exp. by John C. Beckham (Toronto: University of Toronto Press, 2007), 124 §326; Westermann, *Genesis 1–11*, 389, 392; GKC, 382 §119w, n. 2; Paul Joüon and Takamitsu Muraoka, *A Grammar of Biblical Hebrew*, 3rd repr. of 2nd ed. with corrections, SubBi 27 (Rome: Gregorian & Biblical Press, 2011), 460 §133e.

[15] See G. R. Driver, "The Resurrection of Marine and Terrestrial Creatures," *JSS* 7 (1962): 12–22, here 14, http://dx.doi.org/10.1093/jss/7.1.12.

[16] Richard Whitekettle, "A Communion of Subjects: Zoological Classification and Human/Animal Relations in Psalm 104," *BBR* 21 (2011): 173–87.

IV. Fish and Air in Israel

With regard to who among the Israelites believed that fish do not breathe air, several things can be noted. First, although they are few in number, the texts that evince the belief that fish do not breathe air are varied in nature: Gen 1:30 is part of a creation story; Gen 6:17, 7:14–15, and 7:21–23 are parts of a narrative text; and Ps 104 is a hymnic text; Gen 1:30, 6:17, and 7:14–15 are often regarded as Priestly texts, while Gen 7:22–23 is often regarded as Yahwistic material. Second, aquatic animals (or matters related to them) are mentioned elsewhere in texts of different types, times, and traditions (e.g., Gen 1:20–23; 7:14–15, 21–22; Exod 7:14–24; Lev 11:9–12; Num 11:22; Deut 14:9–10; Job 40:31 [Eng. 41:7]; Pss 8:9b [Eng. 8b]; 104:25–26; 105:29; Eccl 9:12; Isa 19:8; 50:2; Ezek 26:5, 14; 29:4–5; 32:3; 47:1–12; Amos 4:2; Jonah 2:1 [Eng. 1:17]; 2:11 [Eng. 10]; Hab 1:14–17). Third, there is archaeological evidence for the consumption, use, and trade of aquatic animals and aquatic animal products in the territory where the Israelites lived.[17] In sum, knowledge of and about aquatic animals was part of the general Israelite thought world and was not confined to fisherfolk and mariners or to one school of thought or literary tradition. Given this, and since the belief that fish do not breathe air is a basic piece of information about their existence (which would be given, for example, in response to a child's question about why fish do not drown), it would appear that it was a general Israelite belief.

An examination of how people from elsewhere in the ancient eastern Mediterranean world thought about fish and air lends support and nuance to this claim.[18]

---

[17] See, e.g., Oded Borowski, *Every Living Thing: Daily Use of Animals in Ancient Israel* (Walnut Creek, CA: AltaMira, 1998), 167–84; Ronny Reich, Eli Shukron, and Omri Lernau, "Recent Discoveries in the City of David, Jerusalem," *IEJ* 57 (2007): 153–69, here 157–60, 163; Paula Wapnish and Brian Hesse, "Faunal Remains from Tel Dan: Perspectives on Animal Production at a Village, Urban and Ritual Center," *Archaeozoologica* 4 (1991): 9–86, here 14, 17, 18; James W. Hardin, "Understanding Domestic Space: An Example from Iron Age Tel Halif," *NEA* 67 (2004): 71–84, here 75–77, 80, 82, http://dx.doi.org/10.2307/4132363.

[18] The amount of information in the Israelite textual record regarding the physiology of blood, breath, and fish is limited. Material from elsewhere in the ancient eastern Mediterranean world can fill in conceptual gaps in the Israelite data. There is no textual evidence for the influence and/or borrowing of ideas regarding these physiologic matters between Israel and nearby cultures. Yet skeletal remains of Mediterranean and Nile fish species have been found at Iron Age sites located in the area occupied by the ancient Israelites (see, e.g., Borowski, *Every Living Thing*, 172–76). It is quite possible, then, that some Israelites may have shared with others in the ancient eastern Mediterranean world an understanding of how these common objects of consumption existed when they were alive, an understanding developed at the water's edge, along trade routes, and in marketplaces, as fisherfolk, merchants, consumers, and neighbors exchanged products, money, and ideas. In light of this possibility, I assume here, cautiously and tentatively and for heuristic purposes (1) that there was some amount of common ground regarding the physiology of blood, breath, and fish across the cognitive environment of the ancient eastern Mediterranean

According to Aristotle, Anaxagoras of Clazomenae (prob. 500–428 BCE) believed that when fish "discharge water through their gills, air is formed in the mouth … and it is by drawing in this that they respire."[19] Also according to Aristotle, Diogenes of Apollonia (fifth century BCE) believed that when fish "discharge water through their gills, they suck the air out of the water surrounding the mouth … for he believes there is air in the water."[20] Plato (ca. 429–347 BCE) says in *Timaeus* that aquatic animals, "in place of breathing the fine and clean air … inhale the muddy water of the depths."[21] Aristotle (384–322 BCE) believed that aquatic animals with lungs (e.g., dolphins) breathed atmospheric air but that those with gills (e.g., fish) took in only water.[22]

From this review, one can assume that there was a consensus among Greek thinkers that fish did not take in atmospheric air (this is explicit in Aristotle and implicit in others). The consensus about this form of breathing from elsewhere in the ancient eastern Mediterranean world lends support to the idea that the Israelites in general did not think that fish breathed air, at least not atmospheric air.

Though there was a consensus among Greek thinkers that fish did not breathe atmospheric air, there were different opinions about whether fish breathed aquatic air (i.e., air found in water). Anaxagoras and Diogenes thought they did, while Aristotle thought they did not. Aristotle criticized Plato for not explaining whether, according to his theory of respiration, all animals or only land animals breathe air.[23] It is unclear, then, whether Plato thought that fish take in air found in the muddy water they inhale.

The Presocratic philosophers Anaxagoras and Diogenes thought that fish were able to breathe aquatic air because they believed that air was present in water, a belief based on their conceptions of matter. For Anaxagoras, "The entities [e.g., air and water] in the original mix [of the world] are ingredients of the phenomenal things … in the world around us; these phenomena are mixtures, produced by the mixture and breaking up of the things that separate off from the original mix."[24]

---

world, and (2) that ideas regarding these physiologic matters found among some of the people who lived nearby can shed light on how the/some Israelites thought about these matters. Regarding the idea of common ground across a cognitive environment, see John H. Walton, *Ancient Near Eastern Thought and the Old Testament: Introducing the Conceptual World of the Hebrew Bible* (Grand Rapids: Baker Academic, 2006), 21, and more broadly 15–28.

[19] Aristotle, *Resp.* 470b33–471a2, trans. G. R. T. Ross, in *The Works of Aristotle*, vol. 3, ed. W. D. Ross (Oxford: Oxford University Press, 1931).

[20] Aristotle, *Resp.* 471a2–5 (Ross, *Works of Aristotle*).

[21] Plato, *Tim.* 92b, trans. Francis Macdonald Cornford, in *Plato's Cosmology: The Timaeus Translated with a Running Commentary* (New York: Humanities Press, 1952), 358.

[22] Aristotle, *Hist. an.* 504b27–29, 589a31–589b22; *Part. an.* 668b33–669a13, 676a26–29, 697a14–24; *Resp.* 475b29–476a15, 480b12–20.

[23] Aristotle, *Resp.* 472b6–473a2. See David Ross, *Aristotle, Parva Naturalia: A Revised Text with Introduction and Commentary* (Oxford: Oxford University Press, 1955), 310–12.

[24] Patricia Curd, *Anaxagoras of Clazomenae, Fragments and Testimonia: A Text and*

Thus, "every stretch of matter [is] a mixture ... of all substances, but in varying concentrations."[25] For Diogenes, "The phenomenal stuffs of the world result from alterations of a basic kind of matter, namely air."[26] Air is "the material of which all the world is composed.... it penetrates everywhere, and it 'steers' everything and 'disposes' everything."[27]

Aristotle thought that fish did not breathe aquatic air because of the following empirical observations: (1) lungs are necessary for breathing air, and fish lack lungs; (2) there is no evidence of inhaled air in the bodies of fish; (3) there is no evidence of the exhalation of air from the bodies of fish; (4) fish die in the air, which shows that they do not breathe air; (5) terrestrial animals (i.e., land and aerial animals) cannot breathe when submerged in water, which shows that there is no air in the water for them to breathe; and (6) water does not contain air, as evidenced by the fact that air introduced into water does not stay there but rises to the surface and exits.[28]

The Israelite conception of matter does not appear to match the thinking of either Anaxagoras or Diogenes. For example, the foundational creation story in Gen 1 understands the present world to be the result of a process in which the various elements of the world were separated from one another and are now kept separate. While the author (or authors) of Gen 1 was presumably aware that elements could overlap (e.g., water + earth = mud), the focus in Gen 1 on the separation of elements suggests, at least, that the author did not share Anaxagoras's idea that every stretch of matter was a mixture of substances or Diogenes's idea that everything is suffused with air. This in turn suggests that the author of Gen 1 did not think that there was air in water for fish to breathe, at least not on the basis of an Anaxagorean/Diogenean conception of matter.

As for the thinking of Aristotle, some Israelites knew that fish die when they are not in water, which suggests that they knew that fish die in the air (Isa 19:5–8; 50:2; Hab 1:14–17), and some knew that terrestrial creatures cannot breathe when submerged in water (Gen 6:17; 7:14–15, 21–23; Jonah 1:13–16).[29] Moreover, in view of the anatomical knowledge that would have come from sacrificial and culinary butchering, it can be assumed that some Israelites knew that the lungs of terrestrial animals were involved with the inhalation of air and that fish did not

---

Translation with Notes and Essays, Phoenix Pre-Socratics 6 (Toronto: University of Toronto Press, 2007), 198.

[25] Daniel W. Graham, *Explaining the Cosmos: The Ionian Tradition of Scientific Philosophy* (Princeton: Princeton University Press, 2006), 198.

[26] Ibid., 289.

[27] David Furley, *The Formation of the Atomic Theory and Its Earliest Critics*, vol. 1 of *The Greek Cosmologists* (Cambridge: Cambridge University Press, 1987), 65.

[28] Aristotle, *Resp.* 471a5–471b29, 475b29–476a15; *Sens.* 443a3–6.

[29] On Hab 1:14–17, see Richard Whitekettle, "Like a Fish and Shrimp out of Water: Identifying the *Dāg* and *Remeś* Animals of Habakkuk 1:14," *BBR* 24 (2014): 491–503.

have lungs. Thus, empirical observations, akin to those of Aristotle, were likely present in the Israelite thought world, which, in the absence of an Anaxagorean/Diogenean conception of matter, would support an Aristotle-like belief that there was no air in water for fish to breathe.

In sum, taking into account the evidence in the Israelite textual record, both in itself and in light of the material from ancient Greece, a robust case can be made that the Israelites generally believed that fish (and other aquatic animals) do not breathe air of any sort or in any way.

Even if it was not a general belief, however, such an idea can be assumed to have been part of the Levitical/Priestly thought world. Three of the texts that evince a belief that fish do not breathe air—Gen 1:30, 6:17, and 7:14–15—are often regarded as Priestly texts. In Gen 7:21–23, verse 21 is often regarded as Priestly material, and verses 22–23 as Yahwistic material. Verse 22, however, which is where breath is mentioned, is in apposition to verse 21 and forms a chiasm with it (verb–subject–subject–verb). Thus, the Priestly verse 21 and the Yahwistic verse 22 form an integrated whole in the current text.

V. Breath and Blood

Two aspects of Levitical/Priestly thought regarding the bodies of edible animals have been noted thus far: (1) Lev 7:26 and 17:10–14 prohibit the consumption of land/aerial animal blood but allow the consumption of fish blood; (2) the tradents behind Lev 7:26 and 17:10–14 believed that land/aerial animals breathe air but that fish do not:

	Breathe Air	Consumption of Their Blood
Fish	no	permitted
Land/Aerial	yes	prohibited

The juxtaposition of these two aspects of Levitical/Priestly thought suggest an explanation for the zoological parameters of Lev 7:26 and 17:10–14: the blood of land/aerial animals was not to be consumed because they breathe air, while the blood of fish could be consumed because they do not.

Of course, for this to be the correct explanation, it would have to be the case that the Levitical/Priestly tradents thought that the breath of a land/aerial animal made its blood different in some way from the blood of a fish. Note, then, how people from elsewhere in the ancient eastern Mediterranean world thought about the relationship between blood and inhaled air. In ancient Egypt, "the heart was viewed as the center of an elaborate network of … vessels … comprising veins [and] arteries.… Within this system flowed blood, water, air, mucus."[30] Air was involved

---

[30] Robert K. Rittner, "The Cardiovascular System in Ancient Egyptian Thought," *JNES* 65 (2006): 99–109, here 100, http://dx.doi.org/10.1086/504985. See also John F. Nunn, *Ancient*

in this system by being "drawn in through the nose into the lungs. It was then transmitted to the heart and thence circulated to all parts of the body."[31] While these ideas are found in texts dated to circa 1550 and 1300 BCE, scholars believe that Egyptian medical thought stayed much the same from pharaonic times down through the latter part of the first millennium BCE.[32] It is reasonable to assume, then, that the belief in a physical, intracorporeal association between blood and inhaled air was maintained in the Egyptian thought world throughout this time.

In ancient Greece, the earliest thinkers did not distinguish between arteries and veins and believed that inhaled air/*pneuma* and blood moved within the same vessels of the body's vascular system. This is found in the thinking of such figures as Empedocles (ca. 492–432 BCE), Diogenes of Apollonia (fifth century BCE), and the Hippocratic Corpus (late fifth century BCE and after).[33] A little later, Aristotle believed that inhaled air did not enter into blood vessels,[34] while Praxagoras of Cos (latter half of the fourth century BCE), and Erasistratus after him (ca. 315–240 BCE), distinguished arteries from veins and believed that arteries contained only inhaled air/*pneuma* while veins contained only blood.[35] But Herophilus (ca.

Egyptian Medicine (Norman: University of Oklahoma Press, 1996), 44–49, 55; Charles R. S. Harris, *The Heart and the Vascular System in Ancient Greek Medicine: From Alcmaeon to Galen* (Oxford: Oxford University Press, 1973), 114–15.

[31] Nunn, *Ancient Egyptian Medicine*, 55. See also Rittner, "Cardiovascular System," 101; Harris, *Heart and the Vascular System*, 114–15.

[32] Robert K. Rittner, "Innovations and Adaptations in Ancient Egyptian Medicine," *JNES* 59 (2000): 107–17, http://dx.doi.org/10.1086/468799; Philippa Lang, "Medical and Ethnic Identities in Hellenistic Egypt," *Apeiron: A Journal for Ancient Philosophy and Science* 37 (2004): 107–31, here 112 n. 12; Nunn, *Ancient Egyptian Medicine*, 121, 206.

[33] David J. Furley, "Theories of Respiration before Galen," in *Galen on Respiration and the Arteries*, ed. David J. Furley and J. S. Wilkie (Princeton: Princeton University Press, 1984), 3–39, here 3–16, http://dx.doi.org/10.1515/9781400855155.1; Friedrich Solmsen, "Greek Philosophy and the Discovery of the Nerves," *MH* 18 (1961): 150–97, here 153–55; Harris, *Heart and the Vascular System*, 16–20, 26–28, 40–44, 52, 59, 63–66, 68, 71–72, 84, 90–91, 104–7; Abraham P. Bos and Rein Ferwerda, *Aristotle, On the Life-Bearing Spirit (De Spiritu): A Discussion with Plato and His Predecessors on Pneuma as the Instrumental Body of the Soul; Introduction, Translation, and Commentary* (Leiden: Brill, 2008), 67, 74, 97, 99; Cornford, *Plato's Cosmology*, 307.

[34] Michael Boylan, "The Digestive and 'Circulatory' Systems in Aristotle's Biology," *Journal of the History of Biology* 15 (1982): 89–119, here 110, 114–17, http://dx.doi.org/10.1007/BF00132006; Michael F. Frampton, "Aristotle's Cardiocentric Model of Animal Locomotion," *Journal of the History of Biology* 24 (1991): 291–330, here 307–15, http://dx.doi.org/10.1007/BF00209433; Solmsen, "Greek Philosophy," 170, 174, 177, 179 n. 2, 183, 190; Bos and Ferwerda, *Aristotle, On the Life-Bearing Spirit*, 4, 24, 26–28, 56, 74, 94–95, 111, 113; Harris, *Heart and the Vascular System*, 121; A. E. Taylor, *A Commentary on Plato's Timaeus* (Oxford: Oxford University Press, 1928), 545.

[35] Vivian Nutton, *Ancient Medicine*, Sciences of Antiquity (London: Routledge, 2004), 126; Michael Boylan, "Galen: On Blood, the Pulse, and the Arteries," *Journal of the History of Biology* 40 (2007): 207–30, here 215, 217, 221, 225–26, http://dx.doi.org/10.1007/s10739-006-9116-2; Heinrich Von Staden, *Herophilus: The Art of Medicine in Early Alexandria; Edition, Translation,*

330–260 BCE), a student of Praxagoras and near contemporary of Erasistratus, while accepting the distinction between arteries and veins, may have believed that both inhaled air/*pneuma* and blood moved through the arteries and possibly the veins as well.[36] Later, Galen (129–ca. 216 CE), while working with the by-then-standard distinction between arteries and veins, believed that both inhaled air/*pneuma* and blood moved through the arteries and probably also the veins.[37] Thus, the idea that inhaled air/*pneuma* and blood were physically associated with each other within the body was the earliest belief in ancient Greece (e.g., Empedocles, Diogenes, the Hippocratic Corpus), an idea from which thinking diverged for a time among some (e.g., Aristotle, Praxagoras, Erasistratus), but to which Greek thinking eventually returned (e.g., Galen) and perhaps never entirely left (e.g., Herophilus).

In sum, the earliest and enduring understanding of the physiology of breath and blood from elsewhere in the ancient eastern Mediterranean world was that inhaled air and blood were physically associated with each other in the body. It is possible, then, that this is what the Levitical/Priestly tradents behind Lev 7:26 and 17:10–14 thought—that inhaled air and blood were physically associated with each other in the body of a land/aerial animal and that they formed a breath/blood amalgam. If so, it is possible that such a belief lies behind the differential treatment of land/aerial animal blood and fish blood, since the tradents also believed that fish did not breathe air. Is there, however, any evidence for a belief in a breath/blood amalgam in ancient Israel?

VI. Breath and Blood in Israel

The word נפש is used in all of the rationale statements that explain why a land/aerial animal's blood must not be consumed:

---

and Essays (Cambridge: Cambridge University Press, 1989), 262–63; Solmsen, "Greek Philosophy," 178–80; Furley, "Theories of Respiration," 22–37; Harris, *Heart and the Vascular System*, 108–13, 195–233.

[36] James Longrigg, "Superlative Achievement and Comparative Neglect: Alexandrian Medical Science and Modern Historical Research," *History of Science* 19 (1981): 155–200, here 170–73, http://dx.doi.org/10.1177/007327538101900301; James Longrigg, "Anatomy in Alexandria in the Third Century B.C.," *British Journal for the History of Science* 21 (1988): 455–88, here 467–69, http://dx.doi.org/10.1017/S000708740002536X; Von Staden, *Herophilus*, 262–67; Furley, "Theories of Respiration," 24–26; Boylan, "Galen: On Blood," 216–17.

[37] Owsei Temkin, "On Galen's Pneumatology," *Gesnerus* 8 (1953): 180–89; Furley and Wilkie, *Galen on Respiration*, 190, 258 n. 2, 260 n. 11, 264 n. 39; Rudolph E. Siegel, *Galen's System of Physiology and Medicine: An Analysis of His Doctrines and Observations on Bloodflow, Respiration, Humors and Internal Diseases* (Basel: S. Karger, 1968), 29–30, 37, 39, 59, 62–63, 81–82, 87, 96–97, 142, 154–60, 184, 191–92; Nutton, *Ancient Medicine*, 233–34; Boylan, "Galen: On Blood," 211–12, 217–19, 227; Harris, *Heart and the Vascular System*, 275, 281, 283, 296–99, 301, 305, 307, 320, 328–29, 332, 336–39, 353, 363, 365–66.

Gen 9:4	בשר בנפשו דמו	the flesh with its נפש, that is, its blood
Lev 17:11a	נפש הבשר בדם הוא	the נפש of the flesh is in the blood
Lev 17:14a	נפש כל־בשר דמו בנפשו הוא	the נפש of all flesh—its blood is with its נפש
Lev 17:14b	נפש כל־בשר דמו הוא	the נפש of all flesh is its blood
Deut 12:23a	הדם הוא הנפש	the blood, that is the נפש
Deut 12:23b	הנפש עם־הבשר	the נפש with the flesh

נפש is usually understood to refer to life in these passages. Note several things, however.[38] First, in all of these passages, נפש and blood are conceptually and physically intertwined (e.g., the נפש is the blood [Gen 9:4; Lev 17:14a, 14b]; the נפש is in the blood [Lev 17:11a]; the blood with its נפש [Lev 17:14a]; the blood is the נפש [Deut 12:23a]). Second, in addition to being used to refer to life, נפש was also used to refer to breath (see, e.g., the references in n. 11). Third, there is nothing in the Israelite textual record that rules out a belief in a breath/blood amalgam. Fourth, there is no evidence in the textual record for a theory regarding the physiology of breath and blood other than a breath/blood amalgam.

In light of these four points, it is possible that נפש refers to breath (or perhaps life-breath) in these passages and that the relationship between נפש and blood described in these passages is that of a breath/blood amalgam. If so, then the rationale statements should be read in the following way:

Gen 9:4	בשר בנפשו דמו	the flesh with its breath, that is, its blood
Lev 17:11a	נפש הבשר בדם הוא	the breath of the flesh is in the blood
Lev 17:14a	נפש כל־בשר דמו בנפשו הוא	the breath of all flesh—its blood is with its breath
Lev 17:14b	נפש כל־בשר דמו הוא	the breath of all flesh is its blood
Deut 12:23a	הדם הוא הנפש	the blood, that is the breath
Deut 12:23b	הנפש עם־הבשר	the breath with the flesh

As is apparent, the four-point interpretive framework outlined in the preceding paragraph yields coherent and compelling readings of the rationale statements, readings that reflect a belief in a breath/blood amalgam.

In addition, reading the rationale statements in this way resolves two interpretive puzzles. First, there is the puzzle of the syntax/meaning of נפש הבשר בדם הוא in Lev 17:11a, a passage that has been interpreted in two very different ways. One approach to the passage has been to understand the preposition ב as indicating location and the word נפש as referring to "the animating soul that was believed to reside in the blood," or something akin to that, like spirit or life force.[39] Another

---

[38] For thinking along lines similar to some of what follows, see Léopold Sabourin, "Nefesh, sang et expiation (Lv 17,11.14)," *ScEccl* 18 (1966): 25–45, esp. 34–36.

[39] Feder, *Blood Expiation*, 202.

approach has been to understand the preposition ב as indicating identity (*bet essentiae*), the word נפש as referring to life, and the passage as meaning that "the life of the flesh *is* the blood."[40] While the existence of these two, seemingly plausible explanations suggests that the precise meaning of the passage is ultimately elusive, this is not the case. If one reads the preposition ב as indicating location and the word נפש as referring to breath, then נפש הבשר בדם הוא reads "the breath of the flesh is in the blood," and the passage is seen to indicate that the breath of a land/aerial animal is physically and materially located *in* the animal's blood. Thus, the נפש-and-blood relationship is seen to be a breath/blood amalgam.[41]

Second, there is the puzzle of the syntax/meaning of דמו בנפשו הוא in Lev 17:14a, a passage that has always been considered difficult and problematic. Among the explanations that have been offered are the following: (1) בנפשו is a scribal error, having been brought down from verse 11; (2) בנפשו and דמו should be reversed in accord with verse 11; (3) the preposition ב in דמו בנפשו is a *bet essentiae* for a rendering of "its blood is its life"; (4) the preposition ב should be taken as "with" for a rendering of "its blood is with its life," which means that "its blood is attached to, inseparable from, its life."[42] While the variety of opinions about דמו בנפשו הוא certainly suggests that the passage is difficult and problematic, this is not the case. If one reads the preposition ב as "with" and נפש as breath, then דמו בנפשו הוא reads "its blood with its breath," and the נפש-and-blood relationship is seen to be a breath/blood amalgam.

In sum, the four-point interpretive framework outlined above makes excellent sense of the rationale statements. Of course, this way of interpreting the statements is not unassailable. It involves some circular reasoning in that evidence for a belief in a breath/blood amalgam can be seen in the rationale statements if the statements are interpreted as reflecting a belief in an amalgam. And just because people elsewhere in the ancient eastern Mediterranean world believed in a breath/blood amalgam does not necessarily mean that any Israelites did. Finally, the amount of textual

---

[40] Gilders, *Blood Ritual*, 169; see also 22.

[41] The idea that the breath is physically and materially located in the blood raises many questions about how this was thought to work. For example, how was the breath thought to enter the blood after it was inhaled and exit the blood before it was exhaled? Was the blood thought to act as a carrier that conveyed the breath throughout the body, or did the blood act as a medium through which the breath moved throughout the body on its own? And why was it thought that a unit of breath left the body in exhalation? Was it thought that its vivific qualities had been spent or exhausted and that a new unit of breath was needed to replace it? Unfortunately, the textual record provides us with no readily apparent answers to these and other questions. Thus, our understanding of the idea that the breath of a land/aerial animal was physically and materially located in the animal's blood is somewhat limited.

[42] Jacob Milgrom, *Leviticus 17–22: A New Translation with Introduction and Commentary*, AB 3A (New York: Doubleday, 2000), 1483. For the various explanations of the syntax, see ibid., 1483–84; John E. Hartley, *Leviticus*, WBC 4 (Dallas: Word, 1992), 263; Feder, *Blood Expiation*, 199–200 n. 117.

data to work with is small. Nonetheless, a robust case can still be made that (1) there was a belief in ancient Israel that breath and blood formed an amalgam in the body of a land/aerial animal; (2) this belief was held by Levitical/Priestly tradents and perhaps by all Israelites; (3) this belief lies behind the rationale statements that explain why the blood of land/aerial animals should not be consumed; (4) the word נפש refers to breath in these rationale statements; (5) there was a belief in ancient Israel that the blood of fish was simply blood and not a breath/blood amalgam since fish did not breathe air; (6) this belief was held by Levitical/Priestly tradents and perhaps by all Israelites; and (7) this belief lies behind the permission to consume the blood of fish.[43]

VII. Concluding Observations

Assuming that the preceding seven points are correct, several concluding observations can be made. First, the thing that made a land/aerial animal's breath/blood amalgam different from a fish's blood was the land/aerial animal's breath. Thus, by prohibiting the consumption of a land/aerial animal's breath/blood amalgam while allowing the consumption of a fish's blood, it would appear that the Levitical/Priestly tradents were focused on prohibiting the consumption of the breath that was amalgamated with a land/aerial animal's blood.

Second, there seems to have been a general Israelite belief that a terrestrial creature becomes alive when it starts to breathe, that it is alive when it is breathing, and that it is dead when it no longer breathes (e.g., Gen 2:7; 25:8, 17; 35:18, 29; 49:33; Deut 20:16; 1 Kgs 15:29; 17:17–22; 2 Kgs 8:14–15; Job 27:3; 32:8; 33:4; 34:14–15; Pss 104:27–30; 146:4; 150:6; Eccl 3:19; Isa 2:22; 42:5; Jer 10:14; Ezek 37:5–10; Hab 2:19). Thus, in Israelite thought, breath was of the essence of life. By prohibiting its consumption, the Levitical/Priestly tradents hallowed a terrestrial animal's breath (and by extension a human being's breath) and established a way to solemnize and express in tangible form the profound existential significance of a terrestrial creature's breath.

Third, there seems to have been a general Israelite belief that breath was something that was given to a terrestrial creature by God and was taken back by God at the creature's death (e.g., Gen 2:7; 1 Kgs 17:17–22; Job 12:10; 27:3; 32:8; 33:4; 34:14–15; Ps 104:27–30; Eccl 12:7; Isa 42:5; Ezek 37:5–10). It was understood, then, that

---

[43] The Levitical/Priestly character of several rationale statements indicates that the beliefs mentioned in nos. 1 and 5 were Levitical/Priestly beliefs. Several things suggest that they were general Israelite beliefs as well. First, the Deuteronomic character of one rationale statement shows that they were more than just Levitical/Priestly beliefs. Second, knowledge of animals, including aquatic animals (see the first paragraph in section IV), was widespread. Third, the rationale statements were, in theory at least, directed at a general audience; it was presumably believed, then, that they would make sense to such an audience.

God had complete and exclusive sovereignty over a terrestrial creature's breath. Thus, by prohibiting its consumption, the Levitical/Priestly tradents divested themselves of any authority and right to use the breath for their own purposes/benefit and, it would appear, established a way to act out a belief that, although they were allowed to control and manipulate a terrestrial animal's living body or dead carcass, they were not allowed to do that with a terrestrial animal's breath, because the authority and right to do that belonged to God alone.

Fourth, it is unclear how the Israelites thought that God vivified fish and other nonbreathing aquatic animals without the use of breath. They identified some water as "living water" (מים חיים [Gen 26:19; Lev 14:5, 6, 50, 51, 52; 15:13; Num 19:17; Cant 4:15; Jer 2:13; 17:13; Zech 14:8]), and they knew that some water could kill or not sustain living things (Exod 7:14–24; 15:22–25; 2 Kgs 2:19–22; Ps 105:29; Ezek 47:1–12). It could be, then, that they believed that water vivified nonbreathing aquatic animals in the same way that air vivified terrestrial creatures. If so, this suggests that the Israelite understanding of physiology and physical space was that every creature drew its life from the medium within which it was situated and through which it moved. That is to say, terrestrial creatures and plants drew their life from the air within which they were situated and through which some of them walked or flew, while nonbreathing aquatic animals drew their life from the water within which they were situated and through which some of them swam.[44] If this was, in fact, how they understood the physiology of nonbreathing aquatic animals, the question is, did they believe that water and blood formed an amalgam in the body of a fish in the way that breath and blood formed an amalgam in the body of a terrestrial creature? If so, why did the presence of the "breath of life" in the blood of a land/aerial animal disqualify its blood for consumption, while the presence of the "water of life" in the blood of a fish did not disqualify its blood for consumption? Such matters, however, are beyond the scope of this article and will have to be left for another time.

---

[44] Isaiah 50:2 describes fish that are not in water as dying from thirst (צמא).

The Ground That Opened Its Mouth: The Ground's Response to Human Violence in Genesis 4

MARI JØRSTAD
mari.jorstad@duke.edu
Duke University, Durham, NC 27701

It has almost become a truism that the ground in Gen 1–11 is a character in its own right. While many scholars repeat this insight, few describe the underlying rationale. In this article I address this question by looking closely at the story of Cain and Abel in Gen 4:1–16. My central claim is that this passage responds to an important question raised in Gen 1 and 2: Does the intimate connection between humans and the ground mean that the ground mirrors or aids human action, regardless of the nature of that action? By looking at the interactions of Cain, Abel, God, and the ground in Gen 4:1–16, I argue that Gen 4 presents the ground as an agent responsive first and foremost to God's will, thus resisting and frustrating human disobedience and violence.

It has almost become a truism that the ground in Gen 1–11 is a character in its own right.[1] While many scholars repeat this insight, few consider the underlying rationale. What is gained by presenting the ground as a character, an agent capable of interacting with others? What motivates the writer of Genesis to make the ground a third party in the human–divine drama? In this article I address these questions by looking closely at the story of Cain and Abel in Gen 4:1–16, with particular attention to verses 9–12. I begin by relating Cain to the characters of Adam and Noah in order to highlight the way in which themes and issues appear

[1] See, e.g., Kristin M. Swenson, "Care and Keeping East of Eden: Gen 4:1–16 in Light of Gen 2–3," *Int* 60 (2006): 373–84, here 381, http://dx.doi.org/10.1177/002096430606000402; Terence E. Fretheim, *God and World in the Old Testament: A Relational Theology of Creation* (Nashville: Abingdon, 2005), 38; Michael Welker, *Creation and Reality*, trans. John F. Hoffmeyer (Minneapolis: Fortress, 1999), 42. For a premodern example of this line of interpretation, see Bruce N. Fisk, "Gaps in the Story, Cracks in the Earth: The Exile of Cain and the Destruction of Korah in Pseudo-Philo (*Liber Antiquitatum Biblicarum* 16)," in *Of Scribes and Sages: Early Jewish Interpretation and Transmission of Scripture*, ed. Craig A. Evans, 2 vols., LSTS 50–51 (London: T&T Clark, 2004), 2:20–33.

and reappear across the Primeval History. Second, I look at Gen 4:1–16 in detail. Finally, I put my reading of Gen 4 into conversation with Gen 1:28, especially the verbs שכב and רדה.

I. Adam, Cain, and Noah: Establishing a Pattern

One way to read the stories of Adam, Cain, and Noah is to see them as three attempts to address a single set of problems. Rather than saying that Gen 3 addresses alienation between God and humanity and Gen 4 addresses alienation between brothers, I read Gen 3, 4, and 6–8 as recapitulating each other.[2] By establishing a close and unique connection between Adam, Cain, Noah, and the ground, Gen 1–11 ruminates on the nature of the relationship between humanity and the ground and the extent to which the ground is available to human choice and control.

The narrative connects Adam, Cain, and Noah to the ground by means of names and vocational titles. The story of Adam provides the most expansive description of the intimate association of humanity and the ground. God forms Adam from the ground (2:7) and later informs him that he will return to the ground (3:19). The name Adam (אדם) is itself a pun on the word אדמה ("ground"), and Gen 2 ties the creation of humanity to the need for someone to work the ground (see 2:5).[3] Finally, after the expulsion from Eden, we are reminded of Adam's work and origin: "The Lord God sent him from the garden of Eden, to work the ground from which he was taken" (3:23). The stories of Cain and Noah evoke the connection with אדמה through shorthands. Cain is a worker of the ground (עבד אדמה), while Noah is a man of the ground (איש האדמה).

Adam, Cain, and Noah also share an association with curses, specifically ones that involve the ground. Because of Adam, the ground is cursed and farming becomes arduous and difficult. Furthermore, God tells Adam that his life will end in a return to the ground (Gen 3:19). Cain is cursed "from the ground" (4:11) after

---

[2] This argument is similar to that of Thomas L. Brodie when he describes the spiraling structures of Genesis: "The text tells a brief story ... then circles around as it were before coming back to tell another, larger story" (*Genesis as Dialogue: A Literary, Historical and Theological Commentary* [Oxford: Oxford University Press, 2001], 13, http://dx.doi.org/10.1093/0195138368 .001.0001) Also instructive is Matthew Richard Schlimm's view of anger in Genesis: "Presenting readers with a dozen episodes involving anger, the texts of Genesis begin to do justice to the manifold perspectives necessary for approximating the truth about this emotion.... They present a variety of perspectives on this emotion in order to promote a greater understanding of its complexity" (*From Fratricide to Forgiveness: The Language and Ethics of Anger in Genesis*, Siphrut 7 [Winona Lake, IN: Eisenbrauns, 2011], 121).

[3] Kristin M. Swenson notes, "Part of the problem, we read, is that there was no human being to ʿbd the ground (Gen 2:5).... Reference to human beings is introduced out of concern for the land—that the land has the attention it needs in order to produce plant life" ("Care and Keeping East of Eden," 375).

he murders Abel, and, despite Cain's continued efforts to work the ground, the ground will no longer yield him its strength (4:20). Noah is the first person to utter a curse, but he is also connected to the curse of the flood. While the flood is never explicitly called a curse, God's statement after the flood associates it with Gen 3 and 4: "I will not again curse the ground on account of humanity ... nor will I again wipe out all life that I have made" (Gen 8:19). Furthermore, Lamech relates Noah to the curse on the ground at Noah's birth, expressing the hope that Noah will bring humanity rest from their work out of the ground (Gen 5:29).[4] In each case, the curse entails a separation from the ground, and this separation intensifies through each story. God tells Adam that his life as a farmer will require toil and sweat; God banishes Cain from the face of the ground; and God brings about the flood that extinguishes all life from the face of the ground.

Another similarity between Adam, Cain, and Noah is that each is in some way an archetype, a father of humanity. Adam and Noah play this part in a literal way. Adam is the first human, and Noah serves a similar role as the first person of postdiluvian humanity. Cain's line, on the other hand, comes to an end at the flood, since Noah descends from Seth. The narrator compensates for this lack of genealogical continuation by making Cain and his descendants the creators of human culture and industry.[5] Cain, himself a farmer, builds the first city and fathers the first cattle-raising nomads, metal workers, and musicians (Gen 4:20–22).[6] Though Cain's line is extinguished, Cain is nonetheless the source of human culture, especially human professions. The fact that Adam, Cain, and Noah are all in some way fathers of humanity suggests that their stories apply to all people, and that the claims made in these stories hold for any and all audiences. No one is outside the obligations and limitations outlined by Gen 1–11.

---

[4] Genesis 5:29b is variously translated "This one will console us for the pain of our hands' work *from the soil* which the LORD cursed" (Robert Alter, *The Five Books of Moses: A Translation with Commentary* [New York: Norton, 2008], 29; emphasis mine); "This one will provide us relief from our work and from the toil of our hands, *out of the very soil* which the LORD placed under a curse" (Nahum M. Sarna, *Genesis* בראשית: *The Traditional Hebrew Text with the New JPS Translation*, JPS Torah Commentary [Philadelphia: Jewish Publication Society, 1989]; emphasis mine); see also E. A. Speiser, *Genesis: Introduction, Translation, and Notes*, AB 1 (Garden City, NY: Doubleday, 1964), ad loc.; and "This same shall comfort us concerning our work and toil of our hands, *because of the ground* which the LORD hath cursed" (KJV). The uncertainty is about the relationship of מן־האדמה to the rest of the clause—is the ground a potential source of relief or is it what makes relief necessary in the first place?

[5] Some scholars take Cain's city building as evidence of an antiurban bias (see André LaCocque, *Onslaught against Innocence: Cain, Abel, and the Yahwist* [Eugene, OR: Cascade, 2008], 127–30). In contrast, Claus Westermann sees the advances of civilization as a blessing from God, though one with a potential for abuse (*Genesis: A Practical Commentary*, trans. David Green, Text and Interpretation [Grand Rapids: Eerdmans, 1987], 38).

[6] Sarna states, "The three pillars of seminomadic culture, as set forth in verses 20–22, are ... said to have originated with the descendants of Cain" (*Genesis*, 31).

II. Cain and the Ground

My interest in the use of אדמה in Genesis began with 4:11: "And now, cursed are you from the ground that opened its mouth to take the blood of your brother from your hand."[7] Several features of this verse are curious. First, the verse uses body parts (or fluids) to name three principal characters in the story: the mouth of the ground, the blood of Abel, and the hand of Cain. The attribution of a body part to the ground suggests that the ground is an actor, not simply a setting, and makes possible an exchange between Cain and the ground. Second, the ground is the only subject of an active verb in this verse.[8] It *opens* its mouth to *take* the blood. English translations tend to use the word "receive" rather than "take," and, while not incorrect, this represents only one of the possible meanings of לקח. The verb can refer to a passive or unwilling act of receiving something from someone else (see, e.g., Isa 40:2), but it usually denotes active taking or acceptance. Genesis uses the phrase "take from the hand" eight additional times: four times referring to characters transporting objects (22:6; 32:14; 43:12, 15), twice to characters persuading someone to accept a gift (21:30; 33:10), one to recovering property (38:20), and one to seizing spoils in war (48:22). Furthermore, the grammatical construction of the verse suggests a purpose clause. The ground opens its mouth in order to take the blood; it is not passively covered in blood.[9] The ground's activity is particularly startling because it appears to work in concert with Cain's violence. In other words, the ground is potentially an accomplice in the murder of Abel.

We know from 4:10 that the ground is not Cain's accomplice but is instead the location from which Abel's blood cries out to God. Nevertheless, we should not miss the oddity of 4:11 and its suggestion that the ground could potentially serve as a partner in crime. In other instances in which the ground or the earth (ארץ) acts by means of a mouth, it is always in accordance with God's will.[10] By highlighting the

---

[7] It is grammatically possible to translate this verse as "more cursed are you than the ground, which ...." Though this translation makes sense in relation to 3:17, it fails to connect with what follows, namely, that the ground will withhold its strength from Abel. The issue is separation, not relative degrees of accursedness (see Anne Marie Kitz, "Curses and Cursing in the Ancient Near East," *Religion Compass* 1 [2007]: 619, http://dx.doi.org/10.1111/j.1749-8171.2007.00039.x).

[8] Abel is not the subject of any verb in 4:11, while Cain is the subject of a passive participle (ארור).

[9] Umberto Cassuto overstates the case when he writes that the earth "greeted [Cain's] deed with joy, greedily opening its mouth to drink his brother's blood from his hand" (*A Commentary on the Book of Genesis,* 2 vols., Publications of the Perry Foundation for Biblical Research in the Hebrew University of Jerusalem [Jerusalem: Magnes, 1961–1964], 1:220). The text raises the possibility of the ground's willing collusion but does not make an absolute or clear statement to that effect.

[10] For אדמה + בלע, see Num 16:30; for ארץ + בלע, see Ps 106:17; for ארץ + פצה, see Num 16:32, 26:10, Deut 11:6; for ארץ + קיא, see Lev 18:25, 28.

agency of the ground at the beginning of the canon, Gen 4:11 raises an important question: does the intimate connection between humans and the ground mean that the ground mirrors or aids human action, regardless of the nature of that action? More specifically, to what extent does the ground participate in human disobedience?

Genesis 4:1–16 addresses these question by means of a dual emphasis. First, the story highlights humanity's intimate connection with the ground by explicitly naming Cain an עבד אדמה ("worker of the ground") and implicitly by fusing Abel's identity with the ground. Second, it stresses the separation between Cain and the ground.

Cain's identification with the ground is clear, as I have already mentioned, from his title עבד אדמה. Cain himself declares his connection with the ground when he offers God "fruits of the ground" (מפרי האדמה). While I do not wish to enter into the discussion of why God rejects Cain's gift, it is important to note that Cain's gift is a direct extension of his identity.[11] Cain brings to God the product of his occupation, of who he is. When God declines to "look on" Cain and his gift, God confronts Cain with a serious challenge. It would be a mistake to consider Cain's anger an overblown reaction to a minor slight; God's refusal to look on Cain's gift strikes directly at Cain's basic identity, an identity that the writer of Genesis has taken pains to emphasize.

The references to the ground in verses 2 and 3 begin a pattern whereby every important turn of the story includes a similar reference. After the murder of Abel, his blood cries out "from the ground" (4:10); God responds to the murder of Abel by cursing Cain "from the ground" (4:11–12); and finally Cain despairs at his exile from "the face of the ground" (4:13). Not an accidental pattern, this careful use of the word אדמה serves to intertwine Cain and the ground as closely as possible, making the separation in 4:11–12 all the more severe.

Like Cain, Abel is associated with the ground. In 4:9, after Cain kills Abel, God initiates a dialogue with Cain: "The Lord said to Cain, 'Where is Abel, your brother?' He said, 'I don't know. Am I my brother's keeper?'" The word keeper (שמר) echoes Gen 2:15, "The Lord God took the human and settled him in the garden of Eden, to work [עבד] it and keep [שמר] it." Genesis 2:15 in turn harks back to 2:5, which says that there was no one to work (עבד) the ground. From the beginning, humans receive a dual responsibility from God, to keep and to work. Though this

---

[11] For an overview of the history of interpretation of God's rejection of Cain's gift in Christian and Jewish sources, see Jack P. Lewis, "The Offering of Abel (Gen 4:4): A History of Interpretation," *JETS* 37 (1994): 481–96; and John Byron, *Cain and Abel in Text and Tradition: Jewish and Christian Interpretations of the First Sibling Rivalry*, TBN: Jewish and Christian Traditions 14 (Leiden: Brill, 2011), http://dx.doi.org/10.1163/ej.9789004192522.i-268. I adopt Swenson's suggestion: "God's behaviour and speech suggest that what is at issue is not what Cain might have done or not done to deserve God's reaction, but what Cain should do to manage his anger and disappointment in circumstances that seem unfair" (Swenson, "Care and Keeping East of Eden," 379).

responsibility clearly applies to the garden, it is not clear if it also applies to other humans. Paul A. Riemann has persuasively argued that, of the more than 450 uses of the verb שמר, none refers to an instance "where a man's keeping another man is an expressed covenant norm or even a recognized social obligation."[12] Riemann argues that "guard" may be a clearer translation of שמר, so that Cain's question is not a disavowal of responsibility but an insistence that he has not exercised inappropriate or excessive power over his brother.

Does this mean that, according to Gen 4, Cain ought not to keep his brother? Does the fact that the word שמר nowhere else describes responsibilities between brothers mean that it has no prescriptive function here? In Gen 2:18, God decides to make the man a helper (עזר). The noun and verbal forms of the root עזר refer almost exclusively to divine or military help. Nowhere else does it describe aid from a spouse. This suggests that the writers of the non-Priestly sections of Genesis use unusual words to describe familial relations and responsibilities. Paying attention to the use of שמר in the context of the Primeval History, Kristin Swenson makes the following argument about Cain's question: "In a deft reintroduction of the term *šmr* that completes the two part mandate for human beings to *ʿbd* and *šmr*, the story leads its readers to conclude … that guarding the welfare of Eden's garden is inseparable from guarding the welfare of others."[13] Cain's question in Gen 4 does not refer to an established social norm; instead the author uses parallelism and association to mold norms. The verbal parallelism builds a connection between care for the garden and care for other humans. The agricultural vocation of humanity extends to a responsibility toward people, especially those with whom we interact closely and intimately. No neat distinction exists between responsibility toward the ground and responsibility toward Abel.

The distinction between Abel and the ground further disintegrates when the ground swallows Abel's blood. After Cain replies to God, God exclaims, "What have you done?! The voice of your brother's blood cries out to me from the ground" (4:10). As Gen 9:4–6 points out, the blood of a creature is its life. The ground swallows Abel's life, and, by so doing, lends voice to Abel. It is as if Abel and the ground have become one being. The ground opens its mouth and takes Abel's blood, and Abel, in response, uses the mouth of the ground to cry out to God.

Abel's return to the ground through the violence of his brother provides the impetus for the second movement of Gen 4:1–16, namely, the separation of Cain from the ground. We learn of this separation by its explicit mention but also by the way in which the ground increasingly comes to exercise agency independent of Cain. In 4:11, God curses Cain "from the ground" (מן־האדמה). The phrase

---

[12] Paul A. Riemann, "Am I My Brother's Keeper," *Int* 24 (1970): 483, http://dx.doi.org/10.1177/002096437002400404. See also Kenneth M. Craig, "Questions outside Eden (Genesis 4.1–16): Yahweh, Cain and Their Rhetorical Interchange," *JSOT* 24 (1999): 107–28.

[13] Swenson, "Care and Keeping East of Eden," 381.

מִן־הָאֲדָמָה has already occurred three times in Genesis, in each instance referring to God forming or drawing life out of the ground—first humans, then trees, then animals (2:7, 9, 19). When the phrase recurs in Gen 4, first to describe Abel's blood crying out from the ground and then to describe Cain's curse, it highlights the extent to which God's initial order has been overturned. The proper use of the ground is as a means, a material, or a partner for creation. What rises from the ground in the case of Cain and Abel is the result of violence and destruction, of un-creation. Because Cain's use of the ground conflicts with its proper purpose, God separates Cain from the ground.[14]

The next verse spells out the implication of Cain's separation from the ground: "For you will work the ground, but it will not again give its strength to you. You will be a vagrant and a wanderer on the earth" (4:12a). The curse, though brief, follows a logic similar to that of futility curses (see, e.g., Deut 28:38–43, Mic 6:14–16).[15] Cain will continue to work the ground, but the ground will no longer yield produce to him. Cain's identity as an עֹבֵד אֲדָמָה remains, but he can no longer count on the cooperation of the ground—he must wander about without a settled connection with the earth. In other words, the ground is not a passive material that Cain can control through work. Instead, the ground actively chooses whether or not to respond to Cain's efforts and, as a result, has the power to determine the form of Cain's life.

Word choice also emphasizes the independent agency of the ground. The use of the construction כֹּחָהּ ("its strength") to refer to produce, while not unique to this context, is nonetheless uncommon and does not appear elsewhere in reference to the word אֲדָמָה.[16] In a range of contexts, כֹּחַ denotes the ability to perform actions, in particular actions that require effort, and it is especially associated with God, youth, and military personnel.[17] The word suggests that produce is not primarily the product of Cain's work but rather the product of the ground's work. The curse on Cain does not limit the ground's ability to put forth vegetation, but it makes this ability unavailable to Cain. Having put the ground to a violent and destructive use, Cain can no longer access its creative functions or live a peaceful and settled life on its face.

---

[14] Kitz claims, "Every malediction … ultimately seeks to establish a division between oppositional forces in an effort to restore divine order" ("Curses and Cursing," 619).

[15] By making Cain an embodied futility curse and placing him at the beginning of the canon, Genesis suggests that the connection between covenant faithfulness and agricultural fertility is not random but instead is woven into the fabric of divine–human relations from the beginning.

[16] See Job 31:39 and possibly Hos 7:9. Note that the logic of Job 31:39 is similar to that of Gen 4:11–12: the consequence of inappropriate use of the ground is frustrated agriculture and poor yield.

[17] Christo H. J. Van Der Merwe, "Lexical Meaning in Biblical Hebrew and Cognitive Semantics: A Case Study," *Bib* 87 (2006): 91.

III. Reading Genesis 1 in Light of Genesis 4

Norman C. Habel claims that Cain's curse is a punishment of the ground:

> The response of God to the killing of Abel amounts to several new curses, each of which affects the Earth. Earth, who provides the body to mediate Abel's voice, suffers because of the way that God articulates the punishment. As frequently in the Scriptures, the judgment on humans involves cruel collateral damage on creation.[18]

Habel's view of the ground as "collateral damage" does not account for the complexities of Gen 1–11, especially its emphases on the intimate connection between humanity and the ground and the ground's autonomous agency. The term *collateral damage* suggests that the ground gets stuck in the middle of a fight between humanity and God. The narrative, however, presents a much more active ground, not a bystander but a participant in the unfolding drama of creation. Viewing the ground simply as a victim fails to take seriously the potentially disastrous implications of the intimate connection established between humanity and the ground at creation. When humans choose to disobey God and to act destructively, will they do so with the aid of the ground, or does the ground's loyalty lie elsewhere? I argue that the presentation of the ground in Gen 1–11 creates room for the ground as a moral agent, rather than a victim, a counterweight to human violence.

Already in 1:28 Genesis raises the issue of the ground's availability and responsiveness to human will: "Fill the earth and subdue [שכב] it, and rule [רדה] over the fish of the sea and the birds of the heavens and all the animals that teem upon the earth." Both שכב and רדה often occur in military contexts, and, although scholars have attempted to show how each word can have a nonoppressive meaning, it is hard to purge them of their violence. The verse seems to extend to humans a power over the earth and its creatures akin to the power of a victorious army over its conquered enemy. The statement resonates negatively for us in the present day because of our concern for humanity's sustained abuse of the earth. This sentiment also does not square well with the rest of the biblical corpus. Humans may not do whatever they please with God's creation.[19] So why does Genesis lead off with such a violent command?

Scholars sometimes explain the curse of the ground in Gen 3 as an etiology for the hardships of agriculture.[20] I believe that Gen 1:28 alludes to such a theme

---

[18] Norman C. Habel, "The Beginning of Violence: An Ecological Reading of Genesis 4," in *Ecumenics from the Rim: Explorations in Honour of John D'Arcy May*, ed. John O'Grady and Peter Sherle, TEIR 1 (Münster: LIT, 2007), 83.

[19] For example, Israel's life in the land depends on covenant fidelity, including fidelity to agricultural laws (see, e.g., Lev 26:27–35, 2 Chr 36:20–21).

[20] Carol Meyers writes, "In the Hebrew Bible, human disobedience in the Eden episode

but in a context preceding human disobedience. In Gen. 1 and elsewhere, human agriculture and husbandry are inherently violent.[21] This violence is not necessarily wrong, however, any more than the violence of a wolf or a tiger is wrong, provided that humans observe the limits of the created order. After all, Abel is not faulted for killing a sheep from his flock in order to sacrifice to God. Genesis 1 is problematic not because of the violence of שכב and רדה but because this chapter does not spell out limits on human power. This is where chapters 2–11 come in. Through the characters of Adam, Cain, and Noah, chapters 2–11 provide a narrative response to chapter 1. The response is not a rejection of Gen 1 but an attempt to answer the questions left open by the first account of creation and to set limits on human control over the earth.

This takes us back to Habel and the curse on Cain. Habel assumes that the curse on Cain frustrates the purpose of the ground.[22] The implicit assumption undergirding this view is that the purpose of the ground begins and ends with producing vegetation, specifically vegetation that is good to eat. My reading of Gen 4 suggests, however, that the ground's purpose extends beyond this; the ground has a responsibility to act in accordance with God's created order. The connection between the ground and humanity is so intimate that it is necessary to explain how the ground might act independently of humans and what form such action might take. The curse on Cain is not primarily a punishment of the ground; it is, rather, an expression and description of the ground's loyalty to God's will. If humans attempt to use the ground for destructive and noncreative ends, the ground will resist. It will sprout that which humans cannot eat and will refuse to lend its strength to human injustice. As I have already noted, many scholars point out that the ground is a character in Gen 1–11, but this insight is rarely taken far enough. Just as the creation of humanity in chapter 2 is a response to a lack of the ground, so the agency of the ground is a response to a lack of humanity—this time a moral lack. The mandate given to humanity in the words שכב and רדה does not connote limitless power. Rather, when humans exercise power in such a way as to make chaos of creation, the ground will oppose that power.

All this is not to say that Habel is entirely wrong. The ground itself is cursed

---

explains the hardships of agrarian life" ("Food and the First Family: A Socioeconomic Perspective," in *The Book of Genesis: Composition, Reception, and Interpretation*, ed. Craig A. Evans, Joel N. Lohr, and David L. Petersen, VTSup 152 [Leiden: Brill, 2012], 156, http://dx.doi.org/10.1163/9789004226579_007).

[21] Daniel Stulac speaks to this point: "I find it thoroughly improbable that Genesis 1 portrays a type of agriculture— as Barr supposes—that sifts tilling from the effects of weed control, or shepherding from the reality of consuming animals and animal products.... Nothing about sustainable food production negates the fact that chewing and swallowing are inherently acts of destruction, meaning life to the eater and death to the eaten" ("Hierarchy and Violence in Genesis 1:26-28: An Agrarian Solution" [paper presented at the Annual Meeting of the Society of Biblical Literature, Baltimore, Maryland, 23-26 November, 2014], 20).

[22] Habel, "Beginning of Violence," 83.

in Gen 3 and the flood wipes out all life from the face of the earth. Given that humanity and the ground are created for companionship, for mutual dependence and benefit, the disobedience of the one inevitably affects the other. Genesis 3 and 6–9 show the stark and sorrowful consequences of human wrongdoing—that the world, intended for intimate relationship with humans, is pulled into human suffering. While Gen 4 highlights a new gulf between humanity and the ground, the curse of the ground and the flood indicate the ongoing potency of humanity's tie with the ground. This connection is reaffirmed when, following the flood, the narrator names Noah a man of the ground.[23] Not severed, the connection between humanity and the ground, which begins in perfect harmony, has become nuanced and troubled. On the one hand, the two remain linked in mutual dependence and responsibility, while, on the other, the ground stands in opposition to human wrongdoing.

IV. Conclusion

I began this article by laying out the similarities between Adam, Cain, and Noah. Though I have focused on Cain, I believe studies of Adam and Noah would corroborate my point. Each story struggles with the question of how to maintain the moral integrity of the ground in the face of human disobedience. None of the stories provides an easy answer or resolves the tension between the world's responsiveness and opposition to human action. Instead, the stories circle around the problem, probe it from different angles, and mull over the mystery of how a world, tied so closely to humanity, will respond to human violence.

I end with a quotation from Marilynne Robinson's *Housekeeping*:

> In the newness of the world God had perhaps not Himself realized the ramifications of certain of his laws, for example, that shock will spend itself in waves; that our images will mimic every gesture, and that shattered they will multiply and mimic every gesture ten, a hundred, or a thousand times. Cain, the image of God, gave the simple earth of the field a voice and a sorrow, and God Himself heard the voice, and grieved for the sorrow, so Cain was a creator, in the image of his creator.[24]

---

[23] Gerhard von Rad and others argue for an "uncursing" of the ground after the flood (Gerhard von Rad, *Genesis: A Commentary*, trans. John H. Marks, rev. ed., OTL [Philadelphia: Westminster, 1972], 122). This argument misses the narrative logic of the story and provides an overly mechanical interpretation. The curses deal with the difficulty of agriculture and the common problem of the extent to which the ground mirrors human disobedience. In Gen 8:21, God sets a limit on how human violence will affect the ground, but God does not remove the curse.

[24] Marilynne Robinson, *Housekeeping* (New York: Farrar Straus Giroux, 1980), 193.

The potential problem of Gen 1–11 is this "spending in waves," the possibility that the ground will endlessly echo our violence. Instead, the ground, Abel's blood, cries out against Cain, who is not a creator but an anticreator, and protests against Cain's attempt to implicate the ground in his act of destruction. Sadly, Robinson's words give voice to the more common experience, that the world does mirror our destructive behavior and that violence echoes across generations, places, and times, replicating itself. Though we increasingly feel the effects of our abuse of the world, it must be recognized that these effects, whether floods, drought, deforestation, or other natural disasters, disproportionately affect plant and animal diversity and the world's poor, who already suffer from the myriad consequences of human folly and violence. With this in mind, I suggest that Gen 1–11 is not a description of the world as it is, the world as we currently experience it. Like prophetic and eschatological images in which the natural world becomes the perfect expression of God's justice, so Gen 1–11 presents a ground actively imposing God's limits on human behavior. It is an image of hope but also of challenge. The ground does not bear witness to every human injustice, nor does God arrive to personally address each murderer. Rather, humans are called to live as if this were the case, called to imagine what the ground might say if asked about human conduct, and to act accordingly.

SBL PRESS

New and Recent Titles

WOMANIST INTERPRETATIONS OF THE BIBLE
Expanding the Discourse
Gay L. Byron and Vanessa Lovelace, editors
Paperback $49.95, 978-1-62837-152-9 402 pages, 2016 Code: 060688
Hardcover $64.95, 978-0-88414-185-3 E-book $49.95, 978-0-88414-184-6
Semeia Studies 85

PSYCHOANALYTIC MEDIATIONS BETWEEN MARXIST AND POSTCOLONIAL READINGS OF THE BIBLE
Tat-siong Benny Liew and Erin Runions, editors
Paperback $38.95, 978-1-62837-141-3 250 pages, 2016 Code: 060684
Hardcover $53.95, 978-0-88414-167-9 E-book $38.95, 978-0-88414-166-2
Semeia Studies 84

BIBLE THROUGH THE LENS OF TRAUMA
Elizabeth Boase and Christopher G. Frechette, editors
Paperback $33.95, 978-1-62837-145-1 270 pages, 2016 Code: 060689
Hardcover $48.95, 978-0-88414-173-0 E-book $33.95, 978-0-88414-172-3
Semeia Studies 86

HOW JOHN WORKS
Storytelling in the Fourth Gospel
Douglas Estes and Ruth Sheridan, editors
Paperback $46.95, 978-1-62837-131-4 Forthcoming, 2016 Code: 060392
Hardcover $61.95, 978-0-88414-148-8 E-book, $46.95, 978-0-88414-147-1
Resources for Biblical Study 86

CLOSE ENCOUNTERS BETWEEN BIBLE AND FILM
An Interdisciplinary Engagement
Laura Copier and Caroline Vander Stichele, editors
Paperback $48.95, 978-1-62837-158-1 342 pages, 2016 Code: 060690
Hardcover $63.95, 978-0-88414-197-6 E-book $48.95, 978-0-88414-196-9
Semeia Studies 87

SBL Press • P.O. Box 2243 • Williston, VT 05495-2243
Phone: 877-725-3334 (toll-free) or 802-864-6185 • Fax: 802-864-7626
Order online at www.sbl-site.org/publications

Different Dreams: Two Models of Interpretation for Three Pairs of Dreams (Genesis 37–50)

JONATHAN GROSSMAN
jonathan.grossman@biu.ac.il
Bar-Ilan University, Ramat Gan, Israel, 5290001

It is generally agreed that the motif of dream-pairs is one of the unifying elements of the Joseph narrative. Each scene in question features not one dream but two. Different theories have been proposed regarding the contribution of these dream-pairs to the narrative, and regarding the relationship between the dreams of each pair. Joseph interprets the Pharaoh's two dreams as "one and the same," but he presents a different interpretation for each of the ministers' dreams. The narrative does not explicitly indicate whether Joseph's own dreams share a meaning or have separate meanings; indeed, there are different scholarly approaches to this question. This article proposes that the relationship between Joseph's dreams is a fundamental question in the narrative, and the two models presented later in the story are two possible interpretations between which Joseph himself has the power to choose.

It is generally agreed that the three pairs of dreams featured in the Joseph narrative (Joseph's dreams [ch. 37]; the ministers' dreams [ch. 40]; and Pharaoh's dreams [ch. 41]) testify not to a fusion of sources or traditions but to a unity of composition: "The relationship of the three pairs of dreams to each other in chapters 37; 40; and 41 is alone sufficient to show that the Joseph story is the composition of a single author; it reveals a well-thought-out plan."[1] Many have noted that the connection between the different pairs of dreams is further reinforced by the phrase "I have dreamed a dream" (חלום חלמתי), which appears in all three instances. "The three dream-pairs seem to be tightly connected,"[2] and they play an important

---

[1] Claus Westermann, *Genesis 37–50: A Continental Commentary*, trans. John J. Scullion (Minneapolis: Fortress, 1986), 78.

[2] Ron Pirson, *The Lord of the Dreams: A Semantic and Literary Analysis of Genesis 37–50*, JSOTSup 355 (Sheffield: Sheffield Academic, 2002), 52. Compare Jean-Marie Husser, *Dreams and Dream Narratives in the Biblical World*, trans. Jill M. Munro, BibSem 63 (Sheffield: Sheffield

role in plot development and the protagonist's movement. Joseph's dreams exacerbate his brothers' envy, which leads to his being sold and taken to Egypt ("we shall see what comes of his dreams!" 37:20); Joseph's accurate interpretation of the ministers' dreams in prison leads to the cupbearer's recommendation of Joseph to Pharaoh, which results in his release from prison and his rise to greatness in Egypt.[3] It has even been claimed that the dreams are the key unifying elements of the entire narrative: "The dreams unify the story and are the glue that hold its parts together. Without them, the story is no longer comprehensible."[4]

Upon first reading, one might think that a single dream would have sufficed in each case. For this reason it is important to examine the contribution made by a *pair* of dreams at each point.[5] Some have proposed that this doubling is inherent in the "literary duplication" of the Joseph narrative's structure (the brothers twice descend to Egypt; both Reuben and Judah attempt to convince Jacob; Joseph accuses his brothers twice—of spying, and of thievery; and so on). According to this theory, the fact that each scene contains a *pair* of dreams is but the tip of the iceberg; the narrative's broader tendency to doubling is what requires explanation.[6]

My own premise differs; I will show that the dream-pairs play a decisive role in the story. The fundamental question concerns the correlation between the two

---

Academic, 1999), 106; Robert Karl Gnuse, *Dreams and Dream Reports in the Writings of Josephus: A Traditio-Historical Analysis*, AGJU 36 (Leiden: Brill, 1996), 70; Nili Shupak, "A Reexamination of the Dreams of the Egyptian Officials and of Pharaoh in the Joseph Narrative (Gen 40–41)" [in Hebrew], *Shnaton* 15 (2005): 63; Jörg Lanckau, *Der Herr der Träume: Eine Studie zur Funktion des Traumes in der Josefsgeschichte der Hebräischen Bibel*, ATANT 85 (Zurich: TVZ, 2006), 254. It should be noted that the expression "dream a dream" appears elsewhere in dream accounts (e.g., Deut 13:2, 4, 8; Judg 7:18; Joel 3:1; Dan 2:1, 3), but not in all biblical dream accounts. Whether the expression serves to link the scenes within the narrative is, therefore, open to debate.

[3] W. Lee Humphreys, *Joseph and His Family: A Literary Study*, Studies on Personalities of the Old Testament (Columbia: University of South Carolina Press, 1988), 39, 70.

[4] Shaul Bar, *A Letter That Has Not Been Read: Dreams in the Hebrew Bible*, trans. Lenn J. Schramm, HUCM 25 (Cincinnati: Hebrew Union College Press, 2001), 54 n. 41.

[5] "Dream-pairs" are also found in Mesopotamian literature; for example, Gilgamesh dreams two dreams before meeting Enkidu (Tablet I, lines 273–74). On this phenomenon in biblical and Near Eastern literature, see Cyrus H. Gordon, *The Common Background of Greek and Hebrew Civilizations* (New York: Norton, 1965), 64–65; Donald B. Redford, *A Study of the Biblical Story of Joseph: Genesis 37–50*, VTSup 20 (Leiden: Brill, 1970), 89–91, 138–86.

Shupak shows that the model of three dreams also existed in the ancient East ("Reexamination of the Dreams," 63). God's two revelations to Balaam should not be considered an example of the phenomenon of "dream-pairs" because each of these revelations plays a different role in the development of the plot: God first forbids Balaam to go, and then permits him. See Ruth Fidler, "*Dreams Speak Falsely?" Dream Theophanies in the Bible: Their Place in Ancient Israelite Faith and Traditions* [in Hebrew] (Jerusalem: Magnes, 2005), 112.

[6] See esp. R. Norman Whybray, "The Joseph Story and Pentateuchal Criticism," *VT* 18 (1968): 522–28; Yairah Amit, "The Repeated Situation: A Poetic Principle in the Modeling of the Joseph Narrative" [in Hebrew], *Te'uda* 7 (1991): 55–66; Robert Alter, *Genesis: Translation and Commentary* (New York: Norton, 1996), 210.

dreams in each of the three scenes—what is the nature of the relationship of the dreams in each pair, and can the doubling of dreams in one scene illuminate the duplication in another? This question is especially relevant given the explicit interpretation of this phenomenon in regard to Pharaoh's dreams. Presenting his solution, Joseph asserts that this doubling has no bearing on the meaning of the dreams' content: "Pharaoh's dreams are one and the same" (41:25); Joseph perceives the phenomenon only as a sign that the dreams will soon come to pass (41:32). Can this interpretation also be applied to the other dream-pairs in the story? Obviously, this cannot be true of the ministers' dreams, as each has a different meaning, but can this be said of Joseph's own dreams?

Hermann Gunkel holds that Joseph's dreams have an identical meaning: "Both of Joseph's dreams mean the same thing. The narrator may have had the brothers' two trips to Egypt in mind in narrating two dreams."[7] Others of this opinion explicitly refer to the fact that Pharaoh's dreams are interpreted as one: "Like Pharaoh's two dreams, which are said to be one (41:25), it seems likely that both Joseph's dreams are making a single point, namely that his family will one day bow down to him, not that they will do so on two occasions."[8]

In contrast, Ron Pirson claims that the relationship between the dreams in each of the three pairs develops over the course of the story: Joseph's dreams have two completely different interpretations; the ministers' dreams have different meanings, but they take place at the same time, while Pharaoh's dreams are indeed "one and the same."[9] In his opinion, Joseph's pair of dreams is the ultimate expression of two completely different dreams.

Two models of interpretation are explicitly integrated into the narrative: the ministers' dreams present two divergent meanings, while Pharaoh's dreams converge. The relationship between Joseph's dreams, however, remains undefined in the text. My thesis is that these two explicit models are intentionally presented in the story, while the ambiguity regarding the relationship between Joseph's dreams is one of its fundamental themes. Not only is the matter intentionally left open to interpretation, but the characters themselves must determine the relationship between the dreams. In order to clarify this developing motif, I will examine each pair of dreams.

---

[7] Hermann Gunkel, *Genesis: Translated and Interpreted*, trans. Mark E. Biddle from 9th German ed. of 1977, Mercer Library of Biblical Studies (Macon, GA: Mercer University Press, 1997; orig. 1910), 390. See also George W. Coats, *Genesis, with an Introduction to Narrative Literature*, FOTL 1 (Grand Rapids: Eerdmans, 1983), 270; Meir Sternberg, *The Poetics of Biblical Narrative: Ideological Literature and the Drama of Reading*, Indiana Literary Biblical Series (Bloomington: Indiana University Press, 1985), 397.

[8] Gordon J. Wenham, *Genesis 16–50*, WBC 2 (Dallas: Word, 1998), 351. Kenneth A. Mathews expresses a similar idea: "These two dreams are like Pharaoh's dual dreams, 'one and the same' (41:25)" (*Genesis 11:27–50:26*, NAC [Nashville: Broadman & Holman, 2005], 691).

[9] Pirson, *Lord of the Dreams*, 58–59.

I. The First Pair: Joseph's Dreams

In contrast to the narrative's other pairs, no interpretation scene is devoted to Joseph's dreams. Rather, these visions are deciphered over the course of the plot, their solutions implied through the characters' reactions.[10] Through the brothers' angry words, the reader learns how they have interpreted the first dream: "Do you mean to reign over us? Do you mean to rule over us?" (37:8); and Jacob's chiding of Joseph reveals his reading of the second dream: "Are we to come, I and your mother and your brothers, and bow low to you to the ground?" (37:10).[11] The fact that these readings are not presented as actual solutions but rather as the characters' reactions, leads the reader to question their accuracy. The implied solutions certainly fit with the dream's tone and main components—after all, the brothers' inferior sheaves bow down before Joseph's sheaf—but the reliability of each speaker influences how their words resonate with the reader. Moreover, both "interpretations" are phrased with skepticism—"Do you really believe that this will happen?!"—which lends these readings further implausibility. As the characters present the solution, the reader grasps their doubt in regard to the dream and its apparent solution. Even if this is due to the family's strained relationship (which is especially apparent in the narrator's description of Jacob's reproach [37:11]), this skepticism still casts the speakers' own words in doubt, leaving the reader to question the irked characters' proposed solutions.[12]

Indeed, scholars have offered various interpretations that differ from the characters' own readings of these dreams.[13] Even if we ultimately accept the solutions

---

[10] Westermann, *Genesis 37–50*, 78.

[11] I find Husser's interpretation—that the interpretation seemed obvious to Jacob and the brothers, whereas Joseph understands this interpretation only when the brothers come and bow before him in Egypt—unconvincing (Husser, *Dreams and Dream Narratives*, 113).

[12] Compare Lanckau, *Der Herr der Träume*, 182–85, who notes that the question of the credibility of Jacob's solution also pertains to whether the eleven stars logically represent Joseph's brothers. As Jacob relates to Rachel as if she were alive, he argues that this scene takes place when Joseph is still young, before Rachel's death and Benjamin's birth, in which case it is unclear why the eleven stars stand for Joseph's brothers. See his discussion.

[13] A good example is Pirson's suggestion that in the second dream the celestial bodies do not symbolize family members, but, like the symbols in the ministers' and Pharaoh's dreams, they show when the dream will come to pass: thirteen years (eleven stars + sun + moon). Indeed, after thirteen years, the first dream begins to be fulfilled: Joseph rises to power in Egypt, and all bow and submit to his "sheaf." See Ron Pirson, "The Sun, the Moon, and Eleven Stars: An Interpretation of Joseph's Second Dream," in *Studies in the Book of Genesis: Literature, Redaction and History*, ed. André Wénin, BETL 155 (Leuven: Leuven University Press, 2001), 561–68; and Pirson, *Lord of the Dreams*, 55–59. Gunkel and Gerhard von Rad already claimed that the stars do not reflect the family members; rather, "the number eleven must be connected with the ancient notion of the eleven signs of the zodiac" (von Rad, *Genesis*, 2nd ed., trans. John H. Marks, OTL [London: SCM, 1963], 347; Gunkel, *Genesis*, 390). Some scholars even claim that the solution to Joseph's dreams

presented in the story, the fact that they are expressed by emotionally wrought characters (which is not the case in the other two scenes) affects the reader's attitude toward these dreams, which remain without authoritative interpretation at the end of chapter 37.

Does the narrative design of this dream-pair allow us to determine whether these dreams share a single meaning or have two separate meanings? On the one hand, the second dream opens with the expression "*another* dream" (ויחלם עוד חלום, 37:9), which implies continuity and cohesion; additionally, both dreams feature bowing down to Joseph or his sheaf, which encourages comparison between them. The difference between sheaves and celestial elements does not seem greater than the difference between Pharaoh's ears of grain and cows rising out of the Nile, which are charged with divine associations in Egyptian culture.[14] Nonetheless, Joseph determines that Pharaoh's two dreams are one and the same, so the reader may easily infer that here, too, although the dreams feature different symbols, their meaning is identical.

Pirson, however, who claims that Joseph's dreams have two completely different meanings, draws attention to the fact that the second dream is introduced with the phrase "another, *different* dream" (ויחלם עוד חלום אחר): "Therefore it is possible that the word 'אחר', does not simply mean 'another, following', but rather indicates that Joseph dreamed a dream which is completely distinct from the first."[15] Note that in the second dream, other entities besides the brothers are represented through celestial bodies (the sun and the moon, besides the stars), which may encourage a different interpretation. Similarly, in the first dream, Joseph, like his brothers, is symbolized by a sheaf, while in the second dream, the sun, moon, and stars bow down to Joseph himself.[16]

The characters' interpretation of Joseph's dreams reinforces the position that the dream-pair has a single meaning, as both Joseph's brothers (after the first dream) and his father (after hearing the second) see the dreams as portents of

---

anticipates other biblical stories beyond the Joseph cycle. See esp. Yair Zakovitch, *I Will Utter Riddles from Ancient Time: Riddles and Dream-Riddles in Biblical Narrative* [in Hebrew], Aron sefarim Yehudi (Tel Aviv: Am Oved, 2005), 41; Benjamin D. H. Hilbert, "Joseph's Dreams, Part One: From Abimelech to Saul," *JSOT* 35 (2011): 259–83, http://dx.doi.org/10.1177/0309089210386019; Hilbert, "Joseph's Dreams, Part Two: From Saul to Solomon," *JSOT* 35 (2011): 435–61, http://dx.doi.org/10.1177/0309089211402178. Pierre Gilbert even claims that Joseph's sheaf surrounded by his brothers' sheaves hints at the male erection, which symbolizes his power. According to Gilbert, the dream reflects the brothers' impotence compared to Joseph (*Le récit biblique de rêve: Essai de confrontation analytique*, Série biblique 3 [Lyon: Profac, 1990], 45).

[14] E. A. Wallis Budge, *From Fetish to God in Ancient Egypt* (London: Oxford University Press, 1934), 228–29.

[15] Pirson, *Lord of the Dreams*, 50.

[16] Lanckau, *Der Herr der Träume*, 169. Amit notes that the first dream, with its large number of verbs, differs from the second, which is more static and describes a situation rather than an event ("Repeated Situation," 59).

Joseph's dominion over his family. These readings reflect the tension and conflicting interests of members of the household. Because these interpretations are not "official" solutions, the reader may be skeptical of them.

At this stage of the reading, then, the possibilities remain open, and it is difficult to determine if the dreams, like Pharaoh's, are one and the same, or if each dream, like the ministers', has its own interpretation.

II. The Second Pair: The Ministers' Dreams

Scholars have noted that this dream-pair is the most sophisticated, containing most of the components that conventionally appear in dream narratives.[17] Even if this is correct from the perspective of a "literary form," it does not require that this pair be considered a prototype for the other two dream-pairs, as I will shortly clarify. Yairah Amit opens her discussion of this dream-pair with the statement that "between the additional dream-pair that appears in chapter 40, the differences are immediately apparent."[18] In light of Joseph's interpretations, there is no doubt that these two dreams have opposite meanings: one heralds life, and the other death. In the first dream, the minister appointed over the king's cup supervises his drink, while in the second the minister responsible for the king's food fails to do his duty, allowing the birds to consume his goods (in contrast, for example, to Abram in Gen 15).[19] The difference between the dreams is also expressed through the narrative techniques of their solution: while Joseph interprets the cupbearer's dream literally (in three days he will serve wine to the king, just as he does in his dream), he reads the chief baker's dream on a symbolic level (the dream figure of the baker represents the gallows; the baskets of food consumed by the birds signify the baker himself, whose flesh will soon be eaten by scavenger birds of prey).[20] The different modes of interpretation of each dream emphasize the differences between them. Moreover, the very fact that this dream-pair is dreamed by two different dreamers reinforces Amit's claim that the reader is immediately struck by the differences between them.

Nonetheless, the narrator employs several methods of misleading the reader, creating the illusion that the two dreams share a single interpretation—until Joseph's words reveal that the two dreams are antithetical in meaning. It is therefore more accurate to state that, initially, the reader anticipates that the two dreams are

---

[17] Wolfgang Richter, "Traum und Traumdeutung im Alten Testament: Ihre Form und Verwendung," *BZ* 7 (1963): 202–20; Husser, *Dreams and Dream Narratives*, 106–7.

[18] Amit, "Repeated Situation," 60. See also Westermann, *Genesis*, 3:75–77.

[19] Mathews, *Genesis 11:27–50:25*, 750.

[20] In contrast, von Rad claims that the meaning of the baker's dream is not interpreted symbolically (*Genesis*, 366).

one and the same, but eventually it becomes clear that their differences emerge. This development employs several devices:

1. The initial description of the ministers characterizes them as an indistinguishable pair:

> Some time later, the cupbearer and the baker of the king of Egypt gave offense to their lord the king of Egypt. Pharaoh was angry with his two courtiers, the chief cupbearer and the chief baker, and put them in custody.... The chief steward assigned Joseph to them, and he attended them. (40:1–4)

Their joint description creates the impression that the two sinned together,[21] angered Pharaoh together, were punished together, were together served by Joseph, and served the same sentence—both were "in custody for some time" (40:4).[22]

2. This impression is reinforced by the description of their dreaming:

> Both of them dreamed a dream in the same night, each his own dream and each dream with its own meaning—the cupbearer and the baker of the king of Egypt, who were confined in the prison. (40:5)

Both dream "in the same night," and the narrator once again emphasizes that the characters inhabit the same narrative space: "who were confined in the prison." In addition, the two have a similar role in the Egyptian government: both are responsible for the victuals "of the king of Egypt." Two dreams are dreamed at the same time, in the same place, by two figures of a similar position.

3. Given the narrator's apparent intentions, it should come as no surprise that the singular form of the word *dream* is used rather than the plural. It is not related that the two "dreamed dreams" but rather that each "dreamed a dream" (40:5). While this is grammatically acceptable—each dreamed his own dream—this language nonetheless creates the impression that the two dreams might be one and the same. The singular form is even more salient in the ministers' appeal to Joseph: "And they said to him, 'We have dreamed *a dream*, and there is no one to interpret *it*'" (40:8). The implication is that, even if each minister dreamed his own dream, the two are deeply connected. In fact, the description that each dreamer is distraught at the same time and that they reply to Joseph's question as one, "Why do you appear downcast today?" (40:7) sustains the impression that their dreams are essentially the same, with a single interpretation.

---

[21] In the LXX, even v. 1 reads, "the chief cupbearer of the king of Egypt and the chief baker *sinned*"—in the singular (see Moshe A. Zipor, *The Septuagint Version of the Book of Genesis* [in Hebrew] [Ramat Gan: Bar-Ilan University Press, 2005], 483).

[22] Compare the similar description of Ahasuerus's two chamberlains (Esth 2:21–23). The two meet the same end. Concerning the connection between the two ministers in Genesis and the two chamberlains in Esther, see Jon D. Levenson, *Esther: A Commentary*, OTL (Louisville: Westminster John Knox, 1997), 65; Timothy S. Laniak, *Esther*, in Leslie C. Allen and Timothy S. Laniak, *Ezra, Nehemiah, Esther*, NIBCOT (Peabody, MA: Hendrickson, 2003), 213.

4. At first glance, the ministers' dreams seem to hint at the same prediction; each minister dreams about three items related to his position:[23] three branches of a vine and three openwork baskets. In the cupbearer's dream, a cup of wine is served to Pharaoh, which seems to correspond to the food being consumed by the birds in the chief baker's dream. In many contexts, birds function as symbols of royalty, the king in particular.[24] For example, the Egyptian god Horus, patron of the pharaohs, was viewed as the founder of the true royal line and was depicted as having the head of a falcon. He was also known as Nekheny, meaning "falcon." While understanding the fowl in the baker's dream as a symbol of Egypt's king is not necessary, it *is* possible; and, given the profound connections between this dream-pair, Joseph could easily have interpreted the scene in this manner. Yair Zakovitch also correctly observes that, because Joseph uses the word *head* when he predicts that the cupbearer will return to his former position (40:13), using the same word in his answer to the chief baker increases the reader's anticipation (and presumably the baker's) that the baker's head, too, will be lifted up and his position restored.[25]

5. The narrator's inclination to present the two dreams similarly is apparent not only in the recounting of the dreams but also in the interpretation (at least initially). Despite the two different interpretations that Joseph ultimately offers, his first words continue to generate anticipation that the two dreams have an identical meaning. The solution to the cupbearer's dream begins with a chronological description: "The three branches are three days" (v. 12). Likewise, Joseph also responds to the chief baker thus: "The three baskets are three days" (v. 18); to both of them, he continues, "in three days ..." (vv. 13, 19). He then describes what will befall each of them with a similar expression: he informs the cupbearer that "in three days, *Pharaoh will lift your head* up and restore you to your post" (v. 13). Echoing this interpretation, he tells the chief baker, "in three days, *Pharaoh will lift your head* off" (v. 19). The reader can imagine the baker holding his breath as Joseph repeats the same words he used to foretell the cupbearer's happy fate, only to have these illusions shattered with the addition of the word *off*. The metaphor of "head lifting" is cruelly reduced to its literal meaning; the baker's head will be lifted not up but off, off of his body.[26]

---

[23] Theoretically, this divergence can be read as an element that differentiates the dreams, but essentially it also creates a connection between them. Each one dreams about his own life. If the two ministers are restored to their former posts, each will resume his life.

[24] Zakovitch, *I Will Utter Riddles*, 41. See further Rozenn Bailleul-LeSuer, ed., *Between Heaven and Earth: Birds in Ancient Egypt*, OIMP 35 (Chicago: Oriental Institute of the University of Chicago, 2012).

[25] Ibid.

[26] Shupak is correct that the masoretic version of the text can remain in its current form, with no need to omit the word מעליך due to dittographical error ("Reexamination of the Dreams," 74–75 n. 77). Many have noted the verse's wordplay. See esp. David Marcus, who shows that this wordplay is usually lost in translation ("'Lifting Up the Head': On the Trail of Word Play in Genesis 40," *Proof* 10 [1990]: 17–27). See also Scott B. Noegel, who notes other wordplays in this scene

Through this careful reading, it is clear that, although the two dreams have an opposite meaning—one portends life and the other death—the narrative has been constructed to generate surprise: the dreams and their interpretations are initially presented similarly. Indeed, as many have commented, the misleading likeness between the two dreams emphasizes the wisdom of Joseph, who is able to make fine distinctions, differentiating even between dreams that appear to be one and the same. This design is not intended merely to serve Joseph's characterization as a wise interpreter of dreams, however; it plays a crucial role in plot development and in Joseph's appearance before Pharaoh.

In the next scene, the reader encounters Egyptian magicians who are unable to solve Pharaoh's dreams ("but none could interpret them for Pharaoh," 41:8). There is no explanation why the king was dissatisfied with other proposed interpretations (assuming that others were offered),[27] but this is important background information for the recommendation of the cupbearer, who suddenly remembers Joseph after two years. The cupbearer's words clarify why this particular situation is what reminds him of the long-forgotten Hebrew youth (40:23). In his address he repeatedly recalls the baker, who dreamed along with him:

> He placed me in custody in the house of the chief steward, together with the chief baker. We had dreams the same night, he and I, each of us a dream with a meaning of its own ... when we told him our dreams, he interpreted them for us, telling each of the meaning of his dream. And as he interpreted for us, so it came to pass: I was restored to my post, and the other was impaled." (41:10–13)[28]

The fact that Pharaoh dreams two dreams reminds the chief cupbearer of the two dreams that Joseph interpreted years before. Pharaoh summons Joseph because the cupbearer mentions his expertise in solving a *pair* of dreams; his ability to distinguish between two similar dreams is precisely what Pharaoh needs. In prison, Joseph proved that he is able to differentiate between a dream signifying that its

---

(*Nocturnal Ciphers: The Allusive Language of Dreams in the Ancient Near East*, AOS 89 [New Haven: American Oriental Society, 2007], 128–32). Zakovitch proposes that the unusual term in the baker's dream, "openwork baskets," hints at Pharaoh's wrath (סלי חרי – חרון אף) (*I Will Utter Riddles*, 43). Regarding the third appearance of the phrase "lift the head" (40:20), James A. Montgomery comments that it is a technical expression that means "counted, took account" (*A Critical and Exegetical Commentary on the Books of Kings*, ICC [Edinburgh: T&T Clark, 1960], 569). This claim is correct, and E. A. Speiser shows that this is also the meaning of the Akkadian phrase *rēšam našûm* ("Census and Ritual Expiation in Mari and Israel," *BASOR* 149 [1958]: 17–25). The third appearance of this phrase, however, even if having a different meaning, further reinforces the wordplay of this passage. See also Menahem Zevi Kaddari, *A Dictionary of Biblical Hebrew* [in Hebrew] (Ramat Gan: Bar-Ilan University Press, 2006), 734, s.v. נשא.

[27] Westermann proposes that the magicians sensed that these dreams were an omen of disaster and did not dare propose this to the king (*Genesis*, 3:88).

[28] Regarding the connection between the cupbearer's words to Pharaoh (41:11) and the narrator's description of the prison scene (esp. 40:5), see Lanckau, *Der Herr der Träume*, 253.

dreamer's head will be lifted *up*, and one signifying that its dreamer's head will be lifted *off*; this endowment is what summons him to Pharaoh.[29]

III. The Third Pair: Pharaoh's Dreams

Ironically enough, Joseph's special knack for distinguishing pairs of dreams (dreamed the same night) is not utilized when he presents a solution to Pharaoh. In contrast to his interpretation of the ministers' dreams, Joseph determines that Pharaoh's two dreams are one, and he even explains why this is so: "As for Pharaoh having had the same dream twice, it means that the matter has been determined by God, and that God will soon carry it out" (41:32). That is, this doubling pertains not to the dreams' actual interpretation but rather to when this interpretation will come to pass.

The narrative design of Joseph's interpretation indicates that the dream-pair has a single meaning. When he deciphers that the cows and ears represent seven years, he fuses the two dreams together:

   A   And Joseph said to Pharaoh, "Pharaoh's dreams are one and the same: God has told Pharaoh what he is about to do.
      B   The seven healthy cows are seven years, and the seven healthy ears are seven years;
         C   it is the same dream.
      B´   The seven lean and ugly cows that followed are seven years, as are also the seven empty ears scorched by the east wind; they are seven years of famine.
   A´   It is just as I have told Pharaoh: God has revealed to Pharaoh what he is about to do." (41:25–28)

The framework of Joseph's words (A–A´) emphasizes the supreme principle of the solution: Pharaoh's dreams are a message from God, informing him of events about to unfold.[30] The heart of the solution pits seven years of abundance (B) against seven years of famine (B´),[31] and here Joseph clearly merges the symbols from both

---

[29] See further Jonathan Grossman, *Text and Subtext: On Exploring Biblical Narrative Design* [in Hebrew] (Tel Aviv: Hakibbutz Hameuchad, 2015), 174–76.

[30] Mathews, *Genesis 11:27–50:25*, 760. The combination of the words *told* (הגיד, mentioned in A) and *showed* (הראה, mentioned in A´) is based on the relationship between the senses of hearing and sight, which is a frequent combination in biblical narrative. See, e.g., Amos Frish, "שמ"ע and רא"ה as a Pair of Leitwörter" [in Hebrew], *Proceedings of the Twelfth World Congress of Jewish Studies*, Division A (Jerusalem: World Congress of Jewish Studies, 1999): 89–98. See also Sheri L. Klouda, "The Dialectical Interplay of Seeing and Hearing in Psalm 19 and Its Connection to Wisdom," *BBR* 10 (2000): 181–95; Kenneth T. Aitken, "Hearing and Seeing: Metamorphoses of a Motif in Isaiah 1–39," in *Among the Prophets: Language, Image, and Structure in the Prophetic Writings*, ed. Philip R. Davies and David J. A. Clines, JSOTSup 144 (Sheffield: JSOT Press, 1993), 12–41.

[31] A careful reading of Joseph's message about the years of plenty and the years of famine

dreams: the "seven healthy cows" are mentioned together with the "seven healthy ears" (B) while the "seven lean and ugly cows" appear alongside the "seven empty ears scorched by the wind" (B´).[32] This fusion is explained both in the introduction to his explanation ("Pharaoh's dreams are one and the same") and at the heart of his interpretation, which transports his audience from the years of plenty to the years of famine ("it is the same dream" [C]).

That the two dreams are one is hinted at already in Pharaoh's account to his magicians: "Pharaoh told them his dream, but none could interpret them" (41:8). The transition from singular ("his dream") to plural ("them") resulted in this verse's harmonization in several translations, either through the alteration of "his dream" to the plural form (the Samaritan Pentateuch) or by changing "them" to singular (LXX). Gordon J. Wenham, however, may be correct that this lack of coordination is intentional, hinting to the reader that the two dreams are one.[33] This suggestion is supported by a similar device in Pharaoh's description to Joseph (is Pharaoh aware of this?): "I have had *a dream*, but no one can interpret *it*" (41:15).[34] Pharaoh's use of the singular for two dreams can be explained as the collective form; upon a second reading, however, the reader is able to interpret this language as an allusion to the two dreams being "one."[35]

Pharaoh's second dream is introduced with a new heading: "he dreamed a second time" (41:5), but he retells the dreams without a separate introduction (41:22). Based on this omission, Jörg Lanckau argues that the two dreams are in fact one and that the second dream serves "as a confirmation dream [*Bestätigungstraum*] of the first."[36]

Other such hints become clear upon a second reading. Both cows and healthy ears "came up" (עולות, 41:2, 5); additionally, the adjective "healthy" (בריאות) describes both cows and ears (41:2, 5), even though it is a more appropriate term for fauna than flora. This similar language connects the two dreams.[37]

---

supports Westermann's claim that Joseph emphasizes the years of famine (*Genesis*, 3:91). It is sufficient to compare the lengths of components B and B´ to confirm this.

[32] It may be that Joseph refers to the ears as "lean," which in the dreams only describes the cows, in order to consolidate the two dreams in his answer, so that there is no need to adopt the versions of the LXX, the Samaritan Pentateuch, or the Peshitta, which emend this to read the "shriveled" ears.

[33] Wenham, *Genesis*, 391.

[34] Here, too, the Samaritan Pentateuch, which found the singular form problematic, changed this to the plural form: "I dreamed dreams and there is no one to interpret them."

[35] Sternberg proposes that Pharaoh sensed that the two dreams had a single meaning and therefore rejected the interpretations of his magicians, who did not realize this (*Poetics of Biblical Narrative*, 398). See, similarly, Bill T. Arnold, *Genesis*, NCBC (New York: Cambridge University Press, 2009), 341.

[36] Lanckau, *Der Herr der Träume*, 256–57.

[37] See Susan Niditch and Robert Doran, "The Success Story of the Wise Courtier: A Formal Approach," *JBL* 96 (1977): 186, http://dx.doi.org/10.2307/3265877; Sternberg, *Poetics of Biblical Narrative*, 397.

IV. Joseph's Dreams: One Dream or Two?

Certain differences may be noted between Joseph's dreams and the two other dream-pairs, and some commentators might claim that there is no room for comparison between them. Jean-Marie Husser notes that the introduction to Joseph's dreams differs greatly from the introduction to the ministers' and Pharaoh's dreams. Joseph's dreams begin with the combination of "dream" and "I dreamed" (37:6, 9),[38] while the ministers and Pharaoh introduce their dreams with the expression "in my dream" (40:9, 16; 41:17, 22).[39] Yet, considering that combinations of a verb and a noun from the root חלם feature in both the ministers' and Pharaoh's accounts, this difference seems negligible and can be attributed to aesthetic variation. Nili Shupak claims that the meaning of Joseph's dreams is self-evident and requires no "professional interpretation," unlike the other two pairs.[40] If we adopt an accepted distinction, however, between dreams whose meaning is determined through interpretation of its symbols and dreams with a literal meaning, then even if the interpretation of Joseph's dreams is obvious to the characters, his dream-pair still falls firmly in the former category.[41] The ministers' dream-pair and Pharaoh's were each dreamed on the same night (40:5; 41:11; 41:5–8), unlike Joseph's, but this ought not to delegitimize comparison between the pairs. It remains to be determined which model of interpretation applies to Joseph's dream-pair. Are Joseph's dreams, like Pharaoh's, "one and the same," or do they have two different meanings, like the ministers'?

If the content of the dreams is taken into consideration, the question becomes yet more complex. Each pair shares common features (the prostration before Joseph; the numbers and symbols related to the ministers' positions; the numbers and scenario in Pharaoh's), but at the same time the discrepancies are important to note. The the ministers' dreams indeed have different meanings, and there are also significant dissimilarities between Pharaoh's dreams that could hint at two interpretations (for example, the first dream's emphasis on the Nile,[42] which is not mentioned at all during the second dream). As I established at the beginning, Joseph's dreams show similarities that suggest a single interpretation, as well as differences

---

[38] Concerning this introduction, see Coats, *Genesis*, 269.

[39] Husser, *Dreams and Dream Narratives*, 112.

[40] Shupak, "Reexamination of the Dreams," 56 n. 5. This was claimed also by Ann Jeffers, "Divination by Dreams in Ugaritic Literature and in the Old Testament," *IBS* 12 (1990): 167–83.

[41] Richter is of this opinion ("Traum und Traumdeutung").

[42] Every stage of the dream emphasizes that it takes place next to the Nile: at the beginning of the dream, Pharaoh is "standing by the Nile" (41:1); the healthy cows rise up "from the Nile" (41:2), as well as the lean cows (41:3); and even the description of their standing alongside the healthy cows takes place "on the bank of the Nile" (41:3).

that point to two. I believe that here lies the key question of the Joseph story and that the reader's confusion plays a crucial role in the narrative's development.

Moreover, while the narrative explicitly defines whether the dreams in the two other pairs share one meaning or two, the relationship between Joseph's dreams remains ambiguous, so that it falls to the characters to determine the meaning. The characters themselves have the power to decide whether the two dreams are one and the same, and this power plays a dramatic role in the story.

Despite the reservations of some scholars, I favor the view that Joseph's dream-sheaves symbolize the family's sustenance: the brothers' sheaves bowing down to Joseph's sheaf anticipates their future financial dependence on Joseph.[43] The intriguing fact that Joseph also is represented by an object (a sheaf) may show that the dream describes the brothers' descent to Egypt in order to appeal to the Egyptian ruler, without conceiving that this ruler is their brother Joseph. The dialogue is held between the "sheaves"; it is strictly a business exchange. This widely accepted explanation may account for Joseph's dream of sheaves despite the fact that his family's wealth is based on their flocks.[44]

In contrast, the celestial bodies of the second dream are unrelated to the family's economic welfare. This dream can easily be read as a forecast of Joseph's future dominion over his family, which accounts for their prostration before him. This is an indication of actual leadership rather than of economic power,[45] as in the first dream. This is significant, given that the second dream is devoid of all symbols pertaining to food or sustenance. The other five dreams all contain such symbols: Joseph first dreams of sheaves; the ministers dream of wine and delicacies for Pharaoh; Pharaoh dreams of emaciated cows and ears of grain "consuming" their superior counterparts.[46] Only Joseph's second dream is devoid of the motif of

---

[43] See, e.g., Gunkel, *Genesis*, 390; Coats, *Genesis*, 269; Wenham, *Genesis*, 351; Victor P. Hamilton, *The Book of Genesis: Chapters 18–50*, NICOT (Grand Rapids: Eerdmans, 1995), 410. Ernst Ludwig Ehrlich, for example, is among those who disagree, writing that this interpretation is tempting but "geht aber zu weit" (*Der Traum im Alten Testament*, BZAW 73 [Berlin: Topelmann, 1953], 59). See also John Skinner, who questions whether the connection between the dream of the sheaves and Joseph's economic position is substantial (*A Critical and Exegetical Commentary on Genesis*, 2nd ed., ICC [Edinburgh: T&T Clark, 1930], 445).

[44] Von Rad seeks to prove from the dream of sheaves that, despite the fact that the family were mainly shepherds, they had "agricultural practices." He therefore rules out the connection between the dream and Joseph's economic position over his brothers later on (*Genesis*, 347). Gunkel also concludes from the dream "that Jacob also farmed," but this did not prevent him from linking this dream to the brothers' later dependence on Joseph (*Genesis*, 390).

[45] The fact that those who bow to Joseph are symbolized by celestial bodies emphasizes Joseph's omnipotence from a theological perspective as well: "The most damaging is that this is an idolatrous dream in which Joseph takes the place of the Almighty, thereby worshipping himself. Self-worship is a characteristic of the Pharaoh, who is called the very incarnation of the sun god Ra" (Aaron Wildavsky, *Assimilation versus Separation: Joseph the Administrator and the Politics of Religion in Biblical Israel* [New Brunswick, NJ: Transaction, 1993], 78).

[46] Words related to food and eating are frequent in the Joseph narrative, as shown by Aldina

eating; it is concerned with celestial bodies, not bodily needs. The dream's subject testifies to its anomalous dissociation from economic issues.

The question of whether Joseph's dreams are one or two, therefore, has the power to propel the plot in two entirely different directions. If the dreams are "one and the same," then the second dream serves only to reinforce the extent of Joseph's economic power. Perhaps its function is to establish that not only will Joseph's family depend on him, but the fate of the entire land, from Mesopotamia to Egypt, will hinge on Joseph's economic proficiency. If, however, the dreams have two separate meanings, then Husser is correct in asserting that the second dream hints at Joseph's dominion over his family in addition to his economic authority.[47] According to the second dream, Joseph will rise above his brothers and serve as the family's firstborn—perhaps even as the chosen son. Within this paradigm, the second dream determines family hierarchy beyond the question of economic dependence.

This distinction is not evident in the family's implied interpretation of Joseph's dreams, as at this point no one can possibly conceive of Joseph's future economic responsibility. But, more significantly, the narrator never explicitly relates the dreams' fulfillment in the future (with the exception of a general statement made from Joseph's perspective in 42:9). Husser ascribes this to the story's folkloric origins and resulting lack of narrative interest in dream fulfillment:

> This is simply further evidence of the existence of different narrative perspectives, perhaps of distinct redactional layers, but also, as regards Genesis 37, of a greater proximity to the original folk motif. Nothing tells us where Joseph's dreams come from. Indeed the narrator does not seem to be interested in the question.[48]

Yet it is problematic to claim that the narrator has little interest in the fulfillment of the protagonist's dreams when so much attention is devoted to the description of the other two dream-pairs' interpretations coming to pass. Leaving Joseph's dreams open to interpretation without explicitly recounting their fulfillment is a literary technique that allows both possibilities (that both dreams are of a solely economic nature, or that the second dream is a harbinger of royalty and leadership), which permits the characters to determine their meaning. Presenting two dream-pair models after Joseph's dreams indicates two possible relationships between them.

As the plot unfolds, we learn how the characters resolve this question. The brothers' descent to Egypt fulfills the first dream. The brothers plead before Joseph, imploring him for economic patronage, and Joseph functions like the symbolic sheaf of his dream, sustaining all of Egypt in the time of famine. The second dream

---

da Silva, *La symbolique des rêves et des vêtements dans l'histoire de Joseph et de ses frères*, Heritage et project 52 (Quebec: Fides, 1994), 68.

[47] Husser, *Dreams and Dream Narratives*, 113.
[48] Ibid., 114.

is fulfilled at the very end of the story.⁴⁹ After Joseph reveals his true identity, and only after the brothers have regained financial independence, do they approach Joseph and ask him to rule over them: "His brothers went to him themselves, flung themselves before him, and said, 'We are prepared to be your slaves'" (50:18). In other words, at this moment the brothers determine that the second dream has a separate meaning from the first (albeit unconsciously, as part of the hidden communication between the narrator and reader), and they submit to Joseph's dominion, asking for governance unrelated to economic dependence.⁵⁰ The second dream is about to be realized, but Joseph chooses to identify the two dreams as "one and the same," forfeiting general authority over his brothers and retaining only economic responsibility:

> But Joseph said to them, "Have no fear! Am I a substitute for God? Besides, although you intended me harm, God intended it for good, so as to bring about the present result—the survival of many people. And so, fear not. I will sustain you and your children." Thus he reassured them, speaking kindly to them. (50:19–21)⁵¹

Not only does Joseph reject the brothers' submission before him and their readiness to serve him; he also emphasizes and repeats that his responsibility lies in the economic sphere: "so as to bring about the present result—the survival of many people … I will sustain you and your children" (50:20–21). At first glance, Joseph's offer to provide for his brothers seems unrelated to their dialogue. This exchange, however,

---

⁴⁹ Erhard Blum is correct that there is no reason to see Gen 50:15–21 as a later addition that was not in the original Joseph cycle nucleus (*Die Komposition der Vätergeschichte*, WMANT 57 [Neukirchen-Vluyn: Neukirchener Verlag, 1984], 255), as opposed to Redford, *Biblical Story of Joseph*, 163–64, 179; see also Walter Dietrich, *Die Josephserzählung als Novelle und Geschichtsschreibung: Zugleich ein Beitrag zur Pentateuchfrage*, BThSt 14 (Neukirchen-Vluyn: Neukirchener Verlag, 1989), 68; Westermann, *Genesis*, 3:204. John Van Seters, however, is right that in these verses the perspective has changed and there is no longer a crisis of famine but concern for "the larger destiny of the people of Israel" (*Prologue to History: The Yahwist as Historian in Genesis* [Louisville: Westminster John Knox, 1992], 323). But this change is consistent with the development of the plot.

⁵⁰ Arnold claims that the brothers' language, "We are prepared to be your slaves," recalls the language of the collective people of Egypt to Pharaoh in 47:25: "we shall be slaves to Pharaoh." This further emphasizes that the brothers are willing to accept Joseph's authority, as Egypt accepts Pharaoh's authority over the land (Arnold, *Genesis*, 387–88). For an alternative understanding of the brothers' words in relation to Joseph's dreams at the beginning of the episode, see Jan-Dirk Döhling, "Die Herrschaft erträumen, die Träume beherrschen: Herrschaft, Traum und Wirklichkeit in den Josefsträumen (Gen 37,5–11) und der Israel-Josefsgeschichte," *BZ* 50 (2006): 1–30.

⁵¹ Peter Weimar also believes that Joseph's dreams are fulfilled differently than the family initially believed, but in his opinion the dreams predicted that Joseph would be leader of all Egypt, rather than over his family ("Josef und Juda: Eine Geschichte einer schwierigen Beziehung—Die Josefsgeschichte [Teil 3]," *BL* 82 [2009]: 217–26). I believe that Joseph is free to choose how his dreams will be fulfilled.

conceals the underlying, fundamental key to Joseph's story: Joseph chooses to privilege his economic vocation over the dream that predicted his sovereignty. While by the story's end the brothers have accepted the dichotomy of Joseph's power—represented by two different interpretations of his dreams—Joseph is the one who forfeits the potential symbolized in the second dream by identifying it with the first, thereby choosing that the two are, in fact, "one and the same." He accepts only the mantle of economic responsibility.[52]

In this vein, we can recognize one of the narrative's fundamental themes in its treatment of Joseph's dreams. Whether Joseph's dreams should be considered prophecy and divine tidings of the future,[53] or whether they reflect Joseph's emotions and his interaction with his environment,[54] the dreams function not as an irrevocable decree but as an invitation for human action and initiative.[55] This is especially striking when Joseph does not merely solve Pharaoh's dreams but advises him what action to take in order to prevent the catastrophe that the dreams portend ("one could not tell that they had consumed them," 41:21). This is the most important aspect of Joseph's attitude toward his dreams: he has the power to determine how the dreams will come to pass; he has the power to decide whether the two are "one and the same." Joseph, who began life as a spoiled, ambitious boy with big dreams, ultimately relinquishes the power within his grasp with humility and hard-earned understanding.

---

[52] The two different perspectives—the brothers' and Joseph's—are also related to the different roles of the characters within the broader plot. The brothers, who sold Joseph to Egypt, undergo a process of accepting responsibility and willingness to pay the proper price; Joseph, the victim, learns to forgive and perceive what happened to him as a fulfillment of divine will. See also Jonathan Grossman, "The Story of Joseph's Brothers in Light of the 'Therapeutic Narrative' Theory," *BibInt* 21 (2013): 171–95, http://dx.doi.org/10.1163/15685152-0016A0002. Cf. Uriel Simon, *Joseph and His Brothers: A Story of Change*, trans. David Louvish, Perspectives on Jewish Education 2 (Ramat Gan: Bar-Ilan University Press, 2002). It may be that these two different perspectives are already found in the two narratives that form the story of the sale of Joseph: if the brothers sold Joseph to Egypt, then guilt rests upon their shoulders, but if he was kidnapped by Midianites from the pit he was cast into, then providence intervened in the event. This direction was taken by Edward L. Greenstein, "An Equivocal Reading of the Sale of Joseph," in *Literary Interpretations of Biblical Narratives*, vol. 2, ed. Kenneth R. R. Gros Louis and James S. Ackerman, with Thayer S. Warshaw, Bible in Literature Courses (Nashville: Abingdon, 1982), 114–25.

[53] As Ephraim Tzoref, for example, believes (*Joseph: Deputy Commander of Pharaoh* [in Hebrew], 3 vols. [Jerusalem: Tzor-Ot, 1980], 1:172–76).

[54] See, e.g., Judith Corey, "Dreaming of Droughts: Genesis 37.1–11 in Dialogue with Contemporary Science," *JSOT* 38 (2014): 425–38.

[55] Humphreys, *Joseph and His Family*, 101, 118–31; Laurence A. Turner, *Announcements of Plot in Genesis*, JSOTSup 96 (Sheffield: JSOT Press, 1990), 159–69.

The Poles of the Ark: On the Ins and Outs of a Textual Contradiction

RAANAN EICHLER
raanan.eichler@gmail.com
Tel Aviv University, Tel Aviv, Israel 69978

The ark, the primary cult object in the Hebrew Bible, is described in detail in the Priestly tabernacle pericopes of the Pentateuch. In these texts, a difficult contradiction arises with regard to its בדים, which are universally understood as carrying poles. The commands for the construction of the ark (Exod 25:10–16) specify that the ark's carrying poles are to stay in its rings and never to part from it (בטבעת הארן יהיו הבדים לא יסרו ממנו, v. 15). In the instructions regarding the packing up of the tabernacle (Num 4), however, we read that, in the course of preparing the ark for transport, its carrying poles are to be put in by Aaron and his sons (ושמו בדיו, v. 6). If the ark's poles are always "in," how can they be "put in"? This problem has received a great deal of attention from medieval exegetes and modern scholars. In this article, I review previous proposed solutions and offer a new solution based on material evidence from the ancient Near East.

The ark, the primary cult object in the Hebrew Bible, is described in detail in the Priestly tabernacle pericopes of the Pentateuch. In these texts, a contradiction arises with regard to its בַּדִּים, which are universally understood as carrying poles.[1]

In the commands for the construction of the ark (Exod 25:10–16), after it is specified that the carrying poles are to be inserted into four gold rings at each of the ark's four feet (vv. 12–14), it is added that the poles are to stay in the ark's rings and never to part from it (בטבעת הארן יהיו הבדים לא יסרו ממנו, v. 15). This requirement is not paralleled in the cases of the other three tabernacle objects that have

---

[1] The בדים of the ark are mentioned in Exod 25:13–15, 35:12, 37:4–5, 39:35, 40:20, and Num 4:6. Outside the Pentateuch, they are mentioned in 1 Kgs 8:7–8 // 2 Chr 5:8–9, in the context of the temple in Jerusalem. In the only other biblical occurrences of בדים as solid, human-made objects, they are transportation-facilitating accessories to other major items in the tabernacle: the table (Exod 25:27–28, 35:13, 37:14–15, Num 4:8), the bronze altar (Exod 27:6–7, 35:16, 38:5–7, 39:39, Num 4:14), and the incense altar (Exod 30:4–5, 35:15, 37:27–28, Num 4:11).

733

carrying poles—the table, the bronze altar, and the incense altar—nor is its fulfillment reported in the account of the ark's construction (Exod 37:1–5). It is, however, comparable to two other requirements within the Priestly tabernacle texts: first, that the breastpiece is to be tied to the ephod and is not to come loose from it (Exod 28:28 = 39:21); second, that the robe of the ephod is to have a binding around its opening and is not to tear (Exod 28:32 //≈ 39:23).

The command regarding the poles can be understood to mean that they are to be inserted into the rings in such a way that it is not *possible* for them to part from it. This understanding was proposed by the Amora R. Aha b. Jacob and rejected in the Talmud (b. Yoma 72a). It may also be reflected in the LXX, which has in place of the phrase לא יסרו ממנו the single word ἀκίνητοι, "immovable."[2] But the command is more commonly understood to mean that it is not *permissible* for the poles to part from the ark. Hence, the Amoraim R. Eleazar and Abaye considered their removal a violation of a pentateuchal prohibition (b. Yoma 72a, b. Mak. 22a). Either way, the text creates a picture in which, in practice, the poles never part from the ark. This picture is consistent with the testimony of a separate tradition in Kings that the ark retained its poles when it was at rest in the temple (1 Kgs 8:7–8 // 2 Chr 5:8–9).

In the Priestly instructions regarding the preparation of the tabernacle for transport from place to place in the wilderness (Num 4), however, we read that in the course of preparing the ark for carriage, its carrying poles are to be "put in"[3] by Aaron and his sons (ושמו בדיו, v. 6). The same action is prescribed for the table (v. 8), the incense altar (v. 11), and the bronze altar (v. 14), and these three objects pose no problem. But if the poles of the ark are always "in," how can they be "put in" when preparing the ark for transport? It cannot be answered that the author of Num 4 was adhering heedlessly to a rigid formula, because this is clearly not the case. On the contrary, he included two peculiarities in the instructions for the ark vis-à-vis the other objects: it was to be wrapped in the tabernacle's own screening curtain (v. 5), as opposed to a generic dyed cloth (vv. 7, 9, 11, 12, 13), and its leather covering was to be wrapped again in a "pure blue" cloth (v. 6).

This contradiction has received a considerable amount of attention, beginning around the eleventh century CE and continuing to the present, with modern scholars often repeating—knowingly or unwittingly—solutions already proposed by

---

[2] NETS translates as "fixed." The Greek word, however, may also describe an object that *can* be moved but *should* not be, as in Herodotus, *Hist.* 6.134 (regarding the nefarious intentions of Miltiades in the shrine of Demeter near Paros): κινήσοντά τι τῶν ἀκινήτων, "moving something that should not be moved."

[3] As translated in the following English-language Bibles: Wycliffe (Vulg.: *inducent*), Tyndale, KJV, Challoner, Webster, RV, ASV, RSV, and ESV. Other translations include "draw in" (Douay-Rheims), "put...therein" (Coverdale), "put to" (Geneva), "put *to it*" (Darby), "put in place" (NAB, NIV, NJPS, NRSV, NLT), "place" (Young's Literal Translation), "set" (JPS), and "insert" (NASB, NKJV, NET; cf. LXX: διεμβαλοῦσιν).

medieval Jewish commentators. Attempts thus far to solve the inconsistency can be divided into four groups. (1) Exodus 25:15 does not really mean that the poles are always in the rings.[4] (2) Numbers 4:6 does not really mean that the poles are to be put into the rings.[5] (3) One or the other of the instructions is not universally applicable but is restricted in some way.[6] (4) The ark had two sets of poles, and each passage refers to a different set.[7] Additionally, some modern scholars maintain (5) that the two passages are indeed contradictory and cannot be reconciled with

---

[4] Rather, it means either (a) that the poles are to be fixed firmly in the rings so that the ark does not slide back and forth along them during carriage (see Moses b. Jacob of Coucy, in *Sefer Tosafot hashalem: Commentary on the Bible* [in Hebrew], ed. Jacob Gellis [Jerusalem: Harry Fischel Institute, 1993], 41 par. 4; see also Joseph Bekhor Shor, in *Mikra'ot Gedolot 'Haketer': Exodus* [in Hebrew], ed. Menahem Cohen [Ramat Gan: Bar-Ilan University Press, 2007], 73); or (b) that they are to be fixed in such a way that the ark does not *accidentally* fall off of them altogether (see Arnold Ehrlich, *Randglossen zur hebräischen Bibel: Textkritisches, sprachliches und sachliches*, 7 vols. [1908; repr., Hildesheim: Olms, 1968], 1:366–67; Cornelis Houtman, *Exodus III*, COT [Kampen: Kok Pharos, 2000], 378–79).

[5] Rather, it means either (a) that the poles are to be adjusted in some way within the rings (see Saadia b. Joseph Gaon, in *Torat Chaim: Numbers* [in Hebrew], ed. Mordechai L. Katzenelnbogen [Jerusalem: Mossad Harav Kook, 1991], 22; Eliakim b. Meshullam of Speyer, in *Commentarius in Tractatum Yoma: Auctore R. Eliaqim* [in Hebrew], ed. Dov Genachowski [Jerusalem: Mekize Nirdamim, 1964], 222; Rashi, in a gloss published in *Mikra'ot Gedolot 'Haketer': Numbers* [in Hebrew], ed. Menachem Cohen [Ramat Gan: Bar-Ilan University Press 2011], 18–19; Nahmanides, ibid., 19; Meir of Rothenburg, in Tosafot on b. Yoma 72a, s.v. בתיב, published, e.g., in Gellis, *Tosafot*, 41–43 par. 6; Isaac b. Judah Halevi, ibid., 41 par. 5; anonymous tosafist, ibid., 43–44 par. 10; Menachem Meiri, in *Beit Habhira on Tractate Yoma* [in Hebrew], ed. Haim B. Ravitz [Bnei Brak: Ktavim, 1969–1970], 214–15; Hezekiah b. Manoah, in *Hizkuni: The Torah Commentaries of Hezekiah b. R. Manoah* [in Hebrew], ed. Chaim D. Chavel [Jerusalem: Mossad Harav Kook, 1981–1982], 289, 431; George Buchanan Gray, *A Critical and Exegetical Commentary on the Book of Numbers*, ICC [Edinburgh: T&T Clark, 1903], 34–35; Benno Jacob, *Der Pentateuch: Exegetisch-kritische Forschungen mit Figuren und zwei Tafeln* [Leipzig: Veit, 1905], 166; Julius H. Greenstone, *Numbers: With Commentary*, Holy Scriptures 3 [Philadelphia: Jewish Publication Society, 1939], 34); or (b) that they are exposed (see Meyuhas b. Elijah, in *Rabbenu Meyuhas b. R. Elijah: Commentary on the Book of Numbers*, ed. Shlomo Freilich [Jerusalem: Mossad Harav Kook, 1977], 8); or (c) that they are placed on the shoulders of the ark's porters (see Abraham Ibn Ezra, in Cohen, *Numbers*, 19; Jacob of Orleans, in Gellis, *Tosafot*, 41–43 par. 6 at 42 col. 1; Eleazar b. Judah of Worms, in *Rokeach: A Commentary on the Bible by Rabbi Elazar of Worms* [in Hebrew], ed. Julius Klugmann and Sons, 3 vols. [Bnei Brak: ha-Va'ad le hotsa'at sifre Rabenu ha-Rokeah, 1981], 3:15).

[6] Either (a) Num 4:6 is a one-time command (see Joseph Bekhor Shor, in Cohen, *Exodus*, 73); or (b) Exod 25:15 does not apply to the disassembly of the tabernacle (see Abraham Ibn Ezra, ibid., 72; C. F. Keil and F. Delitzsch, *Commentary on the Old Testament* [repr., Grand Rapids: Eerdmans, 1986], 1.3:25; A. Noordtzij, *Numbers*, trans. E. van der Maas, BSC [Grand Rapids: Zondervan, 1983], 44).

[7] Isaiah di Trani, in Gellis, *Tosafot*, 43 par. 7; see also 41 par. 3; Hezekiah b. Manoah, in Chavel, *Hizkuni*, 431; see also Abraham Ibn Ezra, in Cohen, *Exodus*, 72.

each other.[8] In what follows, I offer a new solution along the lines of group 2, based on semantic analysis and an examination of relevant material and iconographic data.

I. The Semantics of וְשָׂמוּ

Exodus 25:15 and Num 4:6 are contradictory only if ושמו in Num 4:6, 8, 11, and 14 is understood in the sense of "put in." But this sense calls for an indirect object (e.g., *ושמו עליו בדיו), which is absent here. Every other time the verb שים appears in the tabernacle pericopes without an indirect object, it conveys the broader sense of "set up." These occurrences are all in Exod 40: in verse 8, the verb pertains to the tabernacle's court, and it is paralleled in verse 33 by ויקם, "erect." In verse 18 it pertains to the frames, and in verse 21 it pertains to the curtain. To these we should probably add two parallel occurrences in verses 5 and 28, which pertain to the entrance screen, though in these instances the word למשכן might be understood as an indirect object rather than as part of the name of the screen.

These data suggest that the four occurrences of ושמו בדיו in Num 4 do not mean "and they shall put in its poles," but rather "and they shall set up its poles."[9] In other words, Aaron and his sons should perform whatever actions are necessary so that the poles of each object are in the proper position for their use, that is, for transporting the objects, just as in Exod 40 Moses is to perform whatever actions are required for the various parts of the tabernacle to be in the proper position for their use, that is, for enshrining the divine presence. The author of Num 4 need not have had in mind that the precise physical operations involved in setting up the poles would be identical in all cases.[10] The poles of the table and the altars might very well need to be inserted into their rings, while "setting up" those of the ark might only involve positioning them correctly within the rings.

II. Material and Iconographic Data

But what sort of positioning of the poles of the ark could the Priestly writer have had in mind? I have recently argued that the ark is properly understood as a

---

[8] Either (a) Exod 25:15 is a gloss (Arnold B. Ehrlich, *Mikrâ ki-Pheschutô: Der Pentateuch* [in Hebrew] [Berlin: M. Poppelauer, 1899], 188–90); or (b) Exod 25:15 and Num 4:6 belong to different strata of P (see Gray, *Numbers*, 2–3, 34–35; Martin Noth, *Numbers: A Commentary*, trans. James D. Martin, OTL [London: SCM, 1968], 41–42); or (c) the Priestly writer erred or there was a contradiction in his sources (see William H. C. Propp, *Exodus 19–40: A New Translation with Introduction and Commentary*, AB 2A [New York: Doubleday, 2006], 383).

[9] Indeed, these occurrences of שים are listed in BDB, s.v. שום under the definition "*put in position*," and in *DCH*, under "set, put in position."

[10] *Pace* Jacob Milgrom, *Numbers* במדבר: *The Traditional Hebrew Text with the New JPS Translation*, JPS Torah Commentary (Philadelphia: Jewish Publication Society, 1990), 301 n. 8.

portable wooden chest made in typical Egyptian style, and that extant chests from the ancient Near East, particularly Egypt, reveal parallels to almost every detail of the ark as described in Priestly and other biblical texts.[11] Thus, consideration of actual chests from the ancient Near East may provide the answer. Indeed, there is one such object that is equipped with carrying poles: a gable-lidded chest found in the tomb of the fourteenth-century pharaoh Tutankhamun (fig. 1).[12]

FIGURE 1. Red chest from the tomb of Tutankhamun, equipped with carrying poles, shown with poles extended. Burton photograph 1557. From Jaromir Malek, director, *Tutankhamun: Anatomy of an Excavation*, n.p., http://tinyurl.com/jbl1354b. Copyright: Griffith Institute, University of Oxford. Used by permission.

This chest exhibits general similarities to the ark as described in the Priestly account. All three of its dimensions are based on the cubit, and its width equals its height, as is the case with the ark (Exod 25:10 = 37:1).[13] The chest is also crowned with a cavetto cornice, a feature that has been identified with the זר that adorns the ark in the Priestly account (Exod 25:11 = 37:2),[14] and, like the ark, the chest is made of wood (cf. Exod 25:10 = 37:1; also Deut 10:1, 3). Noting that the chest's wood is red, certain scholars have asserted that it is "probably" or "certainly" cedar.[15] In this regard, the chest would differ somewhat from the ark, whose wood type is said to be acacia (Exod 25:10 = 37:1; Deut 10:1, 3). But the authors of a recent study on wood types in ancient Egypt present two conclusions that may be pertinent: first, that many identifications of wood from Egyptian objects as cedar are almost certainly mistaken; and, second, that acacia wood, which is also red, was widely used to make Egyptian furniture.[16]

---

[11] Raanan Eichler, "The Ark and the Cherubim" (PhD diss., Hebrew University of Jerusalem, 2016).

[12] Object no. 32 in Howard Carter's system. See Jaromir Malek, director, *Tutankhamun: Anatomy of an Excavation*, n.p., http://tinyurl.com/jbl1354b.

[13] Eichler, "Ark and the Cherubim," 58–61

[14] Raanan Eichler, "The Meaning of zēr," *VT* 64 (2014): 1–15, http://dx.doi.org/10.1163/15685330-12341106.

[15] *Treasures of Tutankhamun* (London: Trustees of the British Museum, 1972), exhibition catalogue, exhibit 14 (n.p.); Geoffrey Killen, *Boxes, Chests and Footstools*, vol. 2 of *Ancient Egyptian Furniture* (Warminster: Aris & Phillips, 1994), 51.

[16] Rowena Gale, Peter Gasson, and Nigel Hepper, "Wood [Botany]," in *Ancient Egyptian*

A British Museum catalogue entry on the chest displays a photograph of its poles (fig. 2) and includes the following description:

> Unlike the other chests found in the tomb this chest, no doubt because of its size and weight when full, was provided with four poles so that it could be carried by bearers on their shoulders. Each pole slides backwards and forwards through two bronze rings, attached to boards which are fixed at the bottom of the box. A collar at the back end of the pole, greater in circumference than the ring, prevents the pole from slipping forward through the inner ring.[17]

FIGURE 2. Underside of same chest as in fig. 1, showing rings and (removed) carrying poles. From *Treasures of Tutankhamun*, exhibit 14 (n.p.), credited to the Cairo Museum.

The Priestly account has usually been understood to mean that the ark had two poles, each of which was fitted through two rings at different corners and was long enough to protrude both in front of the ark and in back. Neither this account, however, nor any other text in the Hebrew Bible actually states how many poles the ark (or the table and altars) had.[18] In light of the meticulous and number-loving character of the Priestly author, the absence is understandable only if he assumed that the number of poles would be obvious to the reader. The fact that in his account the golden altar has poles (in the plural), though it only has *two* rings (Exod 30:4–5 = 37:27–28), reveals that he envisioned—and expected the reader to envision—that each pole is held by only one ring. This indicates that the Priestly author, who gave the ark four rings, meant to portray it as having four poles, like the Tutankhamun chest.[19]

Materials and Technology, ed. Paul T. Nicholson and Ian Shaw (Cambridge: Cambridge University Press, 2000), 334–71, esp. 335–36, 349.

[17] *Treasures of Tutankhamun,* Exhibit 14.

[18] Oddly, the question of how many poles the ark and the other objects of the tabernacle had is almost never directly addressed by commentators. Meiri (in Ravitz, *Beit Habhira,* 214–15) explicitly wrote that the ark had two poles as described above. Other medieval Jewish scholars did not say so explicitly, but it can be inferred from their comments that they thought the same. Keil and Delitzsch (*Commentary,* 1.2:167) casually stated that the ark had four poles. Propp (*Exodus: A New Translation,* 378–79) is silent in his comments but includes two illustrations (figs. 1a, 1b), each showing the ark with two poles.

[19] The Tutankhamun chest actually has a pair of adjacent rings at each corner, eight rings in all. In this feature it differs from the ark, which, according to any view of its poles, has one functioning ring at each of its four corners. The purpose of the ring doubling is presumably to keep the poles straight. This aim could be achieved using only one ring for each pole either by ensuring a tight fit or by giving the bands that form the rings substantial width.

The photograph and description express several other details in which the poles of the Tutankhamun chest are similar to those of the ark as described in Exodus: they are made of wood (cf. Exod 25:13 = 37:4); they are slid through metal rings near each of the chest's four feet (cf. Exod 25:12 = 37:3); and they are aligned along the chest's long sides (cf. Exod 25:14 = 37:5). They are also fashioned and positioned in a way that would make it difficult to slide them out of the rings and remove them entirely from the chest, recalling Exod 25:15.

Most significant for our discussion, these carrying poles are retractable: "When the chest was not being carried, the poles could be pushed back until the collars of two axially opposite poles were touching each other and the poles were then entirely concealed from view."[20] In other words, the poles could be slid under the chest, in the space between its underside and the bottoms of its feet, while still held by the metal rings (figs. 3a, 3b). When the chest was to be carried, the poles could be drawn out again in preparation, still held by the rings.

FIGURE 3A. Same chest as in fig. 1, shown with poles in retracted position. Burton photograph 0090. From Jaromir Malek, director, *Tutankhamun: Anatomy of an Excavation*, n.p., http://tinyurl.com/jbl1354b. Copyright: Griffith Institute, University of Oxford. Used by permission.

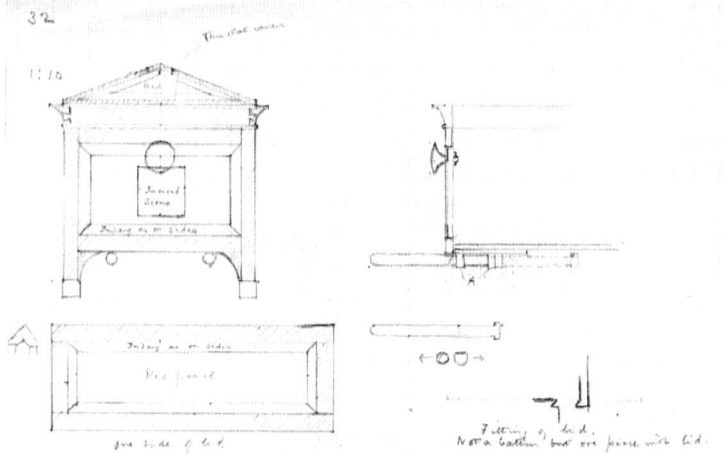

FIGURE 3B. Diagram of same chest as in fig. 1 illustrating pole retraction. Carter card 032-5. From Jaromir Malek, director, *Tutankhamun: Anatomy of an Excavation*, n.p., http://tinyurl.com/jbl1354b. Copyright: Griffith Institute, University of Oxford. Used by permission.

[20] *Treasures of Tutankhamun*, Exhibit 14.

Earlier depictions of chests equipped with carrying poles exist from Old Kingdom Egypt. Some of these have sufficient detail to show the poles slid through rings like those of the Tutankhamun chest (fig. 4), which demonstrates, in the judgment of Geoffrey Killen, that the poles were designed to slide underneath the chests in the same manner.[21]

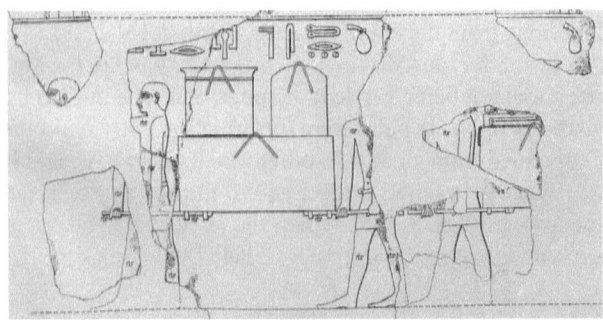

Figure 4. Sixth-Dynasty depiction of a chest with carrying poles. From Ludwig Borchardt, *Das Grabdenkmal des Königs Śaḥu-Reʻ*, 2 vols., WVDOG 26 (Leipzig: Hinrichs, 1910–1913), vol. 2, pl. 60.

III. Conclusion

If carrying poles on ancient Egyptian-type chests were *normally* retractable, as Henry Fischer seems to conclude from the evidence just adduced,[22] or at least if this was the practice with which the author of Num 4:6 was acquainted, then both the biblical author and his audience would most naturally expect that the ark's poles would need to be "set up" in preparation for transport, even if they had never been removed from it. They would still need to be drawn out from underneath it so that they could be grasped by its porters. If this is the case, Exod 25:15 does not contradict Num 4:6. As stipulated by the former verse, the poles of the ark were indeed never to part from it or to leave its rings; and ושמו בדיו in the latter verse simply means that, in preparation for transport, they were to be drawn out, while still in their rings, from underneath the ark's body.

This possibility may also explain why the requirement that the carrying poles remain affixed applies to the ark but not to the table and the altars.[23] Only chests

---

[21] Killen, *Ancient Egyptian Furniture*, 2:20, fig. 40.

[22] Henry G. Fischer, "Möbel," *Lexikon der Ägyptologie*, ed. Wolfgang Helck and Eberhard Otto, 7 vols. (Wiesbaden: Harrassowitz, 1972–1992), 4:180–89, here 182.

[23] The most attractive explanation for the requirement in the first place is that it is a measure to prevent people from touching the body of the ark, an action that, according to a tradition in 2 Sam 6:6–7, is fatal (see Bekhor Shor on Exod 25:15, in Cohen, *Exodus*, 73). The Priestly text

are shaped in such a way that their carrying poles can be hidden from sight while still attached to them, as their feet create a low, narrow space between their lower surface and the ground. Thus, only in the case of the ark would such a requirement be compatible with the goal of an aesthetic tabernacle. The carrying poles of the table and altars would presumably need to be removed and stowed elsewhere.[20]

This study demonstrates how the observation that the biblical ark is described as a portable wooden chest, aided by an investigation of actual and depicted objects of that type from the ancient Near East, can help solve an exegetical difficulty in the biblical text. It also adds an important element to the image of the ark that the Priestly writer apparently intended to convey, one that those familiar with ancient Near Eastern crafts would have understood unaided.

---

[20] Num 4:15, however, indicates that it would be fatal even for a designated porter to touch the body of any of the major tabernacle objects; by the same token, therefore, the table and altars should have permanently attached poles as well.

NEW in BIBLICAL STUDIES

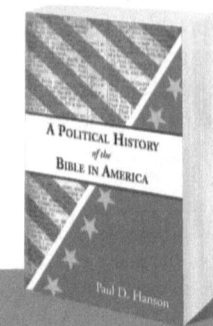

An Introduction to Womanist Biblical Interpretation
Nyasha Junior
November • Paper
$30.00

John
A Commentary
NEW TESTAMENT LIBRARY
Marianne Meye Thompson
November • Hardback
$60.00

A Political History of the Bible in America
Paul D. Hanson
Paper • $50.00

Micah
OLD TESTAMENT LIBRARY
Daniel L. Smith-Christopher
November • Hardback
$50.00

I & II Thessalonians
NEW TESTAMENT LIBRARY
M. Eugene Boring
Hardback • $50.00

A Chorus of Prophetic Voices
Mark McEntire
Paper • $30.00

The Letters of Paul, Sixth Edition
Calvin J. Roetzel
November • Paper • $35.00

Interpreting Prophetic Literature
James D. Nogalski
Paper • $25.00

WJK WESTMINSTER JOHN KNOX PRESS

1.800.523.1631 • www.wjkbooks.com

JBL 135, no. 4 (2016): 743–761
doi: http://dx.doi.org/10.15699/jbl.1354.2016.156763

Sing Me a Parable of Zion: Isaiah's Vineyard (5:1–7) and Its Relation to the "Daughter Zion" Tradition

REBECCA W. POE HAYS
R_Hays@baylor.edu
Baylor University, Waco, TX 76706

The figure of Daughter Zion and her relationship to the larger Zion tradition have emerged as important areas of inquiry in recent decades. This essay argues that the parabolic "Song of the Vineyard" in Isa 5:1–7 falls within this tradition of Jerusalem's female personification and constitutes part of Daughter Zion's larger story in Isaiah. Ancient Near Eastern woman–vineyard associations are well attested, and the love-song elements in the opening verses of the parable invite reading Isaiah's vineyard as a figure for a woman. The parable's depiction of the "beloved's" devotion to the vineyard resonates strongly with the Zion tradition's notions of divine choice of, presence in, provision for, and protection of Jerusalem. The combination of these associations in and around Isa 5:1–7 suggests that the vineyard-woman of the parable is Daughter Zion herself. The self-interpretation of the parable in Isa 5:7, coupled with the following series of woe oracles, makes the basic meaning of this text clear, but reading the Song of the Vineyard as part of Isaiah's larger story of Daughter Zion sheds greater light on the relationship between YHWH and the people he has chosen.

Given the dramatic narrative arc of the anticipated destruction, traumatic exile, and glorious restoration of Jerusalem and its inhabitants presented in the biblical book of Isaiah,[1] the centrality of Zion and Zion theology to the prophetic

---

[1] Biblical exegetes have long noted difficulties with the notion that a single, eighth-century prophet authored the entire book of Isaiah (see Uriel Simon, "Ibn Ezra between Medievalism and Modernism: The Case of Isaiah XL–LXVI," in *Congress Volume: Salamanca 1983*, ed. J. A. Emerton, VTSup 36 [Leiden: Brill, 1985], 257–71). Real challenges to single authorship, however, began in the eighteenth century, with Johann Christoph Döderlein, *Esaias: ex recensione textus hebraei ad fidem codd. quorundam MSS et versionum antiquarum latine vertit notasque varii argumenti* (Altorfi: Venum prostat in officina Schupfeliana, 1775). Building on Bernhard Duhm's classic expression of multiple authorship, most critical scholars now recognize that the canonical form of Isaiah represents material from at least three historical periods in Israel's history. Chapters 1–39

743

message is unsurprising.[2] In recent decades, the figure of בת־ציון (Daughter Zion) and her relationship to the larger Zion tradition have emerged as important areas of inquiry.[3] Isaiah 1:8 introduces Daughter Zion as a woman left standing alone

---

constitute "Proto-Isaiah" (PI) and reflect an eighth-century context. Chapters 40–55, or "Deutero-Isaiah" (DI), reflect the concerns of an exilic community, and chapters 56–66, or "Trito-Isaiah" (TI), reflect those of a postexilic community (Bernhard Duhm, *Das Buch Jesaia*, 5th ed. [Göttingen: Vandenhoeck & Ruprecht, 1968]; for a good overview of the primary theories regarding Isaiah's composition history, see H. G. M. Williamson, *The Book Called Isaiah: Deutero-Isaiah's Role in Composition and Redaction* [Oxford: Clarendon, 2005], 1–16).

In this article, I proceed with the assumption of three primary stages of Isaian composition, but I understand each subsequent stage to be shaping and building on the previous material so that common themes emerge and develop throughout the whole book. For similar views, see Ronald E. Clements, "The Unity of the Book of Isaiah," *Int* 36 (1982): 117–29; and Rainer Albertz, "Das Deuterojesaja-Buch als Fortschreibung der Jesaja-Prophetie," in *Die Hebräische Bibel und ihre zweifache Nachgeschichte: Festschrift für Rolf Rendtorff zum 65. Geburstag*, ed. Erhard Blum, Christian Macholz, and Ekkehard W. Stegemann (Neukirchen-Vluyn: Neukirchener Verlag, 1990), 241–56. In contrast to the hitherto majority opinion that Isa 5:1–7 is eighth-century material, Jacques Vermeylen has argued that it is a Deuteronomistic insertion; even if Vermeylen's assessment is correct, however, this text would still predate much of the other Isaiah material. See Vermeylen, *Du prophète Isaïe à l'apocalyptique: Isaïe, I–XXXV, miroir d'un demi-millénaire d'expérience religieuse en Israël*, EBib (Paris: Gabalda, 1977), 159–68; and Kirsten Nielsen, *There Is Hope for a Tree: The Tree as Metaphor in Isaiah*, JSOTSup 65 (Sheffield: JSOT Press, 1989), 114–16. While Isa 5:1–7 is probably relatively early material, therefore, its present placement in the book of Isaiah reflects later editorial shaping (so Hans Wildberger, *Isaiah 1–12*, trans. Thomas H. Trapp, CC [Minneapolis: Fortress, 1991], 179; Nielsen, *Hope for a Tree*, 88). In this study, I will focus on the current literary location of Isa 5:1–7 and its function in that place. Though I recognize that the text might have had—and probably did have—a different function in earlier stages of Isaiah's composition history, space constraints demand that I largely leave aside matters of historical composition for another time.

[2] Jacob Stromberg has suggested that "Zion's destiny is arguably the most pervasive theme in [Isaiah], and a key metaphor depicting it is 'Zion as woman'" (*An Introduction to the Study of Isaiah*, T&T Clark Approaches to Biblical Studies [London: T&T Clark, 2011], 62). Numerous scholars have noted the importance of Zion theology in Isaiah. See, e.g., Gary Stansell, *Micah and Isaiah: A Form and Tradition Historical Comparison*, SBLDS 85 (Atlanta: Scholars Press, 1988), 39–66; John J. Schmitt, "The City as Woman in Isaiah 1–39," in *Writing and Reading the Scroll of Isaiah: Studies of an Interpretive Tradition*, ed. Craig C. Broyles and Craig A. Evans, 2 vols., VTSup 70 (Leiden: Brill, 1997), 95; Ulrich Berges, "Die Zionstheologie des Buches Jesaja," *EstBib* 58 (2000): 167–98; Bernard Wodecki, "Jerusalem-Zion in the Texts of Proto-Isaiah," *PJBiR* 1 (2000): 89–106. This Zion theology is not flat or static. For example, Wodecki organizes the Zion-related texts in Proto-Isaiah into three categories: those dealing with the idealized past, those addressing the "present" (i.e., eighth-century BCE) difficulties, and those looking toward a future restoration of Zion and the place of God's presence. He observes that DI and TI will continue to develop these themes in new ways.

[3] Finding appropriate terminology for personified Zion is difficult. "Daughter Zion" is a literal rendering of the common expression בת־ציון, but understanding the woman Zion as "Daughter" causes problems in texts that depict the YHWH–Zion relationship as a marriage. "Lady Zion" is antiquated English but allows for more flexibility for the image and communicates

amid the desolation of an enemy attack; then 1:21–31 describes her as a once faithful woman-turned-whore in need of God's purification and restoration. The story of Daughter Zion's experience of this process weaves throughout the remainder of Isaiah.[4]

In this article, I argue that the parabolic "Song of the Vineyard" in Isa 5:1–7 constitutes part of the story of Daughter Zion in Isaiah and falls within the tradition of Jerusalem's female personification. To this end, I will survey the existing scholarship on Isa 5:1–7 with particular attention to how scholars have located it generically and how they have interpreted its application. Then, I will examine the traditional ancient Near Eastern association of vineyards with women in order to demonstrate the validity of reading the vineyard in Isa 5:1–7 as a woman. With this foundation in mind, I will draw connections between Isa 5:1–7 and the Zion tradition by exploring the lexical and conceptual links between Isa 5:1–7 and the Daughter Zion passages in Isa 1–4. Finally, I will demonstrate what the inclusion of the parable of Isa 5:1–7 contributes to its interpretation and to the Daughter Zion tradition in Isaiah. While one can derive meaning from the parable without connecting it to the Daughter Zion tradition, recognizing its relationship to Daughter

---

something of the exalted status that the larger ancient Near Eastern tradition of the personified city connotes (see Aloysius Fitzgerald, "The Mythological Background for the Presentation of Jerusalem as a Queen and False Worship as Adultery in the OT," *CBQ* 34 [1972]: 403–16; Mark E. Biddle, "The Figure of Lady Jerusalem: Identification, Deification, and Personification of Cities in the Ancient Near East," in *The Biblical Canon in Comparative Perspective*, ed. K. Lawson Younger Jr., William W. Hallo, and Bernard F. Batto, Ancient Near Eastern Texts and Studies 11 [Lewiston, NY: Mellen, 1991], 173–94).

One of the first scholars to attend extensively to the female personification in the Zion tradition, the beginning of which he dates to the exilic period, was Odil Hannes Steck (see, e.g., his "Zion als Gelände und Gestalt: Überlegungen zur Wahrnehmung Jerusalems als Stadt und Frau im Alten Testament," *ZTK* 86 [1989]: 261–81). Christl Maier has produced perhaps the most extensive study of this tradition. She argues that the female personification of the city Jerusalem interacts with spatial and gendered perspectives to create a new image of Zion that ultimately develops into a symbol of salvation. In contrast to Steck, she traces the origins of the "Daughter Zion" figure to preexilic times (*Daughter Zion, Mother Zion: Gender, Space, and the Sacred in Ancient Israel* [Minneapolis: Fortress, 2008], 4 and passim). See further discussion below.

[4] Most scholars rightly understand Isa 1 to be some sort of "preview" or "overview" of the rest of Isaiah, though the composition date of this material remains a debated issue. For example, Leon J. Liebreich, Georg Fohrer, Uwe Becker, Réme Lack, Marvin A. Sweeney, and Anthony Tomasino consider Isa 1 to be a later recapitulation of the whole message of Isaiah. In contrast, Otto Kaiser, Lars Gösta Rignell, and Jacques Vermeylen identify Isa 1 as a Deuteronomistic (sixth-century BCE) prologue to Isaiah. Either way, this opening chapter resonates with the major themes of Isaiah and, as it pertains to Isa 5:1–7, can shed light on how a later editor was interpreting the existing Isaiah material (including 5:1–7) and arranging the surrounding material in accordance with this interpretation. See Joseph Blenkinsopp, *Isaiah 1–39: A New Translation with Introduction and Commentary*, AB 19 (New York: Doubleday, 2000), 175–81.

Zion imbues both the parable itself and the larger narrative of Daughter Zion in Isaiah with deeper nuance and significance.[5]

I. Isaiah 5:1–7 in Previous Scholarship

While scholars generally agree on the basic meaning of Isa 5:1–7 (i.e., God will punish "the house of Israel and the men of Judah," as v. 7 explains), the discussion continues regarding the exact genre of the text and the details of its interpretation. These two issues deserve a closer look.

First, the matter of genre has been a point of debate. In his landmark essay on the topic, John T. Willis surveys the various genres that scholars have proposed for Isa 5:1–7 in an effort to determine the correct generic identification for the text. He systematically examines and eliminates the following possibilities: "uncle's song,"[6] satirical polemic against Palestinian fertility cults,[7] the prophet's song about his own vineyard or about the troubles of his friend YHWH, drinking song, song of a wedding party member (bride, groom, or groom's friend), lawsuit, fable, and allegory.[8] Willis concludes that Isa 5:1–7 is in fact a parable that utilizes song and legal

---

[5] I see this interpretation of the text as an interim reception of Isa 5:1–7, not necessarily as the original meaning of the passage. This interpretation reflects the way in which the editor who arranged the material in chapters 1–5 (at least) understood the text, and his arrangement of the material therefore impacted the way that subsequent readers/editors/authors understood the text (see the discussion of Isa 27 in the conclusion below). Nielsen follows a similar method of interpretation (i.e., noting how the text took on new meaning for later readers) in her study (*Hope for a Tree*, 114–23).

[6] Building on early translations of דודי as "my uncle" (see Lev 10:4, Num 36:11, 1 Sam 10:14, Jer 32:7, Amos 6:10), Arnold B. Ehrlich proposed that the whole phrase שירת דודי refers to the genre of Isa 5:1–7. He described an "uncle's song" as an Israelite custom wherein the groom's uncle, often also his father-in-law, would give strong advice and rebuke as necessary (*Randglossen zur Hebräischen Bibel: Textkritisches, sprachliches und sachliches*, 7 vols. [Leipzig: Hinrichs, 1908–1914], 4:19–20). Willis acknowledges the creativity of this interpretation, but he notes that there is little evidence to support it ("Genre of Isaiah 5:1–7," *JBL* 96 [1977]: 337–38). Blenkinsopp translates the phrase שירת דודי as "my lovesong" rather than "the song of my beloved" (*Isaiah 1–39*, 207).

[7] So William Creighton Graham, who takes דוד to be a divine name ("Notes on the Interpretation of Isaiah 5:1–14," *AJSL* 45 [1929]: 167–78, here 169, http://dx.doi.org/10.1086/370227).

[8] Willis, "Genre of Isaiah 5:1–7," 337–56. Willis draws clear distinctions among fables, allegories, and parables. Fables, according to Willis, take "inanimate natural objects" as their subjects (352) and generally involve "fanciful" happenings such as plants or animals speaking (357). Allegories ascribe to each story element a unique correspondence to reality, in contrast to the "single truth" orientation of parables (353). He notes that few modern scholars have attempted to allegorize the whole of Isa 5:1–7, though some will allegorize portions of the text (354). Hans Wildberger, for example, interprets the משוכה ("hedge") and גדר ("wall") of 5:5 as YHWH's protection of Israel from the Canaanites (*Isaiah 1–12*, 186–87). In contrast to this general move

elements in order to catch and hold the attention of the readers.⁹ Critical of the approaches that have been unable to produce consensus, H. G. M. Williamson draws a distinction between the genres of the text (i.e., a song in vv. 1–2 and a lawsuit in vv. 3–6) and its form (i.e., parable).¹⁰ Though scholars continue to debate the "dominant" genre of Isa 5:1–7, most agree that the text contains at least hints of a love song, a lawsuit, and narrative elements of analogy, parable, and metaphor.¹¹

Second, the interpretive details regarding the object of condemnation and punishment remain somewhat debated, though scholars have almost universally agreed that Isa 5:7 holds the key to the interpretation of this pericope ("For the vineyard of the LORD of hosts is the house of Israel, and the people of Judah are the planting of his delight").¹² Most scholars simply—and rightly—take the two collectives, as well as the pair in 5:3 (איש יהודה and יושב ירושלם), as roughly identical references: Jerusalem/Judah is the recipient of both the condemnation and the punishment.¹³ Another line of interpretation distinguishes between the two collectives in 5:7. While the distinction between Israel and Judah is problematic in this context, some of these interpretations draw attention to the rhetorical strategy of

---

away from allegory, Marvin A. Sweeney identifies the genre of Isa 5:1–7 as "allegory," in which YHWH is the vineyard's owner, Israel is the vineyard, and Judah is the "planting of his delight." Sweeney rejects the "parable" designation because this passage merely announces judgment rather than conveying a moral or maxim (*Isaiah 1–39: With an Introduction to Prophetic Literature*, FOTL 16 [Grand Rapids: Eerdmans, 1996], 126).

⁹Willis, "Genre of Isaiah 5:1–7," 358–62.

¹⁰H. G. M. Williamson, *A Critical and Exegetical Commentary on Isaiah 1–27*, 3 vols., ICC (London: T&T Clark, 2006–2014), 1:327–28. Blenkinsopp seems to adopt a similar approach to categorizing the material (*Isaiah 1–39*, 206).

¹¹See Nielsen, *Hope for a Tree*, 89. Gale A. Yee, for example, has argued that the genres are not mutually exclusive and that this pericope represents the combination of a song with a juridical parable ("A Form-Critical Study of Isaiah 5:1–7 as a Song and a Juridical Parable," *CBQ* 43 [1981]: 31). Brevard S. Childs and John Oswalt simply label Isa 5:1–7 a "parable" (Childs, *Isaiah*, OTL [Louisville: Westminster John Knox, 2001], 45; Oswalt, *The Book of Isaiah, Chapters 1–39*, NICOT [Grand Rapids: Eerdmans, 1986], 151). Walter Brueggemann calls the text a "love song-become-dispute-become-judgment," though he notes the similarity to Jesus's parables, particularly the parable of the tenants in Matt 21:33–41 (*Isaiah*, 2 vols., WeBC [Louisville: Westminster John Knox, 1998], 1:48–49). John Goldingay describes Isa 5:1–7 as a "mock love song," and he likewise notes that the pedagogical-rhetorical strategy is similar to that of Jesus's parables (*Isaiah*, NIBCOT 13 [Peabody, MA: Hendrickson, 2001], 52–53).

¹²Schmitt argues that the shift from first person to third person in 5:7 "suggests that v. 7 is not the original identification of the referent for the vineyard" ("City as Woman," 99), but the speaker has already changed once (from third person to first person in 5:3), and such changes in speaker are typical for ancient Near Eastern love poetry (see discussion of the genre below).

¹³So Childs, *Isaiah*, 45; Wildberger, *Isaiah 1–12*, 184; Blenkinsopp, *Isaiah 1–39*, 207–8. Wildberger argues that, like יהוה צבאות, the early uses of בית ישראל were related to the ark of the covenant (1 Sam 7:2; 2 Sam 6:5, 15; see also Ezek 3:1, 4–5). While he acknowledges that בית ישראל came to be a reference to the northern kingdom, it still maintained a broader denotation in some contexts.

the text.[14] For example, while Gale Yee acknowledges that the song also condemns Judah in some way,[15] she also distinguishes sharply between Israel and Judah and argues that the initial identification of the vineyard with Israel is a key rhetorical element of the juridical parable:[16]

> The dynamics of the text are such that the Judeans are led to believe that the vineyard is Israel, that they judge and condemn it and witness Yhwh's prediction to wipe it out. Moreover, the interpretation reveals that the vineyard is indeed Israel. However, with an ironic twist the interpretation also discloses that Judah, whose own situation was analogous to the north's, is the real transgressor in the song. This brief disclosure has the same overwhelming impact as Nathan's short declaration to David: "You are the man."[17]

While Yee's contention that the "decoy" element is key to juridical parables is valid, one does not need to accept her sharp distinction between Israel and Judah in order to preserve the decoy element's presence in Isa 5:1–7. The decoy is the vineyard: Isa 5:3 invites Jerusalem/Judah to consider the parable about YHWH and a vineyard, and then 5:7 forces them to apply the story to themselves.

Kirsten Nielsen agrees with Yee's insistence on the "decoy" or "false trail" in Isa 5:1–7, but she rightly challenges Yee's interpretation of "house of Israel" as equivalent to the northern kingdom on two grounds. First, Yee's separation of the

---

[14] Marvin Sweeney represents an extreme form of this position: the condemnation comes against the northern kingdom alone, with the judgment of Israel merely a warning to Judah. Sweeney argues that the collectives בית ישראל and איש יהודה refer to separate groups. Sweeney's sharp distinction between the two groups results, in part, from his aforementioned allegorization of the text: the vineyard (בית ישראל) and the vines within it (איש יהודה) are separate story elements, each with its own distinct meaning. Sweeney further supports his argument by associating the terms משפח ("bloodshed") and צעקה ("outcry") in 5:7 with murderous activities, which he argues makes more sense in the context of Israel's actions in the Syro-Ephraimite War than it does in the context of Judah's involvement in that episode (*Isaiah*, 130).

[15] Nielsen has rightly challenged Yee's thesis as "imprecise" with respect to the subject of condemnation in the parable (*Hope for a Tree*, 109). See discussion below.

[16] Yee, "Form-Critical Study," 37–38. Like Sweeney, Yee argues that the collectives בית ישראל and איש יהודה refer to separate groups. Yee argues that, by the eighth century, vine imagery was a common means of describing the northern kingdom (cf. Hos 9:10, 10:1, 14:8). She also notes that בית ישראל never appears elsewhere in parallel with איש יהודה or with יושב ירושלם (Isa 5:3). Furthermore, Yee observes that Isaiah's close contemporaries Hosea, Amos, and Micah use בית ישראל exclusively to refer to the northern kingdom (cf. Hos 1:4, 6; 5:1; 6:10; 12:1; Amos 5:1, 3, 4, 25; 6:1, 14; 7:10; 9:9; Mic 1:5; 3:1, 9).

[17] Yee, "Form-Critical Study," 37–39. According to Uriel Simon, a juridical parable is "a realistic story about a violation of the law, related to someone who had committed a similar offense with the purpose of leading the unsuspecting hearer to pass judgment on himself. The offender will be caught in the trap set for him if he truly believes that the story told him actually happened, and only if he does not detect prematurely the similarity between the offence in the story and the one he himself has committed" ("The Poor Man's Ewe-Lamb: An Example of a Juridical Parable," *Bib* 48 [1967]: 220–21; cf. 2 Sam 12:1–14, 14:1–20, 1 Kgs 20:35–43, Jer 3:1–5).

vineyard from the vines overallegorizes the parable and "breaks the unity of the image." Second, Yee's understanding of the northern kingdom's role in the parable is inconsistent:

> Yee says on the one hand that the hearers are lured into believing that the judgment applies to the Northern Kingdom, but discover in the end that it applies to themselves, and on the other hand that the vineyard is in fact the Northern Kingdom. The Northern Kingdom interpretation thus becomes both correct and incorrect.[18]

Instead of the northern kingdom, therefore, Nielsen argues that the "false trail" in Isaiah's metaphorical narrative is the interpretation of the vineyard imagery as the story of a husband and his unfaithful wife (i.e., the vineyard).[19]

The two debated issues of the text's genre and interpretive details (especially those related to rhetorical strategy) come together to suggest a new way to understand the Song of the Vineyard. In what follows, I will draw upon the traditions of vineyard imagery, Zion theology, and the female personification of cities in order to illuminate the rhetorical strategy and meaning of Isa 5:1–7. I propose that Hans Wildberger is right to consider יושב ירושלם (v. 3), בית ישראל, and איש יהודה (v. 7) to be identical recipients of condemnation and judgment but that Yee and Nielsen are right to highlight the importance of the Judean audience's initial identification of the vineyard imagery with some entity other than Judah. Several scholars have elucidated the way that vineyard imagery connotes female imagery as well,[20] and John Eaton and John J. Schmitt have both stated—without developing the argument—that the vineyard in Isa 5:1–7 is Jerusalem.[21] Building on these previous studies, I will demonstrate how the presence of the imagery of Daughter Zion in this pericope coupled with the rhetorical strategy of a juridical parable gives fuller meaning to the text of Isa 5:1–7.

---

[18] Nielsen, *Hope for a Tree*, 109.

[19] Ibid., 107. So also Otto Kaiser, *Isaiah 1–12: A Commentary*, trans. John Bowden, OTL (Philadelphia: Westminster, 1972), 60–62.

[20] See Nielsen, *Hope for a Tree*, 89; Blenkinsopp, *Isaiah 1–39*, 207; Kaiser, *Isaiah 1–12*, 60; Marvin H. Pope, *Song of Songs: A New Translation with Introduction and Commentary*, AB 7C (Garden City, NY: Doubleday, 1977); "Vine, Vineyard," *Dictionary of Biblical Imagery*, ed. Leland Ryken, Jim Wilhoit, and Tremper Longman III (Downers Grove, IL: InterVarsity, 1998), 916; Shalom M. Paul, "A Lover's Garden of Verse: Literal and Metaphorical Imagery in Ancient Near Eastern Love Poetry," in *Tehillah Le-Moshe: Biblical and Judaic Studies in Honor of Moshe Greenberg*, ed. Mordechai Cogan, Barry L. Eichler, and Jeffrey H. Tigay (Winona Lake, IN: Eisenbrauns, 1997), 99–110.

[21] John Eaton, "The Isaiah Tradition," in *Israel's Prophetic Tradition: Essays in Honour of Peter R. Ackroyd*, ed. R. J. Coggins, Anthony Phillips, and Michael A. Knibb (Cambridge: Cambridge University Press, 1982), 72; Schmitt, "City as Woman," 100.

II. Of Vineyards and Women

The association of women with vineyards appears elsewhere in the Hebrew Bible and in the ancient Near East more broadly. The primary questions in relation to the imagery of Isa 5:1–7 concern when vineyards became a recognized image for women and whether Isa 5:1–7 contains sufficient indications that this tradition is indeed present in this text. A brief examination of the vineyard–woman tradition and the text of Isa 5:1–7 reveals that the interpretation of Isaiah's vineyard as a woman is valid.

The importance of vineyards in the ancient Near East for food supplies and economic stability is undisputed, and the importance of a bountiful harvest leads naturally to associations with human fertility.[22] The combination of this fertility association and the social reality that vineyards were a place where men and women could meet lays the groundwork for the use of vineyard imagery as a metaphor for women.[23] A Ugaritic hymn relates the groom's statement "I will make [my bride's] field vineyards [*krmm*], the field of her love orchards," and the Amarna letters compare a field without a tiller to a woman without a husband.[24] By the Greek period, these associations between vineyards, lovemaking, and women had developed into a common artistic motif: the inclusion of vineyards and vine imagery was a key indicator of a scene's erotic nature.[25]

The Hebrew Bible also contains examples of this woman–vineyard association. In his survey of how the association of female fertility with agricultural fertility manifests in the Hebrew Bible, for example, Meir Malul notes the common

---

[22] For an example of the ancient Near Eastern association of sexual fertility with agriculture generally, see "Dawn and Dusk," trans. Dennis Pardee (*COS* 1.87:277–78). Cf. Ronald A. Veenker, "Forbidden Fruit: Ancient Near Eastern Sexual Metaphors," *HUCA* 70–71 (1999): 57–73; Meir Malul, "The Woman–Earth Homology in Biblical *Weltanschauung*," *UF* 32 (2000): 340 and passim. Malul notes, for example, the common ancient Near Eastern metaphor of fruit for human offspring, as with the Akkadian *inbu* ("fruit"), which can refer not only to offspring but also to sexual charm (344–45).

[23] For example, a thirteenth-century BCE Egyptian text suggests that vineyards were viewed as common places for lovers' trysts ("A Satirical Letter," trans. John A. Wilson, *ANET*, 478). See Anselm C. Hagedorn, "Of Foxes and Vineyards: Greek Perspectives on the Song of Songs," *VT* 53 (2003): 344–45. For possible biblical allusions to this notion, see Judg 21:20–23, Song 7:13 (Eng. 7:12).

[24] Cf. Malul, "Woman–Earth Homology," 347; Pope, *Song of Songs*, 324.

[25] Hagedorn, "Of Foxes and Vineyards," 345–48. These Greek examples clearly postdate the composition of Isa 5:1–7 (though at least one example dates to the sixth century BCE), but they help to demonstrate the strength and scope of the tradition. The implication of this evidence for this study is that, by the earliest possible date for the Isaiah material's composition, the tradition of associating women with vineyards was already well established across the ancient Near East. See the following section for further discussion.

image of פרי ("fruit") for human offspring (e.g., Deut 7:13; 28:4, 11, 18; Hos 9:16) and cites the parallelism between vineyards and wives in Deut 20:6-7, 28:30.[26] Psalm 128:3 compares a blessed wife to a fruitful vine. The quintessential examples of the vineyard–woman metaphor in the Hebrew Bible, however, appear in Song of Songs.[27] The female voice laments the darkening of her skin from her labors, which she compares to failing to keep her own vineyard (Song 1:6), and the male voice compares the woman's breasts to "clusters of the vine" (Song 7:9 [Eng. 7:8]).[28] These examples indicate the long-standing association of women with vineyards and their fruit and show precedent in the Hebrew Bible for the depiction of woman as a vine or vineyard.

Is Isaiah's Vineyard a Woman?

Vineyards in the Hebrew Bible do not always represent women. At times, vineyards are simply vineyards or merely symbolize the effects of either divine blessings or curses.[29] As noted above, Yee has argued that the vineyard was a common metaphor for the northern kingdom.[30] Evidence of the vineyard–woman tradition's establishment by the eighth century BCE and indicators in the text of Isa 5:1-7 that the vineyard represents a woman suggest the validity of this interpretation.

Taken together, several factors indicate the likelihood that one should associate the vineyard in Isa 5:1-7 with a woman. First, the preceding examples of early ancient Near Eastern allusions to the vineyard–woman connection show that the

---

[26] Malul, "Woman–Earth Homology," 343–52.

[27] The task of dating Song of Songs presents numerous challenges. While the present form of the book probably dates to late in ancient Israel's history (perhaps even to the third century BCE), many scholars recognize the likelihood that some of the material has early origins. Striking Ugaritic parallels allow for the possibility that at least parts of the book date originally even to pre-Solomonic times. The vineyard–women texts fall into the category of material that likely has earlier antecedents. See Pope, *Song of Songs*, 22–33; Roland E. Murphy, *The Song of Songs: A Commentary on the Book of Canticles or the Song of Songs*, Hermeneia (Minneapolis: Fortress, 1990), 3–5.

[28] See Jill M. Munro, *Spikenard and Saffron: The Imagery of the Song of Songs*, JSOTSup 203 (Sheffield: Sheffield Academic, 1995), 98–102; Tod Linafelt, "Biblical Love Poetry (… and God)," *JAAR* 70 (2002): 326–27, http://dx.doi.org/10.1093/jaar/70.2.323; Pope, *Song of Songs*, 326–27, 631–43. In many ways the imagery of Song of Songs is a "moving target" from an interpretive standpoint. As Linafelt argues, the book is "full of double entendres, on one level the garden most certainly represents the woman's sexuality.… Yet the garden is also *more* than the woman's sexuality, it is the woman *herself*." Pope notes that several interpreters, including the early targums, understand the failure of the woman to keep her own vineyard in Songs 1:6 as a metaphor for Israelite sins such as idolatry, sometimes even connecting this verse with the vineyard image in Isa 5:1-7. See also Song 2:15, 6:11, 7:13 (Eng. 7:12), 8:11–12.

[29] See 2 Kgs 4:25, Isa 36:16, Jer 8:13, Joel 1:11–12, 2:22.

[30] Yee, "Form-Critical Study," 38.

tradition of associating women with vineyards appears across the ancient Near East at least by the tenth century BCE. Recall, for example, that the thirteenth-century Egyptian text and the Ugaritic hymn text, which dates no later than the twelfth century BCE, both associate vineyards with women. The fourteenth-century Amarna letters draw direct comparisons between women and agricultural fields.[31] Precedent therefore exists for interpreting a vineyard as a woman.

Second, the love-song elements that complicate the problem of generic identification in Isa 5:1–7 are the very features that invite an interpretation of Isaiah's vineyard as a woman. Genre and genre indicators function as signals to audiences about how to approach a text.[32] Ancient Near Eastern love poetry generally involves some kind of title for the poem, shifting voices, descriptions of the actions that the lovers take, and—frequently—agricultural imagery such as vineyards and vines.[33] Accordingly, Isa 5:1–7 opens with the declaration that what follows is a שירת דוד ("love song"). The song includes speeches from both the prophetic voice, who describes what the "beloved" did for the vineyard (vv. 1–2), and the voice of the "beloved," who describes what he will do to the vineyard in the future (vv. 3–7).[34] As scholars such as Joseph Blenkinsopp and Nielsen have noted, the proximity of דוד to כרם in Isa 5:1 triggers the familiar associations between vineyards and women and would have prompted the audience to associate the vineyard with the female object of love in the song.[35] That Isa 5:1–7, which quickly degenerates from

---

[31] See "Satirical Letter," *ANET*, 478; Malul, "Woman–Earth Homology," 347; Pope, *Song of Songs*, 324.

[32] Consider, for example, the difference between how one approaches a text that begins "Once upon a time" and a text that begins "Consider the critical scholarship." Using the same number of words, the author prompts the reader to engage with the subsequent material in radically different ways. See Carol A. Newsom's overview of Mikhail Bakhtin's work on generic conventions ("Spying Out the Land: A Report from Genology," in *Bakhtin and Genre Theory in Biblical Studies*, ed. Roland Boer, SemeiaSt 63 [Atlanta: Society of Biblical Literature, 2007], 19–30).

[33] See G. Lloyd Carr, "The Love Poetry Genre in the Old Testament and the Ancient Near East: Another Look at Inspiration," *JETS* 25 (1982): 491–96; Kenton L. Sparks, *Ancient Texts for the Study of the Hebrew Bible: A Guide to the Background Literature* (Peabody, MA: Hendrickson, 2005), 127–43.

[34] While Isa 5:3 marks the shift from romance to accusation, the first person speech, a common marker of ancient Near Eastern love poetry, perhaps works to maintain the link to the love-song idea (see G. Lloyd Carr, "The Old Testament Love Songs and Their Use in the New Testament," *JETS* 24 [1981]: 98).

[35] Blenkinsopp, *Isaiah 1–39*, 207; Nielsen, *Hope for a Tree*, 90–92. Nielsen even proposes that "the beginning of the song reflects a familiar profane song of erotic content, which is now exploited by the prophet for the purposes of the message," but she gives no support for this hypothesis (92). While the term דוד frequently carries erotic connotations (e.g., Prov 7:18; Song 1:2, 4; 4:10; Ezek 16:8; 23:17), in some instances the term refers to an "uncle" or "relative" rather than a lover (e.g., 2 Kgs 24:17, Amos 6:10; cf. Carr, "Old Testament Love Songs," 101). The presence of דוד alone is therefore insufficient evidence that one should relate Isa 5:1–7 to the genre of the love song; coupled with other generic indicators, however, the association is appropriate.

a love song (vv. 1–2) into a more accusatory text (vv. 3–7), clearly begins with the love-song elements suggests the intentionality of the author in guiding the audience into reading the vineyard as a woman.[36]

Third, Isa 5:1–7 has conceptual resonances with Zion theology and specifically the figure of Daughter Zion, both of which have a strong presence in the chapters preceding this pericope and in the larger book of Isaiah. In the next section, therefore, I will explore these resonances with the Daughter Zion tradition in order to place Isa 5:1–7 within this tradition.

III. The Zion Tradition and Its Daughter: Can She Be a Vineyard?

Scholars generally agree regarding the basic content of the Zion tradition.[37] Grounded in the foundational assumption that YHWH is the "great king," the Zion tradition affirms that YHWH chose Jerusalem as his dwelling place. Consequent on this divine selection of and presence in Jerusalem is the notion that Zion is secure from enemy attacks, that Zion is the locus for YHWH's defeat of chaos, and that Zion's people "share in the blessing of God's presence."[38] Conceptually, Isa 5:1–7 reflects several of these traditional Zion theology elements.

---

[36] The suggestive nature itself (as opposed to the "very clear" nature) of this interpretation also coheres with ancient Near Eastern love poetry conventions. As Virginia Lee Davis observes, "Love poetry anywhere tends to depend more for its effect upon connotations than upon meanings, and that is especially characteristic of ancient love poetry.... To translate [for example] Egyptian love poetry in rigid accordance with the dictionary meaning of each word is to lose at least half of the message and quite likely the more important half of it" ("Remarks on Michael V. Fox's 'The Cairo Love Songs,'" *JAOS* 100 [1980]: 111).

[37] While similar consensus regarding the origins of the Zion tradition has yet to emerge, most agree that the basic elements were part of the Israelite consciousness by the time of Isaiah of Jerusalem. Many scholars trace the origins of the Zion tradition to pre-Israelite Jerusalem (so Herbert Schmid, "Jahwe und die Kulttraditionen von Jerusalem," *ZAW* 67 [1955]: 168–97; Edzard Rohland, "Die Bedeutung der Erwählungstraditionen Israels für die Eschatologie der alttestamentlichen Propheten" [ThD diss., Heidelberg, 1956], 142; Gerhard von Rad, *Old Testament Theology*, 2 vols. [New York: Harper, 1962–1965], 1:46–47; John H. Hayes, "The Tradition of Zion's Inviolability," *JBL* 82 [1963]: 419–26). In sharp contrast to this view, Günther Wanke argues that key aspects of the Zion tradition developed in the exilic period (*Die Zionstheologie der Korachiten in ihrem traditionsgeschichtlichen Zusammenhang*, BZAW 97 [Berlin: Töpelmann, 1966], 92). J. J. M. Roberts convincingly critiques both views based on his analysis of the traditional elements, comparisons with ancient Near Eastern theology, and an analysis of the history of ancient Israel. Roberts concludes that the origins of the Zion tradition fit best in the time of David and Solomon and the building of their Jerusalem-based empire ("The Davidic Origin of the Zion Tradition," in *The Bible and the Ancient Near East: Collected Essays* [Winona Lake, IN: Eisenbrauns, 2002], 324–30).

[38] J. J. M. Roberts, "Zion in the Theology of the Davidic-Solomonic Empire," in *Bible and the Ancient Near East*, 331–47; Maier, *Daughter Zion*, 58–59. YHWH's selection of Zion also has

As noted above, the Song of the Vineyard is not an allegory, so one should not seek a one-to-one correspondence between the elements of the Zion tradition and the elements of the story; nevertheless, the overarching image of the "beloved" and his vineyard suggests key aspects of the Zion tradition.³⁹ While these aspects do not correspond to specific entities, nations, or peoples, some analogy with reality is nevertheless present. The image of the "beloved" carefully preparing the ground, clearing away the stones, and planting the best vines there (5:2aα) reflects the Zion tradition's ideas of divine selection and YHWH's subjugation of chaos and enemies. The construction of the tower and the wine vat (5:2aβ) reflects divine presence and protection. Furthermore, the wine vat and the stated expectation of a good harvest due to the "beloved's" care for the vineyard (5:2b, 4) echo promises of divine blessing.⁴⁰ The reverse images that emerge in the second half of the song (5:5–6) similarly reflect the notion that the vineyard's security and success depend on the "beloved's" active, beneficent presence in it. Other Zion tradition texts in Isa 1–39 contain similar ideas couched in various speeches and images,⁴¹ and the resonances of Isa 5:1–7 with the Zion tradition grow stronger with the recognition of female imagery in this pericope.

---

topographical implications: Zion as the peak of the highest mountain and Zion as the source of the paradise river (see Rohland, "Erwählungstraditionen Israels," 142). These two topographical elements have important resonances with the broader ancient Near Eastern tradition into which the Zion tradition falls (see Roberts, "Davidic Origin," 317–21) but are not closely related to the subject matter of this article.

³⁹ Based on her examination of preexilic Zion traditions in Pss 46, 48, Isa 6, and Mic 3, Maier argues that the Zion tradition was "flourishing at least in the second half of the eighth century" (*Daughter Zion*, 59). Though the tradition at this point is still inchoate, the main points of emphasis in these early Zion texts seem to be divine selection, presence, and blessing/protection. Note, however, that the Mic 3 text indicates the early awareness that, while Zion's inviolability is a central aspect of the Zion tradition (see Mic 3:11b), Zion's inviolability is not absolute (*Daughter Zion*, 30–59).

⁴⁰ For passages that associate bountiful harvest with divine blessing, see Deut 7:13, 28:1–14 (esp. vv. 3–4, 11–12), 30:9, Joel 2:18–27, and Zech 8:1–13. This association appears also in the ancient Near East more broadly (e.g., "The Marduk Prophecy," trans. Tremper Longman III [*COS* 1.149:481]).

⁴¹ For example, the speech contrasting what Zion was and should be (i.e., a "faithful city" full of righteousness, silver, and good drink) with what Zion is (i.e., a "harlot" full of injustice) makes explicit YHWH's control over Zion's condition (Isa 1:21–26). In Isa 8:11–22, YHWH is the king who dwells on Zion, and 8:9–10 indicates that enemies cannot stand against him or the city that he protects. Similarly, the image in Isa 14:32 is of Zion as a refuge that YHWH has established for his people, and the military imagery for YHWH's protection of Zion is very strong in Isa 29. An explicit statement (illustrated with nature similes) of YHWH's presence with and protection of his people on Zion comes in Isa 31:5: "Like flying birds, so the LORD of hosts will defend Jerusalem; he will defend and deliver, pass over and rescue."

Zion Becomes Woman

In the book of Isaiah, Jerusalem personified as "Daughter Zion" serves as a primary means of addressing various aspects of the Zion tradition as they relate to Israelite experience(s).[42] In the ancient Near Eastern context of associating cities with patron deities, the female personification of Jerusalem in the Hebrew Bible "becomes a theological device ... allowing for dramatic development, but also setting Jerusalem in proper relation to her God."[43] The images of Zion as a daughter, mother, wife, widow, and harlot that recur throughout the Latter Prophets and Lamentations therefore reflect the shifting dynamics in the relationship between the people of YHWH and YHWH.[44]

Daughter Zion makes her entrance onto the Isaianic stage early and dramatically. As part of the introductory accusations of Judah and Jerusalem in Isa 1, the prophetic voice describes the wayward בת־ציון (Daughter Zion) as "left like a booth [סכה] in a vineyard, like a hut in a cucumber field, like a city besieged" (1:8). Subsequent verses continue to "flesh out" the image of Daughter Zion—whom the text now describes as a whore (1:21a) rather than a daughter—as a once "faithful city" full not only of moral "finery" such as justice and righteousness but also of fine goods such as silver and choice wine (1:21–22). The accusations in Isa 1 suggest that Zion's failure to perpetuate these standards within her walls (i.e., failure to conform to YHWH's expectations as texts such as 1:16–17 outline) precipitates the removal of divine blessing and the resulting condition of Daughter Zion: left abandoned in a vineyard (1:8), she is "like an oak whose leaves wither and a garden that lacks water" (1:30). Isaiah 3 describes further the way that YHWH will "turn aside from Jerusalem and Judah supports of every kind" (3:1), take away all the fine goods the people of Jerusalem previously enjoyed (3:18–24),[45] and leave Daughter Zion

---

[42] The ancient Near Eastern pattern of identifying cities with or as female figures is well documented. Scholars have identified and explored this pattern in West Semitic (e.g., Fitzgerald, "Mythological Background," 403–16), Mesopotamian (e.g., Biddle, "Figure of Lady Jerusalem," 173–94), and Hellenistic (e.g., Elaine R. Follis, "The Holy City as Daughter," in *Directions in Biblical Poetry*, ed. Elaine R. Follis, JSOTSup 40 [Sheffield: JSOT Press, 1987], 173–84) contexts, each of which has some connection to the female personification of Jerusalem in the Hebrew Bible. Comparisons with these traditions indicate that the personification of Jerusalem as a woman in the Hebrew Bible does not always communicate a critique of Zion or her people.

[43] See Biddle, "Figure of Lady Jerusalem," 186–87.

[44] A few psalms also depict Daughter Zion, but the personification here is vague (e.g., Pss 9, 87).

[45] Some of the most striking images related to personified cities involve the stripping or abuse of the woman as an indicator of the city's transgression and a figure for the resulting military defeat. Isaiah 3:17 may connect indirectly with this tradition. While some scholars have interpreted the stripping of an adulterous wife as a regular aspect of ancient Near Eastern divorce proceedings, Nicholas R. Werse argues that this public exposure of a woman does not appear in ancient Near Eastern divorce texts. Rather, this image corresponds to the prophetic pattern of describing the

vulnerable and alone (3:25–26).⁴⁶ The opening chapters of Isaiah thus present a reversal of key Zion theology tenets using female personification.⁴⁷ Significant for the discussion of Daughter Zion's relationship to the Song of the Vineyard, these depictions of Daughter Zion's fallen condition employ agricultural imagery similar to that present in Isa 5:1–7.

Woman Becomes Vineyard; Zion Becomes Woman

Thus far, I have demonstrated how the vineyard imagery in Isa 5:1–7 corresponds to the ancient Near Eastern woman–vineyard tradition, and I have shown how the theological concepts in the Song of the Vineyard resonate with the theological affirmations of the Zion tradition. Furthermore, the opening chapters of Isaiah interweave agricultural imagery with woman imagery in order to announce the failings and consequent judgment of Jerusalem or "Daughter Zion." Careful examination of the lexical and conceptual links between Isa 5:1–7 and Isa 1–4 further establishes the validity of reading Isa 5:1–7 as a text within the Daughter Zion threads in Isaiah.

The present form of the book of Isaiah suggests intentional arrangement and the use of catchwords to join different textual units.⁴⁸ Almost universal agreement exists that Isa 1 serves as a foreshadowing of the major themes that will emerge throughout the rest of the book.⁴⁹ The Song of the Vineyard (כרם) follows on the

---

destruction of a city as the stripping of a woman (e.g., Isa 47:2–3, Jer 13:22–27, Ezek 16:37–39, 23:22–26, Nah 2:8 [Eng. 2:7], 3:5–7). Werse notes that, while the vocabulary varies across these texts, the image itself is consistent ("Where Did She Come From? The Quest For YHWH's Wife In Hosea 2" [paper presented at the Southwest Commission on Religious Studies Regional SBL Conference, Fort Worth, TX, March 8, 2014]). In the case of Daughter Zion, the transgression that prompts the stripping generally pertains to the dissolution of proper relationship with the God who selected, protects, and provides for Jerusalem. While Isa 3:16–17 describes YHWH's actions against the *daughters of* Zion (בנות ציון) rather than against Daughter Zion (בת־ציון), proximity to Daughter Zion imagery (Isa 1:8, 21; 3:25–26) and clear pronouncements of judgment against the city of Jerusalem (Isa 3) allow for the reading of this text within—or at least in relation to—the tradition Werse identifies.

As an interesting continuation of this concept, Meir Malul has drawn connections between the image of removing the hedges and breaking through the walls of the vineyard in Isa 5:1–7 with the image of stripping adulterous women in texts such as Ezek 16:34–41; 23:10, 22–27; Hos 2:5, 12–15; Jer 13:22, 26–27 ("The Relation between Tearing the Fence Down in the Song of the Vineyard [Isaiah 5:1–7] and Stripping the Woman Naked in the Old Testament," *Beit Mikra* 47 [2001]: 11–24).

⁴⁶ Though Isa 3 does not name בת־ציון explicitly, vv. 25–26 refer to the city using feminine singular pronouns, and v. 26 depicts the city as a woman sitting on the ground. Clearly the image is of Zion personified.

⁴⁷ Cf. the similar reversal dynamic in Mic 3:9–12; Maier, *Daughter Zion*, 55–58.

⁴⁸ See Blenkinsopp, *Isaiah 1–39*, 180.

⁴⁹ See n. 4 above.

heels of the promise of Zion's restoration in Isa 4:2–6. This strong Zion passage —which reaffirms YHWH's selection of, presence in, and provision for the city of Jerusalem—ends by describing this Yahwistic presence and provision as a "booth [סכה] for shade from the heat by day and for refuge and shelter from the floods and rains" (4:6). The term *booth* appears here for the first time since 1:8, where the prophetic voice described Daughter Zion as a "booth in a vineyard" (כסכה בכרם). Playing off of the juxtaposition of these catchwords, Isa 5:1–7 returns to the description of Zion as a woman in 1:8 but layers the female personification further in vineyard imagery.

The Song of the Vineyard contains numerous conceptual links to the preceding Daughter Zion passages in Isa 1–4. The dominant common image is of the caretaker (YHWH or the "beloved") removing the protective elements and abandoning the object of care (Daughter Zion or the vineyard) to its fate. For example, the portrait of Daughter Zion in Isa 1:7–8 likens her to a booth or a hut left unprotected from enemy attack; consequently, fires have consumed (שרף) her, and ravaging foreigners have been able to devour (אכל) her and make her desolate (שממה).[50] The prophet declares in Isa 3:18–26 that YHWH will remove (סור) all the fine things from Zion. The "beloved's" plans for his vineyard reflect similar concepts:

> I will remove [סור] its hedge and it will be consumed [בער],[51]
> I will break down its walls and it will become a trampling ground.
> I will make it a wasteland [בתה]: it will not be pruned nor will it be hoed,
>   but thorns and briars will come up;
> And I will command the clouds to keep from raining down the rains upon it.
> (Isa 5:5–6)

While the lexical connections between the Daughter Zion passages and the Song of the Vineyard are few, therefore, the conceptual resemblance both to the larger Zion tradition's notions of divine selection, presence, and protection and to the

---

[50] Maier, *Daughter Zion*, 75–76. Regarding the function of the Daughter Zion metaphor in this passage, Maier observes, "The hut in the fields corroborates the meaning of 'daughter' on the sociological level, namely that Zion needs protection herself. A daughter has to be protected.... A woman alone in a field is in danger of sexual assault or violence (Deut 22:23–29). The metaphors convey that the city cannot protect her inhabitants, but is utterly threatened in her existence and in need of someone to deliver her from imminent assault."

[51] The term בער connotes consumption by fire (see 1 Kgs 14:10, Ezek 21:4 [Eng. 20:28]), which relates conceptually, if not lexically, to Isa 1:7 and the image of Zion burned with fire (שרפות אש). In the *piel*, בער can connote *purifying* fire (see Deut 13:6, 17:7, 22:22, Judg 20:13), which may relate to the metallurgical imagery describing YHWH's purification of Daughter Zion in Isa 1:24–26 (see BDB, s.v. בער). Nielsen argues that the power of tree imagery (she includes vineyards in this category) for Zion and the people of God resides largely in the notion that cutting down a tree or cutting off vines somewhat paradoxically allows for renewal. One could read the "punishment" of the vineyard in Isa 5:1–7, therefore, as a type of purification; the destruction is not absolute (*Hope for a Tree*, 71).

more specific Daughter Zion tradition is striking.[52] Whereas foreign enemies overrun the abandoned and undefended Daughter Zion, invading plant species overrun the abandoned and undefended vineyard.

The efficacy of the ancient Near Eastern city-as-woman metaphor resides in its ability to communicate a wider range of meaning than would be possible from simply naming the city. Christl Maier has explored the way in which the various female roles associated with Zion (e.g., daughter, beloved, wife, mother, widow, harlot) connote various relational, emotionally charged dynamics.[53] The portrayal of a specific human being's situation generally evokes more emotion than does an abstract description of a situation or even the situation of an inanimate object (e.g., a physical city or a vineyard). If the vineyard in Isa 5:1–7 represents Daughter Zion, therefore, consideration of the rhetorical power of Zion's female personification raises the question: Why represent the city as a woman and then filter this representation through vineyard imagery? The final section of this paper will address this question.

IV. Reading the Song of the Vineyard as Part of Daughter Zion's Story

The history of scholarship on Isa 5:1–7 indicates ongoing uncertainty regarding the exact genre designation for this pericope and the specific way one should interpret the meaning of the clearly metaphorical text. I have argued that the longstanding ancient Near Eastern tradition of associating women with vineyards, particularly coupled with the presence of generically confusing love-song elements in the text of Isa 5:1–7, encourages an interpretation of Isaiah's vineyard as a woman. Furthermore, resonances with key aspects of the Zion tradition and conceptual links with Daughter Zion passages in Isa 1–4 suggest that the woman-vineyard in Isa 5:1–7 is, in fact, Daughter Zion. This reading of the text illuminates both Isa 5:1–7 and the Daughter Zion tradition in three primary ways.

First, placing the Song of the Vineyard in the tradition of ancient Near Eastern love poetry and woman–vineyard imagery heightens the intimacy of the YHWH–Zion relationship and the critical importance of YHWH in this relationship. If one begins reading the parable as if one were reading a love song, the care with which the "beloved" clears away the stones and plants the ground with the very best vines underscores the dedication of the "beloved" to his vineyard. Contributing to this image of devoted care is Nielsen's observation that vineyards are among the more

---

[52] Maier notes the similarity between these texts but does not explore them (*Daughter Zion*, 76–77).

[53] Ibid., 73–74 and passim.

"high maintenance" crops and require a high level of human involvement in order to prosper:

> That the vine resembles a lady demanding attention and consideration is not without significance to understanding the frequent use of the vine or vineyard as an image of Israel.... It is scarcely fortuitous that the authors of the Old Testament prefer to use the vine as an image of Israel rather than the hardy and self-reliant olive tree. Used in relation to Israel, the vine is able to connote the election and the greatness as well as the judgment and the insecure position.[54]

The romantic—if not fully erotic—connotations of the agricultural imagery in Isa 5:1-7 thus prompt readers to recognize the bond between YHWH and the city he has chosen more powerfully than in the previous Daughter Zion passages.

Second, depicting Daughter Zion as a vineyard communicates the responsibility Zion has to contribute to the YHWH–Zion relationship. The previous Daughter Zion passages have indicated Zion's failure to "live up to" the expectations of her divine patron, but Isa 5:1-7 presents these expectations using an example that readers in an agriculturally based society could not fail to understand. The economic consequences of a vineyard's failure to produce a good crop after months of labor and toil would be devastating. Thus, the "beloved" can be confident in his appeal to the people of Jerusalem and Judah that they will affirm the justice of his abandonment of the vineyard:[55]

> So now, inhabitants of Jerusalem and men of Judah:
>   judge between me and between my vineyard.
> What more could I have done for my vineyard? And what have I not done in it?
>   Why when I waited for it to produce grapes did it produce wild ones? (Isa 5:3-4)

This reminder that Zion's security depends on its being in right relationship with YHWH is an important corrective to a blanket trust in the inviolability of Jerusalem. The vineyard image provides a relatable, insider perspective on YHWH's "side" of the Zion tradition.

Third, the layering of imagery for Jerusalem in the opening chapters of Isaiah —as a woman, then as a vineyard who is a woman—permits the rhetorical strategy of the juridical parable in Isa 5:1-7 to have its full effect. The text has already presented Jerusalem as a woman, so now a new metaphor becomes necessary in order to "throw off" the audience enough that the necessary self-condemnation can occur.[56]

---

[54] Nielsen, *Hope for a Tree*, 77. Cf. Isa 1:8, 3:14, 5:1-7, 27:2-6, Ps 80:9-13.

[55] Nielsen argues that Isaiah's primary intent in using the vineyard imagery is to demonstrate that the destruction of the vineyard is a righteous judgment (*Hope for a Tree*, 101-2).

[56] See Simon, "Juridical Parable," 220-21; Yee, "Form-Critical Study," 33; Nielsen, *Hope for a Tree*, 101-2. The identity of the "decoy" may have shifted over the course of the text's composition history. The arrangement of Isa 1-4 is critical for understanding the vineyard in Isa 5:1-7 as Daughter Zion. Accordingly, Yee's argument that eighth-century readers might have associated

In short, reading the Song of the Vineyard as a parable about Daughter Zion does not introduce new concepts into the text or the tradition(s), but it does reimage preexisting concepts in new, highly concrete ways as a rhetorical means of increasing the impact on the audience.

V. Conclusion

In this article, I have argued that the vineyard in Isa 5:1–7 is another layer of the metaphorical representation of Jerusalem and has close connections with the Daughter Zion tradition. In Isaiah, the story of Daughter Zion weaves throughout the book and progresses from a picture of abandonment and desolation to one of glorious restoration and divine presence.[57] The Daughter Zion vineyard image in Isaiah similarly exhibits this development. Isaiah 27:2–6 contains another vineyard song in which YHWH the vineyard-keeper declares his care and protection of the vineyard using language and imagery consonant with—but reversing—that of Isa 5:1–7:

> On that day, sing about the pleasant vineyard [כרם]!
> I the Lord keep her, at every moment I water [שקה] her;
> Lest someone injure [פקד] her, by night and by day I guard her.
> I am not wrathful—the one who gives me thorns and briars [שמיר שית] for battle,
>   I will march against her, I will burn her up together [with them]!
> Or let that one cling to my protection: let him make peace with me,
>   let him make peace with me.
> In the coming days, Jacob will take root, Israel will blossom and sprout
>   and fill the face of the world with fruit [תנובה]. (Isa 27:2–6)

In view of the similar language and genre elements (i.e., love song), scholars almost universally recognize this vineyard song's relationship to the vineyard parable that has been the subject of this study. As in Isa 5:1–7, this text does not mention Daughter Zion, nor does it even mention Jerusalem by name. Nevertheless, Schmitt has noted the unique manner in which the author of the text makes implicit the city–vineyard–woman connection: the author changes "the grammatical gender of vineyard from masculine to feminine, to make this passage the only one in the Hebrew

---

the vineyard with the northern kingdom may also have merit: as the text of Isaiah developed, the "decoy" of the parable song could have moved from being the northern kingdom to being Daughter Zion (see Yee, "Form-Critical Study," 38; for other texts that associate the northern kingdom with vineyards, see Ps 80, Hos 9:10, 10:1, 14:8).

[57] Isaiah 1:21–26, as part of the introduction to the book of Isaiah, serves as a foreshadowing of this movement. This pericope opens with the declaration that Zion has moved from faithfulness to whoredom (1:21) but ends with the statement that Zion will once again carry the reputation of a "faithful city" (1:26).

Bible where כרם is feminine."[58] By the time the reader reaches Isa 27, therefore, Daughter Zion the vineyard is at least moving toward restored relationship with her caretaker.[59]

The woman–vineyard associations in the ancient Near East are well attested, and the love-song elements in the opening verses of the parable invite reading Isaiah's vineyard as a figure for a woman. The parable's depiction of the "beloved" and his devotion to caring for and nurturing the vineyard resonate strongly with the Zion tradition's notions of divine choice, presence, provision for, and protection of Jerusalem. The combination of these associations in and around Isa 5:1–7 therefore suggests that the vineyard-woman of the parable is Daughter Zion herself. The self-interpretation of the parable in Isa 5:7 coupled with the following series of woe oracles makes the basic meaning of this text clear: YHWH will punish his people. Reading the Song of the Vineyard as part of the larger story of Daughter Zion, however, sheds greater light on the relationship between YHWH and the people he has chosen.

---

[58] Schmitt, "City as Woman," 114–15. Schmitt further connects Isa 24:2–3 with Isa 5:1–7 by observing that these two texts are the only examples of love songs in Isa 1–39. If nothing else, the connections between these two texts indicate that at a relatively late stage of Isaiah's composition history the editor recognized the feminine aspects of the vineyard in Isa 5:1–7 (for the date of Isa 24–27, see Hans Wildberger, *Isaiah 13–27*, trans. Thomas H. Trapp, CC [Minneapolis: Fortress, 1991], 445–47; Ronald E. Clements, *Isaiah 1–39*, NCBC [Grand Rapids: Eerdmans, 1980], 198–99; Blenkinsopp, *Isaiah 1–39*, 348).

[59] As stated above, the focus of this article is on how the editor(s) of Isaiah understood 5:1–7 during the process of the book's development. The evidence of chapter 27, which most scholars agree is part of the latest additions to the book, therefore supports this interim and/or "final" reading and not the "original" meaning of the text at its time of composition (see Stromberg, *Introduction to the Study of Isaiah*, 11–24).

Wabash Center

for Teaching and Learning in Theology and Religion

2017-18
Workshops & Colloquies
- Early Career Theological School Faculty
- Early Career Asian/North American Asian Religion Faculty
- Theological School Deans
- Writing the Scholarship of Teaching
  Application Deadline: January 15, 2017

Grants up to $30,000
Application Deadlines: March 1 & October 1

Consultants
- Workshops & faculty retreats
- Consultations

Resources
- *Teaching Theology & Religion*
- Religion on the Web
- Teaching Resources
- Over 1800 syllabi

wabash.center

Fully funded by Lilly Endowment Inc.
Located at Wabash College

Walk, Don't Run: Jesus's Water Walking Is Unparalleled in Greco-Roman Mythology

BRIAN D. MCPHEE
bmcphee@live.unc.edu
University of North Carolina, Chapel Hill, NC 27599

Scholarly treatments of Jesus's sea-walking miracle frequently cite several parallel figures "walking on water" in Greco-Roman mythology, such as Poseidon, Orion, Euphemus, and Pythagoras. In fact, however, this "walking" terminology is inaccurate because, contrary to Adela Yarbro Collins and others, Greco-Roman mythology supplies no unambiguous example of a figure *walking* on water in the way that Jesus does in Mark, Matthew, and John. Rather, there are numerous examples—far more than have been recognized—of running, chariot-riding, and flying over water beginning as early as Homer's *Iliad*. Whereas Jesus's feat is presented as a sort of levitation miracle, water running and water riding are understood as a consequence of superhuman speed in the popular Greek conception of physics, with the idea ultimately based on the motion of wind over waves. Flying over water and other surfaces is associated in Greek thought with supernatural travel convenience; it requires speed and flying devices that are entirely foreign to the Gospel narratives. The few examples of Greco-Roman figures purported to walk on water just as Jesus does either have been misinterpreted or are idiosyncratic, Common-Era creations. This article argues that there are no actual Greco-Roman parallels to what Jesus does in the Gospels. Walking on the sea was more novel, more marvelous, and less immediately interpretable for non-Jewish audiences than has been assumed.

In adducing parallels between traditions, it is important to use language precisely in order to avoid overstating the extent of similarity or difference. Just such a distortion is evident in the loose way that the phrase "walking on water" and its variants are sometimes applied to proposed Greco-Roman mythological analogues for Jesus's sea-walking miracle (Mark 6:45–52, Matt 14:22–33, John 6:15–21).[1] In

---

I would like to express my gratitude to Ava Chitwood for inspiring this investigation and especially William H. Race for his helpful comments on several drafts of this article. It has also been greatly improved by the *Journal*'s anonymous referee. All remaining errors are my own.

[1] Thus, e.g., Craig S. Keener asserts, "Various ancient figures reportedly walked on water: Orion, a son of Poseidon; Xerxes, who thereby displayed a divine power; Pythagoras; and a

763

Jesus's case, the "walking" terminology is appropriate. The evangelists describe Jesus "walking on the sea" a total of five times (Mark 6:48, 49; Matt 14:25, 26; John 6:19). In each instance, they represent his movement using no verb but περιπατέω, "walk (around),"[2] and in each case the verb is paired with the prepositional phrase ἐπὶ τῆς θαλάσσης ("upon the sea,"). When Peter attempts to duplicate Jesus's action in Matthew, an inceptive aorist (περιεπάτησεν, "he began to walk") characterizes the motion with the verb περιπατέω yet a sixth time (Matt 14:29).[3] Moreover, Jesus is apparently envisioned standing in place as Peter approaches his position (Matt 14:28–31). These three accounts, therefore, consistently present Jesus's miracle as a sort of levitation, which allows him to walk at a gradual pace or even stand on the

---

Hyperborean magician" (*The Gospel of John: A Commentary*, 2 vols. [Peabody, MA: Hendrickson, 2003], 1:672). Patrick J. Madden is wary of uncritical uses of the "water-walking" terminology in relation to supposed Buddhist parallels, but unfortunately he himself falls prey to the error with phrases like "Orion walked upon the waves" and "a certain Euphemus ... had the ability to walk upon water" (*Jesus' Walking on the Sea: An Investigation of the Origin of the Narrative Account*, BZNW 81 [Berlin: de Gruyter, 1997], 5557). Likewise, George W. Young, characterizing the position of Werner Berg, is careful to distinguish Job 9:8 as the only Hebrew Bible text featuring an "actual walking upon water," but he is not so careful when citing "water-walking episodes" from eleven different Greek authors (*Subversive Symmetry: Exploring the Fantastic in Mark 6:45–56*, BibInt 41 [Leiden: Brill, 1999], 14–15). M. Eugene Boring, Klaus Berger, and Carsten Colpe declare that "Xerxes has this power to walk on the water," and Pythagoras, too, exercises "this wonderful power" (*Hellenistic Commentary to the New Testament* [Nashville: Abingdon, 1995], 99). On the other hand, Adela Yarbro Collins is a model for precise wording on the subject in an article on water walking and in her commentary on Mark, which draws on her earlier work ("Rulers, Divine Men, and Walking on the Water [Mark 6:45–52]," in *Religious Propaganda and Missionary Competition in the New Testament World: Essays Honoring Dieter Georgi*, ed. Lukas Bormann, Kelly Del Tredici, and Angela Standhartinger, NovTSup 74 [Leiden: Brill, 1994], 207–27; *Mark: A Commentary*, Hermeneia [Minneapolis: Fortress, 2007], 328–33), but I will argue that she is misled by certain translations that she cites. At any rate, her careful wording is not always appreciated as, for example, Jason Robert Combs paraphrases her work: "According to Yarbro Collins, those who could walk on water included *living* heroes such as Hercules, Euphemus, and Orion, and also gods such as Neptune, who rides his chariot across the sea" ("A Ghost on the Water? Understanding an Absurdity in Mark 6:49–50," *JBL* 127 [2008]: 349; emphasis original). As I will show, with one or two exceptions, all of the quoted characterizations are inaccurate or uncertain.

[2] BDAG defines the verb περιπατέω thus: "to go here and there in walking, *go about, walk around*" (italics original).

[3] All translations are my own. The text of the New Testament comes from NA[28]. Matthew 14:25 varies the prepositional phrase "upon the sea" with an accusative object (ἐπὶ τὴν θάλασσαν), but the difference in meaning is negligible—the genitive construction ἐπὶ τῆς θαλάσσης appears in the next verse describing the same activity. For Peter's brief walk, the evangelist uses the prepositional phrase "upon the waters" (ἐπὶ τὰ ὕδατα, Matt 14:29), not "the sea," probably because Peter only intends to cover the distance separating him from Jesus. He wants to walk a particular tract of water, not "the sea as such" (John Paul Heil, *Jesus Walking on the Sea: Meaning and Gospel Functions of Matt. 14:22–33, Mark 6:45–52, and John 6:15b–21*, AnBib 87 [Rome: Biblical Institute Press, 1981], 141).

non-solid sea. Conversely, Greek and Roman mythology features numerous examples of supernatural *running* or *flying* over the sea, but in fact it contains no unambiguous reference to *walking* on the sea as Jesus does. To prove this point, I will proceed first by explicating the Greek concept of water running and then of flying over water, in each case distinguishing that idea from what Jesus does in the Gospel narratives. Finally, I will examine a few figures that appear to offer more compelling examples of water walking, though I will argue that none of them represents genuine traditions of water walking that could have interacted with the early Christian traditions. Rather, in a Greco-Roman mythological context at least, Jesus's miracle is unprecedented. I will conclude by considering how this insight affects interpretation of the water-walking narrative.

I. Running on Water

The feat of running on water is at least as old as extant Greek literature, first appearing in Homer's description of the mares of King Erichthonius of Dardania (*Il.* 20.226–229):

αἳ δ' ὅτε μὲν σκιρτῷεν ἐπὶ ζείδωρον ἄρουραν,
ἄκρον ἐπ' ἀνθερίκων καρπὸν θέον οὐδὲ κατέκλων·
ἀλλ' ὅτε δὴ σκιρτῷεν ἐπ' εὐρέα νῶτα θαλάσσης,
ἄκρον ἐπὶ ῥηγμῖνος ἁλὸς πολιοῖο θέεσκον.[4]

When they would bound upon the fruitful plain, they would run atop ears of grain and yet not snap them off; but when they would bound upon the broad back of the sea, they would run on top of the surf of the gray sea.

The siring of these marvelous mares by Boreas, god of the north wind (20.223–225),[5] reveals the inspiration for this fantasy: these horses are "swift as the wind," whose "steps" as it blows can be perceived by the motion of the grain and the waves left in its wake.[6] This hypothesis is further confirmed by the movement of Iris, the messenger goddess of the *Iliad*. Homer never describes her mode of locomotion in detail, but at one point he does have her "running" to her destination (θέουσα,

---

[4] The text of the *Iliad* comes from David B. Munro and Thomas W. Allen, eds., *Homeri Opera*, 3rd ed., 5 vols. (Oxford: Clarendon, 1920).

[5] Divine horses are frequently offspring of the wind gods, as are Achilles's team (*Il.* 16.148–151), Erichthonius's (*Il.* 20.223–225), Ares's (Quintus Smyrnaeus 8.241–244), Erechtheus's (Nonnus, *Dion.* 37.155–161), and Arion, a horse owned by several heroes (Quintus Smyrnaeus 4.568–573); see further Nicholas Horsfall, *Virgil, Aeneid 7: A Commentary,* Mnemosyne Supplement 198 (Leiden: Brill, 2000), ad *Aen.* 7.807. The wind gods could transform into stallions, as Boreas does in the present passage, and sometimes they serve as the horses for Zeus's chariot in late variations of the trope (Quintus Smyrnaeus 12.189–195; Nonnus, *Dion.* 2.420–423).

[6] Cf. *Il.* 14.285, where the treetops quiver as Hera and Hypnos dart over a forest. The image is reminiscent of the wind blowing through the leaves.

23.201), and in another place she explicitly travels across (and then under) the sea (24.77–80). With the regular epithets "swift-footed" (πόδας ὠκέα), "wind-footed" (ποδήνεμος), and "storm-footed" (ἀελλόπος), Iris points up the connection between wind, speed, and running over water in the *Iliad*.[7]

Naturally, Homer was widely imitated, and later poets and mythographers applied his imagery of running on ears of grain and/or waves of the sea, swift as the wind, to several other figures. Thus, Hesiod's Iphiclus can keep pace with the wind and run across grain without breaking the heads (*Ehoeae* frag. 61 [Most, LCL]); Apollonius's Euphemus and Hyginus's Orion are so swift that they can run across the waves, the former without wetting his feet (*Argon.* 1.182–184; *Poet. astr.* 2.34); Ovid's Atalanta and Hippomenes are so fast that you would think they could run over grain or the sea without bruising the heads or wetting their feet (*Metam.* 10.654–655); and Vergil's Camilla can do all three—outpace the winds, speed over blades of grain without bruising them, and race over mid-sea without wetting her feet (*Aen.* 7.807–811).[8] By the time of Nonnus's late, baroque *Dionysiaca* in the fifth century CE, running on water becomes an epic commonplace. For example, in 23.151–161, Nonnus depicts the goat-god Pan, chariots driven by sons of Poseidon, and a bull all running across the Hydapses River (though the aged Sileni must paddle)—and this passage is in no way exceptional.

Nonnus's example indicates a special subcategory of water running, namely, conveyance by water-running animals, usually by chariot. Again, Homer provides the earliest extant example in his description of Poseidon's oversea journey from his palace at Aegae (*Il.* 13.26–30):

> ἑοῦ δ' ἐπεβήσετο δίφρου,
> βῆ δ' ἐλάαν ἐπὶ κύματ'· ἄταλλε δὲ κήτε' ὑπ' αὐτοῦ
> πάντοθεν ἐκ κευθμῶν, οὐδ' ἠγνοίησεν ἄνακτα·
> γηθοσύνῃ δὲ θάλασσα διίστατο· τοὶ δὲ πέτοντο
> ῥίμφα μάλ', οὐδ' ὑπένερθε διαίνετο χάλκεος ἄξων·
> τὸν δ' ἐς Ἀχαιῶν νῆας ἐΰσκαρθμοι φέρον ἵπποι.

and [Poseidon] mounted his chariot and set out to drive it over the waves. Sea monsters gamboled beneath him from all around out of the depths, nor did they fail to recognize their lord, and the sea was gladly parted; they flew very swiftly, and the bronze axle beneath remained dry; and his swift-springing horses were bearing him to the ships of the Achaeans.[9]

---

[7] For example, these epithets appear in *Il.* 2.790, 2.786, and 8.409, respectively. In two places Iris is also dubbed "golden-winged" (χρυσόπτερος, *Il.* 8.398, 11.185), but she does not seem to fly; probably the wings allude to her great speed.

[8] See further Horsfall, *Virgil*, ad *Aen.* 7.808, 810.

[9] The word πέτοντο does not mean that Poseidon's chariot flies through the air, but as in English, "flying" can connote speed in Greek, as LSJ notes, s.v. πέτομαι ("of any quick motion, dart, rush"); cf. Richard Janko, *The Iliad: A Commentary*, vol. 4 (Cambridge: Cambridge University Press, 1992), ad *Il.* 13.27–31. The detail of the parting sea (θάλασσα διίστατο) is taken from sailing imagery, in which a ship "cuts" through the water. For example, the ship of the Phaeacians that

Adela Yarbro Collins implies that there is a connection between Poseidon's mastery over the sea and his riding over it, and that on these grounds he is comparable to YHWH as "a deity controlling wind and sea and making a path through the sea."[10] I find this misleading, because Poseidon's ability does not owe to any special power he might have as a sea god but to his divine horses. For example, when Xerxes invaded Greece, he bridged the Hellespont and crossed it with his chariot in a display of immense power. While Dio Chrysostom compares this feat to Poseidon's action in Homer (*3 Regn.* 30–31), Herodotus compares the power Xerxes demonstrates to Zeus's (*Hist.* 7.56.2). It seems that the ability to travel over water as if it were land is illustrative of divine power in general.[11] In any event, divine horses frequently and famously bound over water or grain,[12] such that the second-century CE satirist Lucian can brand these horses (along with winged ones) as typical examples of poetic nonsense (*Hist. conscr.* 8.9–10).[13] Among water-running horses, the hippocampi deserve special mention. These are the sea-horses that sometimes pull the chariots of the sea gods and their associates through the water, running with equine legs in the front and swimming with piscine tails in the back. For example, hippocampi appear in Roman poets of the first centuries BCE and CE pulling the chariots of Neptune (Statius, *Achill.* 1.59–60, *Theb.* 2.45–47), Proteus (Vergil, *Georg.* 4.388–389), Leucothea (*Ciris* 394–396), and Orion (Valerius Flaccus 2.505–508). Beyond horses, other hooved animals could conceivably run across the water as well. For example, when Zeus abducts Europa off to Crete in the form of a bull, "he

---

bears Odysseus home "was cutting the waves of the sea as it ran" (θέουσα θαλάσσης κύματ' ἔταμνεν, *Od.* 13.88) and is compared to a chariot and a flying hawk, "nimblest of birds" (ἐλαφρότατος πετεηνῶν, 13.87). The text of the *Odyssey* comes from Thomas W. Allen, ed., *Homeri Opera*, 2nd ed., 5 vols. (Oxford: Clarendon, 1917).

[10] Yarbro Collins, *Mark*, 329.

[11] Admittedly, running or riding over water is the sort of feat that sea divinities are more likely to perform than other gods because they have more occasion to be in the sea in the first place. But it is important not to imply that supernatural travel over water must reflect lordship over the sea; for example, Hera is hardly a marine goddess, but she darts across the sea on foot in the *Iliad* (14.225–230).

[12] E.g., *Il.* 13.26–30, 20.226–229; *Od.* 5.380–381; Statius, *Theb.* 6.307–310; Quintus Smyrnaeus 3.748–749, 5.88–96, 8.154–157.

[13] Lucian is here discussing the difference between writing history and writing poetry: "For there [sc. in poetry], there is pure freedom and a single law—the poet's pleasure. For possessed and overcome by the Muses, even if s/he wishes to yoke a chariot to winged horses, or even if s/he sets others to run on water or heads of grain, there is no criticism" (ἐκεῖ μὲν γὰρ ἄκρατος ἡ ἐλευθερία καὶ νόμος εἷς—τὸ δόξαν τῷ ποιητῇ. ἔνθεος γὰρ καὶ κάτοχος ἐκ Μουσῶν, κἂν ἵππων ὑποπτέρων ἅρμα ζεύξασθαι ἐθέλῃ, κἂν ἐφ' ὕδατος ἄλλους ἢ ἐπ' ἀνθερίκων ἄκρων θευσομένους ἀναβιβάσηται, φθόνος οὐδείς). The text of Lucian comes from A. M. Harmon et al., eds. and trans., *Lucian*, 8 vols., LCL (Cambridge: Harvard University Press, 1913–1967).

The second-century CE didactic poet Oppian includes a similar sequence of three horses in his list of extraordinary horses: one that can run on grain without breaking it, another that can run on waves without wetting its hooves, and another, Pegasus, who bore Bellerophon above the clouds (*Cyn.* 1.231–233).

was running like a dolphin, stepping over the broad waves with hooves unwetted" (θέεν ἠΰτε δελφὶς | χηλαῖς ἀβρεκτοῖσιν ἐπ' εὐρέα κύματα βαίνων, Moschus 2.113–114).[14] New Testament scholars typically raise only a few of these mythological water runners as potential parallels for Jesus *qua* water walker, but in fact the trope finds ample exemplification throughout Greek and Roman literature.

None of these references explains the physics by which these figures are supposed to run on water, but the emphasis on speed and the close connection with running on grain are suggestive. It is as if the steps of these runners are so light and rapid that by the time the force of their first footfall breaks the surface tension, they have retracted their foot and are repeating the process with the next step.[15] At the same time, divine horses are sometimes depicted running in midair (e.g., *Il.* 5.767–772, 8.45–49).[16] The concept underlying these feats seems to be that all matter, even liquids and gases, has a certain degree of solidity, which can support speeding feet or hooves at least for a fraction of a second.[17] In any case, whether running on grain, water, or air, the supernatural element is the runner's extraordinary speed; the fact of not bruising, sinking, or falling is itself not supernatural but a theoretical

---

[14] The text of Moschus comes from J. M. Edmonds, ed. and trans., *Greek Bucolic Poets*, LCL (Cambridge: Harvard University Press, 1912). Moschus belongs to the second century BCE.

[15] Cf. Vergil, *Georg.* 3.193–201, where a swift horse barely sets the bottom of its hooves on the sand and is compared to the north wind flying over the sea and fields of grain.

[16] The gods appear to have special control over ἀήρ, the opaque, cloudy portion of the sky, which they can generate or dispel at various densities or degrees of "thickness." Ares can rest his spear and his horses on the substance (*Il.* 5.356); Achilles can stab at "thick mist" (ἠέρα ... βαθεῖαν, *Il.* 20.446); and Hera can spread the same to detain Trojans attempting to flee the battlefield (*Il.* 21.6–7); see Charles H. Kahn, *Anaximander and the Origins of Greek Cosmology* (New York: Columbia University Press, 1960), 140–45. As William H. Race reminds me, Apollonius calls attention to this oddity of mythical physics when he depicts Athena speeding through the air on a light cloud, "which could bear her swiftly, heavy though she was" (ἥ κε φέροι μιν ἄφαρ βριαρήν περ ἐοῦσαν, *Argon.* 2.539; the text of Apollonius comes from William H. Race, ed. and trans., *Apollonius Rhodius: Argonautica*, LCL [Cambridge: Harvard University Press, 2008]). As a result of this peculiar notion, divine horses can run on air as on water or heads of grain, but, in most curious fashion, they can also stand on air in a manner unparalleled for water or grain (*Il.* 5.356; Valerius Flaccus, 5.182–183). Perhaps the gods can thicken air to the point that it can support solid objects.

[17] I have not been able to find evidence of this conclusion in ancient discussions of the materiality of water, but it seems to be implied in poetic descriptions of water running. Interestingly enough, we now know that it is indeed possible to run on water at sufficient speeds, and one animal, the so-called "Jesus" or basilisk lizard, can actually do so for short distances; for a description of the mechanics involved, see S. Tonia Hsieh and George V. Lauder, "Running on water: Three-dimensional force generation by basilisk lizards," *Proceedings of the National Academy of Sciences* 101.48 (2004): 16784–88. According to J. W. Glasheen and T. A. McMahon, a human weighing eighty kilograms would need to achieve a velocity of almost thirty meters per second to be able to run on water, all while maintaining an average power output almost fifteen times greater than the maximum that a human can sustain ("A hydrodynamic model of locomotion in the Basilisk Lizard," *Nature* 380 [1996]: 342).

possibility at sufficient speeds within this worldview. Conversely, Jesus's ambulatory pace indicates a type of levitation miracle, which could hypothetically be executed in the air or over other substances as well. In both cases, the water *per se* is irrelevant to the miracle's execution, so the difference between water running and water walking is really the difference between superspeed and levitation. Put in those terms, the full difference between these purported parallels becomes apparent.

II. Flying over Water

Probably because he is a *theios anēr*, Pythagoras is sometimes viewed as a parallel for Jesus's water walking: in Iamblichus, *De vita pyth.* 91, Pythagoras receives a magical arrow that can carry him over bodies of water, mountains, and other obstacles that hinder ordinary travelers. Such flight bears only the faintest resemblance to Jesus's walking on the Sea of Galilee. In fact, the Pythagorean story is one fantastical variant of the miracle of supernatural flight, which often allows Greek gods and heroes to travel easily over the sea and other treacherous terrain. Once again, Homer supplies the earliest extant example of the trope in question, this time with his description of the sandals that take Hermes and Athena over land and sea (*Il.* 24.340–342 = *Od.* 1.96–98, 5.44–46; cf. Vergil, *Aen.* 4.239–241):

αὐτίκ' ἔπειθ' ὑπὸ ποσσὶν ἐδήσατο καλὰ πέδιλα
ἀμβρόσια χρύσεια, τά μιν <u>φέρον</u> ἠμὲν ἐφ' ὑγρὴν
ἠδ' ἐπ' ἀπείρονα γαῖαν ἅμα πνοιῇς ἀνέμοιο …

Then he immediately bound beneath his feet fine sandals, ambrosial and golden, which would <u>bear</u> him over the sea and over the boundless earth as fast as blasts of wind …

That flight and not water running is at issue here is apparent from *Od.* 5.50–54, in which the traveling Hermes is compared to a cormorant skimming over the waves in search of fish. In later authors, these same sandals bear Perseus in flight to and from the far-flung island of the Gorgons (e.g., Euripides frag. 124 [Collard, Cropp, LCL]). Other gods and heroes employ flying horses, such as the immortal chariot team that can convey Hades through the air over sea, rivers, glens, and mountains (*Hom. Hymn Dem.* 380–383). Less often, other animals serve the same function, like the ram with the golden fleece that bears Phrixus to Colchis.[18] As with water runners, the consistent emphasis on the speed of those who fly over water stands in marked contrast to Jesus's slow walking (περιπατέω). Moreover, Jesus lacks any

---

[18] Many ancient authors clearly represent the ram as flying, but others actually depict him swimming to Colchis. For a survey of the evidence, see D. S. Robertson, "The Flight of Phrixus," *ClR* 54 (1940): 1–8.

wings or other devices that enable him to defy gravity, and Jesus's walking has none of the connotations of speedy travel convenience so prominent in the Greek fantasy.

III. Walking on Water

Are there any genuine water walkers in Greco-Roman mythology? At first glance, there seem to be a few promising candidates. One such figure, according to Yarbro Collins, is Seneca's Hercules, who once "traversed seas on foot" (*maria superavit pedes, Herc. fur.* 324).[19] The phrase initially seems to describe water walking, but in context it assumes a different meaning. An anxious Megara asks Amphitryon how Hercules can return from his labor in the underworld (317–324):

> MEG. Demersus ac defossus et toto insuper
>   oppressus orbe quam viam ad superos habet?
> AMPH. Quam tunc habebat cum per arentem plagam
>   et fluctuantes more turbati maris
>   abît harenas bisque discedens fretum
>   et bis recurrens, cumque deserta rate
>   deprensus haesit Syrtium brevibus vadis
>   et puppe fixa maria <u>superavit pedes</u>.
>
> MEG. Sunk and buried and crushed beneath the whole world above, what way has he [Hercules] to the open air?
> AMPH. The same way he had then when he escaped through the arid tract and the sands flowing like a turbid sea and the gulf twice receding, twice returning, even when, his boat deserted, he was seized and fixed to the shallow shoals of the Syrtes, and, with his ship stuck, he <u>traversed</u> seas <u>on foot</u>.

Our ignorance of this particular adventure of Hercules compounds the usual ambiguity of tragic style, but it is probable that the entire passage refers to the same event, the second *cum* serving a pleonastic function that clarifies the first temporal clause.[20] This conflation of desert and sea would make sense of the story's setting in the Syrtes, sandbanks off the Libyan coast notorious for the dangers that they posed to sailors. Jason's crew find themselves stranded on the Syrtes in Apollonius's *Argonautica*, which are mythically amplified and described most grimly as an inescapable wasteland (4.1232–1240). The Argonauts would have died of dehydration in this marine desert had not Poseidon shown them the way out; the crew carries their ship for twelve days, following the tracks of the god's horse in the sand, until they

---

[19] The text of Seneca comes from John G. Fitch, ed. and trans., *Seneca: Tragedies*, 2 vols., LCL (Cambridge: Harvard University Press, 2002–2004).

[20] So John G. Fitch, *Seneca's Hercules Furens: A Critical Text with Introduction and Commentary* (Ithaca, NY: Cornell University Press, 1987), ad 319–24.

can launch again in deeper waters. The scenario that Seneca envisions is slightly different, but not by much: it seems that, when Hercules was stranded, he abandoned his boat altogether and followed the sandbank all the way to the shore by a different route.[21] Granted, traversing a days-long desert is an achievement,[22] but Hercules does not walk on water in this passage.

I have already mentioned another pair of potential water walkers, Euphemus and Orion, both sons of Poseidon. In Apollonius's third-century BCE *Argonautica*, swift Euphemus runs on water (1.182–184), as does Orion, according to the first- or second-century CE mythographer Hyginus (*Poet. astr.* 2.34). In the *Argonautica* of Valerius Flaccus, the first-century CE Roman poet, however, Orion rides over the sea in a chariot pulled by hippocampi (2.505–508). I should also add here a tradition preserved by Servius, the fourth-century CE Vergilian commentator, in which Orion is so gigantic that he can wade through the sea on foot (Servius ad *Aen.* 10.763).[23]

Yarbro Collins and M. Eugene Boring et al., however, cite other passages in which these heroes purportedly walk on the sea, not run, ride, or wade. First, concerning Orion they cite a passage of the *Catasterismi*, an epitome of an astronomical work attributed to Eratosthenes of Cyrene, a third-century BCE naturalist (Pseudo-Eratosthenes, *Catast.* 32 = Hesiod, frag. 244 [Most, LCL]):[24]

Ὠρίων. τοῦτον Ἡσίοδός φησιν Εὐρυάλης τῆς Μίνωος καὶ Ποσειδῶνος εἶναι, δοθῆναι δὲ αὐτῷ δωρεὰν ὥστε ἐπὶ τῶν κυμάτων <u>πορεύεσθαι</u> καθάπερ ἐπὶ τῆς γῆς.[25]

Orion. Hesiod says he is the son of Euryale, the daughter of Minos, and Poseidon, and that it was given to him as a gift <u>to travel</u> over the waves just as over land.

---

[21] In fact, Apollonius's *Argonautica* appears to allude to just such a tradition. The Argonauts proceed from the Syrtes to Libya in search of water and light upon the Garden of the Hesperides, which Heracles had raided only a day earlier (4.1396–1401). Apollonius indicates that Heracles, too, came to the garden "traveling the land on foot, parched with thirst" (χθόνα πεζὸς ὁδεύων, | δίψῃ καρχαλέος, 4.1441–1442), so Seneca's allusion to Hercules's shipwreck on the Syrtes should probably be situated immediately before his theft of the golden apples.

[22] An allusion to water walking also makes less dramatic sense of Amphitryon's answer to Megara's question: the "way" that Hercules will return home is via his tremendous endurance, which, in the context of his labors, is to be emphasized over the ease afforded by superhuman abilities.

[23] Servius is clarifying the idea that seems to inform Vergil's description of Orion cutting a path through the sea, in which he rises above the waves at his shoulder (*umero supereminet undas*, *Aen.* 10.765; the text of Vergil comes from H. R. Fairclough, trans. and ed., *Virgil*, rev. G. P. Goold, 2 vols., LCL [Cambridge: Harvard University Press, 1999–2000]).

[24] Yarbro Collins, *Mark*, 330; Boring, Berger, and Colpe, *Hellenistic Commentary*, 99.

[25] The text of Hesiod (Pseudo-Eratosthenes) comes from Glenn W. Most, ed. and trans., *Hesiod*, 2 vols., LCL (Cambridge: Harvard University Press, 2006–2007). The scholia ad Nicander, *Ther.* 15 and ad Aratus, *Phaen.* 322 are virtually identical to this fragment.

Both then cite a passage from the *Bibliotheca*, a mythography probably from the first or second century CE once attributed to Apollodorus of Athens (Pseudo-Apollodorus, *Bib.* 1.4.3):

τοῦτον γηγενῆ λέγουσιν ὑπερμεγέθη τὸ σῶμα· Φερεκύδης δὲ αὐτὸν Ποσειδῶνος καὶ Εὐρυάλης λέγει. ἐδωρήσατο δὲ αὐτῷ Ποσειδῶν <u>διαβαίνειν</u> τὴν θάλασσαν.[26]

> They say that he [Orion] was Earth-born and gigantic in stature; but Pherecydes says that he was born of Poseidon and Euryale. Poseidon bestowed upon him the ability <u>to cross</u> the sea.

In both cases, Yarbro Collins and Boring et al. cite Loeb translations that use "walking" terminology.[27] Regarding Euphemus, Yarbro Collins also cites from the scholia to Pindar, ancient commentarial material probably epitomized in the second century CE but with roots in earlier Alexandrian scholarship.[28] Yarbro Collins paraphrases the key words herself as "travel over the sea" or "pass across the sea" (scholium ad Pindar, *Pyth.* 4.61):[29]

φησὶ γοῦν αὐτὸς δῶρον ἔχειν τὸν Εὔφημον παρὰ Ποσειδῶνος, τὴν θάλασσαν ἀπημάντως <u>διαπορεύεσθαι</u> ὡς διὰ γῆς.[30]

> He [Asclepiades] says that Euphemus possessed a gift from Poseidon: <u>to travel</u> across the sea unharmed as if across land.

In all of these cases, the special ability of Orion or Euphemus may loosely be translated as to "walk" or "stride" across the sea as the two Loeb translators have done, likely unaware of the need for any special exactitude. But, in fact, the verbs used (πορεύεσθαι, διαπορεύεσθαι, διαβαίνειν) all have a much wider semantic range. For πορεύομαι, Danker's lexicon offers a primary meaning of "to move over an area, gener. with a point of departure or destination specified, *go, proceed, travel*"; for διαπορεύομαι, "of movement by way of someth., *go, walk through*," or "of movement

---

[26] The text of Pseudo-Apollodorus comes from James George Frazer, ed. and trans., *Apollodorus, The Library, with an English Translation*, 2 vols., LCL (London: Heinemann, 1921).

[27] For the Hesiod fragment, both Yarbro Collins and Boring et al. cite Hugh G. Evelyn-White, who translates "there was given [Orion] as a gift the power of walking upon the waves as though upon land" (*Hesiod: The Homeric Hymns and Homerica*, LCL [Cambridge: Harvard University Press, 1914], 71). For the Pseudo-Apollodorus passage, Yarbro Collins quotes Frazer, who offers, "Poseidon bestowed on him the power of striding across the sea" (*Apollodorus*, 31), but Boring et al. give their own translation of the critical phrase: "to walk through the sea" (*Hellenistic Commentary*, 99). I should note that the current Loeb edition for Hesiod similarly translates, "the gift of walking on the waves just like upon the land" (Most, *Hesiod*, 2:317).

[28] Eleanor Dickie, *Ancient Greek Scholarship* (Oxford: Oxford University Press, 2007), 39.

[29] Yarbro Collins, "Rulers, Divine Men," 215; Yarbro Collins, *Mark*, 329.

[30] The text of Pindar's scholia comes from A. B. Drachmann, ed., *Scholia Vetera in Pindari Carmina*, 3 vols. (Amsterdam: Hakkert, 1964). Tzetzes ad Lycophron 886 is virtually identical to this scholium. The Asclepiades cited as authority for this tradition is probably the fourth-century BCE mythographer from Tragilus.

from one part or locality to another within a geographical area, *pass through*"; and for διαβαίνω, "to proceed from one side to another over a geographical area, *go through, cross*."³¹ These words refer to the fact of travel in general, which could embrace any of the types of movement I have brought up thus far, or even others. For example, Heb 11:29 uses a form of διαβαίνειν for the Israelites crossing the Red Sea (Πίστει διέβησαν τὴν ἐρυθρὰν θάλασσαν ὡς διὰ ξηρᾶς γῆς), but this miracle involves walking between walls of the water of a divided sea.³² More to the point, Hyginus, *Poet. astr.* 2.34 directly translates Pseudo-Eratosthenes, *Catast.* 32 into Latin, and this ancient reader, at least, understood the verb to refer to running:

Ὠρίων. τοῦτον Ἡσίοδός φησιν Εὐρυάλης τῆς Μίνωος καὶ Ποσειδῶνος εἶναι, δοθῆναι δὲ αὐτῷ δωρεὰν ὥστε ἐπὶ τῶν κυμάτων <u>πορεύεσθαι</u> καθάπερ ἐπὶ τῆς γῆς.

Orion. Hesiod says that he is the son of Euryale, the daughter of Minos, and Poseidon, and that it was given to him as a gift <u>to travel</u> over the waves just as over land.

Orion. Hunc Hesiodus Neptuni filium dicit ex Euryale Minois filia natum; concessum autem ei ut supra fluctus <u>curreret</u> ut in terra ...³³

Orion. Hesiod says that he is the son of Neptune by Euryale, the daughter of Minos; moreover, it was granted to him <u>to run</u> over waves as on land ...

The vague language of these texts does not absolutely rule out walking on water, but in light of the mainstream traditions surrounding these figures and the absence of water walking in Greco-Roman myth, other translations should be preferred. The phenomenon of Jesus's walking on the sea, strongly distinguished by the verb περιπατέω, remains unparalleled.

There are, however, two final figures to consider. Unlike the candidates analyzed above, these are genuine water walkers, but they nevertheless cannot represent a viable Greco-Roman background for Jesus's water walking. First, Yarbro Collins advances an aside from the fourth-century emperor Julian (*Or.* 7.219d):

... καὶ τὴν δι' αὐτοῦ πορείαν οἶμαι τοῦ πελάγους ἐπὶ τῆς χρυσῆς κύλικος, ἣν ἐγὼ νομίζω μὰ τοὺς θεοὺς οὐ κύλικα εἶναι, <u>βαδίσαι</u> δὲ αὐτὸν ὡς ἐπὶ ξηρᾶς τῆς θαλάττης νενόμικα. τί γὰρ ἄπορον ἦν Ἡρακλεῖ;³⁴

... and of course [Heracles's fortitude is evident in] his passage across the sea itself on a golden cup, concerning which I myself think, by the gods, that there was no

---

³¹ BDAG, s.vv. πορεύω, διαπορεύομαι, and διαβαίνω.

³² Herodotus's word for Xerxes's crossing the pontoon bridge built over the sea on his chariot is likewise a form of διαβαίνειν (*Hist.* 7.35.2).

³³ The text of Hyginus's *De astronomia* comes from Ghislaine Viré, ed., *Hyginus, De Astronomia* (Stuttgart: Teubner, 1992).

³⁴ The text of Julian comes from Wilmer Cave Wright, ed. and trans., *The Works of the Emperor Julian, with an English Translation*, 2 vols. LCL (London: Heinemann, 1913).

cup, but I believe he walked on the sea as if on dry land. For what was impossible for Heracles?

This passage does accurately reflect Heracles's traditional association with the performance of ἀδύνατα, impossible feats, and water walking is after all impossible. Even so, there are compelling reasons to doubt that Julian here preserves an authentic tradition of Heracles as a water walker. First, Julian cites the standard version of the myth that appears in all other ancient sources, in which Heracles indeed sails to the west in the sun god's golden kylix.[35] Second, Julian does not cite an authority for his own belief that Heracles walked on water; instead, he acknowledges that the idea is idiosyncratic by introducing his opinion with first person singular verbs (νομίζω, νενόμικα), the first of which he emphasizes with the first person singular pronoun (ἐγώ): "I *myself* think."[36] And, finally, because he deviates from the traditional myth, Julian preempts potential objections with the rhetorical question, "For what was impossible for Heracles?" The conceit is "perhaps a passing sneer at the Christians" by the ardently anti-Christian emperor, attributing to Heracles one of Jesus's most distinctive miracles.[37] In any case, given its idiosyncrasy, this late passage does not pass on a genuine tradition of Heracles walking on the sea.

Second, among the absurdities that Lucian invents in his *Philopseudes* ("Lover of Lies") is a Hyperborean magician seen to fly through the air, walk on water (ἐφ' ὕδατος βαδίζοντα), and walk slowly through fire (*Philops.* 13). The magician's one feat does parallel Jesus's, but he is also Lucian's own creation, designed to parody the supernatural (if not the Christian story itself), rather than a genuine mythical figure. In a similar vein, Lucian's Phellopodes ("Corkfeet"), a race of men who run on the sea on feet made of cork (*Ver. hist.* 2.4),[38] represent the author's keen imagination, not a traditional tale. As early as the *Odyssey,* traveling overseas on foot was regarded as a typically impossible task,[39] and Dio Chrysostom, *Troj.* 129 classes walking on the sea (βαδίζειν ἐπὶ τῆς θαλάττης) among the stuff of dreams and

---

[35] On this myth, see Timothy Gantz, *Early Greek Myth: A Guide to Literary and Artistic Sources* (Baltimore: Johns Hopkins University Press, 1993), 404–6.

[36] Cf. LSJ, s.v. ἐγώ: "I at least, for my part, indeed, for myself."

[37] Wright, *Works of the Emperor Julian*, 2:111 n. 4.

[38] Interestingly, although the substance composing their feet is naturally buoyant, the Phellopodes are initially represented running alongside the narrator's ship, not floating on the water. This feature probably better aligns them with the mythical water runners targeted by Lucian's parody. At the end of their brief appearance, however, they turn away and apparently begin to walk (ἐβάδιζον).

[39] When islanders interview strangers at various points in the poem, they formulaically ask how they arrived at the island—"for I hardly suppose you came here on foot" (οὐ μὲν γὰρ τί σε πεζὸν ὀίομαι ἐνθάδ' ἰκέσθαι, *Od.* 1.173; 14.190; 16.60, 224; cf. *Il.* 15.504–505). *Odyssey* 11.158–159 spells out what the other scenes leave unsaid: one would rather need a ship to cross the sea. Cf. the presence of the disciples' ship in the Gospel pericope, which juxtaposes "conventional reality" with Jesus's marvelous walk on the sea (Young, *Subversive Symmetry*, 120).

"incredible lies" (ἀπιθάνοις ψεύσμασιν).[40] Lucian's Hyperborean is therefore outrageous, and the spoof may well reflect the skeptical response the evangelical account garnered in certain circles. It cannot, however, help us to understand the genesis of the evangelical episode. Both of the bona fide Greco-Roman water walkers turn out to be isolated inventions of the Common Era, perhaps inspired by the Christian story itself.

Men, women, gods, and beasts with the power to run or fly over water turn out to be rather common in Greek and Roman mythology, but water walking is not represented by any extant mythological tradition. For a gentile audience receiving the evangelists' stories, Jesus's feat was something new in the realm of supernatural wonders.[41] It may seem that I am splitting hairs by insisting on the distinction between running or flying and walking over water. As Wendy J. Cotter observes, in order to interpret a miracle story,

> the miraculous deed needs a backdrop of similar miracles performed by gods and/or heroes, traditions well known to the ordinary person, Jewish or non-Jewish, who lived in the Mediterranean world. From that set of stories and the significances regularly claimed for them it is possible to create a set of meanings against which the Jesus miracle can be placed to understand the parameters of his power and the meaning of that power.[42]

Poseidon, Orion, Euphemus, and the rest provide such a backdrop for audiences familiar with them, as all types of miraculous locomotion above water are basically similar. But in this instance the differences between Jesus's miracle and that of his Greco-Roman analogues are more significant than the similarities for the way in which ancient audiences would have received the water-walking story. In the Greco-Roman examples I have cited, the means by which someone runs or flies over water is more or less explained: the mares of Erichthonius are so fast that they can run on water; Hermes and Pythagoras have special devices that allow them to fly over the sea; Euphemus and Orion's ability represents the gift of their father Poseidon. In Jesus's case, however, one explanation for his ability to walk on water, that he is a ghost (φάντασμα, Mark 6:49, Matt 14:26), is mistaken, and no alternative

---

[40] The text of Dio Chrysostom comes from J. W. Cohoon and H. Lamar Crosby, eds. and trans., *Dio Chrysostom,* 5 vols., LCL (Cambridge: Harvard University Press, 1932–1951). For walking on the sea as a subject of dreams, see Yarbro Collins, "Rulers, Divine Men," 221–23; Yarbro Collins, *Mark,* 332; Wendy Cotter, *Miracles in Greco-Roman Antiquity: A Sourcebook for the Study of New Testament Miracle Stories* (London: Routledge, 1999), 162–63.

[41] I use the term *gentile* here and below as a shorthand to refer to any audience familiar with Greco-Roman traditions but unfamiliar with Hebraic traditions, which do include examples of water walking (e.g., Job 9:8 LXX). In fact, knowledge of either set of traditions is not exclusive to Jews or to non-Jews.

[42] Wendy J. Cotter, *The Christ of the Miracle Stories: Portrait through Encounter* (Grand Rapids: Baker Academic, 2010), 2.

explanation is given, at least not in the Markan and Johannine accounts.⁴³ In the terms of Vernon K. Robbins's sociorhetorical interpretation, the narration is "rhetographic," or pictorial, offering the image of Jesus simply "walking on the sea" while leaving the audience to induce on their own the "Rule" or premise explaining how he can do so.⁴⁴ The effect of such "thaumaturgical miracle discourse," in the words of L. Gregory Bloomquist, "is often confusion and wonder and uncertainty about how exactly the miracle came about."⁴⁵ In fact, this is the response modeled in Mark by the internal audience, the disciples, who are "utterly astonished" (λίαν [ἐκ περισσοῦ] ἐν ἑαυτοῖς ἐξίσταντο, 6:51) "because they did not understand about the loaves" (οὐ γὰρ συνῆκαν ἐπὶ τοῖς ἄρτοις, 6:52). One of the principal effects of the narration is thus to provoke questioning—how or by what power can Jesus walk on the sea? And, more importantly, who is Jesus that he possesses this power?⁴⁶

Mark and John do not answer, and different audiences may infer different solutions. For example, certain allusions in the text will have been suggestive for

---

⁴³ On the absurdity of the ghost explanation, see Combs, "Ghost on the Water?" Matthew implies that Jesus is able to walk on water because he is "truly a son of God" (ἀληθῶς θεοῦ υἱός, 14:33), as his disciples acclaim him when he climbs aboard the boat, while Peter's (in)ability to imitate Jesus's miracle is related to the amount of faith that he possesses (14:31).

⁴⁴ According to Robbins, such rhetography and inductive reasoning are generally characteristic of early Christian miracle discourse. For a survey of miracles in the Synoptic Gospels analyzed in these terms, see his essay "Sociorhetorical Interpretation of Miracle Discourse in the Synoptic Gospels," in *Miracle Discourse in the New Testament*, ed. Duane F. Watson (Atlanta: Society of Biblical Literature, 2012), 17–84.

⁴⁵ L. Gregory Bloomquist, "The Role of Argumentation in the Miracle Stories of Luke-Acts: Toward a Fuller Identification of Miracle Discourse for Use in Sociorhetorical Interpretation," in Watson, *Miracle Discourse in the New Testament*, 85–124. In this essay Bloomquist distinguishes between "thaumaturgical" miracle discourse, which involves a petition to the deity for help that manifests in a way that is neither controllable nor fully explicable, and "gnostic-manipulationist" miracle discourse, which involves coercing the divine into one's service via certain techniques like special rituals or formulas. The former, which is more characteristic of early Christian miracle discourse, tends to employ paradigmatic or inductive reasoning, while the latter is given to logical or deductive reasoning.

⁴⁶ As Paul J. Achtemeier notes, "A careful study of the miracles will indicate that the significance lies, not in the acts themselves but in the *person* who performs them" (*Jesus and the Miracle Tradition* [Eugene, OR: Cascade, 2008], 2). He adduces the conclusion of the storm-stilling pericope (Mark 4:41, Matt 8:27, Luke 8:25), a similar "nature miracle," by way of illustration: "The reaction of the disciples to this miracle—'Who then is this?'—indicates that it was the person of Jesus which holds the significance" (ibid.). Cf. John P. Meier's interpretation of Mark 6:52, which explains the disciples' astonished reaction to Jesus's water walking: "'for they did not understand [the mystery of who Jesus is] on the basis of [*epi*] the [miracle of the] loaves, but their heart was hardened'" (*Mentor, Message, and Miracles*, vol. 2 of *A Marginal Jew: Rethinking the Historical Jesus*, ABRL [New York: Doubleday, 1994], 907; brackets original). I agree with Meier, among others, in classifying the water-walking miracle as an "epiphany" story, the climax of which is Jesus's self-identification ἐγώ εἰμι, "It is I" or literally, "I am" (Mark 6:50, Matt 14:27, John 6:20), a formula with strong resonances in the Jewish tradition; see the next note.

audiences familiar with the Septuagint,[47] while references to walking on water in certain magical texts suggest that some may have interpreted the act as the feat of a magician.[48] But, as I have shown here, the description of the miracle rules out the explanations that would first occur to an auditor versed in Greco-Roman mythology: Jesus does not use extraordinary speed or a flying device in this episode. The miracle would thus strike a gentile audience as particularly marvelous and incomprehensible. In fact, insofar as Jesus's miracle lacks a clear mechanism and thus seems more "impossible" than the feats of his Greco-Roman analogues, it may have also seemed more impressive and perhaps indicative of greater power. But at the very least, the novelty of this miracle story would have encouraged gentile audiences to keep reading or to keep listening in hopes of learning just who this water walker was and how he could perform such a wonder.

---

[47] On the Jewish background of the water-walking pericope, see, e.g., Meier, *Mentor, Message, and Miracles*, 914–19; Madden, *Jesus' Walking on the Sea*, 62–71.

[48] See Yarbro Collins, "Rulers, Divine Men," 220–21; Yarbro Collins, *Mark*, 331; cf. Lucian's Hyperborean magician.

New and Recent Titles

FOUNDATIONS FOR SOCIORHETORICAL EXPLORATION
A Rhetoric of Religious Antiquity Reader
Vernon K. Robbins, Robert H. von Thaden Jr., and Bart B. Bruehler, editors
Paperback $65.95, 978-1-62837-142-0 Forthcoming, 2016 Code: 067103
Hardcover $85.95, 978-0-88414-169-3 E-book $65.95, 978-0-88414-168-6
Rhetoric of Religious Antiquity 4

EXPLORING PHILEMON
Freedom, Brotherhood, and Partnership in the New Society
Roy R. Jeal
Paper $30.95, 978-0-88414-091-7 262 pages, 2015 Code: 067101
Hardcover $45.95, 978-0-88414-093-1 E-book $30.95, 978-0-88414-092-4
Rhetoric of Religious Antiquity 2

LYDIA AS A RHETORICAL CONSTRUCT IN ACTS
Alexandra Gruca-Macaulay
Paperback $45.95, 978-1-62837-137-6 336 pages, 2016 Code: 064818
Hardcover $60.95, 978-0-88414-160-0 E-book $45.95, 978-0-88414-159-4
Emory Studies in Early Christianity 18

RELIGIOUS COMPETITION IN THE GRECO-ROMAN WORLD
Nathaniel DesRosiers and Lily C. Vuong, editors
Paperback $34.95, 978-1-62837-136-9 346 pages, 2016 Code: 064210
Hardcover $49.95, 978-0-88414-158-7 E-book $34.95, 978-0-88414-157-0
Writings from the Greco-Roman World Supplements 10

THE SBL HANDBOOK OF STYLE, SECOND EDITION
Hardcover $39.95, 978-1-58983-964-9 E-book $39.95, 978-1-58983-965-6

SBL Press • P.O. Box 2243 • Williston, VT 05495-2243
Phone: 877-725-3334 (toll-free) or 802-864-6185 • Fax: 802-864-7626
Order online at www.sbl-site.org/publications

Cruciform Discipleship: The Narrative Function of the Women in Mark 15–16

JEFFREY W. AERNIE
jeff.aernie@gmail.com
Charles Sturt University, North Parramatta NSW 2151, Australia

The purpose of the present essay is to argue for a thematic convergence between Mark and Paul by focusing on the literary function of the named women in Mark 15–16. First, I reconsider the seemingly unexpected conclusion of the Gospel at Mark 16:8, which appears to describe the women's fearful and disobedient flight from the tomb. In contrast to the frequent negative view of their role in the narrative, I offer a positive assessment of the women's role as exemplars of Markan discipleship. Second, I describe how Mark's portrayal of these women as faithful disciples coheres with the theme of cruciform discipleship developed in Pauline theology. The intent of these two steps is to demonstrate that the function of the women in Mark's narrative provides another thematic link between Markan and Pauline theology.

The argument for an intracanonical relationship between Mark and Paul has been proposed since at least the middle of the nineteenth century. Perhaps the seminal contribution to the conversation was the publication of a volume in 1857 entitled *Die Religion Jesu*, by the German scholar Gustav Volkmar.[1] Although Volkmar's monograph argued for a connection between the evangelist and the apostle, he developed the link primarily through the thesis that Mark's Gospel was in fact an allegory in which Jesus represented Paul. Apart from the somewhat positive assessment of Volkmar's work in William Wrede's seminal volume *Das Messiasgeheimnis in den Evangelien*, Volkmar's allegorical arguments have largely been set aside.[2] The strongest opposition to Volkmar's hypothesis was mounted in

---

[1] Gustav Volkmar, *Die Religion Jesu und ihre erste Entwichelung nach dem gegenwärtigen Stande der Wissenschaft* (Leipzig: Brockhaus, 1857).

[2] William Wrede, *Das Messiasgeheimnis in den Evangelien: Zugleich ein Beitrag zum Verständnis des Markusevangeliums*, 4th ed. (Göttingen: Vandenhoeck & Ruprecht, 1969); Eng. trans. *The Messianic Secret*, trans. J. C. G. Greig (Cambridge: James Clarke, 1971). Cf. P. N. Tarazi, *Paul and Mark*, vol. 1 of *The New Testament Introduction* (New York: St. Vladimir's Seminary Press, 1999), 111–237.

779

Martin Werner's 1923 monograph *Der Einfluss paulinischer Theologie im Markusevangelium*.[3] Werner used Volkmar's admittedly odd claims not only to discredit the interpretation of Mark's Gospel as a Pauline allegory but also to argue that there was no immediate connection between Mark and Paul. Werner's thesis has been influential within New Testament scholarship.[4] James Crossley, for example, echoes Werner's major thesis that similarities between Markan and Pauline theology may reflect a shared narrative in early Christianity but not necessarily any form of direct correspondence such as personal interaction or intentional interpretation.[5]

By contrast, Joel Marcus has emphasized the theological and literary connections between Mark and Paul.[6] In assessing both similarities and differences between the two authors, Marcus contends,

---

[3] Martin Werner, *Die Einfluss paulinischer Theologie im Markusevangelium: Eine Studie zur neutestamentlichen Theologie*, BZNW 1 (Giessen: Töpelmann, 1923).

[4] For a helpful summary of Werner's thesis and its impact, see Joel Marcus, "Mark—Interpreter of Paul," *NTS* 46 (2000): 473–87, http://dx.doi.org/10.1017/S0028688500000278.

[5] James Crossley, "Mark, Paul, and the Question of Influences," in *Paul and the Gospels: Christologies, Conflicts, and Convergences*, ed. Michael F. Bird and Joel Willitts, LNTS 411 (London: T&T Clark, 2011), 10–29.

[6] Marcus, "Mark—Interpreter of Paul," 473–87; Joel Marcus, *Mark: A New Translation with Introduction and Commentary*, 2 vols., AB 27, 27A (New York: Doubleday, 2000–2009), 1:73–75. In addition to the scholars discussed below, others who have argued for some form of correlation between Mark and Paul include Benjamin Wisner Bacon, *The Gospel of Mark: Its Composition and Date* (New Haven: Yale University Press, 1925); John C. Fenton, "Paul and Mark," in *Studies in the Gospels: Essays in Memory of R. H. Lightfoot*, ed. Dennis E. Nineham (Oxford: Blackwell, 1957), 89–112; Michael D. Goulder, "Those Outside (Mk. 4.10–12)," *NovT* (1991): 289–302, http://dx.doi.org/10.1163/156853691X00097; Goulder, "Jesus' Resurrection and Christian Origins: A Response to N. T. Wright," *JSHJ* 3 (2005): 187–95, http://dx.doi.org/10.1177/1476869005058195; Heikki Räisänen, "Jesus and the Food Laws: Reflections on Mark 7.15," in *Jesus, Paul and Torah: Collected Essays*, trans. David E. Orton, JSNTSup 43 (Sheffield: JSOT Press, 1992), 127–48; Wolfgang Schenk, "Sekundäre Jesuanisierungen von primären Paulus-Aussagen bei Markus," in *The Four Gospels 1992: Festschrift Frans Neirynck*, ed. F. Van Segbroeck et al., 3 vols., BETL 100 (Leuven: Leuven University Press, 1992), 2:877–904; David Seeley, "Rulership and Service in Mark 10:41–45," *NovT* 35 (1993): 234–50, http://dx.doi.org/10.1163/156853693X00158; W. R. Telford, *The Theology of the Gospel of Mark*, New Testament Theology (Cambridge: Cambridge University Press, 1999), 164–69, http://dx.doi.org/10.1017/CBO9781139163750; Eric Kun Chun Wong, *Evangelien im Dialog mit Paulus: Eine intertextuelle Studie zu den Synoptikern*, NTOA/SUNT 89 (Göttingen: Vandenhoeck & Ruprecht, 2012), esp. 61–130. See also the recent multivolume comparison of the evangelist and the apostle in Oda Wischmeyer, David C. Sim, and Ian J. Elmer, eds., *Two Authors at the Beginning of Christianity*, part 1 of *Paul and Mark: Comparative Essays*, BZNW 198 (Berlin: de Grutyer, 2014); and Eve-Marie Becker, Troels Engberg-Pedersen, and Mogens Müller, eds., *For and against Pauline Influence on Mark*, part 2 of *Mark and Paul: Comparative Essays*, BZNW 199 (Berlin: de Grutyer, 2014), http://dx.doi.org/10.1515/9783110314694.

The most reasonable conclusion would seem to be that Mark writes in the Pauline sphere of activity and shows some sort of Pauline influence on his thought, although he is not a member of a "Pauline school" ... neither is he hermetically sealed off from the influence of Paul, and as a matter of fact in some ways is quite close to him.[7]

To argue for a more specific relationship between Mark and Paul, Marcus, Michael Bird, Clifton Black, and Jesper Tang Nielsen have focused primarily on the prominent role of the theology of the cross for both authors.[8] They demonstrate that Paul's epistolary focus on the theological impact of Jesus as a crucified Messiah and Mark's explicit narrative focus on the cross reflect a shared conceptual and theological worldview. In addition, Michael J. Gorman has suggested that the way in which Mark and Paul formulate the outworking of their emphasis on the cross—namely, its impact on the nature of Christian discipleship—also reflects a shared theological distinctive.[9] Both Mark and Paul establish the cross as paradigmatic for the lives of Jesus's followers, thereby emphasizing cruciform discipleship.

The present article will offer a further piece of evidence for the thematic convergence between Mark and Paul by focusing on the literary function of the named women in Mark 15–16—Mary Magdalene, Mary the mother of James the younger and Joses, and Salome.[10] My primary thesis is that the women in Mark 15–16 function as narrative exemplars of the cruciform discipleship that is a shared thematic emphasis in the theology of Mark and Paul. The first step in developing this thesis involves a reexamination of the literary enigma that constitutes the ending of Mark's Gospel.[11] Most important for the present argument is Mark 16:8, which

---

[7] Marcus, *Mark*, 1:75.

[8] Michael F. Bird, "Mark: Interpreter of Peter and Disciple of Paul," in Bird and Willitts, *Paul and the Gospels*, 30–61, esp. 39–43; C. Clifton Black, "Christ Crucified in Paul and in Mark: Reflections on an Intracanonical Conversation," in *Theology and Ethics in Paul and His Interpreters: Essays in Honor of Victor Paul Furnish*, ed. Eugene H. Lovering and Jerry L. Sumney (Nashville: Abingdon, 1996), 80–104; Marcus, "Mark—Interpreter of Paul," 479–81; Jesper Tang Nielsen, "The Cross on the Way to Mark," in Becker, Engberg-Pedersen, and Müller, *Mark and Paul*, 273–94, http://dx.doi.org/10.1515/9783110314694.273. Cf. Morna Hooker, *Not Ashamed of the Gospel: New Testament Interpretations of the Death of Christ* (Grand Rapids: Eerdmans, 1994), 47–49; Udo Schnelle, "Paulinische und markinische Christologie im Vergleich," in Wischmeyer, Sim, and Elmer, *Paul and Mark*, 283–311, esp. 304–7, http://dx.doi.org/10.1515/9783110272826.283.

[9] Michael J. Gorman, *The Death of the Messiah and the Birth of the New Covenant: A (Not So) New Model of the Atonement* (Eugene, OR: Wipf & Stock, 2014), esp. 33–36, 81–94, 106–11, 114–27.

[10] Although the specific identities of the women are not unimportant, I am concerned primarily with the literary function of the women as a group. For a concise introduction to the historical identity of the women, see Adela Yarbro Collins, *Mark: A Commentary*, Hermeneia (Minneapolis: Fortress, 2007), 774–75.

[11] For a survey of the way in which scholars have understood the literary enigma of Mark's ending, see Ira Brent Driggers, *Following God through Mark: Theological Tension in the Second*

seemingly describes the women fleeing from the tomb in fearful and disobedient silence and failing to report the message of restoration offered in light of Jesus's resurrection:

> καὶ ἐξελθοῦσαι ἔφυγον ἀπὸ τοῦ μνημείου, εἶχεν γὰρ αὐτὰς τρόμος καὶ ἔκστασις· καὶ οὐδενὶ οὐδὲν εἶπαν, ἐφοβοῦντο γάρ.
>
> So they went out and fled from the tomb, for terror and amazement had seized them; and they said nothing to anyone, for they were afraid. (NRSV)

In contrast to the frequent negative assessment of their role in the narrative, I offer a positive assessment of the women's role as exemplars of Markan discipleship.[12] The second step in the argument is to describe how Mark's portrayal of the women as faithful disciples coordinates with the theme of cruciform discipleship developed in Pauline theology. The intent of these two steps is to offer a coherent analysis of the function of the women in Mark's narrative in order to provide evidence for another thematic link between Markan and Pauline theology.[13]

Gospel (Louisville: Westminster John Knox, 2007), 86–96; and Joel F. Williams, "Literary Approaches to the End of Mark's Gospel," *JETS* 42 (1999): 21–35. For the present article, I assume that Mark 16:8 represents the *intentional* ending of the Gospel. For a survey of the text-critical issues, see Kurt Aland, "Bemerkungen zum Schluss des Markusevangeliums," in *Neotestamentica et Semitica: Essays in Honour of Matthew Black*, ed. E. Earle Ellis and M. Wilcox (Edinburgh: T&T Clark, 1969), 157–80; Kurt Aland, "Der Schluss des Markusevangeliums," in *L'Évangile selon Marc: Tradition et rédaction*, ed. M. Sabbe; 2nd ed., BETL 34 (Leuven: Leuven University Press, 1974), 435–70; N. Clayton Croy, *The Mutilation of Mark's Gospel* (Nashville: Abingdon, 2003); Steven Lynn Cox, *A History and Critique of Scholarship concerning the Markan Endings* (Lewiston, NY: Mellen Biblical Press, 1993); James A. Kelhoffer, *Miracle and Mission: The Authentication of Missionaries and Their Message in the Longer Ending of Mark*, WUNT 2/112 (Tübingen: Mohr Siebeck, 2000); Bruce M. Metzger, *A Textual Commentary on the Greek New Testament: A Companion Volume to the United Bible Societies' Greek New Testament (Fourth rev. ed.)*, 2nd ed. (Stuttgart: Deutsche Bibelgesellschaft, 1994), 102–6; Robert H. Stein, "The Ending of Mark," *BBR* 18 (2008): 79–98. For a substantive argument in support of Mark 16:9–20 as the original ending, see Nicholas P. Lunn, *The Original Ending of Mark: A New Case for the Authenticity of Mark 16:9–20* (Eugene, OR: Pickwick, 2014).

[12] The positive assessment of the women developed here is dependent in large part on the constructive proposal advanced by Larry W. Hurtado; see esp. his "The Women, the Tomb, and the Climax of Mark," in *A Wandering Galilean: Essays in Honour of Seán Freyne*, ed. Zuleika Rodgers, with Margaret Daly-Denton and Anne Fitzpatrick McKinley, JSJSup 132 (Leiden: Brill, 2009), 427–50, http://dx.doi.org/10.1163/ej.9789004173552.i-622.122.

[13] The aim, therefore, is not to argue that Mark is repackaging a particular dimension of Pauline theology, but rather to highlight the intersection between Paul's rhetorical emphasis on the cross and its similar importance for the narrative structure of Mark's Gospel. For the notion that the emphasis on the cross in Mark and Paul may have originated independently, see Michael Kok, "Does Mark Narrate the Pauline Kerygma of 'Christ Crucified'? Challenging an Emerging Consensus on Mark as a Pauline Gospel," *JSNT* 37 (2014): 139–60, http://dx.doi.org/10.1177/0142064X14558021.

I. Faithful Exemplars of Markan Discipleship

The interpretation of Mark 16:1–8 as a negative portrayal of the women at the tomb has at times been used to argue that they were not in fact understood by Mark to be disciples of Jesus.[14] Yet, even if the final act of the women described in Mark 16:8 is one of fearful disobedience, their introduction into the narrative in 15:40–41 is evidence of Mark's intentional portrayal of them as disciples. In particular, Mark's assertion that the three named women, along with a much larger group of women, were following (ἠκολούθουν) and serving (διηκόνουν) Jesus throughout his ministry suggests a close connection between their role in the narrative and earlier instances of Jesus's specific teaching on the nature of discipleship, in which the themes of both following and serving play an essential role (i.e., ἀκολυθέω in 8:34–37; διακονέω in 10:42–45).[15] The women's delayed introduction into the narrated events of the Gospel suggests an attempt not to silence their importance in the narrative but rather to emphasize it.[16] The male disciples have abandoned Jesus (14:50–52) and the reader is now introduced to an alternative group of followers.

Interpreters often connect the disciples and the women in terms of broad parallels, such as a perceived narrative arc from faithfulness to failure, and in terms of specific linguistic connections between the story of these women and the preceding narrative of the Gospel.[17] The portraits of the two groups, however, are not uniform. There is both a rhetorical connection between the disciples and the women, and a rhetorical contrast between them. Interpreters are certainly right to see a linguistic connection between the initial description of the women's geographic position at Jesus's crucifixion and Peter's position at Jesus's trial (14:54),

---

[14] See, e.g., Winsome Munro, "Women Disciples in Mark?" *CBQ* 44 (1982): 225–41.

[15] For a discussion of Mark's development of these terms, see Hisako Kinukawa, *Women and Jesus in Mark: A Japanese Feminist Perspective*, Bible and Liberation (Maryknoll, NY: Orbis, 1994), 96–102. See also Ben Witherington III, *Women in the Ministry of Jesus: A Study of Jesus' Attitudes to Women and Their Roles as Reflected in His Earthly Life*, SNTSMS 51 (Cambridge: Cambridge University Press, 1984), http://dx.doi.org/10.1017/CBO9780511520501.

[16] See esp. Hurtado, "Women, the Tomb," 431 n. 20. For the alternative view that Mark intentionally suppressed the role of the women in the narrative, see Munro, "Women Disciples," 225–41.

[17] See, e.g., James A. Kelhoffer, "A Tale of Two Markan Characterizations: The Exemplary Woman Who Anointed Jesus' Body for Burial (14:3–9) and the Silent Trio Who Fled the Empty Tomb (Mark 16:1–8)," in *Women and Gender in Ancient Religions: Interdisciplinary Approaches*, ed. Stephen P. Ahearne-Kroll, Paul A. Holloway, and James A. Kelhoffer, WUNT 263 (Tübingen: Mohr Siebeck, 2010), 85–98; Elizabeth Struthers Malbon, "Fallible Followers: Women and Men in the Gospel of Mark," *Semeia* 28 (1983): 29–48; Francis J. Moloney, *The Gospel of Mark* (Grand Rapids: Baker Academic, 2002), 349; Mary Ann Tolbert, *Sowing the Gospel: Mark's World in Literary-Historical Perspective* (Minneapolis: Fortress, 1989), 288–99.

given Mark's repeated use of the phrase ἀπὸ μακρόθεν ("from a distance").[18] To assert, however, that Mark's description of the women's geographic distance parallels that of Peter and therefore implies the same negative emphasis developed in Peter's situation does not account for the narrative movement of each scene.[19] The negative assessment of Peter's geographic position ἀπὸ μακρόθεν becomes clear only in connection with the wider context concerning his threefold denial (14:66–72) and his subsequent physical absence from the narrative. Peter begins by following Jesus ἀπὸ μακρόθεν and then eventually moves *farther* away from him. In contrast, Mark portrays the women at the crucifixion observing events from a similar distance but then develops their *continued* presence in the narrative. The women follow Jesus's body to its burial site (15:47) and then return on the first day of the week in an apparent demonstration of their continued devotion (16:1). The linguistic connection between the two passages is indeed important, but it does not serve to align the women with Peter. Rather, it functions to create a distinction between them. The women do not move farther away from Jesus, but closer to him.

This contrast also qualifies the potential allusion to Ps 37:12 LXX in Mark's use of the phrase ἀπὸ μακρόθεν.[20] If Mark intends to highlight a connection between the passion narrative and the plight of the righteous sufferer in Ps 37 LXX, whose closest companions abandon him (καὶ οἱ ἔγγιστά μου ἀπὸ μακρόθεν ἔστησαν), then the apparent force of the linguistic connection again develops a contrast between those in the psalm who stand idly by (like Peter in Mark 14:54) and the women in Mark who maintain an ongoing presence in the narrative.[21] The women's continued presence supports R. T. France's view that the phrase ἀπὸ μακρόθεν distinguishes the women *positively* from the mockers and soldiers who are in the immediate presence of Jesus's cross.[22] Indeed, even Paul Danove, who argues for a negative

---

[18] E.g., Malbon, "Fallible Followers," 43; Moloney, *Gospel of Mark*, 332, 348; Joel F. Williams, *Other Followers of Jesus: Minor Characters as Major Figures in Mark's Gospel*, JSNTSup 102 (Sheffield: JSOT Press, 1994), 188.

[19] See Susan Miller, *Women in Mark's Gospel*, JSNTSup 259 (London: T&T Clark, 2004), 168. Miller highlights both the positive behavior of the women and the negative dimensions of the phrase. Yet, if Mark's use of the phrase is seen as an intended contrast with the narrative of Peter, then the ambiguity is avoided.

[20] See, e.g., James R. Edwards, *The Gospel according to Mark*, PilNTC (Grand Rapids: Eerdmans, 2002), 484; Marcus, *Mark*, 1:1068–69; Munro, "Women Disciples," 235.

[21] See Miller, *Women in Mark's Gospel*, 160–61. Miller also notes the important role that the psalms play in the wider development of Mark's passion narrative (see Joel Marcus, *The Way of the Lord: Christological Exegesis of the Old Testament in the Gospel of Mark* [Louisville: Westminster John Knox, 1992], 172–74).

[22] R. T. France, *The Gospel of Mark*, NIGTC (Grand Rapids: Eerdmans, 2002), 663 n. 79. Richard Bauckham also suggests that their distance may stem from the possibility that the Roman soldiers would have prohibited them from approaching the cross more closely (*Gospel Women: Studies of the Named Women in the Gospels* [Grand Rapids: Eerdmans, 2002], 293 n. 94). Elisabeth Schüssler Fiorenza argues that their distance from the cross suggests the reality of their association

progression in Mark's portrayal of the women, asserts that the phrase ἀπὸ μακρόθεν speaks to the women's "positive valuation" given its occurrences prior to this section of the narrative (i.e., Mark 5:6, 8:3, 11:13).[23] The women's presence at Jesus's crucifixion (15:40–41), burial (15:47), and resurrection (16:1–7) highlights their position not as failed or fallible followers but as faithful witnesses of these climactic events.[24]

Most interpreters note the positive value of the women as witnesses in the final section of the narrative in Mark 15 and the initial portion of Mark 16. The more negative assessment of the women that some discern in the phrase ἀπὸ μακρόθεν stems primarily from the culminating events of 16:1–8, particularly in the women's immediate departure from the tomb (ἐξελθοῦσαι ἔφυγον ἀπὸ τοῦ μνημείου, εἶχεν γὰρ αὐτὰς τρόμος καὶ ἔκστασις) and their fearful and apparently disobedient silence (οὐδενὶ οὐδὲν εἶπαν· ἐφοβοῦντο γάρ). The rapid transition from the introduction of the women as essential witnesses to the climactic events of the narrative to their apparent failure seems highly incongruous. Indeed, as France notes:

> for Mark to build up so carefully the women's unique role as the first witnesses of the fact of resurrection only to knock it down in his final sentence by insisting on their complete silence seems bizarre. It is one thing to emphasise and exploit paradoxical elements within the story of Jesus' ministry and passion ... but quite another to conclude his gospel with a note which appears to undermine not only his own message but also the received tradition of the church within which he was writing.[25]

An ancient solution to this literary incongruity was to supply a different ending to the Gospel, either after omitting the reference to the women's apparent failure or simply circumventing it with subsequent material.[26] In light of the near scholarly unanimity that the Gospel ends at 16:8, however, a more recent explanation suggests that the note of fear upon which the Gospel ends is an extension of the theme

---

with Jesus and the potential political danger of being associated with him (*In Memory of Her: A Feminist Theological Reconstruction of Christian Origins* [New York: Crossroad, 1983], 320; cf. Susan Miller, "Women Characters in Mark's Gospel," in *Character Studies and the Gospel of Mark*, ed. Christopher W. Skinner and Matthew Ryan Hauge, LNTS 483 [London: T&T Clark, 2014], 174–93, esp. 188–89).

[23] Paul L. Danove, "The Characterization and Narrative Function of the Women at the Tomb (Mark 15,40–41.47; 16,1–8)," *Bib* 77 (1996): 375–97, here 379. For Danove's wider assessment of the women in Mark 15–16, see also Danove, *The End of Mark's Story: A Methodological Study*, BibInt 3 (Leiden: Brill, 1993), 203–30; and Danove, *The Rhetoric of Characterization of God, Jesus, and Jesus' Disciples in the Gospel of Mark*, JSNTSup 290 (London: T&T Clark, 2005), 127–42.

[24] On the important language of "fallible followers," see Malbon, "Fallible Followers," 29–48.

[25] France, *Gospel of Mark*, 683.

[26] Importantly, however, as Hurtado notes, the earliest readers of Mark—Matthew and Luke—explain the women's silence not in terms of disobedience but in terms of restriction (Hurtado, "Women, the Tomb," 441).

of discipleship failure that is prominent throughout Mark's Gospel.[27] Larry Hurtado offers a helpful summary of this interpretive strategy:

> A number of scholars portray the ending of Mark as a rather sophisticated literary/rhetorical device intended to intrigue, disappoint, frustrate and "trap" the intended Christian readers, drawing them through a sophisticated process into some sort of existential completion of the story, thus compensating for the failures of the disciples in general, and the women of 16:1–8 in particular.[28]

Andrew T. Lincoln argues that the women's failure in 16:8 gives full rhetorical weight to the preceding note of the promise of restoration in 16:7 — "the silence of the women [is] overcome by Jesus' word of promise."[29] In his view, the intent of this redacted ending is to call the audience to review Mark's narrative to understand the interplay between the themes of failure and promised fulfillment. Lincoln argues that this redacted ending will allow the readers to enter into the narrative of the Gospel and determine whether they want to live out the way of the cross or to mirror both the male and female disciples in their fear and disobedience. In Lincoln's words, "the impact of [this] juxtaposition is encouragement to persevere despite failure and disobedience."[30] Therefore, given their own experience and knowledge of the narrative, readers of Mark's Gospel are meant to reverse the action of the women (as well as that of the other disciples) by living out their own lives as faithful

---

[27] See, e.g., Frederick D. Aquino and A. Brian McLemore, "Markan Characterization of Women," in *Essays on Women in Earliest Christianity*, ed. Carroll D. Osburn (Eugene, OR: Wipf & Stock, 1993), 393–424, esp. 423–24; Mary Cotes, "Women, Silence and Fear (Mark 16:8)," in *Women in the Biblical Tradition*, ed. George J. Brooke, SWR 31 (Lewiston, NY: Mellen, 1992), 150–66; Mary Rose D'Angelo, "(Re)Presentations of Women in the Gospels: John and Mark," in *Women and Christian Origins*, ed. Ross Shepard Kraemer and Mary Rose D'Angelo (Oxford: Oxford University Press, 1999), 137–45, esp. 138; Danove, "Characterization and Narrative Function," 395–97; Robert M. Fowler, *Let the Reader Understand: Reader-Response Criticism and the Gospel of Mark* (Minneapolis: Fortress, 1991), 243–53; Joanna Dewey, "Women in the Gospel of Mark," *WW* 26 (2006): 22–29, esp. 28–29; J. David Hester, "Dramatic Inconclusion: Irony and the Narrative Rhetoric of the Ending of Mark," *JSNT* 57 (1995): 61–86, http://dx.doi.org/10.1177/0142064X9501705704; Hooker, *Not Ashamed of the Gospel*, 66–67; Donald Juel, *A Master of Surprise: Mark Interpreted* (Minneapolis: Fortress, 1994), 115–21; Frank Kermode, *The Genesis of Secrecy: On the Interpretation of Narrative*, Charles Eliot Norton Lectures 1977–1978 (Cambridge: Harvard University Press, 1979); Andrew T. Lincoln, "The Promise and the Failure: Mark 16:7, 8," *JBL* 108 (1989): 283–300, http://dx.doi.org/10.2307/3267298; Joan L. Mitchell, *Beyond Fear and Silence: A Feminist-Literary Approach to the Gospel of Mark* (London: Continuum, 2001), 66–115; Norman R. Peterson, "When Is the End Not the End? Literary Reflections on the Ending of Mark's Narrative," *Int* 34 (1980): 151–66, http://dx.doi.org/10.1177/002096438003400204; Tolbert, *Sowing the Gospel*, 295–99; Joseph B. Tyson, "The Blindness of the Disciples in Mark," *JBL* 80 (1961): 261–68, http://dx.doi.org/10.2307/3264783.

[28] Hurtado, "Women, the Tomb," 437.

[29] Lincoln, "Promise and the Failure," 292.

[30] Ibid., 297.

followers of the crucified Messiah in the temporal divide between Jesus's resurrection and parousia.

As Hurtado notes, the primary difficulty with this view is that no other ancient texts exhibit this type of suspended or open ending in which the reader is meant not simply to supply a section of missing information but to reverse an aspect of the narrative's ending in order to supply *alternative* information.[31] If Mark has intentionally redacted a previous tradition to emphasize the theme of discipleship failure, then he has undermined the veracity of the women's testimony and given little support for his introduction of them into the narrative.[32] The difficulty of the rhetorical device developed in the reading of Lincoln and others is not that it recognizes that Mark has ended his Gospel in such a way that it calls readers to enter into a reenactment of the text. The problematic nature of the proposal is its portrayal of the women as negative exemplars who need to be overcome so that the reality of Jesus's cross and resurrection can be known, experienced, and embodied in the community. The call to a form of discipleship that is defined by its relation to Mark's Christology is indeed an essential purpose of the narrative.

The apparent incongruity of the portrayal of the women in Mark 15–16, as well as the problematic nature of some of these recent proposals, has led several scholars to interpret Mark 16:1–8 in a way that maintains a positive assessment of the women.[33] Hurtado has developed a cohesive description of the narrative function of the women as named witnesses of the climactic events of the Gospel. In his conclusion, Hurtado argues:

> Mark 16:1–8 forms a fully satisfactory climactic episode that was designed to thrill and empower intended readers to follow Jesus in mission, through opposition and even their own potentially violent death, confident in an eschatological vindication by resurrection for which Jesus' resurrection was the inspiring model.[34]

---

[31] Hurtado, "Women, the Tomb," 437–38. Proponents of the view developed in Lincoln's essay often point to the essential work of J. Lee Magness in showing that open endings existed in the ancient world (*Sense and Absence: Structure and Suspension in the Ending of Mark's Gospel*, SemeiaSt [Atlanta: Scholars Press, 1986]). Magness, however, never argued for an open ending in which the reader was meant to supply *alternative* information from that developed in the context. In addition, Magness himself argued that the final phrase in Mark 16:8 referred to a temporally constrained silence, not a form of universal failure (100).

[32] So Bauckham, *Gospel Women*, 289: "It is not plausible to read the end of Mark's story of the empty tomb as an ironic device that deconstructs the story's own truth claims." On the function of the women as witnesses in the resurrection narratives, see ibid., 257–310. For an alternative reading of the historical significance of the narrative, see Richard C. Miller, "Mark's Empty Tomb and Other Translation Fables in Classical Antiquity," *JBL* 129 (2010): 759–76, http://dx.doi.org/10.2307/25765965.

[33] See esp. Bauckham, *Gospel Women*, 286–95; and Hurtado, "Women, the Tomb," 429–50.

[34] Hurtado, "Women, the Tomb," 447.

The exegetical crux of this argument is a more positive reading of Mark 16:8 in which the women apparently flee from the tomb in fearful and disobedient silence, failing to report the message of restoration they received (καὶ οὐδενὶ οὐδὲν εἶπαν· ἐφοβοῦντο γάρ). Although most interpreters have understood Mark's assertion that the women "said nothing to anyone" (οὐδενὶ οὐδὲν εἶπαν) as a blanket statement of their failure, this is not the only way in which the phrase may be understood. It has been pointed out by a number of scholars that there is a close syntactical correspondence between the language of 16:8 and the language of 1:44, where Jesus instructs a cured leper not to speak to anyone *except* the priest to whom he was to show himself as a testimony of the healing process (μηδενὶ μηδὲν εἴπῃς ἀλλὰ ὕπαγε σεαυτὸν δεῖξον τῷ ἱερεῖ ... εἰς μαρτύριον αὐτοῖς, "See that you say nothing to anyone; but go, show yourself to the priest ... as a testimony to them" [NRSV]).[35] The close syntactical correspondence between οὐδενὶ οὐδὲν εἶπαν in 16:8 and μηδενὶ μηδὲν εἴπῃς in 1:44 may suggest that the emphasis in 16:8 is on a restricted form of a communication and not a form of universal silence.[36] The thrust of 16:8, therefore, is not that the women remain in perpetual, disobedient silence, but rather that they spoke to no one *except* the disciples to whom they were sent.

That the women's action in speaking to no one (else) is not an act of disobedience is also supported by Mark's use of the term καί to introduce both of the initial clauses in 16:8 (καὶ ἐξελθοῦσαι ἔφυγον ... καὶ οὐδενὶ οὐδὲν εἶπαν). The narrative movement does not stress that their departure or their silence was in *contrast* to the command they received to speak to the disciples, for which the terms δέ or ἀλλά may have been more appropriate.[37] In contrast, the narrative movement suggests simply the consecutive nature of their departure and restricted silence after their reception of the news about Jesus's resurrection and the command to reinform the disciples of Jesus's promise to meet with them in Galilee (cf. 14:28).

---

[35] So Bauckham, *Gospel Women*, 289; Mary Ann Beavis, *Mark*, Paideia (Grand Rapids: Baker, 2011), 246; David Catchpole, "The Fearful Silence of the Women at the Tomb: A Study in Markan Theology," *JTSA* 18 (1977): 3–10; Catchpole, *Resurrection People: Studies in the Resurrection Narratives of the Gospels*, Sarum Theological Lectures (London: Darton, Longman & Todd, 2000), 20–28; Timothy Dwyer, *The Motif of Wonder in the Gospel of Mark*, JSNTSup 128 (Sheffield: Sheffield Academic, 1996), 191–92; Schüssler Fiorenza, *In Memory of Her*, 320–23; Hurtado, "Women, the Tomb," 438–39; Malbon, "Fallible Followers," 45; C. F. D. Moule, "St. Mark XVI.8 Once More," *NTS* 2 (1955–1956): 58–59. On the plural αὐτοῖς in Mark 1:44, see France, *Gospel of Mark*, 119–20; Robert H. Stein, *Mark*, BECNT (Grand Rapids: Baker, 2008), 108. Hurtado also notes a correspondence with Mark 7:36, in which Jesus commands the disciples to speak to no one (διεστείλατο αὐτοῖς ἵνα μηδενὶ λέγωσιν), where in context μηδενί must refer to no one *else* ("Women, the Tomb," 439).

[36] Hurtado, "Women, the Tomb," 439. Cf. Hans F. Bayer, *Das Evangelium des Markus*, HTA (Wuppertal: Brockhaus, 2008), 589.

[37] See the development of this argument in Craig A. Evans, *Mark 8:27–16:20*, WBC 34B (Nashville: Nelson, 2001), 539; Robert H. Gundry, *Mark: A Commentary on His Apology for the Cross* (Grand Rapids: Eerdmans, 1993), 1010; Hurtado, "Women, the Tomb," 439.

Nevertheless, neither the potential parallel with Mark 1:44 nor the minor syntactical argument about the use of καί-consecutives detracts from the other potentially negative elements of Mark's portrait of the women. One such element is the fact that they flee (ἔφυγον) from the tomb. The second is the fear that prevents them from speaking (ἐφοβοῦντο γάρ). Both the terms "flee" (φεύγω) and "fear" (φοβέω) are frequently associated with earlier sections of Mark's narrative that highlight aspects of discipleship failure.[38] For example, the women's rapid departure from the tomb is often connected with the earlier flight of the disciples in Gethsemane in 14:50 (καὶ ἀφέντες αὐτὸν ἔφυγον πάντες, "All of them deserted him and fled" [NRSV]; cf. 14:52), with the result that the women's act of fleeing embodies the same dimensions of failure as are highlighted in the disciples' abandonment of Jesus during his arrest. As with the earlier discussion of the phrase ἀπὸ μακρόθεν in 15:40, it does seem that there is an intended linguistic connection between the narrative of the disciples in Gethsemane and the narrative of the women at the tomb. It seems reasonable to argue, however, that the impact of the linguistic connection is again not one of comparison but of contrast. The direction of the disciples' flight is *away* from Jesus because of the reality of his arrest, but the direction of the women's flight is *toward* the disciples in order to inform them of the reality of Jesus's resurrection. Richard Bauckham here provides a clear assessment of the relationship between the flight of the disciples and the women:

> At first sight it seems plausible that the women's flight parallels that of the men in Gethsemane (14:50, 52), but only so long as we remain at the level of words instead of envisaging the realistic situations Mark depicts. The flight of the men in Gethsemane is a failure to stand by Jesus, a failure to follow him on the way of the cross, through fear of the danger to themselves. But there is no sense in which the women should have remained in the tomb in order to be faithful to Jesus. Their business in the tomb is in any case finished; the young man has told them to go. Their flight can hardly be a failure of discipleship, even if their failure to speak is.[39]

The disciples have fled from Jesus in contrast to the call of discipleship. The women flee from the tomb in response to a direct command to go in order to fulfill the call of discipleship and to bring a message of restoration to those disciples who abandoned Jesus.

The rhetorical import of the women's fearful silence is similarly tied to previous examples of fear in Mark's narrative in which the term φοβέω seemingly reflects a consistently negative connotation (i.e., 4:41; 5:15, 33, 36; 6:20, 50; 9:32; 10:32; 11:18, 32; 12:12; cf. 9:6).[40] Thus, one might argue that, even if the women's silence

---

[38] See, e.g., Danove, "Characterization and Narrative Function," 390–92; Williams, *Other Followers*, 197–98.

[39] Bauckham, *Gospel Women*, 288.

[40] Danove, "Characterization and Narrative Function," 391–92; cf. Lincoln, "Promise and the Failure," 286–87; Moloney, *Gospel of Mark*, 348–49.

was in fact restricted, their fear still represents an example of discipleship failure. Perhaps the most relevant example, given the frequent comparisons between the disciples and the women, is the narrative in Mark 4 in which the disciples' lack of faith during the storm on the sea is closely connected with their fear (vv. 37–41).[41] In the context of chapter 4, the disciples wake Jesus and question his concern for them in the midst of the storm. Jesus responds in verse 40 by rebuking them, questioning their fear (τί δειλοί ἐστε;) and lack of faith (οὔπω ἔχετε πίστιν;). The subsequent note of the disciples' fear in verse 41 (ἐφοβήθησαν φόβον μέγαν), which contains the linguistic parallel with 16:8, however, does not relate to their lack of faith but is rather a description of their response to Jesus's ability to calm the storm.[42] In other words, the disciples' fear in chapter 4 is not an immediate example of discipleship failure but an understandable response to a divine disclosure. It seems likely that it is this aspect of the disciples' experience that is paralleled in Mark 16. The women have encountered an angelic figure, and their experience is marked by the normal pattern of fearful response (cf. Judg 6:22–23; Dan 8:17; 10:7, 12; Luke 2:9–10; Rev 1:17).[43] The entirety of Mark 16:8, therefore, reflects the women's response to their discovery of Jesus's absence from the tomb and the dramatic nature of the message that they have received.[44] The reality of the numinous experience results in a multiplicity of emotional responses—ἐξεθαμβήθησαν ("they were alarmed," 16:5), τρόμος καὶ ἔκστασις, ἐφοβοῦντο ("terror and amazement," "they were afraid," 16:8)—and, in the midst of that powerful experience, the women flee in order to fulfill the specific commission that they have received. That the women are afraid, therefore, represents not their failure or misunderstanding but rather their recognition of the divine drama unfolding before them.[45]

Throughout the narrative of Mark 15–16 these women function as faithful observers of the climactic events of the Gospel—the crucifixion, burial, and resurrection of Jesus. Given this more positive assessment of the women's role in this section of Mark's narrative, it seems reasonable to suggest an amendment to the otherwise measured and helpful reading of the Markan characters developed in the influential work of Elizabeth Struthers Malbon. In her 1983 article "Fallible Followers," Malbon argued that the female characters in Mark's narrative could be

---

[41] Danove, "Characterization and Narrative Function," 391–92.

[42] So Bauckham, *Gospel Women*, 290; cf. Collins, *Mark*, 800; Dwyer, *Motif of Wonder*, 109–11; Marcus, *Mark*, 1:334.

[43] Marcus, *Mark*, 2:1085; cf. Guy J. Williams, "Narrative Space, Angelic Revelation, and the End of Mark's Gospel," *JSNT* 35 (2013): 263–84, esp. 277–80, http://dx.doi.org/10.1177/0142064X12472118. On the notion that the νεανίσκος in 16:5 is in fact an ἄγγελος, see M. Eugene Boring, *Mark: A Commentary*, NTL (Louisville: Westminster John Knox, 2006), 444–48; Collins, *Mark*, 795–96; Dwyer, *Motif of Wonder*, 185–93. On the potential (though unlikely) relationship with the νεανίσκος in Mark 14:51–52, see Marcus, *Mark*, 2:1124–25.

[44] Cf. Collins, *Mark*, 799–800; Hurtado, "Women, the Tomb," 439–40; Olof Linton, "Der vermißte Markusschluß," *TBl* 8 (1929): 229–34, esp. 230–31.

[45] Contra Miller, *Women in Mark's Gospel*, 187.

understood along a spectrum of discipleship that was more extensively developed in the portrait of Jesus's male disciples.⁴⁶ In a slight emendation to her argument, Malbon then argued in her 1994 essay on the minor characters in Mark's narrative that the narrated stories of women prior to Mark 15:40—with the clear exception of Herodias and her daughter (6:14–29)—were all better characterized as *exemplars* of faithful and active discipleship.⁴⁷ Yet, in light of her understanding of the phrase ἀπὸ μακρόθεν in 15:40 and her perception of the women's failed report in 16:8, Malbon continued to assert that the women who appear in chapters 15–16 were fallible followers, demonstrating the same potential for both success and failure that is portrayed in the male disciples.⁴⁸

The preceding argument, however, suggests that Mark may not be focusing on fallibility at all. The late appearance of the women in the narrative (despite their ongoing presence with Jesus in the *non*-narrated story; Mark 15:41⁴⁹) and their presence at the climactic events of Jesus's life imply a specific contrast with the male disciples who have played a prominent role in the narrative but have abandoned Jesus at this crucial stage. The women in Mark 15–16 maintain the same positive portrayal of discipleship that is consistently developed in the previous narratives of female characters (e.g., 5:24–34, 7:24–30, 12:41–44, 14:1–9). This is not to suggest an oversimplified portrait of the male disciples as complete failures or the women as free from the reality of the difficulty of discipleship, but to suggest with Hurtado that the women in Mark 15–16 have a clear *literary* function as faithful witnesses in the narrative.⁵⁰ Or, to build on the language of Malbon, the women who witness Jesus's crucifixion, burial, and resurrection are faithful exemplars of Markan discipleship.

II. Cruciform Discipleship in Mark and Paul

After developing an overtly positive portrait of the women in Mark 15–16, Hurtado returns to the question of the abruptness of the ending of Mark's Gospel. He contends that the absence of developed resurrection appearances—though not the absence of the resurrection itself (cf. 16:7)—is best explained by Mark's emphasis on the central importance of the cross in the development of his Christology. Hurtado argues:

---

⁴⁶ Malbon, "Fallible Followers," esp. 32–35.

⁴⁷ Elizabeth Struthers Malbon, "The Major Importance of the Minor Characters in Mark," in *The New Literary Criticism and the New Testament*, ed. Elizabeth Struthers Malbon and Edgar V. McKnight, JSNTSup 109 (Sheffield: Sheffield Academic, 1994), 58–86, esp. 69 n. 3.

⁴⁸ Malbon, "Minor Characters," 69, 72. This paradigm is largely maintained in Miller, *Women in Mark's Gospel*.

⁴⁹ Cf. Malbon, "Minor Characters," 60–61.

⁵⁰ Hurtado, "Women, the Tomb," 427–49.

> The Markan narrative stresses that the crucifixion of Jesus is not simply overcome in his resurrection, as an ordeal that could now be regarded as a temporary setback like the trials of a Greek hero. Instead, the point is that the risen Jesus remains the same Jesus who was crucified (16:6), and that the events of death, burial and resurrection are together essential in mutually interpreting one another.[51]

Hurtado's emphasis on the importance of the cross for the development of Mark's Christology resonates with his argument in an earlier essay that this emphasis on the cross is in fact the paradigm of Christian discipleship:

> Mark's christological emphasis falls more on the cross as the disclosure of the meaning of Jesus, which is why an accurate understanding of Jesus is withheld from all human characters in Mark's Gospel until the crucifixion. This cross-emphasis in Mark's view of Jesus' mission coheres with his emphasis on Jesus' crucifixion as the paradigm of faithful discipleship. The shortcomings of the Twelve and the positive example of Jesus together form major components in Mark's literary and didactic plan—the Twelve functioning as warning examples of the dangers that readers must avoid and Jesus' example functioning to show what faithful discipleship looks like. Discipleship, Mark emphasizes, means *following* Jesus, with the story of Jesus serving as the paradigm.[52]

Hurtado's summaries represent a constructive explanation of the close connection that is developed between Christology and discipleship throughout Mark's Gospel.[53] What is missing from both, however, is the women of chapters 15–16. In fact, Hurtado stresses that one of the benefits of a positive reading of 16:8 is that it allows "these women to step back quickly out of the public limelight (joining the other disciples, who have been on the sidelines all through the crucifixion-resurrection narratives)."[54] Hurtado is certainly right to stress the christological and cross-shaped emphasis of Mark's narrative. But his sidelining of the women at the end of his argument fails to maintain his discussion of their positive literary function. The fact that their presence with Jesus is narrated only in connection with the passion and resurrection narratives suggests both their close identification with those events and their contrast with the other disciples who are no longer present. Their rapid departure from the narrative is an act not of stepping back but of stepping forward as bearers of the message of restoration. To put it another way, the women's

---

[51] Ibid., 445.

[52] Larry W. Hurtado, "Following Jesus in the Gospel of Mark—and Beyond," in *Patterns of Discipleship in the New Testament*, ed. Richard N. Longenecker, MNTS (Grand Rapids: Eerdmans, 1996), 9–29, here 25; emphasis original. See also Hooker, *Not Ashamed of the Gospel*, 51–55.

[53] The secondary literature on the relationship between Christology and discipleship in Mark is extensive. For an introduction, see Suzanne Watts Henderson, *Christology and Discipleship in the Gospel of Mark*, SNTSMS 135 (Cambridge: Cambridge University Press, 2006), 5–8, http://dx.doi.org/10.1017/CBO9780511487989.

[54] Hurtado, "Women, the Tomb," 443.

role in the narrative is conditioned by the reality of Jesus's crucifixion, death, and resurrection. They are the essential narrative representatives of these central events in the Gospel. In this way the women function as exemplars of discipleship, providing a "narrative exclamation point" for Mark's understanding of the close relationship between Christology and discipleship.[55] Mark portrays the women as narrative exemplars of a form of faithful discipleship that reflects the paradigm established in Jesus by positioning them as participants in the climactic events of the Gospel.

The argument that Markan discipleship embodies the paradigm created in Jesus's life, death, and resurrection is developed in the close association that Mark establishes between Jesus's passion–resurrection predictions and the nature of discipleship. Each of the three passion–resurrection predictions in Mark's Gospel exhibits a rhetorical pattern that connects Jesus's predictions with an instance of discipleship failure and a subsequent call to a reimagined form of discipleship (i.e., 8:31–38, 9:30–37, 10:32–45).[56] Each, therefore, provides both revelatory content about Jesus's ministry and the significance of that ministry for the nature of discipleship. Given the implicitly exhortative nature of this material, Gorman argues that we should refer to each section "not merely as a 'passion prediction' but as a 'passion prediction-summons,' meaning a call to passion-shaped discipleship, or, in a word, cruciformity."[57] Gorman uses this language of "cruciformity" to describe the way in which Christ's own cross-shaped narrative becomes paradigmatic for the life of Christ's followers.[58] Gorman's specific focus on the cross does not diminish the importance of the resurrection but rather emphasizes the revelatory and creative characteristics of the cross itself. It both defines the nature of Christ's identity and creates the community in which this cruciform paradigm is expressed.[59] What develops at these crucial points in Mark's narrative, therefore, is a series of implicit exhortations that position the self-sacrificial character of Jesus's ministry as the essential paradigm for the lives of his followers.

Perhaps the most paradigmatic of these summonses is expressed in Mark 8:34: "If anyone wants to follow me they must deny themselves and take up their cross and follow me." This verse clearly associates Jesus's passion with the life of discipleship—"to follow Christ in the way of the cross is more akin to participating in the reality or life or story of God … than to following someone at a distance or even

---

[55] On Mark's use of "narrative punctuation," see Malbon, "Minor Characters," 72–73.
[56] On Mark's development of this pattern, see, e.g., Schüssler Fiorenza, *In Memory of Her*, 317; Gorman, *Death of the Messiah*, 87; Hurtado, "Following Jesus," 11–15.
[57] Gorman, *Death of the Messiah*, 84.
[58] On the language of cruciformity, see esp. Michael J. Gorman, *Cruciformity: Paul's Narrative Spirituality of the Cross* (Grand Rapids: Eerdmans, 2001); and Gorman, *Inhabiting the Cruciform God: Kenosis, Justification, and Theosis in Paul's Narrative Soteriology* (Grand Rapids: Eerdmans, 2009).
[59] Gorman, *Death of the Messiah*, 34–36.

imitating a master."⁶⁰ Indeed, as Susan Miller notes, the "death and resurrection of Jesus may only be understood by those who follow the way of the cross."⁶¹ Discipleship means *following* Jesus in the way of the cross. Given the emphasis on the theme of following in Mark 8:34, the assertion in 15:40 that the women were following Jesus (ἠκολούθουν) likely harks back to this didactic exhortation and positions them as disciples within the narrative. These women are the only narrative figures who persist with Jesus in the course of these climactic events. Their persistent presence demonstrates their commitment to the shameful paradox of the cruciform nature of Jesus's gospel.⁶²

The final passion–resurrection prediction reflects the same pattern as is developed in Mark 8, focusing on the reality of Jesus's death and resurrection and then summoning the disciples to redefine their ideals about greatness so that they are able to participate in the same form of service that Jesus himself embodies. To lean again on the language of Gorman, Jesus's act of service is both unique and paradigmatic.⁶³ His death and resurrection create a new reality in which disciples are called to live in a way that reflects the same pattern of service (10:42–45). In light of this emphasis on service, the linguistic connection between Jesus's act of service (οὐκ ἦλθεν διακονηθῆναι ἀλλὰ διακονῆσαι, "[the Son of Man] came not to be served but to serve") in 10:45 and the introduction of the women in 15:40–41, who were not only following but also serving (διηκόνουν) are noteworthy. Given the parallel connection with the language of following (8:34, 15:40–41), the repeated use of the verb διακονέω links Jesus and the women.⁶⁴ They are here again introduced into the narrative as positive exemplars of a form of discipleship that evokes Jesus's earlier teaching. Both these specific linguistic connections and the women's narrative position as participants in the story of Jesus's passion and resurrection suggest their function as narrative examples of Mark's wider portrait of cruciform discipleship.

A similar point can be made about the Pauline epistles. Gorman uses the language of cruciformity and cruciform discipleship to argue that Paul's statements about life in Christ establish Christ as the paradigm for Christian existence. Since Christ is the crucified one (1 Cor 1:23; cf. Mark 16:6), participation in the new covenant community he inaugurates through his death and resurrection means participation in that same cross-shaped existence. Gorman defines this participation or *theōsis* as a "transformative participation in the kenotic, cruciform character

---

⁶⁰ Ibid., 36.

⁶¹ Miller, *Women in Mark's Gospel*, 184.

⁶² For this definition of Markan discipleship, see Schüssler Fiorenza, *In Memory of Her*, 316–17; Gorman, *Death of the Messiah*, 87–89; Kinukawa, *Women and Jesus*, 98–99.

⁶³ Gorman, *Death of the Messiah*, 117.

⁶⁴ Mark uses the term only four times (1:13, 31; 10:45; 15:41). Outside of the first occurrence (1:13), which refers to the angels who serve Jesus in the wilderness, all of the occurrences refer either to the activity of women (Simon's mother-in-law in 1:31 and the large group of women in 15:41) or that of Jesus (10:45). This aspect of discipleship is never applied to Jesus's male disciples (cf. Kinukawa, *Women and Jesus*, 100–101; Miller, *Women in Mark's Gospel*, 23).

of God through Spirit-enabled conformity to the incarnate, crucified, and resurrected/glorified Christ."⁶⁵ In other words, the pattern of discipleship that Paul develops is that of an imitation, embodiment, and participation in the narrative of Jesus. Paul's embodiment of Christ's narrative in his suffering represents a crucial element in his proclamation of the gospel. That the embodiment of this particular narrative was essential for Paul is evident from the dramatic statement he makes about the nature of the apostolic ministry in which he and his coworkers engage in 2 Cor 4:10: "We always carry around in our body the death of Jesus, so that the life of Jesus may also be revealed in our body."⁶⁶ Discipleship for Paul is participation in the death and resurrected life of Jesus.

In his work *The Death of the Messiah and the Birth of the New Covenant*, Gorman begins to establish the presence of this cruciform pattern throughout the witness of the wider New Testament corpus. Important for the present article, Gorman develops a strong case for the similar descriptions of discipleship found in both the Pauline epistles and the Markan Gospel narrative.⁶⁷ More specifically, Gorman argues that both Mark and Paul develop their understanding of discipleship in light of the inherent exhortations developed in Jesus's predictions of his death and resurrection.⁶⁸ The paradigmatic nature of discipleship that Gorman develops strongly resonates with the similar emphases elucidated in Hurtado's representative work on Mark's portrait of discipleship. Both Mark and Paul understand Jesus as the ultimate paradigm of discipleship, and consequently call their audiences to live in a way that reflects Jesus's cruciform identity.

As with Hurtado's sidelining of the women, however, Gorman does not draw out the narrative function of the women in connection with his larger thesis about the presence of cruciform discipleship in Mark and Paul. Indeed, although this is a somewhat artificial measure, the last verse that Gorman references from Mark's Gospel is 15:39, immediately prior to the women's entrance into the narrated events of the Gospel (15:40–41). Highlighting Gorman's exclusion of the women is not meant to detract from the importance of his wider thesis, which is both coherent and persuasive. In contrast, it is meant to support the direction of Gorman's argument concerning the theological similarity between Mark and Paul on the topic of

---

⁶⁵ Gorman, *Inhabiting the Cruciform God*, 7.

⁶⁶ On this text, see esp. Steven J. Kraftchick, "Death in Us, Life in You: The Apostolic Medium," in *1 and 2 Corinthians,* ed. David M. Hay, vol. 2 of *Pauline Theology,* ed. Jouette M. Bassler, David M. Hay, and E. Elizabeth Johnson (Minneapolis: Fortress, 1993), 169–77; and Kar Yong Lim, *'The Sufferings of Christ Are Abundant in Us' (2 Corinthians 1.5): A Narrative Dynamics Investigation of Paul's Sufferings in 2 Corinthians,* LNTS 399 (London: T&T Clark, 2009), 64–122; cf. Gorman, *Death of the Messiah*, 58; J. M. F Heath, *Paul's Visual Piety: The Metamorphosis of the Beholder* (Oxford: Oxford University Press, 2013), 109, http://dx.doi.org/10.1093/acprof:oso/9780199664146.001.0001; N. T. Wright, *Paul and the Faithfulness of God,* 2 vols., Christian Origins and the Question of God 4 (Minneapolis: Fortress, 2013), 2:724.

⁶⁷ Gorman, *Death of the Messiah*, esp. 33–36, 81–94, 106–11, 114–27.

⁶⁸ Ibid., 130–31.

discipleship by offering a further example of this thematic convergence. The unique introduction of the women into Mark's narrative both as witnesses to Jesus's crucifixion and burial and as recipients of the news of his resurrection allows them to function as narrative examples of this type of cruciform discipleship. In Mark's narrative, the women are the only ones who are portrayed as faithfully following Jesus in the midst of his suffering, death, and resurrection. To coordinate the narrative of Mark with the rhetoric of Paul is to suggest that Paul's theological emphasis on the theme of participation in Christ—being "in Christ"—is represented in the Markan narrative by these named women whose literary function is to establish, verify, and proclaim the consequence of the climactic events of the Gospel. Mark's portrayal of the women's narrative participation in the crucifixion, burial, and resurrection of Jesus is a thematic parallel to the theme of theological participation developed in the Pauline corpus.

Contra Francis J. Moloney, therefore, Mark has not *"changed the story"* regarding the women and the resurrection in order to highlight a Pauline emphasis on divine agency over against human activity.[69] Rather, the positive interpretation of the women's function in the narrative underlines a thematic connection between Mark and Paul on the nature of discipleship, while the women's rapid departure from the tomb may function as a further emphasis on Mark's theology of the cross, which also constitutes a thematic connection between Mark and Paul.[70] Mark's narrative portrayal of the women in chapters 15–16 as those who follow Jesus faithfully in the midst of his crucifixion, burial, and resurrection constitutes a thematic echo of the portrait of cruciform discipleship that resonates in the narrative theology developed in the Pauline corpus. The named women in Mark 15–16 are narrative examples of the Pauline theme of participation in Christ. In this way, their role in the narrative is a further point of convergence between Markan and Pauline theology. The women are narrative embodiments of the reality of cruciform discipleship at the climax of Mark's Gospel.

III. Conclusion

My intention in the present article was to provide a further example of convergence between Markan and Pauline theology. Although the named women in Mark 15–16 are often seen to move along the same spectrum of faithfulness and

---

[69] Moloney, *Gospel of Mark*, 351 (emphasis original). See also the similar emphasis on divine action in Lincoln, "Promise and the Failure," 293; Miller, *Women in Mark's Gospel*, 186; Sweat, *Theological Role of Paradox*, 173–76.

[70] In addition to Gorman's emphasis on the similarities between the Gospel of Mark and Paul's theology of the cross, see esp. Bird, "Mark: Interpreter of Peter," 39–43; Black, "Christ Crucified in Paul," 80–104; and Marcus, "Mark—Interpreter of Paul," 479–81.

failure that defines Mark's portrayal of Jesus's male disciples, their narrative function in the Gospel can be interpreted more positively as a coherent demonstration of Markan discipleship. The women's late introduction into the narrated story of Mark's Gospel creates a direct association between them and the climactic events of the narrative—Jesus's crucifixion, burial, and resurrection. Their close association with these events establishes their role in the narrative as faithful witnesses and exemplars of those who follow Jesus on the way of the cross. This portrait of the women reflects the cruciform discipleship that is developed both in the preceding narrative of Mark's Gospel and in the Pauline corpus. Both Mark and Paul depict the life of discipleship as conformity to the cruciform existence of Jesus. It is, in the narrative of Mark, a taking up of Jesus's cross (Mark 8:34) and, in the narrative theology of Paul, a participation in Jesus's cruciform suffering (e.g., 2 Cor 4:10–12).

That the shape of Christian discipleship is defined by the paradigm of a crucified Messiah is unique neither to Paul nor to Mark. This particular theological emphasis does not represent a theological distinction within Christian theology. Its *primacy* in both Markan and Pauline theology, however, may suggest that this convergence is more than mere coincidence. There does appear to be support for a mutual engagement with a theology of the cross and its implications. The women of Mark 15–16 embody a narrative presentation of the cruciform discipleship that demonstrates the way in which the cross forces Mark and Paul to reimagine the nature of the new covenant community inaugurated in the Christ event.

The Department of Classics & Ancient Mediterranean Studies (CAMS)
Pennsylvania State University

Post-Baccalaureate Certificate in Ancient Languages

The certificate is for students who want to pursue graduate studies in Classics, Egyptology, Ancient Near East, Biblical Studies, Archaeology, Ancient History.

CAMS offers **Greek**, **Latin**, **Biblical Hebrew**, **Middle & Late Egyptian**, **Akkadian**, **Sumerian**, **Aramaic**, **Coptic**, and **Hittite**, as well as a variety of advanced courses.

Applications for Fall 2017 should be received by **April 7**.

Address inquiries to Prof. Mark Munn (markmunn@psu.edu).
http://cams.la.psu.edu/

What Is Opened in Luke 24:45, the Mind or the Scriptures?

JOSHUA L. MANN
j.l.mann@durham.ac.uk
University of Durham, Durham, UK DH1 3RJ

Until recently, virtually all known readings of Luke 24:45 took for granted a particular underlying Greek syntax that yields the translation, "Then he [Jesus] opened their mind to understand the Scriptures." In an earlier issue of this journal, Matthew Bates proposed an alternative understanding of the Greek syntax, swapping the direct objects of the main verb and infinitive, substantially altering the meaning: "Then Jesus exposited the Scriptures so that the disciples could understand their meaning." In this article, I will show that Bates's reconstruction is syntactically infeasible and otherwise inadequately supported. Further, I present evidence from the broad context of Luke-Acts that supports the traditional reading. Illumination, the opening of the mind of the disciples, is a climactic moment at the end of the Third Gospel.

In the Gospel of Luke, the disciples, who are granted to know the "mysteries of the kingdom of God" (Luke 8:10), nevertheless repeatedly fail to understand the necessity of Jesus's passion.[1] This failure is finally reversed in the conclusion of the narrative when the disciples receive illumination, which enables them to understand Jesus's suffering as a fulfillment of the Scriptures:

> Now [Jesus] said to them, "These are my words which I spoke to you while I was still with you, that it was necessary to fulfill all of the things written about me in the Law of Moses and the Prophets and the Psalms." Then he opened their mind to understand the Scriptures. And he said to them, "Thus it stands written, that the Christ would suffer and rise from the dead on the third day." (Luke 24:44–46)[2]

In a previous issue of this journal, Matthew Bates proposed an alternative understanding of the syntax in Luke 24:45, taking νοῦν ("mind") rather than γραφάς ("Scripture") as the direct object of the infinitive συνιέναι ("to open"), effectively

---

[1] Luke 9:20, 22, 44–45; 18:31–34; 24:11, 37, 41.
[2] All translations are my own unless otherwise specified.

799

recasting Jesus's action of *illumination*, the opening of the mind, with *exposition*, the opening of the Scriptures:

τότε διήνοιξεν αὐτῶν τὸν νοῦν τοῦ συνιέναι τὰς γραφάς·
Then Jesus exposited the Scriptures so that the disciples could understand their meaning.³

While Bates is able to provide semantic support for his rendering of διανοίγω and νοῦς, his reconstruction is nearly impossible on syntactical grounds (for reasons not considered in his article), and it does not fit the context of Luke nearly as well as the traditional reading.

Bates rightly begins with the question, "is the proposed alternative translation syntactically feasible?"⁴ He answers in the affirmative, finding no syntactical objection to taking τὸν νοῦν as the infinitive's direct object (thus, "to understand the meaning").⁵ Yet two significant objections should be raised: (1) Rarely, if ever, in extant Greek literature does the direct object of an articular infinitive *precede* the article of that construction (i.e., direct objects of articular infinitives are not proleptic in *this* way); and (2) where the subject of the infinitive is unspecified, it is normally assumed from the subject of the main verb, thus the implied subject of the infinitive in Luke 24:45 should not be "the disciples" as Bates assumes.⁶

First, in Greek literature adjuncts (including the direct object) of an articular infinitive normally occur either between the article and the infinitive or immediately after the infinitive:⁷

---

³ Matthew W. Bates, "Closed-Minded Hermeneutics? A Proposed Alternative Translation," *JBL* 129 (2010): 537–57, here 539.
⁴ Ibid.
⁵ Ibid. Bates admits that "it is substantially less probable on the basis of word order alone," but he seems unaware of the two issues raised below.
⁶ By the phrase "subject of the infinitive," I refer to the agent of the action denoted by the infinitive. For our purposes, it matters very little to judge whether, strictly speaking, an infinitive takes a subject. See Daniel B. Wallace, *Greek Grammar beyond the Basics: An Exegetical Syntax of the New Testament*, 2nd ed. (Grand Rapids: Zondervan, 1996), 192; BDF §406.
⁷ It seems best to view the article in such constructions as a function marker, making explicit a structural relation of the clause to the rest of the sentence, as can be seen in the examples given here (for a full discussion, see Denny Burk, *Articular Infinitives in the Greek of the New Testament: On the Exegetical Benefit of Grammatical Precision*, New Testament Monographs 14 [Sheffield: Sheffield Phoenix, 2006]). Along these lines, A. T. Robertson twice comments on the article's significance for the infinitive, saying, "I have never seen an articular inf[initive] where the article did not seem in place," and "when the article does occur with the inf[initive], it should have its real force" (*A Grammar of the Greek New Testament in the Light of Historical Research* [Nashville: Broadman & Holman, 1934], 1064, 1065). The older grammarians give no indication that the adjuncts of articular infinitives might occur before the article, but one does find explicit commentary on the occurrence of adjuncts between the article and the infinitive; see, e.g., G. B. Winer and W. F. Moulton, *A Treatise on the Grammar of New Testament Greek Regarded as a Sure*

... καὶ γὰρ πάνυ μοι δοκεῖ ἄφρονος ἀνθρώπου εἶναι τὸ μεγάλου ἔργου ὄντος τοῦ ἑαυτῷ τὰ δέοντα παρασκευάζειν μὴ ἀρκεῖν τοῦτο, ἀλλὰ προσαναθέσθαι τὸ καὶ τοῖς ἄλλοις πολίταις ὧν δέονται πορίζειν. (Xenophon, Mem. 2.1.8)

For considering how hard a job it is to provide for one's own needs, I think it absurd not to be content to do that, but to shoulder the burden of supplying the wants of the community as well. (Marchant, LCL)

... τοῦ μή με θάψαι ἐν Αἰγύπτῳ ... (Gen 47:29 LXX)
... Do not bury me in Egypt. (NRSV)

... τί ἐστιν τὸ ἐκ νεκρῶν ἀναστῆναι. (Mark 9:10)
... what this rising from the dead could mean. (NRSV)

ἐὰν δὲ ἄξιον ᾖ τοῦ κἀμὲ πορεύεσθαι ... (1 Cor 16:4)
If it seems advisable that I should go also ... (NRSV)

This is also true where the construction involves a preposition:

διὰ τὸ αὐτὸν πολλάκις πέδαις καὶ ἁλύσεσιν δεδέσθαι καὶ διεσπάσθαι ὑπ' αὐτοῦ τὰς ἁλύσεις καὶ τὰς πέδας συντετρῖφθαι, καὶ οὐδεὶς ἴσχυεν αὐτὸν δαμάσαι· (Mark 5:4)
for he had often been restrained with shackles and chains, but the chains he wrenched apart, and the shackles he broke in pieces; and no one had the strength to subdue him. (NRSV)

προσεῖχον δὲ αὐτῷ διὰ τὸ ἱκανῷ χρόνῳ ταῖς μαγείαις ἐξεστακέναι αὐτούς. (Acts 8:11)
And they listened eagerly to him because for a long time he had amazed them with his magic. (NRSV)

... εἰς τὸ μὴ ἐκ φαινομένων τὸ βλεπόμενον γεγονέναι. (Heb 11:3)
... so that what is seen was made from things that are not visible. (NRSV)

εἰς τὸ μηκέτι ἀνθρώπων ἐπιθυμίαις ἀλλὰ θελήματι θεοῦ τὸν ἐπίλοιπον ἐν σαρκὶ βιῶσαι χρόνον. (1 Pet 4:2)
so as to live for the rest of your earthly life no longer by human desires but by the will of God. (NRSV)

It has proven difficult to find a single clear exception to this pattern analogous to the one Bates proposes for Luke 24:45, where the direct object of the articular infinitive precedes the article.[8] Crucially, none of the twenty-three examples Bates

---

Basis for New Testament Exegesis, 3rd ed. (Edinburgh: T&T Clark, 1882), 408, 413 n. 3; Robertson, *Grammar*, 1070. The article has a similar function with participial clauses (cf. BDF §474[5]).

[8] Articular infinitive constructions are common in Greek and yet difficult to search exhaustively with software because of their complexity. Without the capacity for an exhaustive search, I cannot say that there are no clear examples of Bates's construction in extant Greek literature. Searching a small corpus like the New Testament is difficult but more manageable where

offers in support of his syntactical construction exhibits the prolepsis of the direct object *before the article* of an articular infinitive construction.⁹

Second, since infinitives without a specified subject normally assume the subject of the main verb, Bates's syntactical construction implies that *Jesus* is the subject of "understand" (συνιέναι), not the disciples, as is inexplicably inserted in his translation.¹⁰ In other words, given the alternative syntax, Jesus opens the Scriptures for *his own* understanding. This of course clashes with the larger narrative, in which the disciples, not Jesus, are in need of understanding. The traditional reading escapes this problem because the subject of the infinitive is easily supplied from the direct object of the main verb, αὐτῶν τὸν νοῦν ("their mind"), a collective singular referring in the context to the mind of the disciples. *Their* understanding, not Jesus's, is the logical outcome of the opening of their mind. In sum, if Bates's reading of Luke 24:45 is correct, one would expect two differences in the Greek text: (1) The proposed direct object of the infinitive would be between the genitive article and the infinitive or just after the infinitive; and (2) the subject of the infinitive would be specified since it is different from the main verb and not otherwise

---

a text is morphologically tagged. Using Accordance Bible Software, for example, of twenty-nine instances in the New Testament where the genitive articular infinitive is preceded immediately by an accusative (Luke 24:45 aside), only once could I find an example that gave pause: Σίμων Σίμων, ἰδοὺ ὁ σατανᾶς ἐξῃτήσατο ὑμᾶς τοῦ σινιάσαι ὡς τὸν σῖτον, "Simon, Simon, listen! Satan has demanded to sift all of you like wheat" (Luke 22:31). But here ὑμᾶς is the direct object of the main verb, as one would expect ἐξαιτέω to take an accusative object (see BDAG, s.v. ἐξαιτέω, 1: "Satan asked for you, to sift you"). The infinitive, specifying the request or its goal, would then assume the same object of the main verb since one is not specified (BDF §396).

⁹ In an errant translation of one example that, like Luke 24:45, concerns the difficulty of understanding Scripture, Bates makes the same two syntactical maneuvers to which I am objecting ("Closed-Minded Hermeneutics?," 539–40 n. 7). The passage is Origen, *Philoc.* 2.3: ἡγοῦμαι γοῦν καὶ τὸν ἀπόστολον τὴν τοιαύτην ἔφοδον τοῦ συνιέναι τοὺς θείους λόγους ὑποβάλλοντα λέγειν … (mistranslated by Bates as "And in fact I think the apostle, in order that [we might] understand this sort of approach, sets down these divine words, saying …"). Bates takes ἔφοδον—notably occurring before the articular infinitive—as the direct object of τοῦ συνιέναι and inexplicably inserts a subject of the infinitive ("we") not implied by the sentence. Further, his translation does not make sense in the context where the apostle is not "setting down divine words" but rather offering a way of understanding divine words (i.e., the Scriptures). The syntax is difficult but not impossible to decipher: The main verb ἡγοῦμαι is followed by an accusative with the infinitive (τὸν ἀπόστολον … λέγειν) (see BDAG, s.v. ἡγέομαι 2). Intervening is a participial phrase (τὴν τοιαύτην ἔφοδον … ὑποβάλλοντα, "suggesting such a way") within which is an epexegetical infinitive that unpacks ἔφοδον (τοῦ συνιέναι τοὺς θείους λόγους, "to understand the divine words"). Compare the translation of George Lewis: "The Apostle, I think, suggested such a way of coming to a knowledge [*sic*] of the Divine words when He said …" (*The Philocalia of Origen: A Compilation of Selected Passages from Origen's Works Made by St. Gregory of Nazianzus and St. Basil of Caesarea* [Edinburgh: T&T Clark, 1911], 32).

¹⁰ Inserted variously with and without brackets (Bates, "Closed-Minded Hermeneutics?," 539, 540). Cf. BDF §§396, 405, 407. In 1 Thess 4:9 the difficulty of the exceptional usage is apparent in the manuscript tradition. On the "subject" of the infinitive, see n. 6 above.

implied in the sentence. These differences might be illustrated with a hypothetical reconstruction fitting Bates's reading:

τότε διήνοιξεν τοῦ αὐτῶν τὸν νοῦν συνιέναι [τοὺς μαθητὰς] τὰς γραφάς·
"Then he opened the Scriptures for the disciples to understand their meaning."

Thus, not only is Bates's proposal syntactically infeasible, it is a far more remote possibility than he suggests.[11]

The other lines of argument given by Bates are unable to overcome the syntactical improbability.[12] First, in Bates's interesting and helpful review of the early reception history of Luke 24:45, not a single example provides clear evidence of the alternative reading, as he admits.[13] Second, what Bates rightly considers the "best evidence" for his proposal, the use of διανοίγω elsewhere in Luke-Acts, especially for the exposition of Scripture (Luke 24:32, Acts 17:2–3), does not provide decisive support of his reading over the other. When discussing two uses of διανοίγω that provide strong support for the traditional reading—where Jesus opens the eyes of two disciples (Luke 24:31) and the Lord opens Lydia's heart (Acts 16:14)—Bates counters that "there are *zero* instances, to the best of my knowledge, in all of antiquity of διανοίγω or the related verb ἀνοίγω with νοῦς as the object prior to the fifth century CE (excluding, of course, the reception history of Luke 24:45 as discussed above)."[14] But this argument from silence is neutralized by the fact that his own reconstruction faces a similar scenario, as described by him: "the author of Luke-Acts appears to be the first extant author to employ this specialized exegetical meaning of διανοίγω."[15] Additionally, why one should exclude a consideration of the reception history at this point is not obvious, for it strongly implies that some ancient readers understood νοῦς as the direct object of διανοίγω.

More compelling is Bates's argument that the context of Luke 24:45 bears closer resemblance to Luke 24:32 and Acts 17:2–3—where αἱ γραφαί is the direct object of διανοίγω—than to Luke 24:31 and Acts 16:14, where διανοίγω is used for opening a faculty of perception.[16] In spite of its relative strength, this argument suffers from a number of problems. To distance Luke 24:45 from the two examples that appear to support the traditional reading, Bates claims that "διανοίγω does *not*

---

[11] I would be reluctant ever to say something is syntactically *impossible*, especially based on word order. As Robertson reminds, "The freedom of the Greek from artificial rules and its response to the play of the mind is never seen better than in the order of words in the sentence" (Robertson, *Grammar*, 417).

[12] I have no problem with Bates's general arguments that διανοίγω can mean "exposit" or νοῦς refer to "meaning." While these arguments are essential to his proposal, they do not support it over against the traditional rendering—hence they will not be discussed at length here.

[13] Bates, "Closed-Minded Hermeneutics?," 545: "There are no absolutely clear-cut cases in which Luke 24:45 was interpreted in accordance with the proposed alternative translation."

[14] Ibid., 547 (emphasis original).

[15] Ibid., 548.

[16] Note that in the case of Acts 17:3, the direct object of διανοίγων is implied.

involve scriptural exposition in either Luke 24:31 or Acts 16:14 in a fashion that might compare with Luke 24:45."[17] Contrary to the weighty impression of this claim, it is true and relevant only if one first grants that διανοίγω denotes exposition of the Scriptures in Luke 24:45. In other words, if διανοίγω refers to the opening of the mind in Luke 24:45, it makes no difference that διανοίγω does not refer to exposition in the other two examples. Perhaps Bates means only to say, as he goes on to argue, that Luke 24:31 and Acts 16:14 lack the sort of exposition present in 24:44–47. But this is not obviously the case. For in Luke 24:31–32, the opening of eyes is connected with the opening of the Scriptures by the consecutive use of διανοίγω.[18] Further, in 24:32, the exposition of the Scriptures is connected to an experience involving a faculty of perception, the burning of the heart: οὐχὶ ἡ καρδία ἡμῶν καιομένη ... ὡς διήνοιγεν ἡμῖν τὰς γραφάς, "were our hearts not burning ... as he opened the scriptures to us?"[19] In fact, it is the two disciples' recognition of Jesus when their eyes are opened that triggers the memory of their burning hearts and the opening of the Scriptures.[20] As for Acts 16:14, Bates weakens his case for its dissimilarity when he says, "Paul presumably did argue to Lydia from the Scriptures."[21] Bates, like any informed reader of Luke-Acts, would rightly presume such, tempering his counterclaim that "the topos of scriptural exposition" is completely absent from the account of Lydia's conversion.[22]

This leaves the use of διανοίγω in Acts 17:2–3 for Paul's exposition of the Scriptures as the most compelling parallel to the alternative reading of Luke 24:45. Indeed, both contexts highlight a christological reading of the Scriptures that

---

[17] Bates, "Closed-Minded Hermeneutics?," 547.

[18] This is noted by, e.g., Robert C. Tannehill, *The Gospel according to Luke*, vol. 1 of *The Narrative Unity of Luke-Acts: A Literary Interpretation*, FF (Minneapolis: Fortress, 1986), 282; Luke Timothy Johnson, *The Gospel of Luke*, SP 3 (Collegeville, MN: Liturgical Press, 1991), 397, 399; Joel B. Green, "Learning Theological Interpretation from Luke," in *Reading Luke: Interpretation, Reflection, Formation*, ed. Craig G. Bartholomew, Joel B. Green, and Anthony C. Thiselton, Scripture and Hermeneutics 6 (Grand Rapids: Zondervan, 2005), 70; Richard B. Hays, *Reading Backwards: Figural Christology and the Fourfold Gospel Witness* (Waco, TX: Baylor University Press, 2014), 13–16.

[19] See I. Howard Marshall, *The Gospel of Luke: A Commentary on the Greek Text*, NIGTC (Grand Rapids: Eerdmans, 1978), 898. The variant reading of κεκαλυμμένη in Codex Bezae does not diminish this connection. For an account of how the theme of comprehension features in Codex Bezae, see Jenny Read-Heimerdinger and Josep Rius-Camps, "Emmaous or Oulammaous? Luke's Use of the Jewish Scriptures in the Text of Luke 24 in Codex Bezae," *RCT* 27 (2002): 23–42, esp. 29–31; see also Eldon Jay Epp, "The 'Ignorance Motif' in Acts and Antijudaic Tendencies in Codex Bezae," *HTR* 55 (1962): 51–62, http://dx.doi.org/10.1017/S001781600002410X.

[20] The narrative is not explicit about if or when the two on the road understood Jesus's exposition of the Scriptures. Given the theme of (mis)understanding outlined above, a case can easily be made that their understanding of the significance of Jesus's exposition was not realized until their eyes were opened (cf. Johnson, *Gospel of Luke*, 399).

[21] Bates, "Closed-Minded Hermeneutics?," 547.

[22] Ibid.

emphasizes Jesus's identification as the Christ and the necessity of his death and resurrection, an important theme in Luke-Acts, as Bates correctly notes. But this does not favor the alternative reading of Luke 24:45 over the traditional one. The necessity of Jesus's messianic suffering is precisely what the disciples *cannot* understand throughout the narrative of the Gospel to this point. Understanding is twice explicitly withheld from them in the wake of passion predictions (9:45, 18:34; cf. 19:42). This concealment of meaning is illustrated by the Emmaus disciples, whose eyes are "seized so as not to recognize Jesus" (οἱ δὲ ὀφθαλμοὶ αὐτῶν ἐκρατοῦντο τοῦ μὴ ἐπιγνῶναι αὐτόν) but later opened, enabling recognition and, as seen above, triggering the memory of their burning hearts at Jesus's exposition of the Scriptures (24:16, 31–32; cf. 24:25–27).[23] Comically, the disciples appear not to understand the meaning of Jesus's death even after the empty tomb and angelic message seen and heard by some of Jesus's followers were reported to them (24:10, 11); after the two on the road to Emmaus told of their experience (24:33–35); and after Jesus himself appeared to them (24:36, 37), offered to be touched (24:39), presented his hands and feet (24:40), and ate food before them (24:41).[24]

The narrative thus raises a question: What will it take for the disciples to understand?[25] Do they simply need exposition, as Bates's proposal would have it? Such a need is not anticipated by the narrative heretofore as the disciples had been subject to Jesus's teaching for some time.[26] It seems better to think that the disciples needed something *in addition to exposition*—they needed the very thing that enabled the Emmaus disciples to see and Lydia to receive:[27]

> Then he opened their mind to understand the Scriptures. And he said to them, "Thus it stands written, that the Christ would suffer and rise from the dead on the third day." (Luke 24:45–46)

---

[23] Indeed, Luke often illustrates his theology, as Richard I. Pervo notes: "One of the important contributions of literary analyses of Luke and Acts has been to indicate that the author communicates theological views by showing rather than telling, through story rather than through exposition" (*Acts: A Commentary*, Hermeneia [Minneapolis: Fortress, 2009], 43).

[24] Note the lingering doubts and misunderstanding spoken of in 24:37, 38, 41.

[25] Green raises a similar question in light of these considerations: "Why are the disciples so slow to comprehend?" ("Learning Theological Interpretation," 69).

[26] That Jesus's earlier teaching included exposition of the Scriptures is not only reasonably assumed but strongly implied by Luke 24:44.

[27] One of the more substantial arguments in this regard can be found in Richard J. Dillon, *From Eye-Witnesses to Ministers of the Word: Tradition and Composition in Luke 24*, AnBib 82 (Rome: Biblical Institute Press, 1978); see also Dillon, "Previewing Luke's Project from His Prologue (Luke 1:1–4)," *CBQ* 43 (1981): 205–27. Although Bates twice mentions Dillon, he does not interact with his arguments. Dillon's major thesis is that the Lukan *Leidensmysterium* remains unresolved until the revelatory action of the risen Christ in Luke 24, which depicts "Easter revelation as the pure gift of God, conveyed only through the personal presence and conclusive word of the risen Christ" (Dillon, *From Eye-Witnesses to Ministers*, ix).

This opening of the mind does not necessarily imply that, for Luke, any and every person stands in need of illumination to understand the Scriptures. Nor does it imply that exposition is unimportant in Luke's hermeneutics. In fleshing out the theological implications of his proposal, Bates implies that one must make a choice between possible ways of understanding, illumination or exposition, presented in the narrative.[28] He argues that the "important point" for Luke is "that someone ... must serve as a *suitable guide* to the reader in order to explain the 'meaning' of the Scriptures."[29] This may in fact be an important point for Luke but not to the exclusion of illumination. First, as the discussion above shows, Luke-Acts gives examples of both illumination and exposition. Second, the examples in Acts of suitable guides providing understanding cannot be read indiscriminately back into the Gospel as Bates does.[30] Even on a strong view of the unity of Luke-Acts, the theme of (mis)understanding functions differently in the narrative of Luke than it does in the book of Acts.[31] Third, suitable guides sometimes *fail* to produce understanding in others, indicating that much more is in play than just suitable guidance in Luke-Acts. Indeed, the penultimate note of Acts is one of fattened hearts and closed eyes in the face of Paul's preaching (Acts 28:24–28). In short, if one wishes to condense a "theology of understanding" from Luke-Acts, it is essential to account for the diversity of factors contributing to characters' understanding.[32] One of those factors is, without a doubt, illumination.

A reading of Luke 24:45 that takes νοῦν as the direct object of συνιέναι ignores normal Greek syntax, and the meaning that results—that Jesus exposits the Scriptures so the disciples will understand their meaning—does not fit the context of the Third Gospel nearly as well as the traditional reading. Indeed, a moment of illumination, not necessarily independent of exposition, resolves the conflict of misunderstanding experienced by the disciples throughout the narrative of Luke.

---

[28] Bates, "Closed-Minded Hermeneutics?," 556; cf. 538.

[29] Ibid., 556 (emphasis original).

[30] Attempting a theology of Luke-Acts (or any corpus) naturally focuses on similarities of passages, sections, books, and so on, at the risk of neglecting distinguishing features of respective parts.

[31] As can be seen, for example, in the role of concealment in the understanding of the disciples, outlined above. The unity question has recently been revisited in Andrew F. Gregory and C. Kavin Rowe, eds., *Rethinking the Unity and Reception of Luke and Acts* (Columbia: University of South Carolina Press, 2010); see also Mikeal C. Parsons and Richard I. Pervo, *Rethinking the Unity of Luke and Acts* (Minneapolis: Fortress, 1993).

[32] As exemplified in Green, "Learning Theological Interpretation," esp. 70–72; Joshua W. Jipp, "The Beginnings of a Theology of Luke-Acts: Divine Activity and Human Response," *Journal of Theological Interpretation* 8 (2014): 23–44; see also Martin Bauspieß, *Geschichte und Erkenntnis im lukanischen Doppelwerk: Eine exegetische Untersuchung zu einer christlichen Perspektive auf Geschichte*, ABIG 42 (Leipzig: Evangelische Verlagsanstalt, 2012).

Acts 9:1–9, 22:6–11, 26:12–18: Paul and Ezekiel

DALE C. ALLISON JR.
dale.allison@ptsem.edu
Princeton Theological Seminary, Princeton, NJ 08540

Although some commentators on Acts observe that a portion of Acts 26:16 borrows from LXX Ezek 2:1, the significance of this has not been grasped. The agreement belongs to a series of parallels between Ezekiel's inaugural vision and the accounts of Paul's call or conversion in Acts 9:1–9, 22:6–11, and 26:12–18. The best explanation for the scattered correlations is that Luke received a tradition or story that likened Paul's vision of Jesus to Ezekiel's vision of the anthropomorphic form of the Lord and indeed identified Paul's Lord with the figure in Ezekiel. It is possible that the apostle himself was responsible for this interpretation of his vision.

In his speech before King Herod Agrippa II, Paul narrates, for the third time in Acts, the story of his call or conversion (26:12–18). When dealing with this account, modern critical commentators typically concern themselves with its relationship to the two other reports of the apostle's vision (Acts 9:1–9, 22:6–11), with the Greek proverb that lies behind "It hurts for you to kick against the goads" (26:14), and with questions about the historicity of attendant events (e.g., How could Luke have known what Festus and Agrippa said to each other in private?). Exegetes also, if only in passing, often call attention to several reminiscences of the LXX. Acts 26:16 (στῆθι ἐπὶ τοὺς πόδας σου, "stand on your feet" [NRSV]) agrees exactly with Ezek 2:1.[1] Acts 26:18 (ἀνοῖξαι ὀφθαλμοὺς αὐτῶν [v.l. τυφλῶν] τοῦ ἐπιστρέψαι ἀπὸ σκότους εἰς φῶς, "to open their eyes so that they may turn from darkness to light" [NRSV]) echoes Isa 42:7 (ἀνοῖξαι ὀφθαλμοὺς τυφλῶν, ἐξαγαγεῖν ... ἐξ οἴκου φυλακῆς καθημένους ἐν σκότει, "to open the eyes that are blind, to bring out ... from the prison those who sit in darkness" [NRSV]) and 16 (ποιήσω αὐτοῖς τὸ σκότος εἰς φῶς, "I will turn the darkness before them into light" [NRSV]).[2] And Acts 26:17 (ἐξαιρούμενός σε ἐκ τοῦ λαοῦ καὶ ἐκ τῶν ἐθνῶν εἰς οὓς ἐγὼ ἀποστέλλω σε,

---

[1] Unless otherwise noted, references to Ezekiel will throughout be to the LXX.
[2] See Gerhard Lohfink, *The Conversion of St Paul: Narrative and History in Acts*, trans. and ed. Bruce J. Malina, Herald Scriptural Library (Chicago: Franciscan Herald, 1976), 70; Robert F.

"I will rescue you from your people and from the Gentiles—to whom I am sending you" [NRSV]) alludes to Jer 1:8 (μετὰ σοῦ ἐγώ εἰμι τοῦ ἐξαιρεῖσθαί σε, "I am with you to deliver you" [NRSV]) and 19 (μετὰ σοῦ ἐγώ εἰμι τοῦ ἐξαιρεῖσθαί σε).[3]

The use of Isaiah is readily explicable. In Acts, Paul is like the servant of Deutero-Isaiah: he is "a light to the nations" (Isa 42:6).[4] As Paul and Barnabas declare in Acts 13:46–47: "We are now turning to the gentiles. For so the Lord has commanded us, saying, 'I have set you to be a light for the gentiles, so that you may bring salvation to the ends of the earth'" (cf. Isa 49:6). The allusion to Jer 1 similarly makes sense. Jeremiah, like Isaiah's servant, was also appointed to be "a prophet to the nations" (Jer 1:5), and his prophetic mission brought him persecution, making for another parallel with Paul (cf. esp. Acts 26:17). What, however, might be the motivation for cutting and pasting a phrase from Ezekiel? That is the topic of this essay.

I. Previous Work

Most of the secondary literature is not very helpful here. Many exegetes fail even to note the parallel with Ezekiel.[5] An equal number cite it without offering comment.[6] A few observe that Luke here adds biblical language or color;[7] oth-

---

O'Toole, *Acts 26: The Climax of Paul's Defense (Ac 22:1–26:32)*, AnBib 78 (Rome: Biblical Institute Press, 1978), 66–67.

[3] See Lohfink, *Conversion of St Paul*, 70–71; Johannes Munck, *Paul and the Salvation of Mankind* (London: SCM, 1959), 27–28; O'Toole, *Acts 26*, 67. Note the extension of the allusion to Jeremiah in Ep. Apost. 31, in its account of Paul's call: "he will be a wall that does not fall" (cf. Jer 1:18).

[4] See C. K. Barrett, *A Critical and Exegetical Commentary on the Acts of the Apostles*, 2 vols., ICC (London: T&T Clark, 1998), 2:1160; and Holly Beers, *The Followers of Jesus as the 'Servant': Luke's Model from Isaiah for the Disciples in Luke-Acts*, LNTS 535 (London: Bloomsbury T&T Clark, 2015), 170–72.

[5] E.g., Hugo Grotius, *Annotationes in Novum Testamentum*, vol. 2, pt. 1 (Erlangen: Tetzschnerum, 1756), 161; Gottfried Schille, *Die Apostelgeschichte des Lukas*, THKNT 5 (Berlin: Evangelische Verlagsanstalt, 1983), 450; Mikeal C. Parsons, *Acts*, Paideia (Grand Rapids: Baker Academic, 2008), 342; Craig S. Keener, *Acts: An Exegetical Commentary*, 4 vols. (Grand Rapids: Baker Academic, 2014), 3:3229–31.

[6] E.g., Johann Albrecht Bengel, *Gnomon Novi Testamentii*, 2 vols. (Tübingen: Ludov. Frid. Fues, 1850), 1:601; Richard Belward Rackham, *The Acts of the Apostles* (London: Methuen, 1901), 468; Eugène Jacquier, *Les Actes des Apôtres*, EBib (Paris: Gabalda, 1926), 711; Kirsopp Lake and Henry J. Cadbury, eds., *The Acts of the Apostles: English Translation and Commentary*, part 1.4 of *The Beginnings of Christianity*, ed. F. J. Foakes Jackson and Kirsopp Lake (London: Macmillan, 1933), 319; Rudolf Pesch, *Die Apostelgeschichte*, 2 vols., EKKNT 5 (Zurich: Benziger; Neukirchen-Vluyn: Neukirchener Verlag, 1986), 2:277; Josef Zmijewski, *Die Apostelgeschichte*, RNT (Regensburg: Pustet, 1994), 847; J. Bradley Chance, *Acts*, SHBC (Macon, GA: Smyth & Helwys, 2007), 481; I. Howard Marshall, "Acts," in *Commentary on the New Testament Use of the Old Testament*, ed. G. K. Beale and D. A. Carson (Grand Rapids: Baker Academic, 2007), 599.

[7] See Ernest Haenchen, *The Acts of the Apostles: A Commentary* (Oxford: Blackwell, 1971),

ers—more helpfully—that his use of Ezekiel's call to depict Paul's call makes the latter a prophet like the former.[8] There is also, however, the view that the perfect word-for-word correlation between Acts 26:16 and Ezek 2:1 is simply a "coincidence."[9] In this case, the parallel is a phantom. It means nothing.

The most interesting discussions of the relationship between Acts 26:12–18 and Ezekiel known to me appear not in the commentaries but in an article by Gilles Quispel and in Alan Segal's monograph *Paul the Convert*.[10] Unfortunately, their proposals, while suggestive, remain brief and undeveloped. Perhaps it is understandable that their work is not yet reflected in the commentary tradition.

According to Quispel, "Luke's story of Paul on the Damascus Road contains some very clear allusions to the visionary experience of Ezekiel."[11] While Quispel does not cite chapter and verse, he clearly has Acts 26 in mind when he goes on to write, "Paul fell to earth and heard a voice saying to stand upon his feet because he is to be sent ... exactly as Ezekiel did." To this he adds one more parallel: "whereas Ezekiel was dumbfounded, Paul was blinded after his vision."[12] Quispel then draws his conclusion: "For those familiar with the meaning and purpose of such hints in

---

686 ("Luke has shaped the words of the exalted Lord ... with the aid of OT expressions"); Jacob Jervell, *Die Apostelgeschichte*, KEK 5 (Göttingen: Vandenhoeck & Ruprecht, 1998), 593; Hilary Le Cornu and Joseph Shulam, *A Commentary on the Jewish Roots of Acts*, 2 vols. (Jerusalem: Academon, 2003), 2:1402 ("biblical overtones"). According to Lohfink, Luke wants Jesus to speak "biblically" (*Conversion of St Paul*, 72). Fergus Kerr offers a compositional explanation: Luke had little information about what happened so he "turned to the Old Testament for examples of how to tell the story of an encounter with the Lord" ("Paul's Experience: Sighting or Theophany?," *NBf* 58 [1977]: 311, http://dx.doi.org/10.1111/j.1741-2005.1977.tb02349.x).

[8] So F. F. Bruce, *The Acts of the Apostles: The Greek Text with Introduction and Commentary*, 2nd ed. (Grand Rapids: Eerdmans, 1952), 444 (like Ezekiel, Paul is "called to prophetic service"); Joseph A. Fitzmyer, *The Acts of the Apostles: A New Translation with Introduction and Commentary*, AB 31 (New York: Doubleday, 1998), 759 ("the addition gives a prophetic nuance to the role that Paul is to play: he is to stand on his feet as did Ezekiel in his inaugural vision"); David G. Peterson, *The Acts of the Apostles*, PilNTC (Grand Rapids: Eerdmans, 2009), 667–68; Josep Rius-Camps and Jenny Read-Heimerdinger, *Acts 18.24–28.31: Rome via Ephesus and Jerusalem*, vol. 4 of *The Message of Acts in Codex Bezae: A Comparison with the Alexandrian Tradition*, LNTS 415 (London: T&T Clark, 2009), 356; Daniel Marguerat, *Les Acts des Apôtres (13–28)*, CNT 5b (Geneva: Labor et Fides, 2015), 337 (Christ calls Paul to service just as YHWH called the prophets to service). O'Toole offers a christological suggestion: Luke is trying to identify Jesus "in some way" with "the Lord of the OT" who called the prophets (*Acts 26*, 65, 68).

[9] "Zufall" is the characterization of Christoph Burchard, *Der dreizehnte Zeuge: Traditions- und kompositionsgeschichtliche Untersuchungen zu Lukas' Darstellung der Frühzeit des Paulus*, FRLANT 103 (Göttingen: Vandenhoeck & Ruprecht, 1970), 128–29.

[10] Gilles Quispel, "Ezekiel 1,26 in Jewish Mysticism and Gnosis," in *Gnostica, Judaica, Catholica: Collected Essays of Gilles Quispel*, ed. Johannes van Oort, NHMS 55 (Leiden: Brill, 2008), 461–74, http://dx.doi.org/10.1163/ej.9789004139459.i-870.138 (this essay originally appeared in *VC* 34 [1980]: 1–13); Alan F. Segal, *Paul the Convert: The Apostolate and Apostasy of Saul the Pharisee* (New Haven: Yale University Press, 1990).

[11] Quispel, "Ezek 1,26," 468.

[12] Ibid.

ancient literature, there cannot be the slightest doubt that the author of Acts is paralleling the vocation of Ezekiel and the vocation of St. Paul. As the *kabod* appeared to the prophet in Babylonia in 593 B.C., so the *kabod* appeared to Saul near Damascus in A.D. 32."[13]

Segal—whose debt to Quispel in this connection is unclear[14]—is like-minded. In his judgment, the "most provocative parallel to Luke's account of Paul's conversion is the commissioning of the prophet Ezekiel."[15] He follows this with a summary description of Ezek 1:18–2:3:

> Ezekiel was granted a vision of a figure shaped like a man, which is called "the likeness of the image of the Glory of God." When Ezekiel beheld the glory of God, he reported, "I fell upon my face, and I heard the voice of one that spoke" (Ezek 1:28). The Lord then ordered Ezekiel to stand, saying, "Stand upon your feet, and I will speak with you.... I send you to the people of Israel, to a nation of rebels, who have rebelled against me" (2:1–3).[16]

This brief recapitulation of a few famous verses in Ezekiel is the backdrop for Segal's equally short summary of Paul's commissioning vision in Acts: "Paul also has a revelation of the Glory of God. Paul hears a voice speaking, and it is clearly a revelatory voice because Paul reacts as Ezekiel did: he falls to the ground. Luke's Paul then rises, but with a significant modification: He receives the charge to go to foreign lands to proselytize a nation of rebels, gentiles rather than Jews as in Ezekiel."[17]

Although Segal fails to supply supporting references to his observations about Luke's Paul, it is easy to fill in the blanks. He is suggesting these parallels:

- Both Paul and Ezekiel see the divine glory: Ezek 1:28, Acts 22:11
- Both hear a revelatory voice: Ezek 1:28–2:8, Acts 9:4–6, 22:7–10, 26:14–18
- Both fall to the ground: Ezek 1:28, Acts 9:4, 22:7, 26:14
- Both then stand on their feet: Ezek 2:1–2, Acts 9:6–8, 22:10–11, 26:16
- Both are charged with a mission, one to Jews, one to gentiles: Ezek 2:3–7, Acts 26:16–18

What does Segal make of these correlations? He offers first that "Luke's reference to Ezekiel illustrates his contention that Paul's mission to the gentiles was contained by his conversion experience itself."[18] That is to say, Acts 9, 22, and 26 do not

---

[13] Ibid.

[14] A couple of pages after discussing Paul's conversion in Acts, Segal (*Paul the Convert*, 40) does name Quispel: Ezek 1 is "a crucial passage informing the christology of the New Testament, as Gilles Quispel has so cogently pointed out." This, however, refers to Quispel's "Hermetism and the New Testament," a piece submitted to the editors of *ANRW* in 1979 and never published. One guesses that there are overlaps between what Quispel says about Luke's Paul in this unpublished paper (which I have not seen) and his article on Ezek 1:26.

[15] Segal, *Paul the Convert*, 9.

[16] Ibid.

[17] Ibid.

[18] Ibid.

recount a conversion experience as opposed to a prophetic commissioning (cf. Gal 1:11–17). They rather interpret Paul's conversion as his divine calling. It follows that "the scholarly distinction between Paul's description of himself as commissioned prophetically and Luke's evaluation of Paul as a convert is thus too sharply drawn."[19]

Segal's second—and for us more important—point, is that the canonical account of Ezekiel's call refers to a vision of "something that seemed like a human form," a form identified as "the likeness of the glory of the LORD" (Ezek 1:26, 28). For Segal, Luke, by alluding to Ezekiel, implies "that the Glory of God was revealed to Paul."[20] As support for this assertion, he observes that early Christian texts often attribute "glory" to Jesus[21] and that Paul himself speaks of God's glory in connection with his conversion (2 Cor 3:16–4:6).[22] Segal goes on to contend that "Luke did not fabricate a relationship between Paul and Ezekiel" because the historical Paul was a mystagogue who belonged to the religious tradition that led to later *merkabah* mysticism, with its interest in Ezekiel's inaugural vision.[23]

Beyond his appeal to later *merkabah* texts and his lack of precision and clarity, several difficulties beset Segal's analysis.[24] One is that he neglects to observe that analogies between what happened to Paul on the Damascus road and the commissioning of any Hebrew prophet would disturb the neat antithesis between conversion and call. So why, if Luke, as Segal suggests, is trying to make that point, did he evoke Ezekiel in particular, or Ezekiel in addition to Isaiah and Jeremiah? Beyond that, Segal, like Quispel, proposes his parallels without looking at the details of texts or even citing them, and he makes no attempt to consider the Greek of Ezekiel or the Greek of Acts.[25] He contents himself with broad parallels of content and sequence without inquiring further. That does not suffice to establish his thesis.

To sum up: Quispel and Segal have, in my judgment, rightly perceived that, in Acts, Paul's calling is indeed akin to Ezekiel's. The following pages are an attempt to establish this point and to explore the consequences.

---

[19] Ibid.

[20] Ibid., 10.

[21] He cites (in this order) Jas 2:1, Phil 3:21, 1 Cor 2:8, Rom 6:4, 9:23, Phil 4:19, Eph 1:18, 3:16, Col 1:27, 2 Cor 4:4, 1 Tim 1:11, Heb 1:3, Eph 1:17.

[22] But whether 2 Cor 3:16–4:6 adverts to Paul's Damascus road experience is uncertain, as an acquaintance with the secondary literature on that passage makes plain. See n. 63 below

[23] Segal, *Paul the Convert*, 11. For a similar conclusion, but on the basis of different—and wholly inadequate—evidence, see J. W. Bowker, "'Merkabah' Visions and the Visions of Paul," *JSS* 16 (1971): 157–73, http://dx.doi.org/10.1093/jss/xvi.2.157.

[24] In addition to what follows, see the pointed criticism of Segal in Colleen Shantz, *Paul in Ecstasy: The Neurobiology of the Apostle's Life and Thought* (Cambridge: Cambridge University Press, 2009), 56–63, http://dx.doi.org/10.1017/CBO9780511581625.

[25] The same complaint can be lodged against Robin Griffith-Jones, *The Gospel according to Paul: The Creative Genius Who Brought Jesus to the World* (San Francisco: HarperSanFrancisco, 2004), 78–88. He makes some of the same observations as Quispel and Segal and then speculates that Paul was, on the Damascus road, meditating on Ezekiel's vision of the divine chariot.

II. Confirming the Parallel

1. The place to begin is Acts 26:16. Here the risen Jesus says to Paul: "Get up and stand on your feet." The Greek is στῆθι ἐπὶ τοὺς πόδας σου. As already observed, the revelatory voice in Ezek 2:1 utters the same words. That this is a coincidence is highly unlikely for the following reasons: (a) In both Ezekiel and Acts, στῆθι ἐπὶ τοὺς πόδας σου belongs to an inaugural call narrative. (b) The precise phrase στῆθι ἐπὶ τοὺς πόδας σου is altogether unattested in secular Greek texts, and it appears only once in the LXX, in Ezekiel. Further, only one extant Hellenistic Jewish work ever uses it, and that is Jos. Asen. 14:8 and 11, where the author is, as we shall see below, clearly dependent on Ezek 1–2.[26] Beyond that, the phrase is confined, in the entirety of Greek literature, to Ezek 2:1 LXX; Acts 26:16; and later Christian texts citing Ezekiel or Acts.

(c) Some commentators have found Acts 26:16—ἀνάστηθι καὶ στῆθι—a bit unexpected. According to C. K. Barrett, it involves "a very unpleasing repetition."[27] In Richard Pervo's words, the Greek is "unnecessarily expanded."[28] Both Pervo and Barrett, however, plausibly account for the redundancy as due to interference from a preformed text, Ezek 2:1.

2. The parallel between Acts 26:16 and Ezek 2:1 does not stand by itself. In Acts 26:14, Paul recounts that he "heard a voice speaking" to him. This resembles two phrases that occur right before and right after Ezek 2:1. One can see this at a glance:

Ezek 1:28	ἤκουσα φωνὴν λαλοῦντος	
Ezek 2:1		στῆθι ἐπὶ τοὺς πόδας σου
Ezek 2:2	ἤκουσον αὐτοῦ λαλοῦντος πρός με	
- - - - - - - - - - -		
Acts 26:14	ἤκουσα φωνὴν λέγουσαν πρός με	
Acts 26:16		στῆθι ἐπὶ τοὺς πόδας σου

3. Acts and Ezekiel share some additional linguistic parallels. By themselves, they would mean nothing, but, given what we have already seen, they should not be overlooked. Both Ezekiel and Paul "see" (εἶδον in Ezek 1:27 and Acts 26:13) a vision in the heavens (οὐρανοί in Ezek 1:1, οὐρανόθεν in Acts 26:13). Both men, upon beholding a supernatural light, fall to the ground (πίπτω in Ezek 1:28, καταπεσόντων in Acts 26:14). Both are divinely commissioned and sent forth with similar first-person declarations (ἐξαποστέλλω ἐγώ σε in Ezek 2:3, ἐγὼ ἀποστέλλω σε in

---

[26] Given that Christian hands copied all the extant texts of Joseph and Aseneth, one cannot exclude the possibility that Acts has influenced the formulations in Jos. Asen. 14:8 and 11.

[27] Barrett, *Acts*, 1159. B omits καὶ στῆθι. Note the simpler Acts 14:10: ἀνάστηθι ἐπὶ τοὺς πόδας σου.

[28] Richard Pervo, *Acts: A Commentary*, Hermeneia (Minneapolis: Fortress, 2009), 632.

Acts 26:17).²⁹ And both individuals are the object of the verb, ἐξαιρέω (ἐξῇρέν με in Ezek 2:2, ἐξαιρούμενός σε in Acts 26:17).

4. In Acts 26:13–14, Paul recalls his dramatic encounter with Jesus by reporting that "at midday along the road ... I saw a light from heaven, brighter than the sun, shining round me and my companions." This is important because, while there are several prophetic call narratives in the Hebrew Bible,³⁰ only one highlights the motif of a heavenly brilliance. It is true that, in Exod 3, God's voice speaks from a burning bush. Here, however, there is no heavenly vision: the bush is on Horeb. It is also the case that Isa 6:3, which belongs to the account of Isaiah's prophetic commission, refers to the divine glory. Yet it is a glory that fills the earth, not a glory that Isaiah is explicitly said to behold. It is only in Ezek 1–2 that the element of heavenly light is emphasized—and that in dramatic and repeated fashion: "brightness around it and fire flashing forth continually, something like gleaming amber" (1:4); "something that looked like burning coals of fire, like torches moving to and fro among the living creatures; the fire was bright, and lightning issued from the fire" (1:14); "shining like crystal" (1:22); "something like gleaming amber, something that looked like fire enclosed all around ... something that looked like fire, and there was splendor all around" (1:27); "splendor all around ... glory" (1:28). The upshot is that, if an early Christian were looking for biblical precedent for, or a parallel to, a story featuring both a supernatural heavenly light and a prophetic call, it is Ezekiel that would come to mind.³¹

5. There is even more to consider. The voice in Acts, as the subsequent narrative reveals, belongs to Jesus, "the Lord" (26:15, ὁ κύριος). There are not two separate things here, a light on the one hand and the Lord on the other. Rather, the light is the glory of Jesus. This is clear from 26:16, which interprets Paul's seeing "a light from heaven" as Jesus having "appeared" (ὤφθεν) to him. Even without this textual prodding, readers familiar with epiphany stories in which heavenly beings shine would have made the equation.³² One recalls in this connection the early Christian

---

²⁹Note Martin Hengel and Anna Maria Schwemer, *Paul between Damascus and Antioch: The Unknown Years* (Louisville: Westminster John Knox, 1997), 405 n. 737: "The ἐγὼ ἀποστέλλω σε [of Acts 26:17] could come from the LXX calls of the prophets in Isa. 6.7 and Ezek. 2.3."

³⁰See, e.g., Exod 3:1–12 (Moses), Josh 1:1–11 (Joshua), 1 Sam 3:1–4:1 (Samuel), Isa 6:1–6 (Isaiah), Isa 49:1–6 (the servant), Jer 1:4–19 (Jeremiah), Ezek 1:1–3:11 (Ezekiel). For discussion, see Dieter Vieweger, *Die Spezifik der Berufungsberichte Jeremias und Ezechiels im Umfeld ähnlicher Einheiten des Alten Testaments*, BEATAJ 6 (Frankfurt am Main: Lang, 1986); Rudolf Kilian, "Die prophetischen Berufungsberichte," in *Studien zu alttestamentlichen Texten und Situationen*, ed. Wolfgang Werner and Jürgen Werlitz, SBAB 28 (Stuttgart: Katholisches Bibelwerk, 1999), 53–76.

³¹It is of interest that Walther Zimmerli viewed the accounts of Paul's call in Acts 9, 22, and 26 as related to the same form-critical *Gattung* as Ezek 1:1–3:15 (*Ezekiel 1: A Commentary on the Book of the Prophet Ezekiel, Chapters 1–24*, Hermeneia [Philadelphia: Fortress, 1979], 110).

³²Note, e.g., Dan 10:6, T. Abr. 2:4, Lat. LAE 9:1, Jos. Asen. 14:9, Liv. Pro. Elijah 2, 2 En. 1:5, Matt 28:3, Luke 2:9, Acts 12:7, Rev 1:14–16.

tradition that the risen Jesus was supernaturally bright[33] as well as the claims in Luke 9:26 ("Those who are ashamed of me and of my words, of them the Son of Man will be ashamed when he comes in his glory") and 21:27 ("They will see the Son of Man coming in a cloud with power and great glory"). So the Lord who calls to Paul is the light, or at least its source.[34]

The situation in Ezekiel is similar. When Ezekiel sees the luminous anthropomorphic form, he hears a voice: "when I saw it [the appearance of the likeness of the glory of the Lord] … and I heard the voice of someone speaking" (1:28). Whose voice is this? Although the text does not say, it is natural to suppose that it comes from the anthropomorphic divinity that Ezekiel has just seen. There is no reference to an angel or any other third character, and the voice addresses the prophet with divine authority in the first person (2:1–8). In Ezekiel as in Acts, then, the heavenly voice comes from "the Lord."

6. One last point about the light. Ezekiel 1:26–28 does not declare that the prophet saw God directly. The verses rather state that he saw "the appearance of the likeness of the glory of the Lord." The convoluted language emphasizes the symbolic, indirect, indistinct nature of the vision, as does the repetition of ὡς (five times in three verses). The targum understandably elaborates with this: "an appearance of glory which the eye is unable to see, and such that it is impossible to look at upward … and downward."[35] Acts 26 is not so different. While Jesus "appears" (ὤφθεν) to Paul (v. 16), the content of this appearance, to judge from verse 13, is "a light from heaven." This light throws Paul to the ground and is "brighter than the sun." The comparison with the sun implies that the apostle could not look at it directly. Indeed, in Acts 22:11, he declares, "I could not see because of the brightness of that light." So here is yet another parallel.[36] Neither Ezekiel nor Paul gazes directly or without qualification at the heavenly "Lord."[37]

---

[33] On this motif, see James M. Robinson, "Jesus: From Easter to Valentinus (or the Apostles' Creed)," *JBL* 101 (1982): 5–37, http://dx.doi.org/10.2307/3260438.

[34] See Philip Doddridge, *The Family Expositor: Or, a Paraphrase and Version of the New Testament* (London: Frederick Westley & A. H. Davis, 1831), 405 (the light "was occasioned by the rays of glory which darted from the body of our Lord"); O'Toole, *Acts 26*, 60 (for Luke, the φῶς in Acts 9:3; 22:6, 9, 11; and 26:13 is "a way of referring to the Christ; Luke knew light as a designation of the Messiah and Savior").

[35] Note also 1 En. 14, which reworks parts of Ezek 1 (see n. 47 below): "It [the vision of the divine throne] was difficult to look at it" (v. 19); "none of the angels was able to come in and see the face of the Excellent and Glorious One; and no one of the flesh can see him" (v. 21).

[36] It may also be pertinent that, if the heavenly light in Ezekiel is "around" things (1:4: κύκλῳ; 1:27: κύκλῳ; 1:28: κυκλόθεν—all for the MT's סביב), the light in Acts "surrounds" Paul (9:3: περιήστραψεν; 22:6: περιαστράψαι … περὶ ἐμέ; 26:13: περιλάμψαν). Rabbinic tradition noticed and expanded this *merkabah* motif; cf. y. Ḥag. 2.1 (77a) ("fire encompassed [הקיפה] them"); b. Ḥag. 14b ("fire surrounded [סיבבה] all the trees"); Mek. R. Shimon b. Yoḥai Nezikin 58.1 ("until fire was glowing around [סביבו] all his sides").

[37] See O'Toole, *Acts 26*, 58–59: "*phōs* strikes us as vague. One cannot claim that he saw

7. Segal proposed a list of parallels between Ezek 1–2 and all three accounts of Paul's call. If, however, we confine ourselves to Acts 26:12–18 and put together the preceding observations, the upshot is a string of coherent parallels that occur in the same order:

Acts 26	Ezekiel 1–2 LXX
13 Paul sees (εἶδον) in heaven (οὐρανόθεν) a bright light that is identified as Jesus or his glory ("a light from heaven, brighter than the sun, shining round me"), or as the "Lord" (κύριε, κύριος)	1:26–28 Ezekiel sees (εἶδον) in heaven (οὐρανοί) a divine man of fire and splendor ("something that looked like fire, and there was a splendor all round") who is the Lord (κυρίου)
14 Paul falls (καταπεσόντων) to the ground	1:28 Ezekiel falls (πίπτω) on his face
14 He hears a voice, that of the Lord, speaking to him: ἤκουσα φωνὴν λέγουσαν πρός με	2:2 He hears a voice, that of the Lord, speaking to him: ἤκουσον αὐτοῦ λαλοῦντος πρός με; cf. 1:28, ἤκουσα φωνὴν λαλοῦντος
16 The voice tells him to stand on his feet: στῆθι ἐπὶ τοὺς πόδας σου	2:2 The voice tells him to stand on his feet: στῆθι ἐπὶ τοὺς πόδας σου
17 The voice commissions Paul with the words, ἐγὼ ἀποστέλλω σε	2:3 The voice commissions Ezekiel with the words, ἐξαποστέλλω ἐγώ σε

While Ezek 1–2 is far from being the only biblical text that has gone into the making of Acts 26:12–18, it has clearly influenced the structure, content, and phrasing of the New Testament passage.

8. If we leave the account of Paul's call in Acts 26 and turn to the variants in chapters 9 and 22, there are additional parallels with Ezekiel. This is important because, in the words of Charles Hedrick, "the complete story of Paul's conversion, as Luke understood it, can only be determined by bringing together features from all three narratives. The entire story is not completely narrated in any one of the three accounts."[38]

a. Acts 9:1–9, the first version of Paul's call, has a phrase—"get up and enter the city, and you will be told what you are to do" (v. 6)—that lines up with Ezek

---

something and describe it more vaguely than by saying he saw a light." O'Toole further suggests that Luke had in mind biblical texts such as Deut 4:12, where God's voice is heard but no form is seen (63).

[38] Charles W. Hedrick, "Paul's Conversion/Call: A Comparative Analysis of the Three Reports in Acts," *JBL* 100 (1981): 432, http://dx.doi.org/10.2307/3265962.

3:22: "Then the hand of the Lord was upon me there; and he said to me, 'Rise up, go out into the valley, and there I will speak with you.'"[39]

Acts 9:6   ἀνάστηθι καὶ εἴσελθε εἰς τὴν πόλιν καὶ   λαληθήσεταί σοι
Ezek 3:22 ἀνάστηθι καὶ ἔξελθε εἰς τὸ   πεδίον καὶ ἐκεῖ λαληθήσεται πρὸς σέ

The combination of verbs, ἀνάστηθι + ἔξελθε + λαληθήσεται, in this order, is attested only once in pre-Christian sources, in Ezekiel, and thereafter only in a single Christian quotation of Ezek 3:22.[40] The comparable sequence in Acts, ἀνάστηθι + εἴσελθε + λαληθήσεται, is almost as rare. It appears only in Acts and in later quotations of Acts.[41] Apart from a few patristic texts, therefore, ἀνάστηθι + εἴσ/ἔξελθε + λαληθήσεται is confined to Ezek 3:22 and Acts 9:6. When one adds that, in both places, εἴσ/ἔξελθε directly precedes εἰς + definite article and that πρὸς σέ or the synonymous σοι immediately follows λαληθήσεται, which refers to the voice of "the Lord," coincidence seems far-fetched. Acts here again borrows from Ezekiel.

One might protest that Ezek 3:22, unlike the other verses already appealed to, is not from the call narrative in Ezek 1–2. This, however, would be an empty objection. Ezekiel 3:23, the verse after 3:22, has this: "So I rose up and went out into the valley; and the glory of the Lord stood there, like the glory that I had seen by the river Chebar; and I fell on my face" (3:23). An event like that in Ezek 3 is an event like that in Ezek 1.

b. In Ezek 1:13, the prophet sees lightning—ἀστραπή—issuing from the heavenly radiance, and twice he uses the related verb, ἐξαστράπτω (vv. 4, 7). Acts 9:3 says that the light from heaven "flashed all around" Paul. The verb is περιαστράπτω. The same verb recurs in the second version of Paul's call, in Acts 22:6: περιαστράψαι φῶς. So the flashing light that Paul sees is akin to that in Ezekiel.[42]

c. Acts 22:11 speaks of the "glory" (δόξης) of the light Paul sees on his way to Damascus. In Ezek 1:28, the prophet sums up his vision of the anthropomorphic form of the Lord with these words: "This was the appearance of a likeness of the glory [δόξης] of the Lord."[43]

---

[39] The vast majority of commentators miss this; exceptions include Edward William Grinfield, *H KAINH ΔIAΘHKH: Novum Testamentum Graecum* (London: Pickering, 1843), 654; Henry Alford, *Acts, Romans, Corinthians*, vol. 2 of *The Greek Testament* (Boston: Lee & Shepherd, 1874), 99; Fitzmyer, *Acts*, 426. None, however, offers comment. Recent editions of the Nestle-Aland Greek New Testament print "Ez 3,22" in the margin beside Acts 9:6.

[40] Theodoret of Cyrrhus, *Ezek.* (PG 86:852).

[41] Chrysostom, *Hom. 1–55 Acts* (PG 50:153); Cyril of Alexandria, *Thesarus de Trin.* (PG 75:500); *Catenae graecorum patrum in novum testamentum*, ed. J. A. Cramer, 8 vols. (Oxford: Typographeo Academico, 1844), 3:152.

[42] This is why Grinfield cites Ezek 1:13 as a parallel to Acts 9:3 (*H KAINH ΔIAΘHKH*, 654).

[43] It is noteworthy that the one-sentence summary of Ezekiel in Sir 49:8 refers to Ezek 1 and to the glory the prophet saw: "It was Ezekiel who saw the vision of glory [δόξης], which God showed him above the chariot of the cherubim."

d. In Acts 9:8–9, after Paul encounters Jesus, he is unable to see for three days (cf. also 22:11), and he neither eats nor drinks. Perhaps it is worth noting that, while the terms and substance are different, Ezekiel's vision and calling likewise leave him overwhelmed and incapacitated.[44] The NRSV translates the end of Ezek 3:15 with these words: "And I sat there among them, stunned, for seven days." The NEB has: "I sat dumbfounded among them there, where they were living, for seven days." The Hebrew verb rendered by "stunned" and "dumbfounded" in these translations is שׁמם. It can also mean "desolated" or "appalled" (cf. Gen 47:19, Ezra 9:3–4). The precise connotations in Ezek 3:15 are unclear. In the targum, Ezekiel is reduced to silence (שׁתיק). The LXX unexpectedly turns שׁמם into ἀναστρεφόμενος, with this result: ἐκάθισα ἐκεῖ ἑπτά ἡμέρας ἀναστρεφόμενος ἐν μέσῳ. The sense of this is unclear. The NETS has this: "I sat there seven days face about among them." This is as hard to fathom as the Greek. In any case, there are witnesses to the notion that, after being called, Ezekiel was temporarily disabled.[45]

9. The odds that one text intentionally recalls another are improved if the latter is prominent in the tradition of the former, and especially if it is cited or alluded to in other, related texts. This matters because recent work has demonstrated the far-reaching influence of Ezek 1–2 on early Jewish and Christian literature.[46] In particular, there was a tradition of assimilating visions and commissioning stories to Ezek 1–2. George Nickelsburg has shown that the description of Enoch's prophetic commissioning in 1 En. 14:8–16:4 relies heavily on Ezek 1–2.[47] The opening vision in Revelation, in chapter 4, is also, as commentators have always seen, full of

---

[44] Cf. Quispel, "Ezekiel 1,26," 469. G. A. Cooke also observes the parallel (*A Critical and Exegetical Commentary on the Book of Ezekiel*, ICC [Edinburgh: T&T Clark, 1936], 43).

[45] If Dan 10:9–10, like Acts, depends on Ezek 1:28–2:1 (see n. 51 below), it is noteworthy that Daniel, after his vision, falls unconscious or into a trance and is speechless (10:15).

[46] For overviews, see Christopher Rowland, "The Visions of God in Apocalyptic Judaism," *JSJ* 10 (1979): 137–54; Rowland, *The Open Heaven: A Study of Apocalyptic in Judaism and Early Christiantiy* (New York: Crossroad, 1982), 94–113; David J. Halperin, *The Faces of the Chariot: Early Jewish Responses to Ezekiel's Vision*, TSAJ 16 (Tübingen: Mohr Siebeck, 1988); Carey C. Newman, *Paul's Glory-Christology: Tradition and Rhetoric*, NovTSup 69 (Leiden: Brill, 1992), 92–104; Quispel, "Ezekiel 1,26," 461–74. One should further bear in mind that some archaeological remains appear to feature *merkabah* wheels, which would be consistent with a far-flung knowledge of Ezekiel; see Mordechai Aviam, "The Decorated Stone from the Synagogue at Migdal: A Holistic Interpretation and a Glimpse into the Life of Galilean Jews at the Time of Jesus," *NovT* 55 (2013): 105–20, http://dx.doi.org/10.1163/15685365-12341433; Aviam, "Reverence for Jerusalem and the Temple in Galilean Society," in *Jesus and Temple: Textual Evidence and Archaeological Explorations*, ed. James H. Charlesworth (Minneapolis: Fortress, 2014), 123–44.

[47] George W. E. Nickelsburg, *1 Enoch 1: A Commentary on the Book of 1 Enoch, Chapters 1–36; 81–108*, Hermeneia (Minneapolis: Fortress, 2001), 254–56. Cf. Rowland, "Visions of God," 140–42.

themes, motifs, and vocabulary from Ezek 1.[48] So too is Abraham's vision in Apoc. Abr. 18:1–19:9.[49] For our purposes, however, the most instructive example of borrowing from Ezek 1–2 appears in Joseph and Aseneth.[50]

In this book's fourteenth chapter, the heavens are split and a great light appears. Aseneth then falls on her face. A heavenly "man," the commander of the host of the Most High, descends and calls to her. When she raises her head to see him, his face is like lightning, his eyes like sunshine, his hair a flame of fire and a burning torch. His hands and feet, which shoot sparks, are like iron shining in fire. Aseneth again falls on her face. But the angel tells her to rise and stand on her feet because he has something to say to her. She does so, and the commander tells her what to do in preparation for her new life. He subsequently grasps her head and shakes it with his right hand, after which he instructs Aseneth to eat a miraculously supplied honeycomb, which she does.

This peculiar text exhibits a number of parallels with the opening chapters of Ezekiel.

Joseph and Aseneth 14–16	Ezekiel 1–3 LXX
14:2 The heavens split: ἐσχίσθη ὁ οὐρανός.	1:1 The heavens open: ἠνοίχθησαν οἱ οὐρανοί.
14:3 A great light appears.	1:4 A great light appears.
14:3, 10 Aseneth falls on her face: ἔπεσεν ἐπὶ πρόσωπον.	1:28 Ezekiel falls on his face: πίπτω ἐπὶ πρόσωπον.

[48] See, e.g., Rev 4:3 with Ezek 1:16, 26–18; Rev 4:6–7 with Ezek 1:5–25; and Rev 10:8–9 with Ezek 2:8; 3:1–3. See esp. Beate Kowalski, *Die Rezeption des Propheten Ezechiel in der Offenbarung des Johannes*, SBB 52 (Stuttgart: Katholisches Bibelwerk, 2004), 75, 102–18, 149–51, 307–24.

[49] See Ryszard Rubinkiewicz, *L'Apocalypse d'Abraham en vieux slave: Introduction, texte critique, traduction et commentaire* (Lublin: Société des Lettres et des Sciences de l'Université de Lublin, 1987), 87, 163. On the apparent debt of Dan 7 to Ezekiel, see those cited in n. 80 below.

[50] For the following I rely on the critical edition of Uta Barbara Fink, *Joseph und Aseneth: Revision des griechischen Textes und Edition der zweiten lateinischen Übersetzung*, FoSub 5 (Berlin: de Gruyter, 2008). The parallels between Jos. Asen. 14 and the stories about Paul in Acts have long been noted; see, e.g., Lohfink, *Conversion of St Paul*, 65–67; Burchard, *Der dreizehnte Zeuge*, 59–88. For our purposes, it does not matter whether Joseph and Aseneth was written at the turn of the era or later, or whether the author was a Christian or (as I am inclined to think) a Jew, or even whether the book at points shows the influence of Acts (a possibility for which there is no clear evidence). It might perhaps matter were one to hold that Acts shows knowledge of the romance. The latter, however, may be as late as the third or fourth century (see Ross Shepard Kraemer, *When Aseneth Met Joseph: A Late Antique Tale of the Biblical Patriarch and His Egyptian Wife Reconsidered* [Oxford: Oxford University Press, 1998]). More importantly, not all of the intertextual links between Ezekiel and Acts are represented in Joseph and Aseneth, nor are all of the intertextual links between Ezekiel and Joseph and Aseneth represented in Acts. This establishes at least partial independent use of the prophet on the part of both books.

Joseph and Aseneth 14–16	Ezekiel 1–3 LXX
14:8 The angel tells Aseneth to stand on her feet so that he can speak to her: στῆθι ἐπὶ τοὺς πόδας σου καὶ λαλήσω πρός σε; so too v. 11.	2:1 The divine voice tells Ezekiel to stand on his feet so that it can speak to him: στῆθι ἐπὶ τοὺς πόδας σου καὶ λαλήσω πρὸς σέ.
14:9 The angel's face is like lightning (ὡς ἀστραπή); it displays splendor (φέγγος); it is as a flame of fire (πυρός); it is like a burning torch or lamp (λαμπάδος παιομένης).	1:4, 7, 13, 27–28 Ezekiel sees lightning (ἀστραπή; v.l.: ὡς ἀστραπή), splendor (φέγγος), fire (πῦρ), and something like lamps or torches (λαμπάδων) coming together.
14:9 The angel's hands and feet shoot sparks (σπινθῆρες ... τῶν ποδῶν αὐτοῦ).	7 The feet of heavenly creatures are wings that shoot sparks (οἱ πόδες αὐτῶν ... σπινθῆρες)
16:1–16 The angel creates a honeycomb (μελίσσης) full of honey (μέλι, μέλιτος) and commands Aseneth to eat it (φάγε); she does (ἔφαγεν).	2:8–3:2 The heavenly voice commands Ezekiel to eat what he hands him (κατάφαγε); he does (ἔφαγον); it tastes as sweet as honey (μέλι).

In light of these correlations, one wonders whether the strange notice in Jos. Asen. 16:12–13, that the angel stretched forth his right hand and grasped Aseneth by her head and shook her—ἐξέτεινε τὴν χεῖρα αὐτοῦ τὴν δεξιὰν καὶ ἔθεγε τὴν κεφαλὴν αὐτῆς καὶ ἐπέσεισε—has something to do with Ezekiel. That the hand of the Lord was upon Ezekiel is a recurring motif in that book (Ezek 1:3, 3:22, 8:1, 33:33, 37:1, 40:1), and in Ezek 8:3, "the likeness of a man" stretches the form of a hand, which lifts up Ezekiel by the top of his head: ἐξέτεινεν ὁμοίωμα χειρὸς καὶ ἀνέλαβέν με τῆς κορυφῆς μου.

Whatever one makes of that possibility, it is of particular interest that, in borrowing from Ezekiel, Joseph and Aseneth, like Acts, makes use of 2:1:

Ezek 2:1   στῆθι ἐπὶ τοὺς πόδας σου καὶ λαλήσω πρὸς σέ
Acts 26:16   στῆθι ἐπὶ τοὺς πόδας σου
Jos. Asen. 14:8   στῆθι ἐπὶ τοὺς πόδας σου καὶ λαλήσω πρὸς σέ

This suggests that the phrase in Ezek 2:1 was indeed memorable and adds to the evidence that the verbal agreement between this text and Acts 26:16 is not coincidental but intentional.[51]

---

[51] Note also the probable use of Ezek 1:28–2:2 in Dan 10:9–10, 18; see Matthias Henze, "The Use of Scripture in the Book of Daniel," in *A Companion to Biblical Interpretation in Early Judaism*, ed. Matthias Henze (Grand Rapids: Eerdmans, 2012), 290–91; Alex P. Jassen, "Apocalypse and Interpretation in the Context of Jewish Scriptural Interpretation," in *The Oxford Handbook of Apocalyptic Literature*, ed. John J. Collins (Oxford: Oxford University Press, 2014), 75–76.

III. Luke or Luke's Tradition?

When attempting to explain why Luke's accounts of Paul's call allude to lines from Isaiah and Jeremiah, scholars often remark on their similar vocations: each is called to be a light or prophet to the nations (see above). This seems correct, and it is confirmed by the fact that Acts uses phrases connected to those two prophets that have to do with their mission. There is, by contrast, no obvious correlation between Ezekiel's mission and Paul's mission, between what God tells Ezekiel to do and what Jesus tells Paul to do.[52] The parallels instead lie in the circumstances surrounding their commissionings: both have the same sort of overwhelming visionary experience. They see and are surrounded by a heavenly light and then are addressed by a heavenly figure.

Perhaps that is all that the text is designed to say: Paul's call was like that of a biblical prophet.[53] Yet one wonders. An intertextually savvy reader who spots the resemblances between Ezekiel and Acts could—like Quispel and Segal—easily go a step further. Later Christians commonly identified the preexistent Christ with figures in various Hebrew Bible theophanies,[54] including the anthropomorphic form of the Lord in Ezek 1:26–28. Justin Martyr wrote that the Son of God was called "a man" (ἀνήρ) by Ezekiel,[55] and Gregory of Nyssa asserted that the one appearing in "human form" (ἀνθρωπικῷ σχήματι) to Ezekiel was also the one who dazzled Paul in light (ὁ ἐν τῷ φωτὶ καταστράψας τὸν Παῦλον).[56] Does Acts already

---

[52] One could draw a parallel between the opposition to Ezekiel (see Ezek 2:1–8) and the Jewish opposition to Paul (Acts 26:21), but the rejection of prophets was a topos, not a theme associated especially with Ezekiel; see Odil Hannes Steck, *Israel und das gewaltsame Geschick der Propheten: Untersuchungen zur Überlieferung des deuteronomistischen Geschichtsbildes im Alten Testament, Spätjudentum und Urchristentum*, WMANT 23 (Neukirchen-Vluyn: Neukirchener Verlag, 1967).

[53] Compare how 2 Bar. 1:1 ("And it came to pass in the twenty-fifth year of [the life of] Jeconiah, king of Judah") dates itself to the same year as Ezek 1:1 ("it was the fifth year of the exile of King Jehoiachin"), and how Sefer Zerubbabel (ed. Jellink, 2:54) locates Zerubbabel's vision by the River Chebar (cf. Ezek 1:1, 3:23, 10:32, 43:3) and has a *rûaḥ* lift him up between heaven and earth (cf. Ezek 8:3). In neither case does the seer's vision significantly resemble what Ezekiel saw.

[54] Note, e.g., Justin, *Dial.* 126–128. The same idea is probably already present in more than one New Testament text; see A. T. Hanson, *Jesus Christ in the Old Testament* (London: SPCK, 1965), 10–47, 136–38; Jarl E. Fossum, "Kyrios Jesus as the Angel of the Lord in Jude 5–7," *NTS* 33 (1987): 226–43, http://dx.doi.org/10.1017/S0028688500022645; Charles A. Gieschen, *Angelomorphic Christology: Antecedents and Early Evidence*, AGJU 42 (Leiden: Brill, 1998), 325–29.

[55] Justin, *Dial.* 126.1; cf. 61.1: the Holy Spirit calls Jesus "the Glory of the Lord."

[56] Gregory of Nyssa, *Adv. Apoll. ad Thpl.*, ed. Mueller, 122. This was a fairly common sentiment; see Angela Russell Christman, *"What Did Ezekiel See?" Christian Exegesis of Ezekiel's Vision of the Chariot from Irenaeus to Gregory the Great*, Bible in Ancient Christianity 4 (Leiden: Brill, 2005), 29–33.

imply this equation?[57] It would be no more surprising than, or rather it would be analogous to, the claim of John 12:41, that Isaiah "saw his glory," that is, the glory of Jesus, and "spoke about him." For this appears to interpret the famous theophany of Isa 6:1–5 as a vision of Jesus, in this case the preexistent Logos.[58]

However one sorts through the christological issue (to which we shall return below), the question of origin remains. Should we ascribe the parallels between Paul and Ezekiel to the author of Acts or to his tradition? The latter option seems the safer bet.

1. Aside from its narratives about Paul's conversion, Luke-Acts makes no clear allusion to Ezekiel's *merkabah* vision.[59]

2. Although the presence of Luke's hand in Acts 26:12–18, 9:1–9, and 22:6–11 is manifest,[60] it is equally obvious that these three passages contain traditional features. This is because some particulars must be judged, on the testimony of Paul, to be historical.[61] The apostle himself believed that he had seen the risen Jesus (1 Cor 9:1, 15:8), and he claimed to have received, through "a revelation of Jesus Christ" (Gal 1:12), a calling to preach to the gentiles (Gal 1:15–16). Further, that this event, which interrupted Paul's persecution of Christians (1 Cor 15:9, Gal 1:13),

---

[57] One might return a negative verdict on the basis of Acts 7:55, according to which Stephen "gazed into heaven and saw the glory of God and Jesus [δόξαν θεοῦ καὶ Ἰησοῦ] standing at the right hand of God." This might be taken to imply a distinction between Christ and the divine glory. This, however, would be to read too much into the Greek. The construction is not unnaturally understood as an instance of hendiadys: Stephen sees Jesus, who is the divine Glory standing at the right hand of God.

[58] So most commentators; see Barnabas Lindars, *The Gospel of John*, NCB (London: Oliphants, 1972), 439 ("John means that the theophany of Isa. 6.1ff. was a sight of the glory of the Logos"), and cf. 4 Bar. 9:20 ("These again are the words that were spoken by Isaiah, son of Amoz, saying, 'I saw God and the Son of God'"); also Asc. Isa. 9:27–32. It is intriguing, given the preceding discussion of Joseph and Aseneth, that Kraemer entertains the possibility that the angelic figure in Joseph and Aseneth, who is called an ἄνθρωπος (17:9), is the divine image on the throne in Ezek 1:26 (*When Joseph Met Aseneth*, 123, 146 n. 105).

[59] See Quispel, "Ezek 1,26," 469. This is not to say that the author of Luke-Acts nowhere else employs Ezekiel. Acts 10:14 seems designed to recall Ezek 4:14, and perhaps there is an echo of Ezek 11:24 in Acts 8:39, or some connection between Ezek 43:1–12 and Stephen's vision of Jesus in Acts 7; see Heike Braun, *Geschichte des Gottesvolkes und christliche Identität: Eine kanonisch-intertextuelle Auslegung der Stephanusepisode Apg 6,1–8,3*, WUNT 2/279 (Tübingen: Mohr Siebeck, 2010), 400–401. My assertion concerns only the initial vision of the *merkabah*. To my knowledge, the only other place occasionally proposed as an allusion to Ezek 1–2 is Acts 10:11, where the heavens are opened and Peter has a vision. As the history of interpretation demonstrates, however, readers of Acts have always been much more likely to move from Acts 10:11 to Luke 3:21 (Jesus's baptismal vision) or to Acts 7:56 (Stephen's vision of the Son of man).

[60] See O'Toole, *Acts 26*, 53–55.

[61] With what follows, cf. Gerd Lüdemann, *The Acts of the Apostles: What Really Happened in the Earliest Days of the Church* (Amherst, NY: Prometheus, 2005), 128–30.

occurred on the road to Damascus (Acts 9:3, 22:6, 26:12) accords with Gal 1:16: "nor did I go up to Jerusalem to those who were already apostles before me, but I went away at once into Arabia, and afterwards I returned to Damascus." Acts, in agreeing with Paul in all these particulars, shows its debt to tradition.[62] The book may also be following tradition in having Paul behold a supernatural light. As the secondary literature attests, 2 Cor 4:6 ("God … has shone in our hearts to give the light of the knowledge of the glory of God in the face of Jesus Christ") might well advert to Paul's foundational vision of Jesus.[63]

3. Acts, as already observed, narrates Paul's experience on the Damascus road with language from Jer 1 and Isa 42. Paul's letters do something similar. In the words of J. Louis Martyn, when the apostle, in Gal 1:15–16, recounts how he became a missionary to the gentiles, "he clearly has in mind the call of Jeremiah," and "equally obvious is the influence on Paul of the 'call tradition' as it is employed in the second servant song of Second Isaiah" (Isa 49:1–6).[64] Given, then, that elsewhere Paul displays his prophetic self-conception by associating his person with phrases from Deutero-Isaiah, including Isa 42,[65] it is likely that Luke did not invent the intertextual links in Acts 26:17 and 18.[66] Surely this increases the odds that the same holds true for the allusions to Ezekiel in the same passage.

4. Although the intertextual links with Ezekiel are strongest in Acts 26:12–18, the other two accounts of Paul's call—9:1–9 and 22:6–11—also echo the prophet, and in ways 26:12–18 does not. The scriptural connections are, in brief, strewn throughout three chapters. This makes it hard for readers to pick up the allusions.

---

[62] In the judgment of Burchard (*Der dreizehnte Zeuge*, 128–29), Acts 26:12–18 in particular is so close to what we know from Paul that it must either go back to Paul himself or reflect knowledge of his letters.

[63] See esp. Seyoon Kim, *The Origin of Paul's Gospel*, WUNT 2/4 (Tübingen: Mohr Siebeck, 1981), 5–13; also Karl Olav Sandnes, *Paul, One of the Prophets? A Contribution to the Apostle's Self-Understanding*, WUNT 2/43 (Tübingen: Mohr Siebeck, 1991), 131–46; Udo Schnelle, *Apostle Paul: His Life and Theology* (Grand Rapids: Baker Academic, 2005), 91 (observing that "from the viewpoint of the history of traditions, the motif of the glory of the chosen one points to a throne room vision [cf. Ezek 1:26, 28; 1 En. 45:1–6; 49:1–4]"). Contrast Victor Paul Furnish, *II Corinthians*, AB 32A (Garden City, NY: Doubleday, 1984), 250–51.

[64] J. Louis Martyn, *Galatians: A New Translation with Introduction and Commentary*, AB 33A (New York: Doubleday, 1997), 156. Cf. Ambrosiaster, *Gal. ad loc.* (CSEL 81.3, ed. Vogels, 14), and Grotius, *Annotationes*, 548; and see further Roy E. Ciampa, *The Presence and Function of Scripture in Galatians 1 and 2*, WUNT 2/102 (Tübingen: Mohr Siebeck, 1998), 111–23.

[65] For Isa 42 as part of Paul's self-conception, see Seyoon Kim, *Paul and the New Perspective: Second Thoughts on the Origin of Paul's Gospel* (Grand Rapids: Eerdmans: 2002), 101–27.

[66] Here the work of Munck remains persuasive (*Paul and the Salvation of Mankind*, 24–33). Contrast Lohfink, who imagines that Paul and Luke forged the links with Jeremiah and Isaiah independently of each other (*Conversion of St Paul*, 71–72).

If, however, all of the verbal parallels were instead together in one place in Acts, matters would be very different. Consider the following chart, with phrases from Acts 9:1–9, 22:6–11, and 26:12–18 on the left, phrases from Ezek 1–3 on the right.

Acts	Ezekiel
οὐρανόθεν, οὐρανοῦ	οὐρανοί
εἶδον	εἶδον
περιήστραψεν, or περιαστράψαι	ἀστραπή, ἐξαστράπτω
δόξης	δόξης
κύριε, κύριος	κυρίου, κύριος
πεσών, ἔπεσα, or καταπεσόντων	πίπτω
στῆθι ἐπὶ τοὺς πόδας σου	στῆθι ἐπὶ τοὺς πόδας σου
ἐξαιρούμενός σε	ἐξῆρέν με
ἤκουσα φωνὴν λέγουσαν πρός με	ἤκουσον αὐτοῦ λαλοῦντος πρός με
ἐγὼ ἀποστέλλω σε	ἐξαποστέλλω ἐγώ σε
ἀνάστηθι καὶ εἴσελθε εἰς τὴν πόλιν καὶ λαληθήσεταί σοι	ἀνάστηθι καὶ ἔξελθε εἰς τὸ πεδίον καὶ ἐκεῖ λαληθήσεται πρὸς σέ

If all the phrases on the left were in a single account of Paul's call, the borrowing would be obvious to all, especially given (a) that the text on the right was well known, (b) that in each case a famous person encounters a supernatural light and hears a heavenly voice, (c) that both times the voice gives that person his prophetic mission, and (d) that the words and phrases occur in mostly the same sequence.[67]

Luke, however, did not put things together like this. Maybe he anticipated hearers who knew the Scriptures so well that they could add fleeting allusion to fleeting allusion and come away with the big picture. The later commentators, however, have not done this, despite so many knowing the Bible inside out. I am inclined to the hypothesis that Luke had a single account of Paul's call which he used at three different points in his narrative[68] and that, in moving its pieces around, he inadvertently scattered the links to Ezekiel, thereby drastically diminishing the odds that readers would espy the allusive anthologizing.

---

[67] The items on the right are listed in the order they occur in Ezekiel. In Acts, οὐρανόθεν, οὐρανοῦ, εἶδον, περιήστραψεν, and περιαστράψαι come at the beginning of their respective call stories, κύριε and κύριος in the middle, and ἐγὼ ἀποστέλλω σε and ἀνάστηθι καὶ εἴσελθε εἰς τὴν πόλιν καὶ λαληθήσεταί σοι after all that.

[68] Cf. Haenchen, *Acts*, 325–28; Hans Conzelmann, *Acts of the Apostles: A Commentary on the Acts of the Apostles*, Hermeneia (Philadelphia: Fortress, 1987), 72.

IV. The Historical Paul?

Should we entertain the possibility that the pre-Lukan links between the story of Paul on the Damascus road and the account of Ezekiel by the river Chebar derive ultimately from the apostle's autobiographical witness?[69] And might he have identified the "appearance of the likeness of the glory of the Lord" (Ezek 1:28) with the Jesus who had appeared to him and called him to missionize gentiles?[70] This is not implausible. Not only did Paul, who could quote from and allude to the book of Ezekiel,[71] write of "the glory of God in the face of Jesus Christ" (2 Cor 4:6),[72] but the scriptural allusions to Isaiah and Jeremiah in Luke's accounts of Paul's call cohere, as we have seen, with the apostle's self-conception, so the same could hold for the allusions to Ezekiel.[73] In addition, Paul was the recipient of multiple visions of his Lord (ὀπτασίας κυρίου, 2 Cor 12:1; cf. Ezek 1:1: ὁράσεις θεοῦ),[74] and he thought

---

[69] That Paul himself narrated his conversion is presupposed by Acts—the accounts in 22:6–11 and 26:12–18 are in the first person—and is consistent with Gal 1:15–16 and 1 Cor 9:1, which perhaps function as allusions to a fuller story. Does Paul not anticipate readers who know more than he is saying?

[70] This is not a claim about what really happened. It should go without saying that Paul must have interpreted his call retrospectively; that is, his subsequent life and opinions would have interpreted and even rewritten his memories of what happened to him on the Damascus road.

[71] Romans 2:24 alludes to Ezek 36:20–23; Rom 14:11 quotes Ezek 5:11; 2 Cor 3:3 alludes to Ezek 11:19; 2 Cor 6:16 quotes Ezek 37:27; 2 Cor 6:17 quotes Ezek 20:34.

[72] See James D. G. Dunn, *The Theology of Paul the Apostle* (Grand Rapids: Eerdmans, 1998), 290: if 2 Cor 4:4–6 alludes "to Paul's Damascus road experience, the inference would be that Paul equated the light from heaven, which struck him down, with the glory of God." Given my conclusions, it is interesting that Edith M. Humphrey finds oblique references to Ezekiel's vision throughout 2 Cor 3–4 ("Ambivalent Apocalypse: Apocalyptic Rhetoric and Intertextuality in 2 Corinthians," in *The Intertextuality of Apocalyptic Discourse in the New Testament*, ed. Duane F. Watson, SymS 14 [Atlanta: Society of Biblical Literature, 2002], 122–25).

[73] Cf. Sandnes, *Paul, One of the Prophets?*, 76: the agreements between Acts 26 and Gal 1:15–16 support the view that the account of Acts is, "in its basic element, derived from tradition as old as Paul's Epistle to the Galatians." Further, of the three reports in Acts, it is 26:12–18 that shows the most contact with Ezekiel. It may then be pertinent that some have thought this account to be the closest to what Paul himself must have thought; so, e.g., Emmanuel Hirsch, "Die drei Berichte der Apostelgeschichte über die Bekehrung des Paulus," *ZNW* 28 (1929): 305–12; and Burchard, *Der dreizehnte Zeuge*, 124–25, 128–29.

[74] Gordon D. Fee, plausibly taking the genitive in ὀπτασίας κυρίου to be objective, writes: "Here is another OT idea that has been taken over by Paul and applied to Christ. Thus Ezekiel begins his prophetic ministry by dating the beginning of what he called 'visions of God' (ὁράσεις θεοῦ), where the 'vision' that immediately follows is ultimately, though indirectly, of God himself. For Paul, Christ is now the one revealed in such experiences" (*Pauline Christology: An Exegetical-Theological Study* [Peabody, MA: Hendrickson, 2007], 194).

of Christ as having a "body of glory" (Phil 3:21), as being enthroned,[75] and as being the ἄνθρωπος ἐξ οὐρανοῦ (1 Cor 15:47).[76] Moreover, that he could, in theory, have imagined his vision to be like Ezekiel's follows his belief in Jesus's preexistence,[77] from his ability to find Jesus in LXX texts about the Lord God,[78] and from 1 Cor 10:1–5, where Jesus is an actor in an old scriptural story.[79] Beyond all this, a number of modern scholars, without detecting or developing the relationship between Acts 26 and Ezekiel, have surmised that Paul identified Jesus with the image of God in Ezek 1:28,[80] or that we should associate the apostle with practices or experiences not unlike those of the later *merkabah* mystics and their fascination with Ezek 1.[81]

[75] This follows from his application of Ps 110:1 to Jesus (Rom 8:34, 1 Cor 15:25) and his equation of the βῆμα θεοῦ with the βῆμα Χριστοῦ (Rom 14:10, 2 Cor 5:10).

[76] It is striking that, in Jos. Asen. 14, the angel who is portrayed in language from Ezek 1 (see above) is called ἄνθρωπος ἐκ τοῦ οὐρανοῦ (v. 3). Cf. Ezek 1:26: ἀνθρώπου ἄνωθεν.

[77] This is, to be sure, a controversial subject, but the conventional view of the matter remains more likely than the alternative; see Lincoln D. Hurst, "Christ, Adam, and Preexistence Revisited," in *Where Christology Began: Essays on Philippians 2*, ed. Ralph P. Martin and Brian J. Dodd (Louisville: Westminster John Knox, 1998), 84–95; Jürgen Habermann, *Präexistenzaussagen im Neuen Testament*, EHS.T 362 (Frankfurt am Main: Lang, 1990), 99–266; Larry W. Hurtado, *Lord Jesus Christ: Devotion to Jesus in Earliest Christianity* (Grand Rapids: Eerdmans, 2003), 118–26.

[78] David B. Capes, *Old Testament Yahweh Texts in Paul's Christology*, WUNT 2/47 (Tübingen: Mohr Siebeck, 1992); Richard Bauckham, *Jesus and the God of Israel*: God Crucified *and Other Studies on the New Testament's Christology of Divine Identity* (Grand Rapids: Eerdmans, 2008) 182–232.

[79] "Paul thinks that Christ was actually the accompanying rock, conceived of as the source of water that saved the Israelites in their desert wanderings." So Joseph A. Fitzmyer, *First Corinthians: A New Translation and Commentary*, AYB 32 (New Haven: Yale University Press, 2008), 383.

[80] See esp. Kim, *Origin of Paul's Gospel*; and Newman, *Paul's Glory-Christology*. Other Jews identified Ezekiel's anthropomorphic figure with exalted intermediaries and eschatological saviors. The "one like a son of man" in Dan 7:13–14 is probably modeled in part on the figure in Ezek 1; see André Feuillet, "Le Fils de l'homme de Daniel et la tradition biblique," *RB* 60 (1953): 170–202; Wolfgang Bittner, "Gott—Menschensohn—Davidssohn: Eine Untersuchung zur Traditionsgeschichte von Dan 7,13f.," *FZPhTh* 32 (1985): 346–49; Markus Zehnder, "Why the Danielic 'Son of Man' Is a Divine Being," *BBR* 24 (2014): 341–42. The same is true regarding the Son of man in 1 En. 46:1 ("whose face was like the appearance of a man"); see Seyoon Kim, *The "Son of Man" as the Son of God* (Grand Rapids: Eermdans, 1983), 18; Quispel, "Ezekiel 1,26," 462; David E. Aune, *Revelation 1–5*, WBC 52A (Nashville: Nelson, 1997), 91. On the angel in Joseph and Aseneth, see n. 58. The vision of Jesus in Rev 1 appears to presuppose that Jesus is the figure from Ezek 1:26; see Kowalski, *Die Rezeption des Propheten Ezechiel*, 83–92. For later possibilities, see Jarl Fossum, "Jewish-Christian Christology and Jewish Mysticism," *VC* 37 (1983): 260–87.

[81] In addition to Bowker, "'Merkabah' Visions," and Segal, *Paul the Convert*, note, e.g., C. R. A. Morray-Jones, "Paradise Revisited (2 Cor. 12:1–12): The Jewish Mystical Background of Paul's Apostolate," *HTR* 86 (1993): 177–217, 265–92; J. M. Scott, "The Triumph of God in 2 Cor 2.14: Additional Evidence of Merkabah Mysticism in Paul," *NTS* 42 (1996): 260–81, http://dx.doi.org/10.1017/S0028688500020737; Edith M. Humphrey, *Joseph and Aseneth*, Guides to Apocrypha

So did Paul liken his call to that of Ezekiel, and did he identify his Lord with the anthropomorphic form of the Lord in Ezekiel? I am inclined to suppose that he did both, that he thought of the Lord who called him as the same Lord who called Ezekiel.[82] We can be fairly confident that someone before Luke likened Paul's Damascus road experience to Ezekiel's inaugural vision and prophetic call, and from what we otherwise know of Paul, he could well be that someone. Regrettably, however, the case falls short of demonstration. The problem is that the apostle fails, in the extant correspondence, to cite or even clearly allude to any part of Ezek 1, 2, or 3. At the same time, it would be imprudent to insist that a person as complex as the historical Paul was nothing more than the sum of the few letters we have from him.

---

and Pseudepigrapha (Sheffield: Sheffield Academic, 2000), 60 (Paul "experienced mystical visions [2 Cor. 12], and used language derived from Ezekiel [perhaps in consonance with a proto-merkavah tradition] in order to describe the Christian life and standing—light versus dark, life from death, transformation into the image, beholding 'the light of the knowledge of the glory of God'").

[82] See Margaret Thrall, "The Origin of Paul's Christology," in *Apostolic History and the Gospel*, ed. W. Ward Gasque and Ralph P. Martin (Grand Rapids: Eerdmans, 1970), 304–16. She urges that Paul would have thought of his Lord as the same Lord who called the biblical prophets.

JBL 135, no. 4 (2016): 827–847
doi: http://dx.doi.org/10.15699/jbl.1354.2016.157466

Γυνὴ τοῦ Πατρός: Analytic Kin Circumlocution and the Case for Corinthian Adultery

JOSHUA M. RENO
renox023@umn.edu
University of Minnesota, Minneapolis, MN 55445

Modern exegesis of 1 Cor 5 has functioned under two assumptions: first, Paul's phrase γυνὴ τοῦ πατρός echoes similar locutions found in Leviticus or Deuteronomy, and, second, sexual liaisons between sons and their stepmothers were considered incestuous in Greco-Roman antiquity. By examining the use of analytic kin circumlocution, this article argues that Paul's periphrasis not only is a standard circumlocution for μητρυιά ("stepmother") but also is constructed to highlight the particularly egregious nature of this affair: it is an inner-οἶκος adultery. Roman, Greek, and Second Temple Jewish data indicate that son–stepmother trysts, while especially offensive, were considered adulterous. By removing this perceived pentateuchal anchor, this article opens new possibilities for reading 1 Cor 5 as a test case in Paul's *homonoia* argument in 1 Cor 1–4 and suggests marriage and the οἶκος as a new latticework for holding together the disparate elements of 1 Cor 5–7.

It is actually heard that among you there is *porneia*, and such *porneia* that is not even among the nations: that some man has his father's wife [ὥστε γυναῖκά τινα τοῦ πατρὸς ἔχειν]. And you are haughty! And should you not have rather mourned, in order that the one having done this deed would be removed from your midst?[1] (1 Cor 5:1–2)

Two assumptions have defined modern exegesis of 1 Cor 5: first, that Paul's phrase γυνὴ τοῦ πατρός ("father's wife") echoes similar constructions found in

---

I wish to extend my great thanks to Melissa H. Sellew for reading multiple drafts of this paper and for offering me valuable insights. I also wish to thank Stephen P. Ahearne-Kroll, David E. Fredrickson, Niklas Jonsson, and Brian J. Reese, all of whom contributed helpful comments on earlier drafts of this paper.

[1] All translations are my own except where otherwise noted.

827

Leviticus and Deuteronomy;[2] and, second, that the instance of πορνεία ("sexual immorality") to which Paul refers is an *incestuous* relationship between a man's son and his, the father's, sexual partner.[3] Several factors, however, militate against such readings. I maintain that the instigating scandal that Paul confronts in 1 Cor 5, ὥστε γυναῖκά τινα τοῦ πατρὸς ἔχειν, is not an oblique echo of Levitical incest prohibitions. Rather, Paul's γυνὴ τοῦ πατρός is a standard locution in antiquity, and, further, what made this particular sexual pairing so egregious to Paul was its location—an inner-οἶκος adultery. Only when Paul's language is decoupled from its presumed Levitical counterpart is 1 Cor 5 able to be read fluidly with both the *homonoia* argument of chapters 1–4 and Paul's continued discourse on marriage and the οἶκος ("household") in chapters 6–7.

I. Analytic Kin Circumlocutions

Kin terms are divided into various subgroups depending on the precise relationship between the two parties associated: consanguineal/affinal, collateral/lineal, and parallel/cross kinship.[4] In these constructions, the two parties are

---

[2] Hans Conzelmann, *1 Corinthians: A Commentary on the First Epistle to the Corinthians*, trans. James L. Leitch, Hermeneia (Philadelphia: Fortress, 1975), 96 n. 25; Gordon D. Fee, *The First Epistle to the Corinthians*, NICNT (Grand Rapids: Eerdmans, 1987), 200; Wolfgang Schrage, *Der Erste Brief an die Korinther*, 4 vols., EKKNT 7 (Zurich: Benziger, 1991–2001), 1:369; Richard B. Hays, *First Corinthians*, IBC (Louisville: Westminster John Knox, 1997), 81; Craig S. de Vos, "Stepmothers, Concubines and the Case of ΠΟΡΝΕΙΑ in 1 Corinthians 5," *NTS* 44 (1998): 104–14, here 105; Kathy L. Gaca, *The Making of Fornication: Eros, Ethics, and Political Reform in Greek Philosophy and Early Christianity*, HCS 40 (Berkeley: University of California Press, 2003), 141 n. 59, http://dx.doi.org/10.1525/california/9780520235991.001.0001; Alistair Scott May, *The Body for the Lord: Sex and Identity in 1 Corinthians 5–7*, JSNTSup 278 (London: T&T Clark, 2004), 64; Paul Hartog, "'Not Even among Pagans' (1 Cor 5:1): Paul and Seneca on Incest," in *The New Testament and Early Christian Literature in Greco-Roman Context: Studies in Honor of David E. Aune*, ed. John Fotopoulos, NovTSup 122 (Leiden: Brill, 2006), 49–62, here 51–52 n. 2; L. William Countryman, *Dirt, Greed, and Sex: Sexual Ethics in the New Testament and Their Implications for Today*, rev. ed. (Minneapolis: Fortress, 2007), 192; Boris A. Paschke, "Ambiguity in Paul's References to Greco-Roman Sexual Ethics," *ETL* 83 (2007): 169–92, here 173; Joseph A. Fitzmyer, *First Corinthians: A New Translation with Introduction and* Commentary, AYB 32 (New Haven: Yale University Press, 2008), 234; Roy E. Ciampa and Brian S. Rosner, *The First Letter to the Corinthians*, PilNTC (Grand Rapids: Eerdmans, 2010), 199; William Loader, *The New Testament on Sexuality* (Grand Rapids: Eerdmans, 2010), 161–63.

[3] Conzelmann, *1 Corinthians*, 96; Fee, *First Epistle*, 194; Schrage, *Der erste Brief*, 1:368; Hays, *First Corinthians*, 81; Bruce W. Winter, *After Paul Left Corinth: The Influence of Secular Ethics on Social Change* (Grand Rapids: Eerdmans, 2001), 47–49; Gaca, *Making of Fornication*, 140; May, *Body for the Lord*, 64–65; Hartog, "Paul and Seneca," 51; Countryman, *Dirt, Greed*, 192–96; Paschke, "Ambiguity in Paul's References," 182; Fitzmyer, *First Corinthians*, 234; Ciampa and Rosner, *First Letter to the Corinthians*, 197; Loader, *New Testament on Sexuality*, 161–63.

[4] Niklas Jonsson, "Kin Terms in Grammar," in *Language Typology and Language Universals*:

separated into anchors and referents. For example, in the phrase "John's brother is tall," John functions as the anchor while his brother is the referent. Anchors are further distinguished between explicit and implicit. The former are explicitly identified, as in the example above. The latter lack any express identification of the anchor, who may be understood contextually or may be intentionally out of focus (e.g., the belligerent brother harped on him).[5] Kin terms are further categorized according to proper/improper use. Proper kin terms reflect actual kin relationships, whereas improper kin terms may connote either a kin connection or some other use outside the kinship system (e.g., her old man). Finally, kin terms are used both in simple kin constructions and analytic kin circumlocutions. Simple kin terms describe kin relations between two people via only one kinsman. On the other hand, Niklas Jonsson defines analytic kin circumlocutions as designating a relationship between two kin members "described by explicitly linking a number of kinsmen to each other" (e.g., Jenna's sister's wife).[6]

Analytic kin circumlocution was a common phenomenon in Greek and Latin literature. As in English, this is a well-known and commonly practiced way of referring to relatives: your brother's husband (i.e., your brother-in-law), her dad's wife (i.e., her stepmother). Often this is a focalizing or clarifying tactic intended to highlight a particular aspect of a tripartite relationship. For instance, the evil stepmother trope is often navigated by distancing tactics: said resentfully, "she's my dad's wife." The intention is to dissociate one party from another through an intermediary. At other times, periphrasis is undertaken to stress one's close relationship to another through an intermediary: "I can't hire him; he's my brother's son." However it is used, periphrasis introduces a third party, which focalizes and contextualizes the relationship between the other two parties. In 1 Cor 5:1 that is precisely what Paul has created: γυναῖκά τινα τοῦ πατρός. Admittedly, this particular phrase might have been familiar to readers of septuagintal Leviticus or Deuteronomy.[7] Leviticus 18:8 reads γυναικὸς πατρός σου ("your father's wife"), and similarly 20:11, γυναικὸς τοῦ πατρὸς αὐτοῦ ("his father's wife"); so also Deut 23:1, τὴν γυναῖκα τοῦ πατρὸς αὐτοῦ ("his father's wife"), and 27:20, γυναικὸς τοῦ πατρὸς αὐτοῦ ("his father's wife").[8] Yet, to suggest that Paul had one specific source text for this phrase is unnecessary, for this expression and others like it were relatively commonplace.

An International Handbook, ed. Martin Haspelmath et al., HSK 20 (Berlin: de Gruyter, 2001), 1203–13, here 1203.

[5] Ibid., 1204–5.

[6] Ibid., 1206.

[7] That Paul is familiar with Leviticus and Deuteronomy in their septuagintal forms is beyond doubt; however, whether Paul's predominantly Greek and Roman audience in Corinth would have read or even been familiar with the Greek Bible is questionable. Much less certain is whether they would have heard γυναῖκά τινα τοῦ πατρός as septuagintal or whether Paul would expect as much from them.

[8] Cf. the MT: אשת־אביך ("your father's wife," Lev 18:8); את־אשת אביו ("his father's wife," Lev 20:11); את־אשת אביו ("his father's wife," Deut 23:1); אשת אביו ("his father's wife," Deut 27:20);

Ancient authors from Homer to Quintus, from Herodotus to Polybius attest similar readings in both literary and epigraphical sources. Homer writes, ἔσκε δὲ πατρὸς ἐμοῖο γυνὴ Φοίνισσ' ἐνὶ οἴκῳ, "Now there was a Phoenician woman of my father in his house" (*Od.* 15.417).[9] Herodotus's recounting of Scyles's inheritance after his father's death reads, Σκύλης δὲ τήν τε βασιληίην παρέλαβε καὶ τὴν γυναῖκα τοῦ πατρός, "And Scyles inherited the kingdom and the wife of his father" (*Hist.* 4.78.2). When Medea sends her sons with deadly gifts to her rival bride, she says, ὦ τέκν', εἰσελθόντε πλουσίους δόμους πατρὸς νέαν γυναῖκα, δεσπότιν δ' ἐμήν, ἱκετεύετ', ἐξαιτεῖσθε μὴ φεύγειν χθόνα, "O children, when you enter the wealthy house, beseech the new wife of your father, my queen, beg that she not exile you from this land" (Euripides, *Med.* 969–971). In every circumstance γυνή is modified by πατρός, and in two of these instances the referent is the father's wife. Yet γυνή is not the only word for wife; in fact, Greek has over twenty-five terms for wife, and thus variations on this wording appear in our sources as well.[10] For instance, εἶδέν τε πατρὸς <u>ἄλοχον</u> φίλαν appears in Bacchylides's *Dithyrambs* 3.109: "And he saw the dear wife of his father." Or Euripides's tragedy *Hippolytus* 26–28, in which the eponymous protagonist rebuffs the advances of his stepmother, Phaedra, reads, πατρὸς εὐγενὴς <u>δάμαρ</u> ἰδοῦσα Φαίδρα καρδίαν κατέσχετο ἔρωτι δεινῷ τοῖς ἐμοῖς βουλεύμασιν, "when Phaedra, his father's well-born wife, saw him her heart was possessed by a terrible love according to my plans."[11] Quintus likewise writes, ἄζετο γὰρ <u>παράκοιτιν</u> ἑοῦ πατρὸς ἀκαμάτοιο, "For he revered the wife of his tireless father" (*Posthom.* 3.128). Finally, circumlocution even functions as the pun of a riddle, οἴνου τὴν ἑτέρην γράφε μητέρα καὶ θὲς ἐπ' ἄρθρῳ ἄρθρον, καὶ πάτρην πατρὸς <u>ἄκοιτιν</u> ὁρᾷς, "Write out the second mother of wine, add an article to an article, and you will see the fatherland of (her) father's wife" (*Anth. Graec.* 5.14.31).

---

and the Vulg.: *uxoris patris tui* ("your father's wife," Lev 18:8); *nouerca sua* ("his stepmother," Lev 20:11); *homo uxorem patris sui* ("his father's wife," Deut 23:1); *uxore patris sui* ("his father's wife," Deut 27:20). Biblical Hebrew does not have a discrete term for stepmother. The same term is used of both mother and stepmother (cf. Gen 30:14 [אמו, "his mother"]; Gen 37:10 [אמך, "your stepmother"]).

[9] A. T. Murray's 1919 LCL translation reads, "Now there was in my father's house a Phoenician woman." While this certainly makes for better English, it misconstrues πατρός as modifying the object of the prepositional phrase (οἴκῳ). At a contextual level this is also untenable, since the reader is incited when the father's sexual property (γυνὴ Φοίνισσ') is seduced (ἠπερόπευον) surreptitiously by the cunning Phoenicians (Φοίνικες πολυπαίπαλοι).

[10] Circumlocution is conceptual; that is, analytic kin circumlocution is one way in which ancient Greeks and Romans conceptualized kin connections. Failure to identify the conceptual nature of periphrasis is a failure to understand its purpose and use. Searching only for precise parallels is unnecessarily restrictive and obfuscates the issue. One need not show that the exact phrase γυνὴ τοῦ πατρός is used widely, though the evidence supports a greater prevalence than is typically acknowledged; rather, one must demonstrate that circumlocution was in general use. By so doing one is able to avoid the pitfall of assuming that Paul is obliquely echoing another author or text.

[11] See also Euripides, *Hipp.* 1072–1073, 1164–1165 (cf. 651–652); *Alc.* 314.

Greek writers were not alone in utilizing periphrasis; Latin authors also follow this practice. When Martial accuses Gallus of a deviant relationship with his stepmother he writes, Privignum non esse tuae te, Galle, novercae, rumor erat, coniunx dum fuit illa patris, "That you were not just the stepson of your stepmother, Gallus, was a rumor, while she was your father's wife" (*Epigr.* 4.16). In a similar vein Calpurnius Flaccus mentions, pater filio pecuniam dedit, ut amatam patris redimeret, "A father gave his son money, so that he could redeem the father's lover" (*Decl.* 37). Apuleius even names the same woman at once as parent, father's wife, and brother's mother! (*Metam.* 10.3; see also Ovid, *Metam.* 10.347). Justinian's *Digest*, though it is admittedly late and likely does not always reflect the reality of the first century CE, provides yet three more examples.[12]

A few more instances are of note. First, the author of the Testament of the Twelve Patriarchs, commenting on Jacob's household, writes, ὠνείδιζον Ῥουβὴμ τὸν ἀδελφόν μου περὶ Βάλλας γυναικὸς πατρός μου, "I upbraided Reuben, my brother, concerning Bilhah, my father's wife" (T. Jud. 13:3).[13] Likewise, Philo, quoting Gen 37:2, refers to Jacob's two concubines as τῶν γυναικῶν πατρὸς αὐτοῦ ("the wives of his father," *Deus* 119). Finally, Josephus, in his comments on Mosaic proscriptions against adultery,[14] says, καὶ μίσγεσθαι δὲ μητράσι κακὸν μέγιστον ὁ νόμος ἀπεῖπεν, ὁμοίως δὲ καὶ πατρὸς συνεῖναι γαμετῇ, "And the law also forbade mixing with mothers as the greatest evil, and likewise also to have intercourse with the father's wife" (*A.J.* 3.274). One additional reference may be the no-longer-extant Greek text of Jubilees (33:10).

Finally, papyrological and epigraphical evidence substantiates the widespread practice of this form of circumlocution. A Delian inscription from the end of the second century BCE offers an exemplar, [βασιλεὺς Πτολε]μα[ῖος βασιλ]έ[ω]ς [Πτολεμαίου] [Εὐ]εργέτου βασίλισσαν Κλεοπάτραν Εὐεργέτιν [τ]ὴν τοῦ πατρὸς μὲν γυναῖκα, ἐμαυτοῦ δ[ὲ] ἀνεψιάν, "King Ptolemy son of the King Ptolemy Euergetes, [set up this statue of] the Queen Cleopatra Euergetes, the wife of my father, and my

---

[12] Paulus, *Dig.* 23.2.14.pr., Adoptivus filius si emancipetur, eam quae patris adoptivi uxor fuit ducere non potest, quia novercae locum habet, "If an adopted son is emancipated, he is not able to marry her who was the wife of his adoptive father, for she has the position of stepmother"; Paulus, *Dig.* 23.2.14.4, quidam novercam per se patris uxorem … intellegunt, "Some understand 'stepmother' to be 'the wife of one's father'"; Neratius, *Dig.* 24.1.44.pr., idemque iuris erit, si is, qui in potestate viri erat, credens se patrem familias esse uxori patris donaverit, "The same legal principle shall stand, if someone, who was under the authority of the husband, thinking himself to be a *paterfamilias*, were to present a gift to his father's wife."

[13] This designation stands in direct contrast to Gen 35:22, Βαλλας τῆς παλλακῆς [MT פלגש] τοῦ πατρὸς αὐτου, "Bilhah the concubine of his father." Cf. Gen 30:4, καὶ ἔδωκεν αὐτῷ Βαλλαν τὴν παιδίσκην [MT שפחתה] αὐτῆς αὐτῷ γυναῖκα [MT לאשה], "And she gave him Bilhah, her handmaid, as a wife for him."

[14] Josephus, *A.J.* 3.274. Μοιχείαν is syntactically secluded as a heading for this section (3.274–275).

own cousin" (I.Délos 1530 = PH63966).[15] A papyrus from Egyptian Thebes (ca. 112 BCE) tells of the grievances experienced at the hands of the author's stepmother, ἀδικοῦμαι ὑπὸ Θεννήσιος τῆς γενομένης τοῦ πατρός μου γυναικ[ό]ς, "I am wronged by Thennesia, the woman who became the wife of my father" (P.Tor.Choach. 3.4–6). Conversely, another Egyptian papyrus (ca. 127–168 CE) recounts the impartiality of the author's stepmother, ἡ γενομένη τοῦ πα[τ]ρ[ό]ς μου γυνὴ Τααρμιῦσις … ἔστερξεν ὡς φυσικὰ τέκνα, "She who became the wife of my father, Taarmiusis … loved us as natural children" (P.Mil.Vogl. 2.73.3–4, 8). Aurelius Apollonius, in a formal complaint to Vettius Gallianus in 216 CE, protests that ἡ γὰρ τοῦ πατρὸς γυνή, Ὀσεαῦς [Φ]ιλήμονος ("For my father's wife, Oseaus, daughter of Philemon") has stolen his inheritance (P.Turner 34.13–14). Finally, a Cyzicene epigram, inscribed on the stylopinakia of the temple of Apollonis (ca. 175–159 BCE), identifies scenes shown in relief.[16] This particular example recounts the myth of Phineas, king of Thrace: ὁ δ' ἔχει Πολυμήδην καὶ Κλυτίον, τοὺς υἱοὺς Φινέως τοῦ Θρᾳκός, οἵτινες τὴν Φρυγίαν γυναῖκα τοῦ πατρὸς ἐφόνευσαν, ὅτι τῇ μητρὶ αὐτῶν Κλεοπάτρᾳ αὐτὴν ἐπεισῆγεν, "The fourth has Polymedes and Clytius, the sons of Phineus the Thracian, who slew their father's Phrygian wife, because he took her to wife while still married to their mother Cleopatra" (Anth. Graec. 1.3.4). As it appears in our sources, then, the use of periphrasis in this instance is relatively common.[17] Indeed, there is consistent evidence for this construction, in multiple media, in both prose and poetry, from the eighth century BCE to well after the first century CE. It is safe to say that analytic kin circumlocution was a regular way of conceptualizing kin connections in Greco-Roman antiquity.

Paul's use of γυνὴ τοῦ πατρός, therefore, need not be restricted by insisting on an oblique septuagintal echo. Had Paul intended to allude to the pentateuchal prohibition, would he not have used κοιμάομαι ("to sleep," Lev 20:11, Deut 27:20) or λαμβάνω ("to take," Deut 23:1)? Or made reference to the father's ἀσχημοσύνη ("disgrace, genitals," Lev 18:8, 20:11) or συγκάλυμμα ("skirt," Deut 23:1, 27:2)? The earliest commentators certainly do not hear this echo. Text-critical evidence offers no variation on ἔχειν ("to have") in 5:1, while ἀρθῇ ("be removed") in 5:2 demonstrates some scribal preference for the Deuteronomic ἐξαρθῇ ("be driven out").[18] Neither do the earliest Christian commentators relate this phrase to the Mosaic proscriptions.[19] Cyril of Alexandria points instead to Amos 2:7, "Father and son go in

---

[15] Théophile Homolle, "Dédicaces déliennes," BCH 4 (1880): 223.

[16] For more information, see Kristoffel Demoen, "The Date of the Cyzicene Epigrams: An Analysis of the Vocabulary and Metrical Technique of AP, III," AnCl 57 (1988): 231–48.

[17] For more similar examples, see Erasistratus, Fr. 2B.1; Polybius, Hist. 31.26.1.

[18] MSS L Ψ 1241. 1505 𝔐; Did. Cf. Deut 17:7, 12; 19:19; 21:21; 22:21, 22, 24; 24:7; 1 Cor 5:13.

[19] The nearest I have been able to find is Tertullian, Marc. 5.7 (ANF 3:443), "I quite admit, that, according to the Creator's law, the man was an offender 'who had his father's wife.' He [Paul] followed, no doubt, the principles of natural and public law" (cf. Cyril of Alexandria, Comm. Proph. Min. 1.405–406). Of course, Tertullian refers to the situation at Corinth as condemned by

to the same girl, so that my holy name is profaned" (NRSV).[20] Indeed, John Chrysostom feels the need to explain that Paul shied away from the disgrace of using the more direct μητρυιά ("stepmother").[21] Given that γυνὴ τοῦ πατρός was a common construction in antiquity, it is dubious to assert that Paul here echoes Mosaic law and even more to suggest that the Corinthian community would have realized it.

Thus far this investigation has been rather narrow, merely demonstrating the existence and prevalence of this linguistic phenomenon. The question remains: why did Paul choose this particular expression over a more direct term (e.g., μήτηρ, μητρυιά, παλλακίς ["concubine"])? Obviously the precise nature of the relationships of the three parties needs to be assessed. Some points, however, may be deduced from γυναῖκά τινα τοῦ πατρός. The most striking feature of Paul's construction is its ambiguity. As one reads along the text, the most natural reading takes τινα as an indefinite adjective with γυναῖκα, "some woman."[22] The resulting reading understands an unexpressed object (e.g., υἱόν): "some woman has the father's (son)." That a *woman* has a *man* would have been intolerable and would have required the reader to do a double take. On second glance, however, it is clear that some man divides his father and stepmother, even at a syntactical level.[23] Such ambiguity minimizes the πόρνος ("fornicator"), allowing Paul to emphasize the other parties involved.

Circumlocution permits Paul to use the expression τοῦ πατρός. Had Paul used

---

the "Creator's law," which is not so much an admission that Paul's phrasing comes from the Pentateuch as it is that Tertullian believes Paul's moral judgment is pentateuchal in origin.

[20] Cyril of Alexandria, *Fr. 1 Cor.*, 261.16–17. Origen (*Fr. Exod.* 12.276.42) relates Paul's discipline of the offender to God's discipline of Pharaoh; see Origen, *Philoc.* 27.8.29–31. See also Thomas Aquinas, *Comm. 1 Cor.* 230, Erat tamen quaedam fornicationis species, quae et apud gentiles illicita habebatur. Et ideo dicit ita ut uxorem patris aliquis habeat, sicut dicitur Gen. XLIX, 4: effusus es sicut aqua, non crescas, quia ascendisti cubile patris tui, et maculasti stratum eius, "There was, however, some instance of fornication, which was considered illicit among the gentiles. And behold thus he says that someone has his father's wife, just as it is said in Gen 49:4: You are poured out as water, may you not thrive, because you mounted your father's bed, and you defiled his sheets." Aquinas does go on to mention Lev 18:8; however, note that it is used to expound Gen 2:24—not 1 Cor 5. Like Tertullian, Aquinas is interested in the prohibition, not the particular expression.

[21] John Chrysostom, *Hom. 1 Cor.* 15.2. Cf. Theodoret of Cyrus, *Int. Ep. Paul.* 82.261; John of Damascus, *Comm. Ep. Paul.* 95.605.50–52.

[22] The placement of τινα is odd in Paul's syntax. It cannot go before γυναῖκα, where it would be read as an interrogative adjective (BDAG, s.v. τίς, τί, 1.a.ב; Philo, *Gig.* 1.23). Yet, immediately after γυναῖκα, it is most naturally read as an indefinite pronominal *adjective*. It cannot separate τοῦ from πατρός, nor would it be natural to place it after the verb ἔχειν. To remove any ambiguity Paul may have written ὥστε τινα ἔχειν γυναῖκα τοῦ πατρός. As it is, however, Paul's phrasing yields a certain ambiguity, which requires the reader to confront the offense a second time.

[23] Hartog suggests that the placement of τινα heightens the ignominy of the offender's crime ("Paul and Seneca," 52 n. 4).

a more direct term, τοῦ πατρός would have been superfluous. The construction's primary anchor shifts from the offender to the father. In place of "some man has *his* stepmother," Paul writes, "some man has (his) *father's* wife." Likewise, Paul separates the γυνή from the offender through an intermediary. The offender is not permitted to be the possessive anchor for the referent woman; rather, his referent becomes the father, further highlighting the son's egregious overstep. Thus, Paul's locution enables him to emphasize the father, who is ultimately the victim of the liaison. Simultaneously, Paul's use of τινα instead of ἄνθρωπον ("man"), ἄνδρα ("man"), υἱόν ("son"), or even ἕνα ὑμῶν ("one of you")[24] deflects focus from the πόρνος, a task further established by the absence of a personal pronoun (cf. Lev 18:8, 20:11, Deut 23:1, 27:20).[25] This form of implicit anchor is correctly designated as intentionally out of focus. Paul obscures the offender; he is not Paul's primary concern.[26] Finally, by using γυνή Paul underscores the formality of the relationship between her and the father. For Paul, it is more important that she be understood primarily in relation to the father; that is, the emphasis falls on her status as the father's sexual property—not as the son's mother or stepmother.[27] Paul's analytic kin circumlocution reifies this at the syntactical level: the father anchors the woman.

The relationship between the father and this shadowy man is, of necessity, father and son. Much ink has been spilled on the relationship of the father to the woman and, consequently, the son to the woman. Contra Craig de Vos, the woman is not likely the father's *concubina* ("concubine").[28] As several have pointed out, de Vos's conclusion rests on an argument from silence and faulty assumptions.[29] In addition, his rationalization for Paul's use of γυνή over παλλακή ("concubine") is

---

[24] E.g., 1 Cor 5:11, 6:1, 7:12, 11:28, 2 Cor 12:2–4.

[25] It is important here to recognize that Paul's rhetorical tactic has undercut and uprooted the man's status. He is outside the Corinthian οἶκος, neither Paul's son to admonish nor the Corinthians' brother to commune. This man is a ξένος ("stranger").

[26] Note Paul's pointed use of personal pronouns throughout 1 Cor 5:1–5. Ὑμεῖς ("You") is used four times and ἐγώ ("I") is used twice. Paul creates an especially forceful contrast between 5:2, καὶ ὑμεῖς ("and you"), and 5:3, ἐγὼ μὲν γάρ ("for I"), both of which are superfluous and intensifying. By contrast, the labels for this offender, τινα (5:1, note also the absence of the personal pronoun αὐτοῦ), ὁ τὸ ἔργον πράξας ("the one having done this deed," 5:2), τὸν οὕτως τοῦτο κατεργασάμενον ("the one thus having done this," 5:3), and τὸν τοιοῦτον ("such a man," 5:5; cf. 5:11), reduce his significance and relegate him to background material. He is tertiary to Paul's major concern: power dynamics between the Corinthian elite and himself.

[27] As opposed to mother, stepmother, or concubine, none of which necessarily ties the woman to the father in a legally binding relationship; that is, one's mother is not necessarily *currently* one's father's wife. Further, a woman could be a concubine with varying degrees of formality and legality. By using γυνή Paul stresses her role as *wife*, and therefore, as the sexual property of her husband, τοῦ πατρός.

[28] De Vos, "Stepmothers, Conclubines," 112–14.

[29] See Paschke, "Ambiguity in Paul's References," 171–72; May, *Body for the Lord*, 64–65, esp. 65 n. 29.

doubtful.[30] It is also unlikely that Paul, a Roman subject, was so ill-informed about Roman practices,[31] nor does an argument from silence provide grounds to believe that Paul did not differentiate *concubinae* and γυναῖκες.[32] Nor is the woman the man's biological mother.[33] Boris Paschke is right that "Paul certainly would have used the word μήτηρ in order to make clear the extreme sinfulness"[34] had that been the case. Some, building off Chrysostom, insist that Paul was embarrassed to speak about such an intolerable act, yet Chrysostom himself goes on to identify the woman as a stepmother (*Hom. 1 Cor.* 15.2), and Paul's explicit purpose is to shock and shame the audience.[35] Further, Paul's locution does not fit this hypothesis. Rather, this type of construction is used most commonly of stepmothers.[36] Paul is therefore referring to the son's stepmother and the father's (at least) second wife, as recognized at least since Origen (*Fr. 1 Cor.* 23.21). This is the general consensus of scholars.[37]

---

[30] De Vos, "Stepmothers, Concubines," 112–13: "The fact that Paul did not use the normal Greek term for a concubine, παλλακή or παλλακίς, is not really significant. For these terms are not found at all in the NT, even though Roman practice of concubinage was very common" (112). Paul on at least 315 other occasions uses New Testament *hapax legomena*, and, as de Vos admits, παλλακή was used frequently in the LXX.

[31] Winter, *After Paul Left Corinth*, 48 nn. 18–19. The inferiority of *concubinae* was deeply rooted in Roman ideas. The *Leges Iuliae* confirmed an established hierarchy; see Thomas A. J. McGinn, *Prostitution, Sexuality, and the Law in Ancient Rome* (New York: Oxford University Press, 1998), 152. Further, if later Roman jurists bear upon the discussion in the way de Vos contends, this sort of *concubina* sharing was frowned upon by the much later Roman jurist Ulpian (*Dig.* 25.7.1.3; cf. Pseudo-Phocylides, *Sent.* 1.181).

[32] De Vos, "Stepmothers, Concubines," 112.

[33] For this view, see Michael Lattke, "Verfluchter Inzest: War der 'Pornos' von 1 Kor 5 ein persischer 'Magos'?," in *Peregrina curiositas: Eine Reise durch den orbis antiquus; Zu Ehren von Dirk Van Damme*, ed. Andreas Kessler, Thomas Ricklin, and Gregor Wurst, NTOA 27 (Göttingen: Vandenhoeck & Ruprecht, 1994), 37. For criticisms, see de Vos, "Stepmothers, Concubines," 104–5, esp. 105 n. 4.

[34] Paschke, "Ambiguity of Paul's References," 170. So also Fitzmyer, *First Corinthians*, 233; Schrage, *Der erste Brief*, 369.

[35] De Vos, "Stepmothers, Concubines," 105; see 1 Cor 6:5. I contend that 1 Cor 5–7 should be understood as Paul's attempt to shame the Corinthian Strong. Paul is concerned to show himself to be their σοφὸς πατήρ ("wise father").

[36] See Herodotus, *Hist.* 4.78.10; Bacchylides, *Dith.* 3.109; Euripides, *Med.* 970; *Hipp.* 26, 1073, 1165; *Alc.* 314; Lev 18:8; 20:11; Deut 23:1; 27:20; Erasistratus, *Fr.* 2B.1; T. Jud. 4.13.3; Philo, *Deus* 119; Quintus, *Posthom.* 3.128; *Anth. Graec.* 5.14.31; Josephus, *A.J.* 3.274; P.Tor.Choach. 3.4–6; P.Mil.Vogl. 2.73.3–4; P.Turner 34.13–14; *Anth. Graec.* 1.3.4; Martial, *Epigr.* 4.16.2; Paulus, *Dig.* 23.2.14.pr; 23.2.14.4.

[37] Conzelmann, *1 Corinthians*, 96; Fee, *First Epistle*, 200; Schrage, *Korinther*, 369; Winter, *After Paul Left Corinth*, 48–49; May, *Body for the Lord*, 64–65; Hays, *First Corinthians*, 80–81; Hartog, "Paul and Seneca," 51–52; Countryman, *Dirt, Greed*, 192; Fitzmyer, *First Corinthians*, 233–34; Ciampa and Rosner, *First Letter to the Corinthians*, 199; Loader, *New Testament on Sexuality*, 161.

The choice of γυνὴ τοῦ πατρός over the more specific μητρυιά is one that is initially difficult to discern. Μητρυιά is not used elsewhere in the New Testament or the LXX; however, Philo consistently uses it when exegeting the law (*Spec.* 3.12, 20, 21), and so also does Pseudo-Phocylides (*Sent.* 1.179–180). The only instance in Josephus is proverbial: μητρυιᾶς χαλεπωτέρα ("crueler than a stepmother," *B.J.* 1.473).[38] In general it is relatively common, appearing eighty-six times in our extant literature prior to the first century CE in epic poets, tragedians, comedians, philosophers, orators, and historians.[39] We can confidently surmise that μητρυιά was not a technical term and that Paul was familiar with it. Paul's preference for γυναῖκά τινα τοῦ πατρός is best explained by the tripartite relationship produced by such a circumlocution, not by appeal to a so-called *biblische Sprache*.[40] The word γυνή underscores the legality of the father's exclusive sexual privilege, and τινα de-emphasizes the significance and identity of the offender, which is further obscured by substantival constructions in 5:2–3.[41] Most importantly, however, by using this construction Paul inserts the father, who would otherwise remain tenebrous, into the equation, at once identifying the victim of the offender's egregious deed and conjuring the image of the οἶκος.[42] The household is an important context for Paul to maintain, an image he builds through 1 Cor 5–7. In particular, Paul's own

---

[38] See also Philo, *Ios.* 1.232; but cf. Philo, *Virt.* 1.224, 225. For the wicked stepmother trope, see Patricia A. Watson, *Ancient Stepmothers: Myth, Misogyny and Reality*, Mnemosyne Supplement 143 (Leiden: Brill, 1995), 22–25, 62–71, 92–134, 140–57.

[39] E.g., Homer, *Il.* 5.389, 13.697, 15.336; Euripides, *Alc.* 305, 309; Menander, *Mon.* 1.127; Plato, *Leg.* 672b, 930b; Lysias, *Diog.* 17.1; Dionysius of Halicarnassus, *Ant. rom.* 1.70.2. The TLG lists 760 instances in its canon: 86 times prior to the first century, 170 before the third century, and 317 before the seventh century. Μητρυιά appears five more times in inscriptions and at least once in documentary papyri.

[40] Dieter Zeller, *Der erste Brief an die Korinther*, KEK 5 (Göttingen: Vandenhoeck & Ruprecht, 2010), 199.

[41] In 5:2, Paul refers to him as ὁ τὸ ἔργον πράξας, and in 5:3 τὸν οὕτως τοῦτο κατεργασάμενον. Cf. τὸν τοιοῦτον in 5:5, 11. See n. 26 above.

[42] The οἶκος is the exclusive property of the male head of household, the father, often referred to as the κύριος. An οἶκος is not merely a physical abode; an οἶκος includes the actual building but also the movable property and all those who inhabit the building (slaves, women, children). A father's γυνή is, in a sense, his property; he holds exclusive rights to her use(s) and role(s), both public and private. Citing this instance in this way, ὥστε γυναῖκά τινα τοῦ πατρὸς ἔχειν, evokes the image of the οἶκος by indicating the appropriate relational parties (γυναῖκά τινα τοῦ πατρός) and use (ἔχειν), albeit in a drastically disturbed way.

Froma I. Zeitlin comments, "The *oikos* is the visual symbol of paternal heredity that entitles sons to succeed their fathers as proprietor of its wealth and movable goods and as ruler over its inhabitants" ("Theater, Theatricality, and the Feminine," in *Sexuality and Gender in the Classical World: Readings and Sources*, ed. Laura K. McClure, Interpreting Ancient History [Malden, MA: Blackwell, 2002], 103–38, here 113–14). Paul depicts this image yet reveals a significant caveat: the son has prematurely succeeded his father's rightful role as sole proprietor of the οἶκος and its inhabitants, even usurping his claim to the sexual use of his γυνή.

self-presentation is as a father organizing and managing his household.⁴³ Here in 1 Cor 5:1–2 Paul invokes the father to highlight the particularly heinous nature of this deed: the offender has not only committed adultery but committed adultery against his own father!⁴⁴ The consequence of this is palpable: this man has brought shame on the whole household through an inner-οἶκος assault:⁴⁵ on his father,

---

⁴³ First Corinthians 4:14–15 makes this explicit: "I am not writing this to make you ashamed, but to admonish you as my beloved children. For though you might have ten thousand guardians in Christ, you do not have many fathers. Indeed, in Christ Jesus I became your father through the gospel" (NRSV). In 5:1–13 Paul presents himself as a benevolent *paterfamilias* who "must set his house in order, discipline unruly members, and, if need be, expel those who will not respond to discipline" (Dale B. Martin, *The Corinthian Body* [New Haven: Yale University Press, 1995], 160). Martin himself, however, does not follow this line of reasoning. Paul handles the legal disputes in 1 Cor 6:1–11 as a father admonishing siblings to get along and resolve their disputes in house; see Margaret M. Mitchell, *Paul and the Rhetoric of Reconciliation: An Exegetical Investigation of the Language and Composition of 1 Corinthians* (Louisville: Westminster John Knox, 1993), 96 n. 186. Paul creates the image of an οἶκος in 1 Cor 6:12–20 in which the Corinthian elite heap shame on the κύριος by entering into illicit marriages without paternal consent. Finally, 1 Cor 7 presents Paul as the benevolent father managing marriage contracts and stipulations for his children.

Recent anthropological studies, in tandem with linguistic analysis, have highlighted the importance of fictive kinship in antiquity. Paul was no stranger to this process. On fictive kinship in antiquity, see Ann-Cathrin Harders, "Kinship Terms, Used Metaphorically," in *The Encyclopedia of Ancient History,* ed. Roger S. Bagnall et al. (Malden, MA: Wiley-Blackwell, 2012), 3771–72. For recent additions to Pauline studies, see Christine Gerber, *Paulus und seine "Kinder": Studien zur Besiehungsmetaphorik der paulinischen Briefe,* BZNW 136 (Berlin: de Gruyter, 2005), 351–435, http://dx.doi.org/10.1515/9783110892963; J. Dorcas Gordon, *Sister or Wife? 1 Corinthians 7 and Cultural Anthropology,* JSNTSup 149 (Sheffield: Sheffield Academic, 1997), 92–98; Jennifer Houston McNeel, *Paul as Infant and Nursing Mother: Metaphor, Rhetoric, and Identity in 1 Thessalonians 2:5–8,* ECL 12 (Atlanta: SBL Press, 2014), 93–95; David M. Bossman, "Paul's Fictive Kinship Movement," *BTB* 33 (2003): 135–47. The Stoic wise man is a father to all: Epictetus, *Diatr.* 3.22.81–82; see Abraham J. Malherbe, *Paul and the Popular Philosophers* (Minneapolis: Fortress, 2006), 54–55.

⁴⁴ There is no reason to assert that the father is dead or divorced. Those who make this assertion (Conzelmann, *1 Corinthians,* 96; Fee, *First Epistle,* 200; de Vos, "Stepmothers, Concubines," 112; Countryman, *Dirt, Greed,* 192; Fitzmyer, *First Corinthians,* 234) do so by fiat or on the fallacious grounds of legality. May points out the double fallacy of assuming that illegality precludes adultery's occurrence and that laws enacted are enforced (*Body for the Lord,* 64). Other scholars (Hays, *First Corinthians,* 80–81; Winter, *After Paul Left Corinth,* 45–52; Paschke, "Ambiguity of Paul's References," 171) have rightly noted that this is insufficient cause to make such a jump. I maintain that Paul's periphrasis stresses the father's claim on the woman, and in so doing suggests that he is still alive and married to the woman. This does not, however, preclude the possibility that he is unaware of the affair. Paul's ὅλως ἀκούεται ("it is actually heard") need not suggest that the affair is common knowledge. Instead, many in the community may yet be unaware, but some must have reported it to Paul (e.g., Chloe's people) and some must have known and done too little (the Strong).

⁴⁵ See Richard L. Rohrbaugh, "Honor: Core Value in the Biblical World," in *Understanding the Social World of the New Testament,* ed. Dietmar Neufeld and Richard E. DeMaris (New York:

whose responsibility it is to guard his women and rear virtuous sons;⁴⁶ on his stepmother, whose honor and fecundity⁴⁷ he has sullied; and on himself, by overstepping his rightful social position.⁴⁸ Yet, for Paul, shame bleeds through the walls of that οἶκος into the hallways of his.

II. The Nature of the Corinthian Πορνεια

If Paul is citing an instance of a son and stepmother engaged in sexual activity, how might this relationship have been understood? Usually this relationship has been labeled incestuous,⁴⁹ though some scholars have preferred the description "adulterous incest."⁵⁰ No doubt this unanimity reflects the misidentification of a pentateuchal echo and modern Western sexual sensibilities. These positions are problematized by ancient sources, which consistently categorize relationships between stepmother and son as simply adulterous. Some scholars have asked: why wouldn't Paul have labeled

---

Routledge, 2010), 109–25, here 112. See also Carolyn Osiek and David L. Balch, *Families in the New Testament World: Households and House Churches*, Family, Religion, and Culture (Louisville: Westminster John Knox, 1997), 38–40: "Male honor consists in maintaining the status, power, and reputation of the male members of a kinship group" (38); and Rohrbaugh, "Honor," 112: "Any offense on a woman's part, however slight, would destroy not only her own honor, but that of all males in her paternal kin group as well." Rohrbaugh later points out that "being shamed was a social catastrophe, especially since shame for one member of the family meant shame for all" (112).

⁴⁶ On women, see Kenneth J. Dover, "Classical Greek Attitudes to Sexual Behavior," in *Sex and Difference in Ancient Greece and Rome*, ed. Mark Golden and Peter Toohey, Edinburgh Readings on the Ancient World (Edinburgh: Edinburgh University Press, 2003), 114–28, here 118. On sons, see S. M. Baugh, "Marriage and Family in Ancient Greek Society," in *Marriage and Family in the Biblical World*, ed. Ken M. Campbell (Downers Grove, IL: InterVarsity Press, 2003), 103–31, here 128; Richard P. Saller, *Patriarchy, Property, and Death in the Roman Family*, Cambridge Studies in Population, Economy, and Society in Past Time 25 (Cambridge: Cambridge University Press, 1994), 143–45.

⁴⁷ Osiek and Balch, *Families in the New Testament World*, 38–39; Carolyn Osiek and Jennifer Pouya, "Constructions of Gender in the Roman Imperial World," in Neufeld and DeMaris, *Understanding the Social World*, 46. Childbearing was perhaps the primary role of the wife. See Osiek and Pouya, "Constructions," 47: "A woman's status and authority increased when she became a mother, particularly a mother of sons." Being labeled an adulteress was tantamount to being infertile: never will an adulteress be able to bear legitimate children; see Loader, *New Testament on Sexuality*, 76–77.

⁴⁸ According to Rohrbaugh, challenging the status of one's social superior was a "failure to know one's proper place" and was considered a grievous circumvention of the social hierarchy ("Honor," 115–16; quotation from 115).

⁴⁹ See the works cited in n. 3 above.

⁵⁰ Fitzmyer, *First Corinthians*, 234; Winter, *After Paul Left Corinth*, 47–49; Gaca, *Making of Fornication*, 140.

this as μοιχεία ("adultery")?[51] Such logic may equally apply to incest, as several Greek words denote such a circumstance (e.g., ἀθεμιτομιξία, "lawless marriage").[52] Or, if Paul was unfamiliar with these rarer, technical terms, Greek provided several other, more circuitous phrases (e.g., ἀνόσιος συνουσία ["godless intercourse"], ἡ χρῆσις παρὰ φύσιν ["unnatural use"]).[53] Whatever the case, Paul nowhere makes explicit his understanding of this relationship. Some evidence suggests, however, that this relationship would likely have been understood as adultery. Quintilian mentions a controversy of Seneca wherein a son and his stepmother are killed when caught by

---

[51] Carolyn Osiek, "Female Slaves, *Porneia*, and the Limits of Obedience," in *Early Christian Families in Context: An Interdisciplinary Dialogue*, ed. David L. Balch and Carolyn Osiek, Religion, Marriage and Family (Grand Rapids: Eerdmans, 2003), 255–74, here 269. Ironically, Paul never once uses μοιχεία in his letters; the substantive μοιχός ("adulterer") occurs once (1 Cor 6:9), the adjective μοιχαλίς ("adulterous") twice (Rom 7:3); and the verb μοιχεύω ("to commit adultery") three times (Rom 2:22; 13:9). Winter argues that those who commit adulterous incest are considered adulterers (μοιχοί) according to Roman law (*After Paul Left Corinth*, 49).

[52] See LSJ, s.vv. μητροκοίτης, an incestuous person (Hipponax, *Fr.* 12.2; Apc. Esdr. 28.28); μητρογαμέω, to marry one's mother ([Ps.-]Clement, *Recogn.* 9.20.9; 9.25.17); μητρομιξία, incest with one's mother (Sextus Empiricus, *Math.* 11.191.2); μητρογαμία, incest with one's mother; μητρογάμος, one guilty of such incest. See also ἀδελφομιξία, marriage of brother and sister; θυγατρογαμία, marriage to one's own daughter; θυγατρογάμος, married to one's own daughter; θυγατρομιξία, incest with a daughter.

Broader terms used in instances of incest include ἀθεμιτογαμία, an unlawful marriage; ἀθεμιτογαμέω, to enter an unlawful marriage ([Ps.-]Clement, *Recogn.* 9.20.10); ἀθεμιτόγαμος, one guilty of such a marriage; ἀθεμιτομιξία, an unlawful union; συγγενής γάμος, intra-kin marriage (Aeschylus, *Prom.* 855); ἀνόσιος συνουσία, unholy sexual intercourse. For later developments, see *PGL*, s.v. αἱμομιξία.

For a word related to our circumstance, see LSJ, s.v. μητρυιογάμος, one who marries his stepmother. Like μητρογάμος, this word is used only once, by Manetho, a third-century BCE Egyptian priest. One should not hastily dismiss γαμ- root words as nuptial (cf. LSJ, s.v. γαμέω, I.2).

Latin also has a group of related words that broadly denote impurity, defilement, or pollution but may be used of incestuous relationships; see *Oxford Latin Dictionary*, 2nd ed., ed. P. G. W. Glare (Oxford: Oxford University Press, 2012), s.vv. *inceste, incestificus, incesto, incestum, incestus, incestuosus*. See also G. Humbert, "Incestum, Incestus," *DAGR* 3.1:455; Bé Breij, "Incest in Roman Declamation," in *New Chapters in the History of Rhetoric*, ed. Laurent Pernot, International Studies in the History of Rhetoric 1 (Leiden: Brill, 2009), 201; and Mark Golden, "Incest," *OCD*, 4th ed., 731.

All of the Greek words listed above are exceedingly rare and, for the most part, relatively late. I have included above all citations that occur prior to the third century CE. In fact, Golden notes that "no general word for incest is found before the Byzantine period" (*OCD*, 731). Most of the words above would not apply to Paul's circumstance (stepmother–son).

[53] See n. 62 below. On ἡ χρῆσις παρὰ φύσιν, see David E. Fredrickson, "Natural and Unnatural Use in Romans 1:24–27: Paul and the Philosophical Critique of Eros," in *Homosexuality, Science, and the "Plain Sense" of Scripture*, ed. David L. Balch (Eugene, OR: Wipf & Stock, 2000), 197–222, here 199–207.

his father in the act of adultery.[54] Certainly incest was a common topic of Roman *controversiae*.[55] Yet Bé Breij's extensive study cautions against assigning legal reality to such declamations: "Roman *controversiae* … often served as a means to explore and finally confirm and adopt contemporary socio-cultural norms.… The Roman values attached to these were eventually accepted, but only after they had been explored in a profound and probing manner."[56] Consequently, the jurists of the second and third century CE take up the issue in earnest. Marcian notes a similar case during Hadrian's reign, where a son was murdered by his father after committing *adultery* with his stepmother.[57] Papinian distinguishes between the two, "if adultery is committed with incest, as for instance with a stepdaughter, daughter-in-law, stepmother," the woman shall also be punished (*Dig.* 48.5.39.pr.).[58] Not all authors, however, employ the same terms. Juvenal (*Sat.* 6.403), for instance, hints and dances about the common trope of stepmother–son adulterous liaisons, whereas Vergil and Apuleius, confronting deviant stepmothers, use the terms *incestum* and *incestare*, respectively.[59] Yet it is not sufficiently clear that incest is meant over the more basic meaning "defile."[60] G. Humbert observes, "Le mot *incestum* comprenait en droit romain, dans un sens large, tout acte immoral ou irréligieux; et, comme adjectif, il avait conservé cette signification. Mais, dans un sens plus étroit, il désignait l'impudicité des vestales et le commerce prohibé entre personnes

---

[54] Quintilian, *Inst.* 9.2.42: ut Seneca in controversia, cuius summa est quod pater filium et novercam inducente altero filio in adulterio deprensos occidit, "As Seneca in his *controversia*, whose plot is that a father, when led in by another son, having caught the [other] son and the [son's] stepmother in adultery, he killed them."

[55] Breij ("Incest in Roman Declamation," 208–9) cites three texts concerning son–stepmother relationships ([Ps.-]Quintilian, *Decl. Min.* 246, 335; Calpurnius Flaccus, *Decl.* 22).

[56] Breij, "Incest in Roman Declamation," 197.

[57] Marcian, *Dig.* 48.9.5.pr: Divus Hadrianus fertur, cum invenatione filium suum quidam necaverat, qui novercam adulterabat, in insulam eum deportasse, "The divine Hadrian is said, when a certain man during a hunt had killed his son, who had committed adultery with his stepmother, to have deported him to an island." See also Modestinus, *Dig.* 48.5.34.1.

[58] Cf. Papinian, *Dig.* 48.5.39.6, though Papinian makes clear that here a marriage had taken place.

[59] Vergil, *Aen.* 10.389: hinc Sthenium petit et Rhoeti de gente vetusta Anchemolum thalamos ausum incestare novercae, "Then Sthenius he assailed; and next Anchemolus of Rhoetus' ancient stock, who dared defile his stepmother's bridal bed"; Apuleius, *Metam.* 10.6.9: illum incestum paterno thalamo, illum parricidam fraterno exitio et in comminata novercae caede sicarium, "that defiler in paternal bed, that murderer with fraternal ruin, and an assassin in the murder of stepmother threatened."

[60] The word *incestum* is formed from *in* + *castus*, literally, "unchaste." Moreover, the precise meaning of the words is complicated by the presence of *thalamus* ("marriage bed"). In both cases, the crime committed assaults the *thalamus*, highlighting the transgressive nature of the relationships—they usurped the father's marriage right—as opposed to the odious quality of the pairing.

unies par un lien de parenté ou d'alliance."[61] Breij notes that incest is fundamentally a religious transgression, a desecration of sacred sexual bonds.[62]

So far all the evidence has been Roman, and relatively late at that, with a conspicuous dearth of Greek authors. Patricia Watson's seminal study *Ancient Stepmothers* helps clarify the issue. She shows that, for the Athenians, sexual intercourse between a son and his stepmother was considered not incestuous but adulterous.[63] So Gustave Glotz observes, "l'inceste donnait lieu à l'exercice de certains droits, en tant que μοιχεία. En cas de flagrant délit, le mari, fils, père ou frère de la coupable pouvait tuer l'amant; le mari pouvait lui infliger l'humiliation du παρατιλμός et de la ῥαφανίοωσις, ou bien lui intenter une γραφὴ μοιχείας."[64] Indeed, no laws are known that prohibited incest even if it was culturally repugnant.[65] So, Watson argues, in his *Thesmophoriazusae*, Aristophanes depicts Euripides's Phaedra as a metonym for adulteress: "you wouldn't call one woman living today a Penelope, but you'd call the whole lot of them Phaedras."[66] The stepmother, as a literary figure and in Athenian imagination, was one consumed by unbridled passion and desire, sometimes for murder, other times for sex. Athenian men apparently suffered considerable anxiety by the thought of their young wives falling for the sons of previous marriages, yet never did they conceive of these affairs as anything but adulterous.[67] By contrast, so Watson argues, the Romans consider sexual

---

[61] Humbert, *DAGR* 3.1:455: "The word *incestum* in Roman law, in a broad sense, included any immoral or irreligious act; and, as an adjective, it retained that meaning. But, in a narrower sense, it designated the vestals' unchastity and the intercourse prohibited between persons united by a kinship or marital bond."

[62] Breij, "Incest in Roman Declamation," 199–200. This, she argues, helps explain why the earliest designations in Greek, especially prior to Christendom, are sacred terms: ἀνήκεστος καὶ ἄνομος γάμος ("ruinous and lawless marriage"), γάμος ἀσεβής ("unholy marriage"), γάμος ἀνόσιος ("unholy marriage") (200 n. 13). Hipponax, *Fr.* 12.2 (μητροκοίτης, "one who beds his mother") is an exception to this rule.

[63] Watson, *Ancient Stepmothers*, 17, 71–90, 256. Cf. Breij, "Incest in Roman Declamation," 201: "it was a form of *moikheia*."

[64] Gustave Glotz, "Incestum, Incestus," *DAGR* 3.1:449–55, here 454–55: "Incest occasioned the exercise of certain rights, as an (instance of) μοιχεία. In cases of *flagrante delicto*, a husband, son, father, or brother of the culpable party could kill the lover; the husband could inflict the humiliation of the παρατιλμός ['forced depilation'] and of the ῥαφανίοωσις ['radish-insertion'], or to bring against him a γραφὴ μοιχείας ['indictment for adultery']."

[65] Glotz, *DAGR* 3.1: 449–50, 455: "Ainsi l'inceste, interdit par la θέμις, entravé par le droit public, n'était punissable que s'il lésait un tiers." So also Paschke, "Ambiguity of Paul's References," 182; Breij, "Incest in Roman Declamation," 201.

[66] Aristophanes, *Thesm.* 540–550. See Watson, *Ancient Stepmothers*, 87–90. On Euripides's *Hippolytus*, see Jean-Baptiste Bonnard, "Phèdre sans inceste: À propos de la théorie de l'inceste du deuxième type et de ses applications en histoire grecque," *RH* 621 (2002): 77–107.

[67] Watson, *Ancient Stepmothers*, 89–90, esp. n. 139.

unions between sons and stepmothers incestuous.⁶⁸ Her basis for this assertion, however, is the Augustan marriage legislation, a notoriously complicated topic.

First, the texts of Augustus's *Leges Iuliae* (18 BCE), and *Lex Papia-Poppaea* (9 CE) are no longer extant, surviving only in the legal commentaries of later jurists.⁶⁹ As Angelika Mette-Dittman notes, "Die Texte dieser Gesetze [*leges Iuliae*] sind nicht in geschlossener Form überliefert, sondern mußten aus verschiedenen literarischen Quellengattungen sowie epigraphischem Material rekonstruiert werden."⁷⁰ This has led some scholars to question whether the Augustan marriage laws prohibited incest at all.⁷¹ Nonetheless, many scholars still cite the Roman jurists as applicable. Of particular note is the Roman jurist Gaius (fl. 130–180 CE),⁷² who wrote in his *Institutes*, "Likewise, (it is not permitted to marry) her who was once my mother-in-law or my daughter-in-law or my stepdaughter or my stepmother."⁷³ Note that Gaius does not label this incest, nor does he repudiate it with the same severity with which he lambasts other close-kin marriages (*nefarias et incestas nuptias*, "impious and defiling marriages").⁷⁴ Further complicating the

---

⁶⁸ Ibid., 137.

⁶⁹ On the Augustan marriage laws, see Judith Evans Grubbs, *Women and the Law in the Roman Empire: A Sourcebook on Marriage, Divorce and Widowhood* (New York: Routledge, 2002), 83–85; Susan Treggiari, *Roman Marriage: Iusti Coniuges from the Time of Cicero to the Time of Ulpian* (New York: Oxford University Press, 1991), 37–80.

⁷⁰ Angelika Mette-Dittman, *Die Ehegesetze des Augustus: Eine Untersuchung im Rahmen der Gesellschaftspolitik des Princeps*, Hist.E 67 (Stuttgart: Steiner, 1991), 15: "The texts of these laws [*leges Iuliae*] do not survive in finished form, rather they must be reconstructed from various literary source-genres as well as epigraphic material."

⁷¹ Ibid., 42: "In der Forschung umstritten ist bis heute die Frage, ob die *lex Julia de adulteriis* ein Verbot inzestuöser Beziehungen einschloß." See also McGinn, *Prostitution, Sexuality*, 140; Paschke, "Ambiguity of Paul's References," 179–84, esp. 181–82; Humbert, *DAGR* 3.1:455: "La loi *Julia de adulteriis* ne paraît pas avoir comblé cette lacune, car elle ne mentionne l'inceste qu'en passant, c'est-à-dire en tant qu'il constituait en même temps un adultère."

⁷² Liselot Huchthausen, ed., *Römisches Recht in einem Band: Zwölftafelgesetz; Gaius, Institutionen; Aus den Digesten; Cicero, Rede für Sextus Roscius aus Ameria, Aus den zwei Büchern Rhetorik*, Bibliothek der Antike: Römische Reihe (Berlin: Aufbau, 1989), xxvi–xxvii: "Das Vorurteil gegen Gaius war wohl teilweise dadurch begründet worden, daß er unter den berühmten 'klassischen' Juristen des 2. und 3. Jahrhunderts u.Z.—Ulpian, Papinian, Paulus, Celsus, Julian— offensichtlich ein Außenseiter war ... aus den erhaltenen Fragmenten können wir erkennen, daß sie sich gegenseitig schätzen: sie zitieren einander, berufen sich aufeinander—den Namen des Gaius erwähnt keiner von ihnen.... Von unserem Autor [Gaius] wissen wir weder, woher er kam, noch wo er lebte und lehrte, nur die Zeit seines Wirkens wird einigermaßen sicher abgegrenzt durch Bestimmungen, die er noch als gültig erwähnt, und Erlasse, die er bereits kannte."

⁷³ Gaius, *Inst.* 1.63: Item eam [uxorem ducere non liquet] quae mihi quondam socrus aut nurus aut privigna aut noverca fuit. See also Paulus, *Dig.* 23.2.14. Concerning slave marriages (already an anachronism?), see Paulus, *Dig.* 23.2.14.2.

⁷⁴ Gaius, *Inst.* 1.59; cf. 1.64. The most natural reading takes 1.64 as rounding again on those marriages prohibited in 1.59. The obvious verbal parallel (*nefarias atque incestas nuptias*) commends this reading. Likewise, Gaius's language is much too pointed to cover all of 1.59–63.

issue, Papinian (ca. 142–212 CE) permits marriages between step-siblings (*Dig.* 23.2.34.2), as does Gaius between adopted siblings postemancipation (*Inst.* 1.61). One must, therefore, ask whether step-relations were even considered incestuous by later jurists.[75]

Moreover, it is dubious to assume that the Augustan marriage laws significantly impacted Paul's Corinthian community. It is well known that Augustus aimed his marriage laws at the Roman senatorial (and to some extent equestrian) elite.[76] Indeed, Russell Dudrey has persuasively argued that 1 Corinthians betrays not the slightest consciousness of the *leges Iuliae*.[77] Instead of arraigning the adulterer as the *leges Iuliae* require, Paul encourages the Corinthians to resolve this adultery in house. This may reflect the self-regulation so famously granted by the Romans to Jewish communities and, by extension, to nascent Christian communities.[78] On the other hand, it may merely provide evidence that the *leges Iuliae* were generally stillborn and completely so at Corinth.[79] The latter is almost certainly true. While it has generally been assumed that Roman Corinth was heavily Romanized, more recent scholarship on Corinthian identity has tended to underscore the criss-crossing identity of the city and its inhabitants, marking a resurgence of Corinth's dominant Greek identity.[80] Archaeological evidence demonstrates that Roman Corinth was rebuilt according to its earlier Greek layout.[81] The Corinthian

---

Gaius notes greater leniency for collateral unions (1.60): exceptions for adopted siblings (1.61) and for paternal uncles and their nieces (1.62). Gaius even tempers his language in 1.63, leaving the reader to supply *uxorem ducere non liquet* ("it is not permitted to marry"; cf. 1.59, *nuptiae contrahi non possunt*, "marriages unable to be contracted"), and feels compelled to justify his position vis-à-vis polygamy. Thus, 1.63 should be taken with 1.60–62, wherein Gaius provides a caveat on various forms of collateral marriages for which *est quaedam similis obseruatio, sed non tanta*, "there is the very same practice, but not to the same degree" (1.60).

[75] The later jurists prohibited these relationships; of this there is no doubt. The question is why. Is it because a stepmother and her stepson are tied too closely by kinship? Why then are step-siblings permitted to marry? Surely they are no closer kin than stepmother and son.

[76] Richard I. Frank, "Augustus' Legislation on Marriage and Children," *CSCA* 8 (1975): 41–52. See also Russell P. Dudrey, "The Social and Legal Setting of 1 Corinthians 7:17–35: De Facto Slave Marriages in the Church at Corinth" (PhD diss., University of Minnesota, 1998), 490–94.

[77] Dudrey, "Social and Legal Setting," 496–98.

[78] Ibid., 467–80. Dudrey well establishes Roman conflation of Christian and Jewish communities during the Julio-Claudian period.

[79] Ibid., 497 n. 90.

[80] The standard text of this resurgence is Simon Swain, *Hellenism and Empire: Language, Classicism, and Power in the Greek World, AD 50–250* (Oxford: Oxford University Press, 1996).

[81] Peter Oakes, "Contours of the Urban Environment," in *After The First Urban Christians: The Social-Scientific Study of Pauline Christianity Twenty-Five Years Later*, ed. Todd D. Still and David G. Horrell (London: T&T Clark, 2009), 21–35, here 33. See also Benjamin W. Millis, "The Social and Ethnic Origins of the Colonists in Early Roman Corinth," in *Corinth in Context: Comparative Studies on Religion and Society*, ed. Steven J. Friesen, Daniel N. Schowalter, and James C. Walters, NovTSup 134 (Leiden: Brill, 2010), 10–33, here 14–15.

colonization included also the revival and/or revitalization of old Corinthian cults, festivals, and cultural symbols, including the return of the Isthmian Games.[82] Surveying the evidence, Benjamin Millis states, "The early colonists of Roman Corinth, whatever their origins, were at pains to emphasize and promote their status not as interlopers but as legitimate successors and inheritors of the Greek city."[83] Further still, however, epigraphical, onomastic, and numismatic evidence from Roman Corinth suggests that Greek identity did, in fact, predominate among Roman Corinth's new inhabitants.[84] This is true, to some extent, even at the political level.[85] Given that Roman administration generally maintained the status quo of local authorities and laws, it is not impossible that Roman Corinth was refounded, as it was architecturally and culturally, in a Greek politico-legal tradition.[86] Therefore, it is doubtful that, if the Augustan marriage laws prohibited incest at all, such decrees even reached the reality of Roman Corinth's principally Greek lower strata.

---

[82] Millis, "Social and Ethnic Origins," 15. Cf. Christine M. Thomas, "Greek Heritage in Roman Corinth and Ephesos: Hybrid Identities and Strategies of Display in the Material Record of Traditional Mediterranean Religions," in Friesen, Schowalter, and Walters, *Corinth in Context*, 114–44, here 119–23.

[83] Millis, "Social and Ethnic Origins," 15.

[84] Ibid., 34. Roman Corinth was not, as often portrayed, a colony inhabited primarily by Roman military veterans; rather, evidence suggests a majority population of Greek freedmen, highly conversant with Roman culture and politics yet maintaining their Greek identity, especially in their private affairs (31).

[85] Oakes notes that, in contrast to other Roman colonies, political leadership at Corinth was sometimes retained by Greeks instead of Romans ("Contours of the Urban Environment," 34).

[86] On Roman administration of foreign cities, see Dudrey, "Social and Legal Setting," 466–67. Dudrey, however, is hostile to the idea that Roman Corinth was governed according to Athenian (read: Hellenistic) law (see 504–5). His argument is by and large unconvincing. He is right to state that evidence for Hellenistic law is slim and thus extrapolated from Athenian law (505 n. 108). Yet his dismissal of Athenian law at Roman Corinth is a bare assertion and does not heed his own concession that the *Leges Iuliae* were not realized at Corinth.

Millis argues that, at Roman Corinth, the elite were composed primarily of Greek freedmen, with a smaller minority of hellenized Romans (e.g., T. Claudius Dinippus), while the lower strata were predominantly of Greek origin ("Social and Ethnic Origins," 32). According to Thomas, Greek provincials, such as Pausanias, actively downplayed Roman influence in favor of Greek continuity, while conversely, Romans tended to emphasize their continuity with their subjugated cities ("Greek Heritage," 142). In this climate, it is not enough to claim Corinth as a Roman colony and therefore subject to Roman law. Such an assertion conflates Roman rule with Roman law.

Dio Chrysostom provides unique evidence that Greek provincial elites actively attempted to prevent Roman intrusions into local politics (see Christopher P. Jones, *The Roman World of Dio Chrysostom*, Loeb Classical Monographs [Cambridge: Harvard University Press, 1978], 95–103). Greek elites preferred to self-legislate, self-regulate, even if they were not permitted to self-rule. At Corinth, despite its colonial status, evidence suggests a much greater emphasis on its Greek identity than other Roman colonies. Therefore, one cannot so quickly dismiss the possibility that Roman Corinth's politico-legal structure was as mixed as its Greek-Roman inhabitants.

The case for Paul's regarding the offense as incest is tenuous. Roman sources regularly identify this type of relationship as adulterous, though some authors do charge offenders with incest. On the other hand, Greek sources stereotype amorous stepmothers as adulteresses par excellence. Jewish sources likewise appear to place these relationships under the rubric of adultery. Philo, for instance, expounding on the adultery commandment (*Spec.* 3.7–8), notes that the Mosaic law prohibits men from mixing with other men's wives and also with widowed stepmothers.[87] The reasons for this restriction are two: on account of the honor (owed) to the father and because the words *stepmother* and *mother* are of a kind (*Spec.* 3.20). The former establishes the father's sexual right to his wife beyond the grave, while the latter secures a guilt by analogy. Philo explicitly acknowledges, however, that the relationships are not equal: "[they are of a kind] even though the passion of the soul is not identical; for the man who has been taught to abstain from others' wives, because concerning his stepmother he was commanded, much more will abstain from his natural mother" (*Spec.* 3.20–21).[88] Likewise, Josephus places relationships between a man and his mother, stepmother, aunt, sister, and son's wives under the category of adultery.[89] Finally, Pseudo-Phocylides, listing this union between an interdict against prostituting one's wife (*Sent.* 1.177–178) and mingling with one's father's concubine,[90] appears to recapitulate conceptions already found in Philo: "Do not touch your stepmother, the second marriage-bed of your family; but honor she who has gone in the footsteps of your mother as your mother" (*Sent.* 1.179–180). The stepmother fills the shoes of one's mother. In the instances of these Jewish authors,

---

[87] Philo, *Spec.* 3.12: εὖ μέντοι καὶ τὰ ἄλλα τὰ περὶ τὰς ὁμιλίας ὁ νόμος διετάξατο. κελεύει γὰρ οὐ μόνον ἀλλοτρίων ἀπέχεσθαι γυναικῶν, ἀλλὰ καὶ χηρευουσῶν μητρυιῶν, αἷς οὐ θέμις συνέρχεσθαι, "Indeed, well does the law establish other regulations concerning intercourse. For it commands that one not only abstain from others' wives, but also from their widowed stepmothers, with whom it is not right to unite."

[88] Again, Philo's concern seems to be that the son honor his father and mother: καὶ εἴ τις διὰ τὴν ἐπὶ τῷ πατρὶ μνήμην αἰδεῖται τὴν ἐκείνου ποτὲ γενομένην γυναῖκα, δῆλός ἐστιν ἕνεκα τῆς εἰς ἀμφοτέρους τοὺς γονεῖς τιμῆς οὐδὲν βουλευσόμενος ἐπὶ τῇ μητρὶ νεώτερον, "And if any one, on account of his father's memory, respects the woman who became his father's wife, it is clear that, on account of the honor for both his parents, he will plot nothing worse against his mother."

[89] Note how Josephus uses bare accusatives and genitives as headings: Josephus, *A.J.* 3.264: τοὺς δὲ λεπρούς ("Now as for lepers"); 3.271: Τὰς δὲ γυναῖκας ("Now as for wives"); 3.274: Μοιχείαν ("As for adultery"); 3.276: Τῶν δ ἱερέων ("Now as for priests"). There is an inherent difficulty produced by 3.275, which must either fall under the rubric of adultery or must be seen as beginning a new section on related but nonadulterous sexual unions. The former option seems untenable; however, given that 3.275 begins a new sentence, opened by a new prohibition (ἐκώλυσε ... μηδέ, "he forbade ... and not"), it is most plausible that Josephus categorized 3.274 as adultery while maintained the material of 3.275 under this heading precisely because Lev 18 lumps these offenses together.

[90] Pseudo-Phocylides, *Sent.* 1.181: μηδέ τι παλλακίσιν πατρὸς λεχέεσσι μιγείης, "Do not mingle with your father's concubines."

their rationale is derivative, and consequently the conceptualization of the proscriptions remains somewhat opaque.[91] Yet there is good cause to understand this prohibition in light of the father's sexual rights; namely, one should not use one's stepmother sexually due to the father's—that is, the husband's—honor.

The case for the offense being adultery over and against incest is preferable. The evidence internal to 1 Cor 5 buttresses this reading. If Paul had intended to underscore the incestuous nature of that sexual union one might expect him to have written μητρυιάν instead of γυνὴ τοῦ πατρός. The cognate word[92] would surely have heightened the sense of offense. Or likewise, Paul may have emphasized the incestuous nature of this union using υἱόν instead of or in addition to τινα. Moreover, Greek offered still other ways to identify and condemn incestuous relationships.[93] Paul utilizes none of these. Yet neither does Paul label this union μοιχεία. In fact, Paul explicitly calls it πορνεία, a term denoting general sexual incontinence, and a term nearly absent from the Pentateuch.[94] The choice of πορνεία is understandable, since its semantic range is broader than μοιχεία, and it is therefore conducive to Paul's larger goals in 1 Cor 5–7.

III. Conclusion

Paul's confrontation with Corinthian πορνεία is anything but transparent to outside readers. For modern readers, for whom incest and adultery are clearly distinguished, a relationship between a stepmother and stepson is recognizably incestuous. For the Greeks and Romans, however, this was not so. I have argued that the relevant Greek, Roman, and Jewish evidence supports the position that such a relationship would have been identified as adulterous. At its core, this was an instance of one man violating the sexual rights of another man. Yet this was a

---

[91] As with Paul, it cannot be assumed that these authors understood the pentateuchal prohibitions as the authors of the Pentateuch intended them. In fact, it is clear that all three of these authors are grappling with the Pentateuch in Greco-Roman contexts, often with apologetic ends. Exegetes do not finish their task by merely identifying a potential source; rather, it is imperative that they determine how the author has understood and utilized the material that is recycled. They cannot assume that Philo understood Leviticus through "Hebrew" eyes, particularly since his major project was to demonstrate the coherence of Jewish Scriptures with Greco-Roman philosophy. Note how Philo frames his exposition of adultery (*Spec.* 3.7–11). Cf. Pseudo-Phocylides, *Sent.* 1.59, 190, 193–194.

[92] Philo, *Spec.* 3.20: διότι μητρυιᾶς καὶ μητρὸς ὄνομα συγγενές, "because the names 'stepmother' and 'mother' are of a kind."

[93] See nn. 52 and 62 above.

[94] See Gen 38:24; Num 14:33. The Pentateuch does use cognates; however, these are all technical uses referring to prostitution (πορνεύω: Deut 23:18; πόρνη: Gen 34:31; 38:15, 21, 22; Lev 21:7, 14; Deut 23:3, 18, 19).

particularly egregious adultery, as evidenced by Paul's use of analytic kin circumlocution. Rather than securing an oblique allusion to pentateuchal incest prohibitions, Paul's phrase, ὥστε γυναῖκά τινα τοῦ πατρὸς ἔχειν, focuses on the woman as the *wife* of the *father*—not as the stepmother of the πόρνος. In fact, it is precisely by concentrating on the woman as the father's wife that it becomes clear exactly what is so heinous about this act: it constituted inner-οἶκος adultery, an assault from within on the health and hierarchy of the social body.

Without an indictment for incest, the case for a pentateuchal echo is crippled, providing less fodder for those who would read 1 Cor 5 against the backdrop of ritual purity. When this obstacle is removed, it is easier to identify 1 Cor 5 as a test case of Paul's *homonoia* argument in chapters 1–4. Further, adultery provides the latticework for drawing 1 Cor 5 together with chapters 6–7. Marriage and the οἶκος draw together the seemingly disparate elements of 1 Cor 5–7.

New and Recent Titles

STEPS TO A NEW EDITION OF THE HEBREW BIBLE
Ronald Hendel
Paperback $45.95, 978-1-62837-157-4 330 pages, 2016 Code: 067010
Hardcover $60.95, 978-0-88414-195-2 E-book $45.95, 978-0-88414-194-5
Text-Critical Studies 10

MAPPING JUDAH'S FATE IN EZEKIEL'S ORACLES AGAINST THE NATIONS
Lydia Lee
Digital open access, 978-0-88414-180-8 316 pages, 2016 Code 062819
http://www.sbl-site.org/publications/Books_ANEmonographs.aspx
Paper $49.95, 978-1-62837-151-2 Hardcover $64.95, 978-0-88414-183-9
Ancient Near East Monographs 15

L'INFLUENCE DE L'ARAMÉEN SUR LES TRADUCTEURS DE LA LXX PRINCIPALEMENT, SUR LES TRADUCTEURS GRECS POSTÉRIEURS, AINSI QUE SUR LES SCRIBES DE LA *VORLAGE* DE LA LXX
Anne-Françoise Loiseau
Paperback $45.95, 978-1-62837-156-7 270 pages, 2016 Code: 060465
Hardcover $60.95, 978-0-88414-193-8 E-book $45.95, 978-0-88414-192-1
Septuagint and Cognate Studies 65

ARMENIAN APOCRYPHA RELATING TO ANGELS AND BIBLICAL HEROES
Michael E. Stone
Paperback $55.95, 978-1-62837-154-3 322 pages, 2016 Code: 063549
Hardcover $75.95, 978-0-88414-189-1 E-book $55.95, 978-0-88414-188-4
Early Judaism and Its Literature 45

METAPHOR, MORALITY, AND THE SPIRIT IN ROMANS 8:1–17
William E. W. Robinson
Paperback $29.95, 978-1-62837-153-6 192 pages, 2016 Code: 064521
Hardcover $44.95, 978-0-88414-187-7 E-book $29.95, 978-0-88414-186-0
Early Christianity and Its Literature 20

SBL Press • P.O. Box 2243 • Williston, VT 05495-2243
Phone: 877-725-3334 (toll-free) or 802-864-6185 • Fax: 802-864-7626
Order online at www.sbl-site.org/publications

JBL 135, no. 4 (2016): 849–857
doi: http://dx.doi.org/10.15699/jbl.1354.2016.3019

An Armenian Fragment of the Gospel of Mark in the *Erkatʿagir* Script: With a Note on Its Codicological Reconstruction

ALIN SUCIU
asuciu@uni-goettingen.de
Akademie der Wissenschaften zu Göttingen,
37085 Göttingen, Germany

This article provides an introduction to and a transcription as well as English translation of a previously unknown Armenian fragment of the Gospel of Mark (15:4b–7a, 11b–14a), which is currently kept in a private collection in the Middle East. The fragment was extracted from the binding of a sixteenth- or seventeenth-century Garšūnī codex that probably came from Diyarbakir in Turkey. The Armenian text is inscribed in the *erkatʿagir* uncial ("iron-forged letters") that can approximately be assigned on paleographical grounds to the late tenth or eleventh century CE. The paper compares the textual variants of the newly identified fragment against the old Armenian text of the Gospel of Mark published by Johannes Zohrap in 1805. Although the text usually agrees with the Zohrap edition, at least one notable difference occurs in Mark 15:5. Finally, the attempt to reconstruct the fragment codicologically raises some questions concerning the format of the manuscript to which it originally belonged.

The Armenian parchment fragment introduced here belongs to a private collection in the Middle East. The fragment is inscribed in the *erkatʿagir* uncial ("iron-forged letters") and features the text of the Gospel of Mark 15:4b–7a, 11b–14a. As the *erkatʿagir* manuscripts are not as numerous as the later minuscule (*bolorgir*), and most of them date before the eleventh century, the importance of the fragment is evident, not least for the knowledge of the Gospel of Mark in the early Armenian codices.[1] Moreover, given that ancient manuscripts in private hands often change

I sincerely thank Dr. Gohar Muradyan and Prof. Dickran Kouymjian, who had the generosity to read and comment an early version of this paper.

[1] Dickran Kouymjian, "Armenian Paleography: A Reassessment," in *Scribes et manuscrits du Moyen-Orient*, ed. Françpos Déroche and Francis Richard, Etudes et recherches (Paris: Bibliothèque nationale de France, 1997), 177–88; Kouymjian, "Notes on Armenian Codicology: Part 2, Armenian Paleography: Dating the Major Scripts," *Comparative Oriental Manuscript Studies*

849

owners, the task of editing them before they vanish again is obviously important. Therefore, this article provides an introduction to and a transcription as well as English translation of the newly recovered Armenian fragment of the Gospel of Mark.

Many *erkat'agir* fragments served as pastedowns or protective sheets and have thus been discovered stitched to the bindings of more recent manuscripts. It is notable that the recycled fragments were usually taken from Gospel manuscripts. This situation was noted long ago by Robert Pierce Casey, who remarked that "Armenians … frequently employed in binding the leaves of gospel manuscripts which they had discarded, and some of the oldest specimens of Armenian paleography are to be found as fly-leaves of much later codices."[2] The same applies to the fragment introduced here, which was retrieved by a private collector from the inner cover of another manuscript in his possession.

I. Provenance of the Fragment

According to a private report, the owner found the fragment pasted down inside the covers of what he thought to be a Syriac paper codex.[3] Inspection of three photographs, however, reveals that, while the manuscript is written in the western Syriac Serto script, the text is actually not in Syriac but rather in Arabic Garšūnī. The codex is inscribed in a beautifully neat hand that can probably be dated to the sixteenth or seventeenth centuries CE. The photographs examined suggest that the manuscript contains various hymns and prayers that may be of Catholic provenance. The only text that has an *incipit* in the photographs I have seen is a "Hail to you, Mary," introduced by a heading written in red ink. Below are the transliterations of the heading and *incipit* into Arabic letters,

طلبه على تدبير المسيحى: تقال كل يوم: وهي عجيبه لمن يتفهمها: وهى تغنى عن طلبات[4] كثيره: لأن كلمه من قُرب اخير من الف كلمه من بُعد

---

[1] *Newsletter* 6 (July 2013): 23–28; Kouymjian, "The Archeology of the Armenian Manuscripts: Codicology, Paleography and Beyond," in *Armenian Philology in the Modern Era: From Manuscript to Digital Text*, ed. Valentina Calzolari, with Michael E. Stone, HdO, Section 8, Uralic and Central Asian Studies 23.1 (Leiden: Brill, 2014), 5–22.

[2] Robert Pierce Casey, "An Early Armenian Fragment of Luke xvi 3–25," *JTS* 36 (1935): 70–73, here 70, http://dx.doi.org/10.1093/jts/os-XXXVI.141.70. See also Arthur Vööbus's remark that the study of the early Armenian Gospel fragments extracted from later manuscripts will revolutionize the research on the Armenian New Testament text, in *Early Versions of the New Testament: Manuscript Studies*, PETSE 6 (Stockholm: Estonian Theological Society in Exile, 1954), 156; S. Peter Cowe, "The Armenian Version of the New Testament," in *The Text of the New Testament in Contemporary Research: Essays on the Status Quaestionis*, ed. Bart D. Ehrman and Michael W. Holmes, 2nd ed., NTTSD 42 (Leiden: Brill, 2013), 253–92, here 260.

[3] The informant mentioned that this manuscript is no longer in his possession.

[4] *Lamed* was initially omitted and added later in black ink.

A supplication for the preparation of the Christian. To be recited every day. And it is miraculous for the one who understands it. And it is more enriching than many supplications. Because a word from near is better than a thousand words from afar.

Incipit:

السلام لكِ ياستى العدرى ام الخلاص اسألك ان تكونى لى شفيعه فى الليل والنهار
السلام لكِ ياستى العدرى ام البهجه والفرح

Hail to you, my Virgin Lady, the mother of salvation, I ask you to be my intercessor day and night.
Hail to you, my Virgin Lady, the mother of joy and happiness.

Apparently, the owner purchased this and other manuscripts that he describes as Syriac and Garšūnī from an antiquities dealer based in Istanbul, who claimed that the entire batch came from Diyarbakir, located in the southeastern Anatolia region of Turkey. This statement is plausible given that Armenian and Syriac Christians coexisted for centuries in that region, until the massacre and deportations that began in 1915 decimated the two communities. It is possible that other *membra disjecta* of the same Armenian manuscript are to be found in the Syriac and Garšūnī codices from Diyarbakir. It is currently not possible to document a more precise provenance that would narrow the search area for other related fragments. The discovery of the fragment in a Garšūnī codex from Diyarbakir, however, does not necessarily imply that the Armenian manuscript was created in that location. Although this hypothesis cannot be ruled out, it may well be that the codex was imported from a scriptorium situated elsewhere.

II. Description and Dating

The hair side (= recto) and the flesh side (= verso) of the parchment are clearly distinguishable, the latter having a lighter color. The fragment currently measures 15.5 cm in height × 10.0 cm in width and preserves a portion of one column of text on each side. When intact, the manuscript must have contained two text columns and was probably about twice as high. The fragment, however, does not retain the whole length of the leaf but appears to be a piece that is probably equivalent to about a quarter of the entire folio.

At first glance, the position of the text columns on the pages can be inferred from the fact that one of the fragment's margins still seems to preserve the fold pattern of the sheet. Thus, the centerfold appears to be visible on the left margin of the recto and on the opposite margin of the verso. In this case, the recto would feature part of the first text column of the page, while the verso would have a portion of the second column of the next page. As will be argued in the last section of this paper, however, it is more plausible that what appears as the spine of the codex may actually not be the real fold pattern of the sheet. This would suggest that the recto accommodates the right-hand column of the first page, while the verso preserves the left-hand column of the second page.

The fragment has vestiges of twelve lines of text on each side. The number of letters per line ranges from thirteen to eighteen, the average being sixteen. The text is written in *scriptio continua*. Like some of the earliest Armenian manuscripts, the only punctuation mark employed is the raised dot. In one place (recto, line 3), the fragment features the common *nomen sacrum* ႘U, Jesus. The letters are monochrome and the ornamentation is simple. On the recto, lines 3 and 7, the letters *eč'* and *ben*, which open verses 5 and 6 respectively, are written in *ekthesis* and are much enlarged. Judging from the length of verso's line 4, it is likely that the letter *da*, which must be restored in the lacuna that opens verse 12, was also in *ekthesis*.

The fragment may tentatively be assigned on paleographical grounds to the late tenth or eleventh centuries CE. The hand looks similar to those of the manuscripts Erevan, Matenadaran Institute, Nos. 7735 (Four Gospels, 986 CE) and 3723 (Four Gospels, 1045 CE). The latter codex was copied by the scribe Yusik kʻahanay, perhaps at Melitene or Sebaste.[5]

Several inscriptions appear on both sides of the parchment indicating that, before it was pasted inside the covers of the Garšūnī codex, the sheet was used for pen-testing. The recto contains letters in Syriac, inscribed upside down between the lines of the Armenian text. At first glance, the two different scripts give the fragment the appearance of a palimpsest. A more careful inspection, however, clearly eliminates this possibility because the skin does not display any specific mark of treatment proper to palimpsests. Moreover, although some of the Syriac letters form ligatures with their neighbors, they do not seem to form words or clauses. On the verso are scribbled some *probatio pennae* in black and blue ink.

III. The Text

The recto of the fragment features Mark 15:4b–7a, and the verso has Mark 15:11b–14a. The text generally conforms to the version of the Gospel of Mark in classical Armenian published by Yovhannes Zohrapian (Johannes Zohrap),[6] although some differences can be identified. This is not surprising given that the text edited by Zohrap does not properly reflect the diversity of the Armenian New Testament manuscripts.[7]

---

[5] See Michael E. Stone, Dickran Kouymjian, and Henning Lehmann, *Album of Armenian Paleography* (Aarhus: Aarhus University Press, 2002), 140–41, 160–61.

[6] The fragment parallels Johannes Zohrap, *Astuacašunčʻ matean hin ew nor ktakaranačʻ* (Venice: Saint Lazarus, 1805), 681–82.

[7] See Claude Cox, "The Textual Character of the Manuscript Printed as Text in Zōhrapean's Bible," *REArm* 18 (1984): 69–83; Joseph M. Alexanian, "The Armenian Version of the New

Among the small variations from the published text, we may note մըշեւ ի on line 5, recto. This is a variant of մինչեւ, which occurs in the Zohrap version. Similarly, on recto, line 7, our fragment has տաւնին instead of տօնի. The difference must be explained by the fact that the letter o entered the Armenian alphabet only in the thirteenth century CE, when it started to replace the digraph աւ. This orthographic feature gives credit to the early dating of our fragment. Other minor differences, most of them purely orthographic variations, include այնոյհետե[ւ] for այնուհետեւ (recto, line 3), կա[յ]եալ for զկայեալ (recto, lines 8–9) and էր for էր (recto, lines 10, 11).

One notable divergence is found in Mark 15:5b (recto, line 6), where the newly identified fragment reads "the judge marveled greatly" (զարմանալ յոյժ դատաւորին) instead of "Pilate marveled greatly" (զարմանալ յոյժ Պիղատոսի), as the text published by Zohrap has.

Mark 15:5 (the new fragment), Եւ Յիսուս այնոյհետե[ւ ոչ]ինչ եւս պատասխա[նի] մըշեւ ի զարմանալ յոյժ դատաւորին

But Jesus did not answer anything from that moment on, so that the judge marveled greatly.

Mark 15:5 (Zohrap), Եւ Յիսուս այնուհետեւ ոչինչ եւս պատասխանի մինչեւ զարմանալ յոյժ Պիղատոսի

But Jesus did not answer anything from that moment on, so that Pilate marveled greatly.

Leaving aside the adverb "greatly" (յոյժ), which is a variant proper to the Armenian version of Mark, the Zohrap version renders precisely the parallel Greek text, θαυμάζειν τὸν Πιλᾶτον. Our fragment's reading "the judge" in Mark 15:5, finds support at least in the manuscript Erevan, Matenadaran Institute, Ms. No. 3784 (olim Ms. 362.G of the Catholicosate in Etchmiadzin [Vagharshapat]). This parchment codex was inscribed by the priest Thomas at Melitene in 1057 CE.[8] The manuscript received the siglum "C" in Frédéric Macler's extensive study of the Armenian versions of the Gospels of Matthew and Mark.[9] According to Macler, this manuscript of the "Mq type" contains many variations compared to the text published by Zohrap, evincing a Greek-oriented revision of the Armenian text, probably due to the Hellenophile translators of the sixth and seventh centuries.[10] The variant in

---

Testament," in Ehrman and Holmes, *Text of the New Testament in Contemporary Research*, 157–72, esp. 158–59.

[8] Description in Frédéric Macler, *Rapport sur une mission scientifique en Arménie russe et en Arménie turque (juillet–août 1909)* (Paris: Imprimerie nationale, 1910), 41–44.

[9] Frédéric Macler, *Le texte arménien de l'Évangile d'après Matthieu et Marc* (Paris: Imprimerie nationale, 1919), 93–167.

[10] On the Hellenophile School of translators, see Charles Mercier, "L'École Hellénistique dans la littérature arménienne," *REArm* 13 (1978–1979): 59–75; Abraham Terian, "The Hellenizing

Mark 15:5, however, was recorded by Macler among the "arbitrary variants," which are those readings without correspondent in the Greek or Syriac versions.[11] Compared to the new fragment, it is only the word order that differs in the Matenadaran manuscript, զարմանալ դատաւորին յոյժ ("the judge marveled greatly").[12] Despite this similarity, the newly discovered fragment is more akin to the Zohrap text than to that of Macler's manuscript C.

The reading դատաւորին ("the judge") in some Armenian manuscripts of Mark 15:5 can probably be explained as a borrowing from the parallel passage in Matt 27:14, մինչեւ զարմանալ դատաւորին յոյժ, "so that the judge marveled greatly." This would justify the occurrence of the adverb "greatly" (յոյժ) in Mark 15:5 in Armenian, because the same adverb is present in the Greek text of Matt 27:14, ὥστε θαυμάζειν τὸν ἡγεμόνα λίαν.

IV. A Codicological Conundrum

Because of the damaged character of the fragment, the codicological reconstruction of the folio remains a conundrum. As I have already mentioned, one of the fragment's margins seems to preserve the folding pattern of the sheet, which suggests that the surviving piece belonged to the inside part of the folio as it was originally bound. The fragment preserves Mark 15:4b–7a on the recto and 15:11b–14a on the verso. Consequently, the lacuna would extend from the first column of the recto to the second column of the verso, a space too large to contain only Mark 15:7b–11a, which occupies about six and a half printed lines in the Zohrap edition. By comparison, the surviving text on the recto—eleven manuscript lines—corresponds roughly to five lines in the Zohrap edition. This makes it unlikely that the missing portion of Mark could fill more than two complete columns of text, which represents the gap between the end of the first column of the recto and the second column of the verso. To further bolster this argument, it is noteworthy that in a Gospel manuscript from the same period, whose facsimile was published by Macler, the entire text of Mark 15:4–14 fits on two columns.[13]

It is likely that our manuscript had a minimum of twenty lines of text per column and that it measured approximately 35 cm in height × 25 cm in width, which is the average size of the Armenian manuscripts of the tenth and eleventh

---

School: Its Time, Place, and Scope of Activities Reconsidered," in *East of Byzantium: Syria and Armenia in the Formative Period (Dumbarton Oaks Symposium, 1980)*, ed. Nina G. Garsoïan, Thomas F. Mathews, and Robert W. Thomson (Washington, DC: Dumbarton Oaks, 1982), 175–86.

[11] Macler, *L'Évangile d'après Matthieu et Marc*, 124–25.

[12] Ibid., 165.

[13] Frédéric Macler, *L'Évangile arménien: Édition phototypique du manuscrit n° 229 de la Bibliothèque d'Etchmiadzin* (Paris: Geuthner, 1920), f. 108r.

centuries CE.[14] The following improbable scenarios show that the arguments that the codex had another format or that it contained only one column of text cannot be sustained.

1. If Mark 15:7b–11a was accommodated by the recto's second column and the verso's first column, the codex could not be very high since the text is too brief. In other words, this would mean that the width of the hypothetical two-column manuscript would be standard, that is, about 25 cm, but its height would be only slightly more than 15.5 cm, which is the current height of the fragment. This would yield an unusual rectangular codex of about 15.5 cm height and 25 cm width. Even if such a manuscript could be imagined, the missing text would still have to fill two columns of about twelve lines, which already exceeds its length.[15]

2. If the codex had only one column of text, Mark 15:7b–11a would have to be placed on the inferior part of the recto and the superior part of the verso. This would yield a codex of normal height (more than 30 cm), but its width would not change much, which means that it would have been only slightly larger than the current 10 cm. The idea of such an unusual format (ca. 30 × 10 cm) must be rejected from the outset.

Unless the portion of the parchment that has disappeared was either erased or unavailable for some other reason for writing, one may speculate that the fragment actually belonged to a lectionary, in which case it is theoretically possible that the text of the Gospel of Mark was separated by another biblical reading. This hypothesis, however, is undermined by the fact that the lectionaries are usually standard collections of biblical readings and, as far as we are aware, Mark 15:4–14 is not divided in the Armenian lectionaries.

There is at least one other possibility that might explain the format of the fragment. If the recto preserved the second column of text, and the verso the first column of the next page, then the missing portion of Mark 15:7b–11a could just be accommodated in the lacuna. In this case, what appears as the centerfold of the sheet on the left side of the recto and on the opposite side of the verso is not the ancient fold of the manuscript but rather an alteration that the piece of parchment suffered after it was cut off from the folio. A few details support this argument. The

---

[14] Dickran Kouymjian, "La structure et illustration des manuscrits arméniens," in *Illuminations d'Arménie: Arts du livre et de la pierre dans l'Arménie ancienne et médiévale*, ed. Valentina Calzolari (Cologne: Fondation Martin Bodmer, 2007), 41–59, here 42. Kouymjian provides a chart with the typical dimensions of Armenian codices during the course of time, based on the examination of 282 dated manuscripts ("Archeology of the Armenian Manuscripts," 9 n. 12). According to this research, the ninth- and tenth-century Armenian codices were typically 34.4 cm in height × 26.7 cm in width. The eleventh-century manuscripts are slightly smaller, 31.3 cm in height × 24.1 cm in width.

[15] My stichometric calculation suggests that Mark 15:7b–11a roughly corresponds to sixteen lines of text in the manuscript.

letter *ečʽ*, which is written in *ekthesis* on line 3, is partly lost, together with the left margin of the fragment. Similarly, the enlarged letter *ben* that opens line 7 appears too much projected into the hypothetical margin of the page. Moreover, the same letter is inscribed almost completely on what seems to be the folding pattern of the sheet. The position of these letters is a significant issue from a codicological point of view because it is quite unlikely that the copyist inscribed them so near to the centerfold of the manuscript. This indicates that the apparently discernible outer spine of the codex may actually be some kind of erosion due to the recycling of the fragment inside the cover of the Garšūnī codex and not the true centerfold.[16] In the absence of any other satisfactory codicological reconstruction of the manuscript, this explanation remains the most likely one.

Unfortunately, the incomplete nature of the fragment precludes any firm conclusion concerning the character of the manuscript to which it originally belonged. I offer below the photographs of the fragment and a transcription and translation of the text, in the hope that someone else will either confirm or disprove my attempts to explain this conundrum and will thereby shed light on the kind of text represented on this fragment.

Transcription and Translation of Gospel of Mark 15:4b–7a, 11b–14a

Recto (Hair Side) Mark 15:4b–7a

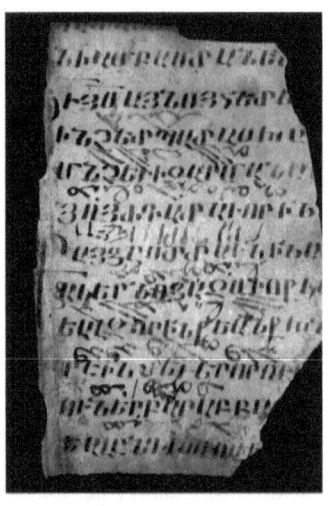

```
15 ⁴[…] […] […] [ՏԵՍ ՔԱ]
   ՆԻ ԱՄԲԱՍՏԱՆԵՆ [ՔԵՆ·]
   ⁵ԵՒ ՅԱ ԱՅՆՈՅՀԵՏԵ[Ի ՈՉ]
   ԻՆՉ ԵՍ ՊԱՏԱՍԽԱ[ՆԻ]
5  ՄՆՉԵԻ Ի ՋԱՐՄԱՆԱ[Լ]
   ՅՈՅԺ ՊԱՏԱԻՈՐԻՆ[·]
   ⁶ԲԱՅՑ ՃԱՍ ՏԱԻՆԻՆ Ա[ՐՁ]
   ԱԿԵՐ ՆՈՅԱ ՋՄԻ ՈՔ ԿԱ[Պ]
   ԵԱԼ ՋՈՐ ԻՆԲԵԱՆՔ ԽՆ[Դ]
10 ՐԵԻՆ· ⁷ԵՒ ԵՐ ՈՐՈԻ[Մ ԱՆ]
   ՈՒՆ ԵՐ ԲԱՐԱԲԲԱ [ԿԱՊ]
   ԵԱԼ ԸՆԴ ԽՌՈՎԻ[ՉԱՆ]
```

---

[16] The owner could not give any clear information concerning the position of the fragment inside the binding of the Garšūnī manuscript that would provide evidence of the relationship of the columns.

Recto 15 ⁴ "... [see how much] they accuse [you]." ⁵But Jesus did not answer anything from that moment on, so that the judge marveled greatly. ⁶But at the feast he released to them one prisoner that they themselves asked. ⁷And there was one whose name was Barabbas, who was bound with the fellow-agitators ...

Verso (Flesh Side) Mark 15:11b–14a

¹¹[...] [...] [...] ՀԱԻԱՆԵ
[ՅՈԻՑ]ԻՆ· ՋԻ ԱՐՁԱԿԵՑԷ
[ՆՈՑ]Ա ՋԲԱՐԱԲԲԱՅՆ·
¹²[ԴԱՐ]ՁԵԱԼ ՊԱՏԱՍԽԱՆԻ
5 [ԵՏ] ՊԻՂԱՏՈՍ ԵԻ ԱՍԷ ՑՆ
   [ՈՍ]Ա· ԻՍԿ ՋԻՆՉ ԿԱՄԻՔ·
   [Թ]Է ԱՐԱՐԻՑ ՋԱՐՔԱՅՆ ՀՐԷ
   [ԻՑ]Ն· ¹³ ԵԻ ՆՈՔԱ ԴԱՐՁԵԱԼ
   [ԱՂ]ԱՂԱԿԵԻՆ ՅՈԻՉԵԱԼՔ Ի
10 [ՔԱՀ]ԱՆԱՅԱՊԵՏԻՑՆ· Ի
   [ԽԱՉ Հ]ԱՆ ՋԴԱ· ¹⁴ ԱՍԷ ՑՆ
   [ՈՍԱ ՊԻԼ]ԱՏՈՍ· ՋԻՆՉ

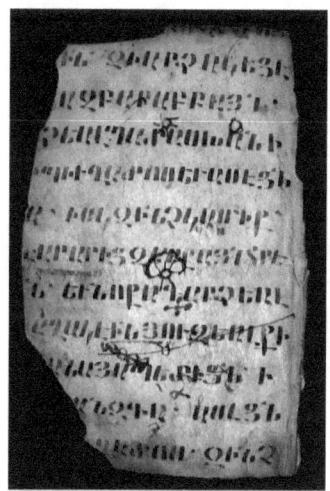

Verso ¹¹ ... they persuade[d] (the crowd), so that he should release Barabbas [for them]. ¹²Pilate answered again and said to them, "But what do you want me [to] do to the king of Jews?" ¹³And they cried out again moved by the archpriests, "[Crucify] him!" ¹⁴Pilate said [to them], "What ...

New from
BEVERLY ROBERTS GAVENTA

978-0-8010-9738-6 • 160 pp. • $22.99c

"No one makes Romans come alive quite like Beverly Gaventa."
—**John M. G. Barclay**, Durham University

"A book the church has long needed . . . . Scholarly and accessible, ancient and contemporary, theological and pastoral."
—**M. Craig Barnes**, president, Princeton Theological Seminary

"A gift to Christians and inquirers alike."—**Susan Grove Eastman**, Duke Divinity School

Baker Academic

bakeracademic.com
Available in bookstores or by calling 800.877.2665

The Apocalypse in Codex Alexandrinus: Exegetical Reasoning and Singular Readings in New Testament Greek Manuscripts

GARRICK V. ALLEN
Garrick.allen@dcu.ie
Dublin City University, Dublin, Ireland

This article explores the ways in which the textual history of the New Testament functions as evidence for its early reception history, and how this layer of reception sheds light on the social realities that stand behind textual transmission. The wording of the book of Revelation in Codex Alexandrinus (A02) serves as an illuminating test case, in that it allows us to focus on singular readings that arose from exegetical reasoning linked to scribal awareness of allusions. I begin by exploring the various social and exegetical motivations that influenced scribes to alter the wording of their *Vorlagen*. I argue that many singular readings can be explained as efforts to explicate the text's deep structure, emphasizing instances where textual variation creates heightened affiliations with antecedent scriptural traditions ("external harmonization"). Next, I examine the wording of Rev 11:4 and 14:9 in A02. The textual evidence indicates that the scribe of A02 was aware of the lexical details of two distinct traditions (OG/LXX Exod 25–26 and 2 Chr 32:12) and that this copyist altered the wording of Revelation in a way that was indicated by the text's implied connection to these traditions. I conclude by offering some observations about the typology of singular readings and scribal awareness of the textual details of the breadth of the scriptural tradition, as well as some reflections on the lessons that New Testament textual critics can learn from the study of the Hebrew Bible in the late Second Temple period.

Textual scholars have long recognized that the wording of their manuscripts contain residues of scribal practices and attitudes. The popular caricature of the scribe as automaton, aiming only at the flawless reproduction of an antegraph, is wholly inappropriate in light of the textual evidence provided by the early Greek manuscript record of the New Testament. Evidence suggests that copyists were also, at times, careful readers who altered the wording of their *Vorlagen* to convey more explicitly a work's meaning (deep structure).[1] For these reasons, textual history functions as a medium for reception history, and actively so. Recently, scholarly interest in the reception of Revelation within its own textual history, focusing primarily on textual variation that appears to be theologically motivated, has intensified.[2] One emphasis of this trend is on the role of singular readings[3] in reception, primarily for their potential to illuminate the theological positions of scribes.[4] While

---

[1] See Barbara Aland, "Sind Schreiber früher neutestamentlicher Handschriften Interpreten des Textes?," in *Transmission and Reception: New Testament Text-Critical and Exegetical Studies*, ed. J. W. Childers and D. C. Parker, TS 4 (Piscataway, NJ: Gorgias, 2007), 114–22; Kim Haines-Eitzen, "The Social History of Early Christian Scribes," in *The Text of the New Testament in Contemporary Research: Essays on the Status Quaestionis*, ed. Bart D. Ehrman and Michael W. Holmes, 2nd ed., NTTSD 42 (Leiden: Brill, 2014), 479–95, esp. 489.

[2] The reasons for this interest are twofold: first, the *Editio Critica Maior* of Revelation is currently in production at the Institut für Septuaginta- und biblische Textforschung at the Kirchliche Hochschule in Wuppertal and, second, the peculiarities of Revelation's manuscript tradition in light of other New Testament works (see n. 7 below) make it an ideal test case for measuring scribal reception. See Juan Hernández Jr., *Scribal Habits and Theological Influences in the Apocalypse: The Singular Readings of Sinaiticus, Alexandrinus, and Ephraemi*, WUNT 2/218 (Tübingen: Mohr Siebeck, 2006); Michael Labahn, "Die Schriftrezeption in den großen Kodizes der Johannesoffenbarung," in *Die Johannesoffenbarung: Ihr Text und ihre Auslegung*, ed. Michael Labahn and Martin Karrer, ABIG 38 (Leipzig: Evangelische Verlagsanstalt, 2012), 99–130; Martin Karrer, "Der Text der Johannesoffenbarung—Varianten und Theologie," *Neot* 43 (2009): 373–98; Martin Karrer, Sigfried Kreuzer, and Marcus Sigismund, eds., *Von der Septuaginta zum Neuen Testament: Textgeschichtliche Erörterungen*, ANTF 43 (Berlin: de Gruyter, 2010), 317–423, http://dx.doi.org/10.1515/9783110240023.

[3] Singular readings in this study are variants that exist only in a single exemplar and have no versional support. They are usually (but not always) considered to be secondary to the initial text.

[4] See particularly Hernández, *Scribal Habits and Theological Influences*; and Karrer, "Der Text der Johannesoffenbarung," 373–98. Singular readings are valuable data since it is probable that they were the creation of the scribe. This perspective does not always reflect the complex reality of transmission, but singular readings are more likely to attest scribal agency than readings with greater attestation in the tradition. See E. C. Colwell, "Scribal Habits in Early Papyri: A Study in the Corruption of the Text," in *The Bible in Modern Scholarship: Papers Read at the 100th Meeting of the Society of Biblical Literature, December 28–30, 1964*, ed. J. Philip Hyatt (Nashville: Abingdon, 1965), 370–89, esp. 372; and Barbara Aland, "The Significance of the Chester Beatty Papyri in Early Church History," in *The Earliest Gospels: The Origins and Transmission of the Earliest Christian Gospels; The Contribution of the Chester Beatty Gospel Codex P45*, ed. Charles Horton, JSNTSup 258 (London: T&T Clark, 2003), 110–11. D. C. Parker cautions against attributing all textual change to scribal activity; one must also consider the function of New Testament texts in the earliest strata of Christianity ("Scribal Tendencies and the Mechanics of Book Production," in *Textual Variation: Theological and Social Tendencies? Papers from the Fifth Birmingham Colloquium on the Textual Criticism of the New Testament*, ed. H. A. G. Houghton and D. C. Parker, TS 3/6 [Piscataway, NJ: Gorgias, 2008], 173–84). I agree that the wording of scriptural texts was fluid in this period due in part to their role in the Christian community; nevertheless, scribes were ultimately responsible for the wording preserved on ancient physical *realia*.

singular readings provide useful data for multiple areas of exploration, an underdeveloped area of inquiry is the possibility that particular singular readings were influenced by external scriptural traditions (predominantly the OG/LXX) and/or the scribe's awareness of allusions to these traditions. If certain singular readings represent scribal awareness of the broader scriptural tradition, then the study of these readings, and of textual variation in the New Testament more generally, provides evidence for the reading practices of ancient tradents, a layer of evidence that speaks to the social realities of textual transmission and attitudes toward the scriptural text.[5] The aim of this article is to examine the possibilities and boundaries of the reception of the OG/LXX in the textual history of the New Testament by examining the text of the book of Revelation in Codex Alexandrinus (A02) as an example. I ask two questions: (1) Do selected singular readings in Apoc. A02 (of which there are eighty-four) suggest the scribe's awareness of antecedent scriptural traditions? (2) If so, how is this awareness manifested in the wording of the manuscript?[6]

I closely examine two singular readings in Apoc. A02 as test cases, emphasizing instances where textual alterations betray an awareness of references to the OG/LXX embedded within Revelation.[7] It is likely that the scribe was aware of the text

---

[5] The exegetical variation of scriptural wording is a well-attested phenomenon in the late Second Temple period (see David Andrew Teeter, *Scribal Laws: Exegetical Variation in the Textual Transmission of Biblical Law in the Late Second Temple Period*, FAT 92 [Tübingen: Mohr Siebeck, 2014]), especially in copies of works that are designed to facilitate understanding at the expense of exact reproduction of wording, but such variation became a more restricted phenomenon as the centuries progressed. The New Testament facilitates comprehension in more subtle ways, in copies that strive by and large for precise replication of wording. A focused study on the boundaries and hermeneutics of textual variation in the New Testament manuscript tradition is needed; the present article is a first step in this direction. On the text as an avenue to social realities, see Bart D. Ehrman, "The Text as Window: New Testament Manuscripts and the Social History of Early Christianity," in Ehrman and Holmes, *Text of the New Testament in Contemporary Research*, 479–95.

[6] For more on the diffusion of singular readings in A02, see Hernández, *Scribal Habits and Theological Influences*, 100 n. 14, 212–15. Additionally, the assumption that scribes are responsible for every reading is, as Ulrich Schmid has argued, faulty or at least difficult to determine ("Conceptualizing 'Scribal' Performances: Reader's Notes," in *The Textual History of the Greek New Testament: Changing Views in Contemporary Research*, ed. Klaus Wachtel and Michael W. Holmes, TCSt 8 [Atlanta: Society of Biblical Literature, 2011], 49–64). The readings explored in this discussion, however, are attributed to the scribe. The importance of this discussion is not attribution but the fact that these textual changes are the result of *someone's* cognitive processes.

[7] I selected A02 for this study because of its recognized quality in terms of the text of the Apocalypse, in light of the relatively few extant early manuscripts of the book of Revelation. See James R. Royse, *Scribal Habits in Early Greek New Testament Papyri*, NTTSD 36 (Leiden: Brill, 2008), 45–46. For a full accounting of the peculiarity and uniqueness of the Greek manuscript traditions of the book of Revelation, see J. Delobel, "Le texte de l'Apocalypse: Problèmes de méthode," in *L'Apocalypse johannique et l'apocalyptique dans le Nouveau Testament*, ed. J. Lambrecht, BETL 53 (Leuven: Leuven University Press, 1980), 151–56; J. K. Elliott, *New Testament Textual Criticism: The Application of Thoroughgoing Principles; Essays on Manuscripts and Textual Variation*, NovTSup 137 (Leiden: Brill, 2010), 145–55, http://dx.doi.org/10.1163/

of writings in the OG/LXX tradition, and it is surprising that external influences on textual variation have not yet been explored in greater detail—particularly since the Apocalypse is notoriously allusive.[8] The reuse of scriptural wording in Revelation suggests concrete relationships with antecedent texts, especially to scribes well versed in the wording of antecedent traditions.

The following examples provide numerous platforms for further discussion. First, this analysis identifies an underappreciated external pressure that shaped the textual history of the book of Revelation: allusion to scriptural traditions already embedded in the composition. Second, it provides information about the producer of Apoc. A02, elucidating the scribe's reading and transcribing practices. If we are able to better understand the scribe's performance (the mechanics and social settings of text production), we can more fully comprehend the textual anomalies present in the copy, which leads to a more comprehensive appreciation of the forces that created textual variation in Christian antiquity.[9]

I. A Typology of Singular Readings

Singular readings are not always the result of intentional cognitive processes; therefore, care must be taken to avoid the assumption of scribal intention where it

---

ej.9789004189522.i-664; H. C. Hoskier, *Concerning the Text of the Apocalypse: Collations of All Existing Available Greek Documents with the Standard Text of Stephen's Third Edition, together with the Testimony of Versions, Commentaries and Fathers; A Complete Conspectus of All Authorities*, 2 vols. (London: Quaritch, 1929); Josef Schmid, *Studien zur Geschichte des griechischen Apokalypse-Textes*, 2 vols. (Munich: Karl Zink, 1955–1956), vol. 2; D. C. Parker, *An Introduction to the New Testament Manuscripts and Their Texts* (Cambridge: Cambridge University Press, 2008), 227–45; Markus Lembke, "Beobachtungen zu den Handschriften der Apokalypse des Johannes," in Labahn and Karrer, *Die Johannesoffenbarung*, 19–69.

One hand was responsible for the production of the Apocalypse in A02. F. G. Kenyon argued that the scribe of this work only produced the Apocalypse and no other works present within A02 (*The Codex Alexandrinus [Royal MS. 1 D v–viii] in Reduced Photographic Facsimile: New Testament and Clementine Epistles* [London: Longmans, 1909], 10). Marcus Sigismund also finds that the paleography of Apoc. A02 is consistent ("Schreiber und Korrektoren in der Johannes-Apokalypse des Codex Alexandrinus," in Karrer, Kreuzer, and Sigismund, *Von der Septuaginta zum Neuen Testament*, 319–38). Although I examine only two examples closely here, there are numerous other examples of singular readings in A02 that were influenced by the Greek text of the Old Testament. For example, Delobel points to the influence of Jer 15:2 and 50:11 in Rev 13:10 ("Le texte de l'Apocalypse," 162–65).

[8] See Juan Hernández Jr., "Recensional Activity and the Transmission of the Septuagint in John's Apocalypse: Codex Sinaiticus and Other Witnesses," in Labahn and Karrer, *Die Johannesoffenbarung*, 83, who notes that "Christian scribes throughout this period [fifth century CE] would have been in a position to identify differences between extant copies of the LXX and the Apocalypse's allusions to it."

[9] See a similar sentiment in Elliott, *New Testament Textual Criticism*, 64.

does not exist. Five distinct but interrelated underlying motivations/mechanics give rise to particular presentations of singular readings.

First, singular readings may reflect the reading in the initial copy or *Urtext*.[10] In this case, the reading was corrupted at an early stage and subsequently transmitted, in one or multiple alternative forms, by the majority of the manuscript tradition. This option is a theoretical possibility, especially for the book of Revelation. The Apocalypse's minimal early attestation in the Greek tradition (in comparison to other New Testament works), as well as the other anomalous features of its transmission, heightens the possibility that a reading from an early witness may be "original."[11] For readings that are grammatically cohesive and logically coherent, this must remain at least initially an open possibility.

Many singular readings in Apoc. A02 are also transcription errors, or examples of variable orthographic practices or itacisms.[12] Vowel/diphthong replacement of one or two graphemes (e.g., Rev 2:6a, 7b; 4:6; 5:9; 7:1a; 8:1; 21:20a), consonantal replacement (12:11, 14:18, 22:8b), and omission of graphemes (3:4) occur in Apoc. A02 in modes commensurate with the transmission of other Greek literatures.[13] Also present are examples of morphological variation (2:14a, 15:6) or the confusion of graphically similar lexemes (2:14b, 6:8a, 8:5, 17:8) that result in nonsensical or incohesive texts.[14] These readings mostly represent *in scribendo* accidents in copying. Though they can illuminate particular transcription processes or linguistic conventions of a specific locale or time period, they provide little useful data pertinent to reception history or the perception of allusions to external traditions. If they are helpful for the question of reception at all, they may provide evidence for the ways that scribes interacted with the substance of their *Vorlage* in the process

---

[10] For a long period, singular readings were considered valuable only insofar as they might accurately reflect the "original" text. See perspectives on the singular readings in A02 in R. H. Charles, *A Critical and Exegetical Commentary on the Revelation of St. John*, 2 vols., ICC (Edinburgh: T&T Clark, 1920), 1:clxxi–clxxii; Delobel, "Le texte de l'Apocalypse," 161–66; Bernhard Weiss, *Die Johannes-Apokalypse: Textkritische Untersuchungen und Textherstellung*, TUGAL 7 (Leipzig: Hinrichs, 1891), 147–48. See also Dirk Jongkind, *Scribal Habits of Codex Sinaiticus*, TS 5 (Piscataway, NJ: Gorgias, 2007), 131–43. The most recent appraisal of singular readings in A02 and the *Urtext* is in Hernández, *Scribal Habits and Theological Influences*, 96–100, 124–25. He suggests that only three singular readings in this manuscript represent the *Urtext* (Rev 12:10 [κατηγωρ]; 13:10 [αποκτανθηναι]; 21:4 [απηλθαν]).

[11] The book of Revelation is preserved in only 307 manuscripts, according to Lembke ("Beobachtungen zu den Handschriften," 21), the vast majority of which derive from the Byzantine period.

[12] This is true for many singular readings in the early New Testament manuscripts more generally. See Peter M. Head, "The Habits of New Testament Copyists: Singular Readings in the Early Fragmentary Papyri of John," *Bib* 85 (2004): 399–408, esp. 407; Colwell, "Scribal Habits in Early Papyri," 374–77.

[13] See Hernández, *Scribal Habits and Theological Influences*, 103–4.

[14] See ibid., 105–6.

of copying, potentially illuminating the textual features that arrested the attention of copyists.

A singular reading may also reflect a desire to explicate the internal discourse of a work, a type of reading that provides evidence for reception.[15] A clear example of this type of explicative variation, although not properly a singular reading, occurs in Apoc. A02 4:3.[16] The vast majority of the manuscripts read "and a rainbow [ἶρις] around the throne," while the minority reading is "and priests [ΙΕΡΕΙC] around the throne."[17] The reading in A02 is clearly secondary, as it disrupts the syntax of the apodosis: the adjectival phrase ὅμοιος ὁράσει σμαραγδίνῳ ("like the appearance of emerald") supposes a singular antecedent.[18] There is no obvious external tradition that influenced the wording of this locution. The change was made based on internal concerns; in this case, the ubiquitous cultic imagery associated with the depiction of the heavenly court in Rev 4–5. It is logical to identify the twenty-four elders as heavenly priests who minister before God, since both are located "around the throne" (κυκλόθεν τοῦ θρόνου) in successive verses (4:3–4). Furthermore, ἶρις occurs elsewhere in the New Testament only in Rev 10:1, and only once in the OG/LXX tradition (Exod 30:24).[19] Its rarity and semantic opacity, perhaps, made it a target for revision to a contextually logical and graphically similar alternative. The effect of this subtle alteration is that the cultic dimensions of the heavenly court are now more pronounced, complete with a heavenly priesthood.[20] Readings that explicate the internal coherence of a word or locution tend, especially at the lexical level, to heighten an already present profile of images attached to a given passage. These singular readings may also create a greater level of grammatical cohesion. In this example, cohesion is sacrificed for the sake of coherence, but this dialectic varies in this type of reading.[21]

An additional category of singular readings includes those that are assimilated to social compunctions or theological attitudes operative at the time of transcription. Hernández suggests that certain singular readings in Apoc. A02 emphasize,

---

[15] E.g., Rev 1:10a, 2:7a, 6:1, 14:1 in A02. This is often called "harmonization to the immediate context." See Peter M. Head, "Observations on Early Papyri of the Synoptic Gospels, especially on Scribal Habits," *Bib* 71 (1990): 240–47; Colwell, "Scribal Habits in Early Papyri," 377–78.

[16] See also ℵ 2329 and the numerous itacistic readings noted by Hoskier, *Concerning the Text*, 2:122–23.

[17] The reading in ℵ was later corrected to "rainbows" (ΙΡΕΙC).

[18] So Karrer, "Der Text der Johannesoffenbarung," 384–86.

[19] ℵ reads θριξ in Rev 10:1, a singular reading. ἶρις in the context of Exod 30:24 refers to botanicals. See LSJ, s.v. ἶρις; and John William Wevers, *Notes on the Greek Text of Exodus*, SCS 30 (Atlanta: Scholars Press, 1990), 499.

[20] Karrer, "Der Text der Johannesoffenbarung," 388.

[21] See, for example, the small-scale addition of material in Apoc. A02 6:6 and 9:11 that creates greater grammatical cohesion. In 9:11, the addition of τὸν ἄρχοντα creates both a heightened level of coherence *and* cohesion. In addition, in Apoc. A02 1:1 and 21:20b, the case of nouns is altered to create greater grammatical cohesion.

albeit subtly, christological aspects of the composition.[22] These alterations are not the result of textual harmonization but reflect the ideological attitude or milieu of the text producer.[23]

Finally, singular readings can reflect the result of scribal awareness of *external* scriptural traditions.[24] This type of reading is the result of a conscious mechanic that draws the text into closer alliance with specific source traditions, based on the scribe's perceived boundaries of the scriptural tradition and knowledge of its wording. These readings differ from internal harmonization in that correlation to external traditions occasionally results in readings that are "nonsense in context" or awkward turns of phrase that may confuse internal discourse, though they often retain a high level of grammatical cohesion. In these cases deference is given to external traditions, sometimes over and above internal coherence and/or cohesion, based on perceived overlap (of either wording or content) between a source tradition and a locution in Revelation. While both internal and external influences can result in singular readings (identical operations), the underlying motivations behind these changes fundamentally differ. This creates a typology of singular readings.[25]

A Typology of Singular Readings	
Type 1	A reading present in the "initial text" that is now transmitted in a single manuscript.
Type 2	A reading that results from a number of different transcription errors or diachronic spelling conventions, often yielding a nonsense readings.
Type 3	Conscious changes to wording that create greater grammatical cohesion and/or discourse coherence based on *internal* criteria, often smoothing rutted texture.
Type 4	Conscious changes to wording based on external social, doctrinal, or theological norms.
Type 5	Conscious changes to wording influenced by external scriptural traditions or the awareness of allusions embedded in the work being transcribed.

---

[22] E.g., A02 1:17; 2:8, 22. See Hernández, *Scribal Habits and Theological Influences*, 126–31.

[23] See the classic work of Bart D. Ehrman, *The Orthodox Corruption of Scripture: The Effect of Early Christian Controversies on the Text of the New Testament* (Oxford: Oxford University Press, 1993), who interacts with Revelation only in a cursory manner.

[24] This phenomenon is prevalent in the Gospels. The wording of Synoptic parallels is often "harmonized to remote parallels." See Head, "Observations on Early Papyri," 246; Colwell, "Scribal Habits in Early Papyri," 377; Elliott, *New Testament Textual Criticism*, 53–64, esp. 54.

[25] Tommy Wasserman also presents a typology of singular readings, focusing on different forms of theological clarification ("Theological Creativity and Scribal Solutions in Jude," in Houghton and Parker, *Textual Variation*, 75–83).

These types of readings reflect, on the one hand, text historical or transcriptional accidents (types 1–2), and, on the other, varying forms of explication or clarification (types 3–5). The final three categories in this typology reveal exegetical or interpretive processes that give rise to textual change, shedding light on the reception of the work by scribal tradents. The remainder of the article focuses on type 5 readings in A02.

II. Scribal Awareness of Embedded Scriptural References

A scribe's awareness of references to Scripture embedded in New Testament works is determined by a number of features.[26] Physical characteristics of manuscripts and paratextual features—indentation, the use of diplés (marginal dots) and other marginalia, paragraph division, and so on—can denote sensitivity to external traditions.[27] These physical and paratextual markers are nonexistent in the test cases examined below (Apoc. A02 11:4 and 14:9), but they remain an important aspect of textual transmission since most facilitating features of the New Testament manuscript tradition take the form of paratexts (e.g., explicit commentary traditions or glosses).[28] In addition to physical characteristics, unique textual readings aid in measuring scribal awareness of an OG/LXX work.[29] The presence of a lexeme located in only a single manuscript that alters the traditional reading(s) toward the wording of a particular OG/LXX tradition suggests that the scribe identified an

---

[26] See Ronald Henry van der Bergh, "The Textual Tradition of Explicit Quotations in Codex Bezae Cantabrigiensis of the Acts of the Apostles" (PhD. diss., University of Pretoria, 2013), 3–5.

[27] On the use of diplés specifically, see Ulrich Schmid, "Die Diplé: Einführung," in Karrer, Kreuzer, and Sigismund, *Von der Septuaginta zum Neuen Testament*, 77–81. See also Johannes de Vries and Martin Karrer, "Early Christian Quotations and the Textual History of the Septuagint: A Summary of the Wuppertal Research Project and Introduction to the Volume," in *Textual History and the Reception of Scripture in Early Christianity / Textgeschichte und Schriftrezeption im frühen Christentum*, ed. Johannes de Vries and Martin Karrer, SCS 60 (Atlanta: Society of Biblical Literature, 2013), 9; and, in the same volume, Alexander Stokowski, "Diplé-Auszeichnung im Codex Vaticanus Graecus 1209 (B): Liste nebst einigen Beobachtungen," 93–113.

[28] Marcus Sigismund confirms that there are no diplés in the Apocalypse of A02 ("Formen und Verwendung der Diplé im Codex Alexandrinus," in Karrer, Kreuzer, and Sigismund, *Von der Septuaginta zum Neuen Testament*, 132). The Greek tradition of Revelation from the sixth century onward is dominated by multiple commentary traditions, especially the commentary associated with Andrew of Caesarea. See Eugenia Scarvelis Constantinou, *Guiding to a Blessed End: Andrew of Caesarea and His Apocalypse Commentary in the Ancient Church* (Washington, DC: Catholic University of America Press, 2013).

[29] Van der Bergh, commenting on the text of Acts in Codex Bezae, notes that "OT awareness can also be shown by a variant reading peculiar to a NT manuscript or group of manuscripts" ("Textual Tradition of Explicit Quotations," 3).

embedded reference to traditional material. It is this lexical criterion that anchors the following investigation.

Revelation 11:4

The first example of a singular reading that is influenced by scribal awareness of the wording of an external text is preserved in Apoc. A02 11:4.

NA[28] οὗτοί εἰσιν αἱ δύο <u>ἐλαῖαι</u> καὶ αἱ δύο λυχνίαι αἱ ἐνώπιον τοῦ[30] κυρίου τῆς γῆς ἑστῶτες

These are the two <u>olive trees</u> and the two lampstands which are standing before the Lord of the earth.

A02[31] ΟΥΤΟΙ ΕΙCΙΝ ΑΙ ΔΥΟ <u>ΑΥΛΑΙΑΙ</u> ΚΑΙ ΑΙ ΔΥΟ ΛΥΧΝΙΑΙ ΑΙ ΕΝΩΠΙΟ͞ Κ͞Υ ΤΗC ΓΗC ΕCΤѠΤΕC

These are the two <u>curtains</u> and the two lampstands which are standing before Kyrios of the earth.

This lexical substitution of ΑΥΛΑΙΑΙ for ἐλαῖαι in Apoc. A02 is exceptional; and, as Hernández notes, "it is difficult to discern what could have prompted the change."[32] The word αὐλαία is not present in the lexical stock of the New Testament, and within the OG/LXX tradition this lexeme functions as a *terminus technicus*, referring almost exclusively to the curtains of the wilderness tabernacle (see Exod 25–26; 37).[33]

Furthermore, Rev 11:4 preserves a clear scriptural reference to Zech 4:14.[34] The verbal connection to this text is obscured by the lexical choice of the singular reading in A02. While this veiling of Zechariah material may suggest that the scribe did not perceive this allusion, it is equally probable that the scribe wished to weight

---

[30] This article is not witnessed in A02 046 1006 1841.

[31] Column 1 leaf 131b lines 29–31.

[32] Hernández, *Scribal Habits and Theological Influences*, 119 n. 110.

[33] The word occurs twenty times in the OG/LXX (Exod 26:2–6; 37:1 [36:8], 2 [36:9], 10 [38:12], 13 [38:15], 14 [38:16]; 40:19). It also occurs in OG Isa 54:2 in a text that recalls tabernacle language embedded in Exod 26; 37. Judith 14:14 employs this lexeme to describe the entrance of the tent of Holofernes following his beheading. The only instance in which the text preserved in Exodus of A02 differs from OG Exodus in reference to the lexeme αυλαια occurs in Exod 37:14 where A02 (and 707 118 537 121) reads πυλαι(αι) for αυλαιαι. See John William Wevers, *Text History of the Greek Exodus*, AAWG 192 (Göttingen: Vandenhoeck & Ruprecht, 1992), 93–103. The term retained its technical character in other Jewish and early Christian Greek literature. See, e.g., Philo, *Mos.* 2.85.1; 2.86.2; Justin, *Dial.* 13.8.5; Eusebius, *Dem. Ev.* 3.2.73.5; Cyril of Alexandria, *Commentarius in xii Propheta Minores* 2.304, among others.

[34] See Garrick V. Allen, "Textual Pluriformity and Allusion in the Book of Revelation: The Text of Zechariah 4 in the Apocalypse," *ZNW* 106 (2015): 136–45, http://dx.doi.org/10.1515/znw-2015-0008.

this locution with the import of an *additional* antecedent tradition: Exod 25–26. The cultic imagery of Zech 4 (gold lampstands, lamps, thrones, bowls, oil) corresponds closely to language in the tabernacle construction narrative, and the reading in A02 preserves connections to both of these related traditions.³⁵ There is a distinct and traceable traditional line from Exodus to Zechariah to Rev 11:4, of which the scribe demonstrates some awareness.³⁶

Nonetheless, in light of the use of αὐλαία as a technical term to refer to a component of the wilderness tabernacle, the identification of the two witnesses as "curtains" is peculiar. Martin Karrer has observed that this singular reading weights the pericope with another example of cultic imagery, but it is not clear how this alteration contributes any literary, cohesive, or ideological value to the narrative of Rev 11.³⁷

Type of Singular Reading

Where in the typology does this singular reading belong? The graphic and morphological similarities of these words (ἐλαῖαι and ΑΥΛΑΙΑΙ) might suggest that the reading is the result of graphic/aural confusion—that is, a transcriptional mistake (type 2). This type of interchange is not uncommon. Nonetheless, it is difficult to envision a scenario in which ΑΥ could have been confused with *epsilon* in the scribe's *Vorlage* based on graphic similarity. Phonological similarity might

---

³⁵ Others have noted that the language of Rev 11:1–5 relates both to Zechariah and to Exodus. See Ferrell Jenkins, *The Old Testament in the Book of Revelation* (Grand Rapids: Baker, 1972), 80–83; G. K. Beale, *The Book of Revelation: A Commentary on the Greek Text*, NIGTC (Grand Rapids: Eerdmans, 1999), 576; Jan Dochhorn, "Beliar als Endtyrann in der Ascensio Isaiae," in *Die Johannesapokalypse: Kontexte – Konzepte – Rezeption*, ed. Jörg Frey, James A. Kelhoffer, and Franz Tóth, WUNT 287 (Tübingen: Mohr Siebeck, 2012), 308; James C. VanderKam, *From Revelation to Canon: Studies in the Hebrew Bible and Second Temple Literature*, JSJSup 62 (Leiden: Brill, 2000), 168–70, 173–76.

³⁶ The scribe's forging of connections between like traditions is an ancient mechanic, which finds evocative parallels in legal exegesis in numerous documents from the Second Temple period. See Teeter, *Scribal Laws*, 175–204. For example, 11QT XLVIII, 7–11 integrates material from Lev 19:28 within a locution from Deut 14:1–2 based on their lexical and thematic overlap (see Moshe J. Bernstein and Shlomo A. Koyfman, "The Interpretation of Biblical Law in the Dead Sea Scrolls: Forms and Methods," in *Biblical Interpretation at Qumran*, ed. Matthias Henze, SDSSRL [Grand Rapids: Eerdmans, 2005], 67–68). The acceptable level of textual alteration is greater in the Temple Scroll and other similar documents, and its presentation much more overt, but the underlying motivation and mechanic is identical to the singular reading in Apoc. A02 11:4: like texts, sharing lexical and thematic features, are combined to form new, multilayered reservoirs of tradition.

³⁷ Karrer, "Der Text der Johannesoffenbarung," 383. See also the emphasis on liturgical language in the Apocalypse as a whole in Gottfried Schimanowski, *Die himmlische Liturgie in der Apokalypse des Johannes: Die frühjüdischen Traditionen in Offenbarung 4–5 unter Einschluß der Hekhalotliteratur*, WUNT 2/154 (Tübingen: Mohr Siebeck, 2002).

account for this reading, but there are no examples (as far as I have been able to ascertain) of αυ | ε confusion in A02.[38] The graphic and aural similarity of these words does not firmly establish this example as a scribal mistake. It is equally probable that the scribe consciously altered this word, replacing it with a word that retained morphosyntactic congruity, as well as graphic and phonological similarity with the lexeme found in his or her *Vorlage*.[39]

Such a procedure stands within the bounds of contemporary scribal behavior, and the restricted nature of transcription means that exegetical alterations usually retain some level of semblance to their *Vorlage*. Examples of explications of opaque narratives, linguistic difficulties, and ideological problems through intentional, yet subtle, textual adjustment are ubiquitous in Jewish and Christian antiquity.[40] It is therefore possible that readings that retain some literal characteristics vis-à-vis the reading in the rest of the manuscript tradition are the conscious creations of transcribers.

An alternative explanation beyond scribal error exists in a solution toward which I have already gestured: the scribe altered this lexeme to draw it into closer lexical alliance with the tabernacle construction narrated in Exod 25:30–26:6 OG.[41] If evidence exists that the alteration was designed to create further lexical parallels between Rev 11 and an external tradition, then the burden of proof falls to one who

---

[38] B. Harris Cowper notes multiple vowel and diphthong substitutions in A02, but no example of αυ | ε confusion (*Codex Alexandrinus: Hē Kainē Diathēkē; Novum Testamentum Graece* [London: Williams & Norgate, 1860], x–xi). Likewise, B. F. Westcott and F. J. A. Hort proffer no evidence of αυ | ε confusion (see "Notes on Orthography," in *The New Testament in the Original Greek* [London: Macmillan, 1885], 512–15). Natalio Fernández Marcos notes that, in the OG/LXX manuscript tradition, scribal mistakes arise from phonological similarities between letters, especially ρ | λ; φ | β; φ | θ; χ | γ (*The Septuagint in Context: Introduction to the Greek Version of the Bible*, trans. Wilfred G. E. Watson [Atlanta: Society of Biblical Literature, 2000], 199). Bruce M. Metzger and James R. Royse note confusion between αι | ε and other similar vowel sounds (ω | ο; ου | υ; etc.), but do not catalog any examples of αυ | ε confusion (see Metzger, *The Text of the New Testament: Its Transmission, Corruption, and Restoration*, 3rd ed. [Oxford: Oxford University Press, 1992], 190–92; and Royse, "Scribal Tendencies in the Text of the New Testament," in Ehrman and Holmes, *Text of the New Testament in Contemporary Research*, 462). Additionally, Royse notes υ | η confusion but, again, not αυ | ε confusion (*Scribal Habits in Early Greek*, 83).

[39] It is possible that a female scribe produced A02, a possibility supported by a tradition that ascribes its copying to a Thecla. I retain the masculine pronoun for the scribe throughout only for the sake of convenience, making no judgment as to this person's gender. See Kim Haines-Eitzen, *Guardians of Letters: Literacy, Power and the Transmitters of Early Christian Literature* (Oxford: Oxford University Press, 2000), 41–52, esp. 50–52.

[40] See, e.g., Emanuel Tov, *The Text-Critical Use of the Septuagint in Biblical Research*, 2nd rev. ed., JBS 8 (Jerusalem: Simor, 1997), 100–103; Alexander Samely, *Rabbinic Interpretation of Scripture in the Mishnah* (Oxford: Oxford University Press, 2002), 406; Royse, *Scribal Habits in Early Greek*, 537–42.

[41] The versification system used in this discussion follows John William Wevers, *Exodus*, Septuaginta 2.1 (Göttingen: Vandenhoeck & Ruprecht, 1991).

would argue that this singular reading is a transcriptional slip. Let us now explore this possibility in detail by examining the Greek text of Exod 25:30–26:6.

The book of Revelation as a whole reuses much of the technical language from the tabernacle construction accounts in Exodus across the entirety of the composition.

Lexical Overlap		
Lexeme	Exod 25:31–26:5, 37:1–6	Book of Revelation
λυχνία	25:30–35	1:12–13, 20; 2:1, 5; 11:4
χρυσίον (καθαροῦ*)	25:30,* 35,* 37,* 38*; 37:4,[42] 6	3:18; 17:4; 18:16; 21:8,* 21*
καλαμίσκος/κάλαμος	25:30–35[43]	11:1; 21:15–16
ἐκπορεύομαι	25:31, 32	1:16; 4:5; 9:17, 18; 11:5; 16:14; 19:15; 22:1
σκηνήν	26:1, 6, 7, 9, 12–15, 17, 18, 22, 23, 26, 27, 30, 35, 36; 37:1, 5	13:6; 15:1; 21:3
αὐλαία	26:1–6; 37:1, 2, 10, 13, 14	11:4
ὑάκινθος	26:4, 14	21:20 (9:17)[44]
πορφύρα	26:1, 31; 37:3	18:12
κόκκινος	26:1, 31, 36; 37:3, 23	17:3, 4; 18:12, 16
πῆχυς	25:9, 16, 22; 26:2, 8; 37:2, 10	21:17
μῆκος	25:9, 22; 26:2, 8, 13; 37:2, 16	21:16
μέτρον (μετρέω)	26:2, 8	21:15, 17 (11:1, 2)[45]
βύσσος/βύσσινος	26:1, 31, 36; 37:3, 7, 16, 21	18:12, 16; 19:8, 14[46]
στῦλος	26:15–37 (25x); 37:4, 6, 8, 10, 12, 13, 15, 17	3:12; 10:1
κεφαλίς/κεφαλή	26:24, 32, 37 37:4, 6	1:14; 4:4; 9:7, 17, 19; 10:1; 12:1, 3; 13:1, 3; 14:14; 17:3, 7, 9; 18:19; 19:12
θυσιαστήριον	20–40[47]	6:9; 8:3, 5; 9:13; 11:1; 14:18; 16:7
αὐλή	27:9, 12, 13, 16–19; 37:7, 13–16[48]	11:2

[42] χρυσίον is omitted in A02 in this verse.

[43] καλαμίσκος occurs elsewhere in the entirety of the OG/LXX tradition only in Exod 38:14–15. This lexeme is used only in the context of the branches of this lampstand. See Wevers, *Notes on the Greek Text*, 405–7.

[44] Revelation 9:17 contains ὑακίνθινος. These cognate words occur in the New Testament only in these two locutions in Revelation.

[45] See the verbal form μετρέω in Rev 21:15–17 as well.

[46] The lexeme βύσσινος is unique to the book of Revelation in the New Testament.

[47] This lexeme does not occur in Exod 25–26 or 37 but is ubiquitous elsewhere in Exod 20–40, occurring fifty-four times.

[48] This lexeme does not occur in Exod 25:30–26:5, 37:1–6, but is attested in other locations cataloged in the chart, as well as in Exod 38:19–21; 29:9, 20; 40:6, 33.

This recurrent employment of identical lexemes served as the platform from which the scribe identified language in certain textual segments of the Apocalypse with the tabernacle construction instructions in OG Exodus.[49] For a scribal expert with an intimate knowledge of scriptural traditions, the lexical relationship between these antecedent texts and segments of Revelation (namely, 11:1–5, 19:1–14, 21:12–22:1) was not difficult to identify.

With Rev 11:1–6 in closer focus, numerous lexemes that recur in Exod 20–40 (esp. 25–27) are present:

Lexical Overlap		
Lexeme	Exod 25:31–26:5, 37:1–6	Revelation 11
λυχνία	25:30–35	11:4
καλαμίσκος/κάλαμος	25:30–35	11:1
ἐκπορεύομαι	25:31, 32	11:5
αὐλαία	26:1–6; 37:1, 2, 10, 13, 14	11:4
μέτρον (μετρέω)	26:2, 8	(11:1, 2)
θυσιαστήριον	20–40	11:1
αὐλή	27:9, 12, 13, 16–19; 37:7, 13–16	11:2

More specifically still, the tradition underlying the description of the two witnesses in A02 (Rev 11:4) as "the two curtains [αὐλαίαι] and the two lampstands [λυχνίαι]" can be traced to OG Exod 25:30–26:5, where these terms occur in clusters elsewhere unparalleled in the Jewish Greek scriptural tradition. The juxtaposition of these terms is unique to OG Exod 25:30–26:5 and Rev 11:4. Forms of λυχνία occur nine times in OG Exod 25:30–38, a segment that immediately precedes Exod 26:1–6, where αὐλαία occurs eleven times.[50] This parallels the description of the two witnesses in Rev 11:4 as "two curtains [αὐλαίαι] and the two lampstands [λυχνίαι]."

The status of αὐλαία as a technical term and its overwhelming occurrence in Exod 26 suggest that the scribe altered the wording of Rev 11:4 to connect the identification of the two witnesses to the tabernacle account. The absence of αὐλαία in the New Testament and its rarity in OG/LXX suggest that its occurrence in A02 is not a phonological mistake. This textual alteration heightens the lexical consistency between Exod 25–26 and Rev 11:4, and clarifies the traditional material that

---

[49] The presence of a cluster of similar lexemes represents one of a number of textual features that activate intertextual awareness. The presence of "allusive keywords" (so Aaron Koller, *Esther in Ancient Jewish Thought* [Cambridge: Cambridge University Press, 2014], e.g., 174) or a quantity of shared words often signaled interpretive engagement in ancient Jewish and Christian literature. A similar criterion based on Richard Hays's work on allusion in Paul ("volume") has been plied recently in so-called Old Testament in the New Testament studies to identify the presence of allusions and echoes (see Hays, *Echoes of Scripture in the Letters of Paul* [New Haven: Yale University Press, 1993], 30).

[50] αὐλαία also occurs three times in Exod 37:1–2 but forms of λυχνία are not present.

the scribe identified as underlying Rev 11:4. The resultant singular reading is the residual evidence of the scribe's attentiveness to and knowledge of external scriptural traditions activated in the process of copying. The act of transcription was not passive but was undertaken in connection with the scribe's past scriptural engagements.[51] This change, which may have been premeditated (i.e., planned before transcription), was created based on the scribe's knowledge of the scriptural tradition, learned in part through past experience of copying. The lexical clusters within Revelation that correspond to Exod 25–26 OG factored into this example of lexical substitution.

This singular reading was a shrewd procedure that allowed the scribe to remain faithful to his *Vorlage* in terms of syntax and phonology, while simultaneously altering the lexical value of his *Vorlage* to cause Rev 11:4 to cohere more closely with a perceived allusion. The scribe intuited an allusion and altered the wording of Revelation to conform to this intuition, perhaps creating an allusion where one did not clearly exist.[52] This alteration, based in part upon the scribe's awareness of Exod 25–26, is, to borrow a phrase from Karel van der Toorn, a vigorous "display of scribal dexterity."[53]

Revelation 14:9

An additional example of a reading that was created due to the awareness of external scriptural traditions is found in Apoc. A02 14:9.

NA[28] 14:9 Καὶ ἄλλος ἄγγελος τρίτος ἠκολούθησεν αὐτοῖς λέγων ἐν φωνῇ μεγάλῃ· εἴ τις προσκυνεῖ τὸ <u>θηρίον</u> καὶ τὴν εἰκόνα αὐτοῦ καὶ λαμβάνει χάραγμα ἐπὶ τοῦ μετώπου αὐτοῦ ἢ ἐπὶ τὴν χεῖρα αὐτοῦ

And another angel, a third, followed them saying in a loud voice: "if anyone worships the <u>beast</u> and his image and receives a stamp on his forehead or his hand ..."

A02 14:9 [ΚΑΙ Α]ΛΛΟC ΑΓΓΕΛΟC ΤΡΙΤΟC ΗΚΟΛΟΥΘΗ[CΕ]Ν ΑΥΤΩ ΛΕΓΩΝ ΕΝ ΦΩΝΗ ΜΕΓΑΛΗ [ΕΙ] ΤΙC ΠΡΟCΚΥΝΕΙ ΤΟ <u>ΘΥCΙΑCΤΗΡΙΟΝ</u> [Κ]ΑΙ ΤΗΝ ΕΙΚΟΝΑ ΑΥΤΟΥ ΚΑΙ ΛΑΜΒΑΝΕΙ [Χ]ΑΡΑΓΜΑ ΕΠΙ ΤΟΥ ΜΕΤΩΠΟΥ ΑΥΤΟΥ Η ΕΠΙ [Τ]ΗΝ ΧΕΙΡΑ ΑΥΤΟΥ

---

[51] See Klaus Junack, "Abschreibpraktiken und Schreibergewohnheiten in ihrer Auswirkung auf die Textüberlieferung," in *New Testament Textual Criticism: Its Significance for Exegesis; Essays in Honour of Bruce M. Metzger*, ed. Eldon Jay Epp and Gordon D. Fee (Oxford: Clarendon, 1981), 277–95.

[52] See also Karrer, "Der Text der Johannesoffenbarung," 388, who argues that this reading must be considered when constructing the main text of the *Editio Critica Maior* of Revelation based on transcriptional probability, even though singular readings are usually considered to be secondary intrusions into the tradition.

[53] Karel van der Toorn, *Scribal Culture and the Making of the Hebrew Bible* (Cambridge: Harvard University Press, 2007), 40.

And another angel, a third, followed him saying in a loud voice: "if anyone worships the <u>altar</u> and its image and receives a stamp on his forehead or on his hand …"

Numerous explanations for this singular reading have been proffered. David Aune argues that the scribe understood θηρίον as an abbreviation of θυσιαστήριον,[54] but there are no examples of this abbreviation in the manuscript evidence.[55] Hernández categorizes this reading as an insignificant singular that is "nonsense in context"— in its immediate literary context this reading complicates the sense of the locution and is not explicable on internal grounds.[56] These observations do not, however, necessarily make this reading insignificant.

Again, like the previous example, the reading is graphically and phonologically similar (ΘΗΡΙΟΝ | ΘΥϹΙΑϹΤΗΡΙΟΝ) to the reading preserved in the rest of the manuscript tradition, and it is difficult to deduce a procedure by which the scribe altered this reading based on internal evidence. This reading becomes more difficult to explain when the preeminence of the lexeme θηρίον in the texts immediately preceding and following Rev 14:9 is noted.[57] Attributing this reading to a transcriptional error is an unlikely answer, since the alteration remains grammatically cohesive and there are no clear local textual features that would trigger this expansion. The lexical substitution does not seem to reflect care for the internal discourse of the pericope.

I suggest that a yet unexplored solution may lie in an external textual harmonization to 2 Chr 32:12 OG.

2 Chr 32:12[58] οὐχ οὗτός ἐστιν Εζεκιας, ὃς περιεῖλεν τὰ <u>θυσιαστήρια</u> αὐτοῦ καὶ τὰ ὑψηλὰ αὐτοῦ καὶ εἶπεν τῷ Ιουδα καὶ τοῖς κατοικοῦσιν Ιερουσαλημ λέγων Κατέναντι τοῦ <u>θυσιαστηρίου</u> τούτου <u>προσκυνήσετε</u> καὶ ἐπ' αὐτῷ θυμιάσετε

Is this not Hezekiah who took away his altars and his high places and he said to Judah and to those dwelling in Jerusalem saying: "<u>worship before this altar</u> and on it make an incense offering."

Like the previous example, 2 Chr 32 OG evidences significant lexical overlap with the book of Revelation.

---

[54] David Aune, *Revelation 6–16*, WBC 52b (Nashville: Nelson, 1998), 787.

[55] Hernández, *Scribal Habits and Theological Influences*, 106 n. 45.

[56] Ibid., 105–6. Weiss suggests that this reading is a "reine Schreibfehler" (*Die Johannes-Apokalypse*, 60).

[57] See 11:7; 13:1–4, 11, 12, 14, 15, 17, 18; 14:11; 15:2; 16:2, 10, 13; 17:3, 7, 8, 11–13, 16, 17; 19:19, 20; 20:4, 10.

[58] The Greek text of 2 Chronicles is taken from Alan England Brooke, Norman McLean, and H. St. John Thackeray, *The Old Testament in Greek according to the Text of Codex Vaticanus*, 3 vols. in 9 (Cambridge: Cambridge University Press, 1932), vol. 2.3. I have changed the text in this edition where A02 is in disagreement with B, most notably the inclusion of οὐχ.

Lexical Overlap		
Lexemes	2 Chronicles	Revelation
πολεμέω	32:2	2:16, 12:7, 13:4, 17:14, 19:11
πρεσβύτερος	32:3, 31	4:4; 10; 5:5, 6, 8, 11, 14; 7:11, 13; 11:16; 14:3; 19:4
ὕδωρ + πηγή	32:3, 4	7:17, 8:10, 14:7, 16:4, 21:6
ἔξω(θεν) τῆς πόλεως	32:3	14:20
ποταμός	32:4	8:10; 9:14; 12:15, 16; 16:4, 12; 22:1, 2
ὕδωρ + πολύς	32:4	1:15, 14:2, 17:1, 19:6
τεῖχος	32:5, 18	21:12, 14, 15, 17–19
Ἰερουσαλήμ	32:2, 9, 10, 12, 18, 19, 33	8:12; 21:2, 10
θυσιαστήριον	32:12	6:9, 8:3, 14:9 (A02)
Κατοικέω	32:12	2:13; 3:10; 6:10; 8:13; 11:10; 13:8, 12, 14; 17:2, 8
Προσκυνέω	32:12	3:9; 4:10; 5:14; 7:11; 9:20; 11:1, 16; 13:4, 8, 12, 15; 14:7, 9, 11; 15:4; 16:2; 19:4; 10, 20; 20:4; 22:8, 9
θυμιάω/θυμίαμα	32:12	5:8; 8:3, 4; 18:13
σῖτος	32:28	6:6, 18:13
οἶνος	32:28	6:6; 14:8, 10; 16:19; 17:2; 18:3, 13; 19:15
Βαβυλών	32:31	14:8; 16:19; 17:5; 18:2, 10, 21

The lexical overlap specifically between 2 Chr 32 and Rev 14 is also impressive.

Lexical Overlap		
Lexemes	2 Chronicles	Revelation 14
πρεσβύτερος	32:3, 31	14:3
ὕδωρ + πηγή	32:3, 4	14:7
ἔξω(θεν) τῆς πόλεως	32:3	14:20
ὕδωρ + πολύς	32:4	14:2
θυσιαστήριον	32:12	14:9 (A02)
προσκυνέω	32:12	14:7, 9, 11
οἶνος	32:28	14:8
Βαβυλών	32:31	14:8

More important still, in 2 Chr 32:12, the translator of OG Chronicles twice placed forms of the lexeme θυσιαστήριον in the mouth of Sennacherib: once as part of a prepositional phrase serving as the indirect object of the imperative προσκυνήσετε ("worship"). A similar, although inexact, collocation of verb and object occurs in Apoc. A02 14:9: ΠΡΟCΚΥΝΕΙ ΤΟ ΘΥCΙΑCΤΗΡΙΟΝ ("worship the altar"). In the remainder of the OG/LXX tradition outside of 2 Chr 32:12 προσκυνέω and θυσιαστήριον do not occur in such close proximity; the clause in 2 Chr 32:12 is unique in this regard. Again, the exclusive occurrence of these words in a clause and the larger lexical points of connection between 2 Chr 32 and Rev 14 suggest that the scribe altered Rev 14:9 to correspond more closely to 2 Chr 32:12 and its surrounding co-texts. The scribe substituted the lexeme attested in all other copies for one that was graphically and phonologically similar, yet retained a different semantic sense.

This alteration creates greater linguistic correspondence between 2 Chr 32 and Rev 14, a move that alerts text users to the antecedent material. The singular reading is the residual evidence of the scribe's perception of a relationship between the Sennacherib story of 2 Chr 32 and the narrative of Rev 14, clarifying his perception of an allusion in Rev 14:9.

This singular reading highlights an analogy between Sennacherib in 2 Chr 32 and the beasts described in Rev 13–14. Beyond lexical overlap, these accounts share numerous plot features:

Plot Alignment	
2 Chronicles	Revelation
Sennacherib attacks Judah (32:1)	Beast makes war with God's people (13:7)
Hezekiah's assertion of military dominance (32:7)	Appearance of the Lamb's army (14:1–5)
Appeal to God for protection (32:8)	Call for endurance and worship (14:7; 12)
Blaspheming of God by Assyrians (31:9–19)	Beast blasphemes God (13:5–6)
Angelic deliverance of Jerusalem; judgment of the Assyrians (32:20–23)	Angelic judgment scene (14:14–20); beasts judged (19:20)

Although the plot elements do not align chronologically within both narratives, the presence of these features suggests a connection. This correlation of elements is similar to typological elements identified by Michael Fishbane in the Hebrew Bible, particularly "typologies of a historical nature," in which historical events function as prototypes for present or future events.[59] It seems that the scribe read

---

[59] Michael Fishbane, *Biblical Interpretation in Ancient Israel* (Oxford: Oxford University Press, 1985), 358–68. The solidification of this typology by lexical change in this example draws an interesting parallel between scribal habits in early Christian manuscripts and interpretive elements native to the Hebrew Bible and Second Temple Jewish literature.

Revelation with a similar interpretive mind-set, which strengthens the typological relationship between 2 Chr 32 and Rev 13–14 based on already extant lexical overlap/borrowing and parallel plot features in order to provide another point of contact between narratives. In each account, the enemies are menacing and powerful, yet victory is assured through faithfulness to God. The accounts ultimately conclude with the defeat of these frightening foes by divine judgment. For a reader of Revelation in A02 who is conscious of the story of the defeat of the Assyrian army in 2 Chr 32, the defeat of the beasts in Rev 13 is assured at the outset. The singular reading in Rev 14:9 not only elucidates a potential allusion to Rev 13–14 but also provides the reader with an intrinsic approach to reading this text in conversation with the 2 Chr 32.

The skill of the scribe's intervention in the text of Revelation is manifest. This lexical alteration was made within the graphic and phonological confines of the remainder of the tradition—the altered lexeme retains each grapheme of the lexeme in the scribe's *Vorlage* in identical order, with an additional six graphemes inserted into the middle of the word. An identical mechanic is operative in the alteration of ἶρις to ΙΕΡΕΙC in Apoc. A02 4:3 (cf. ℵ 2329). The phonetic value of the source lexeme (θηρίον) and the singular reading (ΘΥCΙΑCΤΗΡΙΟΝ) retain an identical consonance. The scribe explicated a traditional source that was in some sense already implied in the wording of the Apocalypse.

III. Exegetical Reasoning and Second Temple Jewish Literature

The conclusion that both of these readings are the result of the scribe's awareness of antecedent scriptural wording stands in contrast to the prevailing position in New Testament textual studies. Scholars tend to explain the majority of textual variation as either the result of (premeditated) theological reasoning or *in scribendo* transcriptional error. Karrer, for example, suggests that the readings in Apoc. A02 11:4 and 14:9 are explicable on ideological grounds (type 4).[60] The primary thrust of Karrer's article—that the Greek text of Revelation is in serious need of a critical reevaluation, and that the nexus of theology, textual criticism, and textual history is a burgeoning area of inquiry—is both perceptive and important.[61] He also accurately observes the existence of an interesting pattern, in which these textual alterations in A02 create more cultic imagery. Lacking in Karrer's argument, however, is attentiveness to the external traditions that influence some of the textual

---

[60] Karrer, "Der Text der Johannesoffenbarung," 383–88. He also holds open the possibility that the reading in 11:4 may have a claim for originality (type 1).

[61] See also Martin Karrer, "The Angels of the Congregations in Revelation—Textual History and Interpretation," *Journal of Early Christian History* 1 (2011): 64–66.

anomalies in Apoc. A02; his argument therefore disregards the possibility that exegetical reasoning gave rise to these readings. Ideology and awareness of external textual traditions need not be mutually exclusive categories, and it is impossible to divorce theology from ancient scriptural reading. But the evidence in the preceding examples suggests that the variation in Rev 11:4 and 14:9 in A02 is primarily the result of exegetical reasoning perhaps deployed to particular theological ends.

It is at this juncture that the study of the transmission of the Hebrew Bible in the late Second Temple period can provide assistance in understanding the shape of textual variation in the New Testament. It is well documented that perceived connections between scriptural texts were a primary factor leading to changes and development in the wording of writings in the Hebrew Bible, however minute the intuited connection may have been.[62] The influence of external traditions on the text of a particular work was authorized by various textual hermeneutics, including the "awareness of an interrelated, sacred scriptural whole."[63] This awareness is operative in the fifth century, especially when the scriptural whole is codified in a single physical entity like A02. This presupposition of Scripture as a collection of sacred works, an attitude largely absent in the praxis of modern text-critical endeavors, demands that scholars also consider textual variation as the remnants of ancient exegetical encounters. Singular readings or other textual anomalies should be considered beyond their value in establishing a hypothetical *Ausgangstext*. Scholars should emphasize any potential external scriptural traditions that might have influenced the shape of strangely worded texts, especially when the text contains explicit or implicit references to other scriptural works. Studies on the reuse and transmission of Scripture in the late Second Temple period, including engagement with the scrolls from the Judean Desert, have the potential to provide New Testament scholars with helpful avenues of inquiry in this regard.[64] It is not that scholars have failed to consider exegetical reasoning altogether, but that this explanation for textual change has been downplayed in favor of emphasizing

---

[62] The most recent and comprehensive study of this issue is located in Teeter, *Scribal Laws*, 7–174.

[63] Ibid., 204; see also Eugene Ulrich, *The Dead Sea Scrolls and the Origins of the Bible*, SDSSRL (Grand Rapids: Eerdmans, 1999), 79–98.

[64] From the many studies that explore Second Temple Jewish texts, I will point to only a representative sample, including Teeter, *Scribal Laws* (2014); William A. Tooman, *Gog of Magog: Reuse of Scripture and Compositional Technique in Ezekiel 38–39*, FAT 2/52 (Tübingen: Mohr Siebeck, 2011); Molly M. Zahn, *Rethinking Rewritten Scripture: Composition and Exegesis in the 4QRewroked Pentateuch Manuscripts*, STDJ 95 (Leiden: Brill, 2011), http://dx.doi.org/10.1163/ej.9789004193901.i-282; Henze, *Biblical Interpretation at Qumran* (2005); Henze, ed., *A Companion to Biblical Interpretation in Early Judaism* (Grand Rapids: Eerdmans, 2012); Martin Jan Mulder, ed., *Mikra: Text, Translation, Reading and Interpretation of the Hebrew Bible in Ancient Judaism and Early Christianity*, CRINT, Section 2, Literature of the Jewish People in the Period of the Second Temple and the Talmud 1 (Assen: Van Gorcum, 1988).

transcriptional issues or theological scruples. Exegetical reasoning is intricately connected to these other factors, but a distinct phase in the process.

VI. Conclusions

The preceding discussion leads to the following conclusions. First, there is a diverse range of motivating factors that created singular readings in the textual history of the New Testament, factors that illuminate aspects of textual production, the social realities of scribalism, and the reception of New Testament works in late antiquity. Transcription errors and assimilation to internal grammatical or discourse conventions are assuredly the most prevalent explanations for singular readings. Additionally, changes based on theological perceptions also exist in the manuscript record. Yet another motivation—assimilation to external traditions based on awareness of lexical and thematic relationships—provides a further scribal proclivity that gives rise to exegetical textual variation (sometimes in the form of singular readings) in particular manuscripts. This variation is not unbridled or whimsical but is controlled by the scribe's understanding of the copied text, namely, the influence of allusions that underlie particular locutions in Revelation.[65] In this way, the alterations introduced into the tradition, although not precise representations of the wording of an antegraph, are faithful to the text insofar as they represent the scribe's understanding of the text's meaning—the scribe is faithful to his own perceived interpretation of the text, not necessarily always to its wording. This reality is not specific to A02 for the Apocalypse. The text of Revelation in Codex Sinaiticus (ℵ) contains numerous and egregious scribal errors alongside a number of readings that seem to preserve an interest in theological nuance and awareness of external tradition.[66] Awareness of antecedent traditions in this manuscript is even more obvious than in A02. Regardless of which exemplar one examines, the typology of singular readings presented above provides a critical tool for evaluating these readings and their causes within the textual history of the New Testament generally, and in the Apocalypse specifically.

Second, the scribe was aware of antecedent Greek scriptural traditions and the subtle textual details therein. The examples explored above were created in response to lexical overlap with texts in the OG/LXX and the alignment of typological features. Numerous textual and linguistic cues coalesced to suggest that Exod 25–26 and 2 Chr 36 stood behind Rev 11:4 and 14:9 respectively.[67] Multiple conflicting

---

[65] See Haines-Eitzen, *Guardians of Letters*, 105–27.

[66] See Juan Hernández Jr., "Codex Sinaiticus: An Early Christian Commentary on the Apocalypse?," in *Codex Sinaiticus: New Perspectives on the Ancient Biblical Manuscript*, ed. Scot McKendrick et al. (London: British Library, 2015), 107–26.

[67] In regard to the association of Exod 25 with Rev 11:4, Beale also makes this connection, mentioning Exod 25:30–31 (*Book of Revelation*, 576).

tendencies are present in these textual alterations: a conservative desire to remain faithful to the wording of the *Vorlage* and an impulse to explicate the presence and identity of the traditional sources alluded to in the book of Revelation. On the one hand, these readings retain literal relationships to their sources graphically, phonologically, and, in the case of Rev 14:9, its serial presentation of graphemes. On the other hand, the scribe's copy is not precisely literal to its *Vorlage* in terms of lexical items. The lexical alterations retain some formal resemblance to the *Vorlage*, while altering the semantics of the phrase. That these alterations may result in unintuitive turns of phrase (e.g., "worship the altar") suggest that the scribe was constrained by the norms of acceptable textual intrusion and the type of alteration allowable by his form of transmission. A full appraisal of variant readings in Apoc. A02 is required to determine the extent and form of socially acceptable textual reworking in this period.[68]

Finally, the features of these alterations intimate parallels between the scribal handling of New Testament documents and earlier examples of the interpretation and transmission of the Hebrew Bible in the Second Temple period. A helpful avenue for New Testament textual scholars to describe exegetical textual variation in the Greek manuscripts is the study of textual variation in the Hebrew Bible in the late Second Temple period. Observations from this field raise interesting comparative questions regarding the relationship between the production of copies and transmission of the works within these corpora and the shared facets of an ancient scribal tradition. The modes of transmission witnessed in Apoc. A02 and Second Temple literature both preserve facilitating tendencies within textual cultures that tend, to differing degrees, to privilege the precise replication of wording.[69] Michael Segal's observation pertaining to "Rewritten Bible" compositions also holds true, to some degree, for the scribe of our text: "the active intervention of scribes in these texts was accepted in this period and was not viewed as an affront to the sanctity of the text."[70] The socially permitted level of textual interference is admittedly minimized by the fifth century CE, but the scribe retained a limited freedom to alter the wording of copies in quantitatively small ways. For the most part, this occurs

---

[68] Some significant work has been done in this area in regard to different early manuscripts, but more is needed. See Royse, *Scribal Habits*. Hernández (*Scribal Habits and Theological Influences*) also makes a profitable step in this direction, and his work is a helpful tool in accessing data pertaining to singular readings in the early codices that preserve Revelation.

[69] See especially Teeter, who suggests that two concurrent models of scriptural transmission existed in this period: one devoted to improving the readability of the tradition, and another that privileged the precise replication of wording (*Scribal Laws*, 208–10). This second model is the prevailing mode of transmission of New Testament manuscripts, but features of facilitation exist within this model.

[70] Michael Segal, "Between Bible and Rewritten Bible," in Henze, *Biblical Interpretation at Qumran*, 16. The boundaries of acceptable intervention in early New Testament documents are what require further exploration.

at the lexical level, although some omissions of multiple words are also present.[71] Recourse to information about the habits of scribes from the Second Temple period ought to be considered with caution, since the scribe and these tradents stand on very different chronological, ideological, and social planes; however, this endeavor may provide solutions to textual anomalies in the New Testament manuscript record. In my view, the scribe is not merely a copyist, and scribal operations—rather than simply being limited to acts of transcription—reflect also acts of interpretation and explication. Because of this, it is not always possible to distinguish between scribe and exegete, just as it is not always possible to contrive the boundary between textual and reception history.[72]

---

[71] See Apoc. A02 7:1b, 4; 8:10.

[72] See also the problematizing of the boundary between biblical criticism and reception history in Brennan W. Breed, *Nomadic Text: A Theory of Biblical Reception History*, ISBL (Bloomington: Indiana University Press, 2014), esp. 1–14.

www.ingramcontent.com/pod-product-compliance
Lightning Source LLC
Chambersburg PA
CBHW020836020526
44114CB00040B/1223